A·N·N·U·A·L E·D·I·T·I·O·N·S

The Family

Twenty-Seventh Edition

01/02

EDITOR

Kathleen R. Gilbert
Indiana University

Kathleen Gilbert is an associate professor in the Department of Applied Health Science at Indiana University. She received a B.A. in Sociology and an M.S. in Marriage and Family Relations from Northern Illinois University. Her Ph.D. in Family Studies is from Purdue University. Dr. Gilbert's primary areas of interest are loss and grief in a family context, trauma and the family, family process, and minority families. She has published several books and articles in these areas.

McGraw-Hill/Dushkin
530 Old Whitfield Street, Guilford, Connecticut 06437

Visit us on the Internet
http://www.dushkin.com

Credits

1. Varied Perspectives on the Family
Unit photo—© 2001 by Cleo Freelance Photography.
2. Exploring and Establishing Relationships
Unit photo—© 2001 by Cleo Freelance Photography.
3. Finding a Balance: Maintaining Relationships
Unit photo—Dushkin/McGraw-Hill photo.
4. Crises—Challenges and Opportunities
Unit photo—© 2001 by Cleo Freelance Photography.
5. Families, Now and Into the Future
Unit photo—© 2001 by Cleo Freelance Photography.

Copyright

Cataloging in Publication Data
Main entry under title: Annual Editions: The Family. 2001/2002.
1. Family—United States—Periodicals. 2. Marriage—United States—Periodicals. I. Gilbert, Kathleen, *comp.*
II. Title: The family.
ISBN 0–07–243294–2   301.42'05   74–84596   ISSN 0272–7897

Twenty-Seventh Edition

Cover image © 2001 by PhotoDisc, Inc.

Printed in the United States of America   1234567890BAHBAH54321   Printed on Recycled Paper

Members of the Advisory Board are instrumental in the final selection of articles for each edition of ANNUAL EDITIONS. Their review of articles for content, level, currentness, and appropriateness provides critical direction to the editor and staff. We think that you will find their careful consideration well reflected in this volume.

EDITORS

Kathleen R. Gilbert
Indiana University

ADVISORY BOARD

Gloria W. Bird
Virginia Polytechnic Institute and State University

Judith Bordin
California State University, Chico

Sari G. Byrd
Suffolk Community College

Marie J. Corey
Michigan State University

Donna K. Crossman
Ohio State University

Bernard Davidson
Medical College of Georgia

Preston M. Dyer
Baylor University

Anita Farel
University of North Carolina Chapel Hill

David J. Hanson
SUNY at Potsdam

Dennis Johnson
Monterey Peninsula College

Rita Krasnow
Virginia Western Community College

Marcia Lasswell
California State Polytechnic University, Pomona

William C. Marshall
Brigham Young University

Janette K. Newhouse
Radford University

N. Catherine Norris-Bush
Carson-Newman College

Dorothy Seiden
San Francisco State University

George F. Stine
Millersville University

Robert M. Walsh
Illinois State University

Charles West
University of Mississippi

Editors/Advisory Board

Staff

To the Reader

In publishing ANNUAL EDITIONS we recognize the enormous role played by the magazines, newspapers, and journals of the public press in providing current, first-rate educational information in a broad spectrum of interest areas. Many of these articles are appropriate for students, researchers, and professionals seeking accurate, current material to help bridge the gap between principles and theories and the real world. These articles, however, become more useful for study when those of lasting value are carefully collected, organized, indexed, and reproduced in a low-cost format, which provides easy and permanent access when the material is needed. That is the role played by ANNUAL EDITIONS.

The purpose of *Annual Editions: The Family 01/02* is to bring to the reader the latest thoughts and trends in our understanding of the family, to identify current concerns as well as problems and possible solutions, and to present alternative views of family process. The intent of this anthology is to explore intimate relationships as they are played out in the family and, in doing this, to reflect the family's changing face.

The articles in this volume are taken from professional publications, semiprofessional journals, and popular lay publications aimed at both special populations and a general readership. The selections are carefully reviewed for their currency and accuracy. In some cases, contrasting viewpoints are presented. In others, articles are paired in such a way as to personalize the more impersonal scholarly information. In the current edition, a number of new articles have been added to reflect reviewers' comments. As the reader, you will note the tremendous range in tone and focus of these articles, from first-person accounts to reports of scientific discoveries as well as philosophical and theoretical writings. Some are more practical and applications-oriented, while others are more conceptual and research-oriented.

This anthology is organized to cover many of the important aspects of the family. The first unit looks at varied perspectives on the family. The second unit examines the beginning steps of relationship building as individuals go through the process of exploring and establishing connections. In the third unit, means of finding and maintaining a relationship balance are examined. Unit 4 is concerned with crises and ways in which these can act as challenges and opportunities for families and their members. Finally, unit 5 takes an affirming tone as it looks at families now and into the future.

Instructors can use *Annual Editions: The Family 01/02* as a primary text for lower-level, introductory the family classes, particularly when they tie the content of the readings to basic information on the family. This book can also be used as a supplement to update or emphasize certain aspects of standard the family textbooks. Because of the provocative nature of many of the essays in this anthology, it works well as a basis for class discussion about various aspects of the family relationships.

As in previous editions, this edition of *Annual Editions: The Family* contains *World Wide Web* sites that can be used to further explore topics addressed in the articles. These sites are cross-referenced by number in the *topic guide*.

I would like to thank everyone involved in the development of this volume. My appreciation goes to those who sent in *article rating forms* and comments on the previous edition as well as those who suggested articles to consider for inclusion in this edition. To all of the students in my Marriage and Family Interaction class who have contributed critiques of articles, I would like to say thanks.

Anyone interested in providing input for future editions of *Annual Editions: The Family* should complete and return the postage-paid *article rating form* at the end of this book. Your suggestions are much appreciated and contribute to the continuing quality of this anthology.

Kathleen R. Gilbert
Editor

Contents

UNIT 1

Varied Perspectives on the Family

Three articles explore different views
on where our images of family come
from and how they are influenced
by our life experiences as well as
societal and cultural constraints.

UNIT 2

Exploring and Establishing Relationships

Ten articles address
factors that influence the
formation of close relationships,
both romantic and generative.

The concepts in bold italics are developed in the article. For further expansion please refer to the Topic Guide and the Index.

The concepts in bold italics are developed in the article. For further expansion please refer to the Topic Guide and the Index.

UNIT 3

Finding a Balance: Maintaining Relationships

Seven articles consider the complex issues relating to relationships. From marriage to parent/child relationships to sibling relationships, maintaining relationships requires thought and commitment from members.

UNIT 4

Crises— Challenges and Opportunities

A wide variety of crises, normative and catastrophic, are detailed in 16 articles. From family violence, stress, and chaos to the intimate crises of infidelity, divorce, caregiving, and death, these articles provide accounts of devastation and hope.

The concepts in bold italics are developed in the article. For further expansion please refer to the Topic Guide and the Index.

The concepts in bold italics are developed in the article. For further expansion please refer to the Topic Guide and the Index.

UNIT 5

Families, Now and Into the Future

Five articles examine ways of establishing and/or maintaining health and healthy relationships within families.

The concepts in bold italics are developed in the article. For further expansion please refer to the Topic Guide and the Index.

The concepts in bold italics are developed in the article. For further expansion please refer to the Topic Guide and the Index.

This topic guide suggests how the selections in this book relate to the subjects covered in your course.

The Web icon (🌐) under the topic articles easily identifies the relevant Web sites, which are numbered and annotated on the next two pages. By linking the articles and the Web sites by topic, this ANNUAL EDITIONS reader becomes a powerful learning and research tool.

TOPIC AREA	TREATED IN	TOPIC AREA	TREATED IN
Abuse	21. Anatomy of a Violent Relationship 22. Resilience in Development 🌐 *1, 9, 13, 18, 19, 22, 24, 30*		38. Getting the Word 🌐 *9, 14, 19, 20, 22, 24, 28, 29*
Aging	10. How Old Is Too Old to Have a Baby? 23. Sex & Marriage 34. Elder Care 35. Bereavement Events Among Elderly Men 39. What's Ahead for Families 🌐 *17, 25, 26, 27, 31, 32, 33, 34*	**Culture**	2. American Family 13. Our Babies, Ourselves 20. Family Matters 41. Rituals for Our Times 🌐 *5, 6, 7, 24, 31, 35*
		Dating/Mate Selection	6. Flirting Fascination 7. What Is Your Love Story? 🌐 *13, 14, 19, 20, 24, 31*
Attachment	16. Will Your Marriage Last? 18. Father Love and Child Development 20. Family Matters 🌐 *13, 14, 19, 20, 22, 29*	**Divorce**	28. Should You Leave? 29. Is Divorce Too Easy? 30. Smart Plan to Save Marriage 31. Children of Divorce 32. Divorced? Don't Even Think of Remarrying 39. What's Ahead for Families 🌐 *19, 22, 23, 24, 28, 29*
Beliefs	13. Our Babies, Ourselves 38. Getting the Word 40. Power of Secrets 41. Rituals for Our Times 🌐 *3, 4, 8, 9, 19, 24, 31*	**Family Systems**	1. Intentional Family 31. Children of Divorce 34. Elder Care 38. Getting the Word 40. Power of Secrets 41. Rituals for Our Times 🌐 *19, 20, 22, 23, 24, 28, 29, 31*
Bereavement	35. Bereavement Events Among Elderly Men 36. Failing to Discuss Dying Adds to Pain of Patient and Family 🌐 *3, 4, 25, 26, 31, 32, 34*	**Family Therapy**	1. Intentional Family 15. Science of a Good Marriage 16. Will Your Marriage Last? 🌐 *19, 22, 24*
Biological Issues	5. Sex Differneces in the Brain 6. Flirting Fascination 8. Protecting Against Unintended Pregnancy 9. Brave New World of Parenting 10. How Old Is Too Old to Have a Baby? 11. Shaped by Life in the Womb 19. Do Parents Really Matter? 🌐 *2, 10, 12, 14, 15, 16*	**Finances, Family**	12. Cost of Children 17. Men, Women & Money 34. Elder Care 39. What's Ahead for Families 🌐 *33, 35*
		Future of Family	2. American Family 9. Brave New World of Parenting 37. To See Your Future Look Into Your Past 39. What's Ahead for Families 🌐 *19, 20, 22, 29, 31, 35*
Children/ Childcare	4. Boys Will Be Boys 12. Cost of Children 13. Our Babies, Ourselves 18. Father Love and Child Development 22. Resilience in Development 26. Do Working Parents Make the Grade? 31. Children of Divorce 🌐 *3, 4, 5, 10, 18, 20, 21, 22, 23, 24, 28, 29, 31*	**Gender/Gender Roles**	4. Boys Will Be Boys 5. Sex Differences in the Brain 17. Men, Women & Money 18. Father Love and Child Development 25. Politics of Fatigue 35. Bereavement Events Among Elderly Men 🌐 *1, 2, 3, 4, 5, 6, 7, 8, 9, 11, 16*
Communication	6. Flirting Fascination 15. Science of a Good Marriage 16. Will Your Marriage Last? 36. Failing to Discuss Dying Adds to Pain of Patient and Family	**Grandparents**	34. Elder Care 39. What's Ahead for Families 🌐 *26, 27, 33, 34, 35*

● AE: The Family

The following World Wide Web sites have been carefully researched and selected to support the articles found in this reader. The sites are cross-referenced by number and the Web icon (●) in the topic guide. In addition, it is possible to link directly to these Web sites through our DUSHKIN ONLINE support site at *http://www.dushkin.com/online/*.

The following sites were available at the time of publication. Visit our Web site—we update DUSHKIN ONLINE regularly to reflect any changes.

General Sources

1. American Psychological Association
http://www.apa.org/psychnet/
Explore the APA's "Resources for the Public" site to find links to an abundance of articles and other resources related to interpersonal relationships throughout the life span.

2. Encyclopedia Britannica
http://www.ebig.com
This huge "Britannica Internet Guide" leads to a cornucopia of informational sites and reference sources on such topics as family structure and other social issues.

3. Penn Library: Sociology
http://www.library.upenn.edu/resources/subject/social/sociology/sociology.html
This site provides a number of indexes of culture and ethnic studies, population and demographics, and statistical sources that are of value in studies of marriage and the family.

4. Social Science Information Gateway
http://sosig.esrc.bris.ac.uk
This is an online catalog of Internet resources relevant to social science education and research. Sites are selected and described by a librarian or subject specialist.

Varied Perspectives on the Family

5. American Studies Web
http://www.georgetown.edu/crossroads/asw/
This eclectic site provides links to a wealth of resources on the Internet related to American studies, from gender to race and ethnicity to demography and population studies.

6. Anthropology Resources Page
http://www.usd.edu/anth/
Many cultural topics can be accessed from this site from the University of South Dakota. Click on the links to find comparisons of values and lifestyles among the world's peoples.

7. Human Rights Report—India
http://www.usis.usemb.se/human/human1998/india.html
Read this U.S. Department of State 1998 report on India's human-rights practices for an understanding into the issues that affect women's mental and physical health and well-being in different parts of the world.

8. Men's Health
http://www.menshealth.com/new/guide/index.html
Men's Health presents many links to topics about men, AIDS/STDs, impotence and infertility, and vasectomy. It includes discussions of relationship and family issues.

9. Women's Studies Resources
http://www.inform.umd.edu/EdRes/Topic/WomensStudies/
This site provides a wealth of resources related to women and their concerns. You can find links to such topics as body image, comfort (or discomfort) with sexuality, personal relationships, pornography, and more.

Exploring and Establishing Relationships

10. Ask NOAH About Pregnancy: Fertility & Infertility
http://www.noah.cuny.edu/pregnancy/fertility.html
NOAH (New York Online Access to Health) seeks to provide relevant, timely, and unbiased health information for consumers. At this site, the organization presents extensive links to a variety of resources about infertility treatments and issues.

11. Bonobos Sex and Society
http://songweaver.com/info/bonobos.html
This site, accessed through Carnegie Mellon University, contains an article explaining how a primate's behavior challenges traditional assumptions about male supremacy in human evolution. Guaranteed to generate spirited debate.

12. Go Ask Alice!
http://www.goaskalice.columbia.edu/index.html
This interactive site of the Columbia University Health Services provides discussion and insight into a number of personal issues of interest to college-age people—and those younger and older.

13. The Kinsey Institute for Research in Sex, Gender, and Reproduction
http://www.indiana.edu/~kinsey/
The purpose of the Kinsey Institute's Web site is to support interdisciplinary research in the study of human sexuality.

14. Mysteries of Odor in Human Sexuality
http://www.pheromones.com
This is a commercial site with the goal of selling a book by James Kohl. Look here to find topics of interest to nonscientists about pheromones. Check out the diagram of "Mammalian Olfactory-Genetic-Neuronal-Hormonal-Behavioral Reciprocity and Human Sexuality" for a sense of the myriad biological influences that play a part in sexual behavior.

15. Planned Parenthood
http://www.plannedparenthood.org
Visit this well-known organization's home page for links to information on the various kinds of contraceptives (including outercourse and abstinence) and to discussions of other topics related to sexual and reproductive health.

16. The Society for the Scientific Study of Sexuality
http://www.ssc.wisc.edu/ssss/
The Society for the Scientific Study of Sexuality is an international organization dedicated to the advancement of knowledge about sexuality.

17. Sympatico: HealthyWay: Health Links
http://www.ab.sympatico.ca/Contents/Health/
This Canadian site meant for consumers will lead you to many links related to sexual orientation. It also addresses aspects of human sexuality over the life span as well as reproductive health.

Finding a Balance: Maintaining Relationships

18. Child Welfare League of America
http://www.cwla.org
The CWLA is the United States' largest organization devoted entirely to the well-being of vulnerable children and their families. This site provides links to information about such issues as teaching morality and values.

19. Coalition for Marriage, Family, and Couples Education
http://www.smartmarriages.com
CMFCE is dedicated to bringing information about and directories of skill-based marriage education courses to the public. It hopes to lower the rate of family breakdown through couple-empowering preventive education.

20. Family.com
http://www.family.com
According to this site, Family.com is an online parenting service that offers comprehensive, high-quality information and a supportive community for raising children.

21. The National Academy for Child Development
http://www.nacd.org
The NACD, dedicated to helping children and adults reach their full potential, presents links to various programs, research, and resources into a variety of family topics.

22. National Council on Family Relations
http://www.ncfr.com
This NCFR home page leads to valuable links to articles, research, and other resources on issues in family relations, such as stepfamilies, couples, and children of divorce.

23. Positive Parenting
http://www.positiveparenting.com
Positive Parenting is an organization dedicated to providing resources and information to make parenting rewarding, effective, and fun.

24. SocioSite
http://www.pscw.uva.nl/sociosite/TOPICS/Women.html
Open this site to gain insights into a number of issues that affect family relationships. It provides wide-ranging issues of women and men, of family and children, and more.

Crises—Challenges and Opportunities

25. Alzheimer's Association
http://www.alz.org
The Alzheimer's Association, dedicated to the prevention, cure, and treatment of Alzheimer's and related disorders, provides support to afflicted patients and their families.

26. American Association of Retired Persons
http://www.aarp.org
The AARP, a major advocacy group for older people, includes among its many resources suggested readings and Internet links to organizations that deal with social issues that may affect people and their families as they age.

27. Caregiver's Handbook
http://www.acsu.buffalo.edu/~drstall/hndbk0.html
This site is an online handbook for caregivers. Topics include medical aspects and liabilities of caregiving.

28. Children & Divorce
http://www.hec.ohio-state.edu/famlife/divorce/
Open this site to find links to articles and discussions of divorce and its effects on the family. Many bibliographical references are provided by the Ohio State University Department of Human Development & Family Science.

29. Parenting and Families
http://www.cyfc.umn.edu/Parenting/parentlink.html
By clicking on the various links, this site of the University of Minnesota's Children, Youth, and Family Consortium will lead you to many resources related to divorce, single parenting, and stepfamilies, as well as information about other topics of interest in the study of marriage and family.

30. Sexual Assault Information Page
http://www.cs.utk.edu/~bartley/saInfoPage.html
This invaluable site provides dozens of links to information and resources on a variety of sexual assault-related topics, from child sexual abuse, to date rape, to incest, to secondary victims, to offenders.

31. A Sociological Tour Through Cyberspace
http://www.trinity.edu/~mkearl/index.html
This extensive site, put together by Michael C. Kearl at Trinity University, provides essays, commentaries, data analyses, and links on such topics as death and dying, family, the sociology of time, social gerontology, and social psychology.

32. Widow Net
http://www.fortnet.org/WidowNet/
Widow Net is an information and self-help resource for and by widows and widowers. The information is helpful to people of all ages, religious backgrounds, and sexual orientation who have experienced a loss.

Families, Now and Into the Future

33. Economic Report of the President
http://www.library.nwu.edu/gpo/help/econr.html
This report includes current and anticipated trends in the United States and annual numerical goals concerning topics such as employment, income, and federal budget outlays. The database notes employment objectives for significant groups of the labor force.

34. National Institute on Aging
http://www.nih.gov/nia/
The NIA presents this home page that will take you to a variety of resources on health and lifestyle issues that are of interest to people as they grow older.

35. The North-South Institute
http://www.nsi-ins.ca
Searching this site of the North-South Institute—which works to strengthen international development cooperation and enhance gender and social equity—will lead to a variety of issues related to the family and social transitions.

We highly recommend that you review our Web site for expanded information and our other product lines. We are continually updating and adding links to our Web site in order to offer you the most usable and useful information that will support and expand the value of your Annual Editions. You can reach us at:
http://www.dushkin.com/annualeditions/.

www.dushkin.com/online/

5

Unit Selections

1. **The Intentional Family,** William J. Doherty
2. **The American Family,** Stephanie Coontz
3. **The Family: What Do We Really Want?** Michael Rustin

Key Points to Consider

❖ What is the nature of your family in terms of closeness and strong ties? What might you do to strengthen your family? What would you suggest for others?

❖ Why, in the face of strong evidence that the "good old days" weren't all that good, do we cling to the view that life in the past was superior to the present? What are some of the common beliefs about the past in contrast with the present? What is the truth about the quality of life in earlier times?

❖ What are your expectations for the family as an institution? How do personally held views of family influence policy? What might be the effects of this?

 **Links**   **www.dushkin.com/online/**

These sites are annotated on pages 4 and 5.

Our image of what family is and what it should be is a powerful combination of personal experience, family forms we encounter or observe, and attitudes we hold. Once formed, this image informs decision making and interpersonal interaction throughout our lives. It has far-reaching impacts: On an intimate level, it influences individual and family development as well as relationships both inside and outside the family. On a broader level, it affects legislation as well as social policy and programming.

In many ways, this image can be positive. It can act to clarify our thinking and facilitate interaction with like-minded individuals. It can also be negative, because it can narrow our thinking and limit our ability to see that other ways of carrying out the functions of family have value. Their very differentness can make them seem "bad." In this case, interaction with others can be impeded because of contrasting views.

This unit is intended to meet several goals with regard to perspectives on the family: (1) to sensitize the reader to sources of beliefs about the "shoulds" of the family—what the family should be and the ways in which family roles should be carried out, (2) to show how different views of the family can influence attitudes toward community responsibility and family policy, and (3) to show how views that dominate one's culture can influence awareness of ways of structuring family life.

In the first selection, "The Intentional Family," William Doherty explores a model of family life that is intended to build strong ties among family members. Next, Stephanie Coontz, in "The

American Family," takes a historical perspective to examine the contrast between common beliefs about the past and the reality of the time. In the final reading in this section, "The Family: What Do We Really Want?" Michael Rustin continues this broader view to address the evolution of the family as a legal, social, cultural, and economic institution.

Varied Perspectives on the Family

The Intentional Family

William J. Doherty, Ph.D.

W E REINVENTED FAMILY LIFE in the twentieth century but never wrote a user's manual. Have no doubt about the reinvention. This century has witnessed a revolution in the structures and expectations of family life. The changes in family structures are by now familiar: A child is as likely to grow up in a single-parent family or stepfamily as in a first-married family; an adult is likely to cohabitate, marry, divorce, and remarry; and most mothers are in the paid labor force.

The revolution in expectations of family life is less widely recognized. A scene from the 1971 film *Lovers and Other Strangers* captures this cultural shift. Richie, the adult son of Italian immigrant parents, tells them that he and his wife are divorcing. The stunned parents want to know "What's the story, Richie?" When he tells them he is not "happy," the answer does not compute. "Happy?" the father retorts, "What? Do you think your mother and I are happy?" A startled Richie asks, "You mean you and Mom aren't happy?" The parents look at each other, shrug, and with one voice respond, "No. We're content." Richie storms off with the testimonial of his generation: "Well, if I'm not going to be happy, I'm not going to stay married." But the memorable line from this vignette comes from the mother, played by Beatrice Arthur: "Don't look for happiness, Richie; it'll only make you miserable."

These fictional immigrant parents represented the remnants of the Institutional Family, the traditional family based on kinship, children, community ties, economics, and the father's authority. For the Institutional Family, the primary goals for family life were stability and security; happiness was secondary. Ending a marriage because you were not "happy" made no sense. An elderly British lord expressed the values of the Institutional Family when, upon learning that I was a family therapist he commented: "A frightful mistake so many people are making these days [is] throwing away a perfectly good marriage simply because they fall in love with somebody else."

The Institutional Family was suited to a world of family farms, small family businesses, and tight communities bound together by a common religion. The dominant form of family life for many centuries, it began to give way during the Industrial Revolution of the nineteenth century, when individual freedom and the pursuit of personal happiness and achievement began to be more important than kinship obligations, and when small farms and villages started to give way to more impersonal cities. During the 1920s, American sociologists began noting how an historically new kind of family—what I term the Psychological Family—was replacing the Institutional Family of the past. This new kind of family was based on personal achievement and happiness more than on family obligations and tight community bonds. In the early twentieth century, Americans turned a corner in family life, never to go back.[1]

By the 1950s, the Psychological Family had largely replaced the Institutional Family as the cultural norm in America. In ideal form, the Psychological Family was a nuclear unit headed by a stable married couple with close emotional ties, good communication, and an effective partnership in rearing children in a nurturing atmosphere. The chief goals of this kind of family life were no longer stability and security. Instead, the overarching goal was the satisfaction of individual family members. Men's and women's roles ideally were "separate but equal," with men being experts on the "world" and women being experts on the home.

Current social debates about the Traditional Family generally center around this Psychological Family, which did not come into full flower until the 1950s. Its supporters praise its traditional values, while its critics decry its conformity and unequal gender roles. Both sides miss an important point: the Psychological Family was radical in its own right when it supplanted the Institutional Family as the dominant family form. Its emergence threatened historical family values by reversing the importance of the individual and the family. The family's main job now was to promote the happiness and achievement of individual family members, rather than individual family members' main job being to promote the well-being of the family unit. To paraphrase: Ask not what you can do for your family; ask what your family can do for you. No more radical idea ever entered family life, but it is one we now take for granted in mainstream American culture.

If you doubt this shift in family values, try to imagine a contemporary American man choosing a wife because his family thinks the match would be good for the family. Or imagine a young woman announcing that she will never marry in order to stay home to care for her aging parents. Or a young adult deciding not to have sex before marriage in order not to bring embarrassment to his or her family. Most of us would assume that there was much more to these stories; someone was not telling the truth, or there was some personal or family pathology at work. We would have trouble imagining that a healthy adult would sacrifice important personal goals for the sake of family duties. Although most Americans continue to assume that parents, especially mothers, should place family needs over personal needs while the children are being raised, all bets are off for young people's obligations to their parents and extended family. And the perceived absence of happiness in marriage is a widely acceptable reason to divorce and try again for the kind of satisfying intimate relationship that has become a cultural birthright.

From its beginning, the Psychological Family was germinating the seeds of its own destruction. It harbored a profound contradiction: the value of individual happiness for both men and women, coupled with the value of family stability. For marriage, this meant commitment based on getting one's personal needs met in an equal relationship—a dicey combination for couples that lacked the skills required for such unions. When the feminist and sexual revolutions exploded in the late 1960s and later joined with the "Me Generation" of the 1970s, the Psychological Family began to fracture. The power of high expectations for marriage overwhelmed couples' abilities to cope at a time when divorce was losing its social stigma. The divorce rate skyrocketed along with nonmarital births and single-parent and stepfamilies. The cultural image of the two-parent nuclear family from cradle to grave splintered into a montage of family forms.

> We now have the first society in human history without a clear social consensus about what constitutes a "real" family and "good" family. And I don't see one emerging anytime soon.

The eclipse of the shared cultural ideal of the Psychological Family gave rise to the Pluralistic Family, which has dominated the last three decades of the twentieth century. Unlike the Institutional and Psychological Families, the Pluralistic Family does not offer an ideal for what constitutes a good family. Instead, the working assumption is that people create, or find themselves in, a wide variety of family configurations. No family form is inherently better than another, and all should be supported by the broader society. The traditional two-parent family becomes one lifestyle alternative among others, including cohabitation, single parenting, remarriage, and gay and lesbian families. The Pluralistic Family ideal is to let a thousand family forms bloom as families creatively respond to the modern world.

The Pluralistic Family carries forward the Psychological Family's emphasis on personal satisfaction but adds the new value of *flexibility*: to be a successful sailor in the seas of contemporary family life requires the ability to shift with the winds that come your way and the willingness to change boats when necessary. Essentially, you can never tell which kind of family structure you or your children may end up in, so be flexible.[2]

There is intense debate over the merits of the Pluralistic Family ideal in contemporary society. These cultural debates reflect a struggle between adherents to the Psychological Family and the Pluralistic Family. (Hardly anyone wants to go back to the Institutional Family because the value of personal satisfaction in family life ranks high among virtually all groups in American society, with the exception of recent immigrants.) But the very existence of the cultural debate shows the strength of the idea of the Pluralistic Family: the two-parent Psychological Family competes as just one lifestyle ideal among others. We now have the first society in human history without a clear social consensus about what constitutes a "real" family and "good" family. And I don't see one emerging anytime soon.

Following these staggering twentieth-century changes in family life, we now live in the best and worst of times for families. The worst of times because families have historically followed the guidance of their community and culture in shaping marriage, childrearing, and the countless other elements of family living; and now the

The natural drift of family life in contemporary America is toward slowly diminishing connection, meaning, and community.

community and culture are unable to provide a coherent vision or set of tools and supports. Families are left to struggle on their own. We also live in the best of times because we understand better what makes families work, and because now we have unprecedented freedom to shape the kind of family life we want, to be *intentional* about our families.

DEFINING THE INTENTIONAL FAMILY

Sometimes with my therapy clients, I use an analogy of the Mississippi River, which flows just a couple of miles from my office. I say that family life is like putting a canoe into that great body of water. If you enter the water at St. Paul and don't do anything, you will head south toward New Orleans. If you want to go north, or even stay at St. Paul, you have to work hard and have a plan. In the same way, if you get married or have a child without a working plan for your family's journey, you will likely head "south" toward less closeness, less meaning, and less joy over time. A family, like a canoe, must be steered or paddled, or it won't take you where you want to go.

The natural drift of family life in contemporary America is toward slowly diminishing connection, meaning,

Only an Intentional Family has a fighting chance to maintain and increase its sense of connection, meaning, and community over the years.

and community. You don't have to be a "dysfunctional" couple to feel more distant as the years go by, or a particularly inept parent to feel that you spend more time disciplining your children than enjoying them. You are not unusual if you feel you have too little time for meaningful involvement with your community. Lacking cultural support and tools for shaping the kinds of families we want, most of us end up hoping the river currents carry us to somewhere we want to go. In the "anything goes" world of the Pluralistic Family, where specifically do we want to go, and how in the world do we get there?

Only an Intentional Family has a fighting chance to maintain and increase its sense of connection, meaning, and community over the years. An Intentional Family is one whose members create a working plan for maintaining and building family ties, and then implement the plan as best they can. An Intentional Family rows and steers its boat rather than being moved only by the winds and the current.

At heart, the Intentional Family is a ritualizing family. It creates patterns of connecting through everyday family rituals, seasonal celebrations, special occasions, and community involvement. An Intentional Family does not let mealtimes deteriorate into television watching. It does not let adolescents "do their own thing" at the expense of all family outings. It is willing to look at how it handles Christmas or bar mitzvahs in order to make them work better for everyone. It has the discipline to stick with good rituals, and the flexibility to change them when they are not working anymore.

The Entropic Family

The opposite of the Intentional Family is the Entropic Family. Entropy is the term for the tendency of a physical system to lose energy and coherence over time, such as a gas that expands and dissipates until there is little trace left. Similarly, the Entropic Family, through lack of conscious attention to its inner life and community ties, gradually loses a sense of cohesion over the years. Its maintenance rituals such as meals and birthdays lose their spark, and then degenerate. Individual family members may have active lives in the world, but the energy of the family itself slowly sweeps away.

Contemporary society creates Entropic Families by two means. First is our lack of support for couples to make marriage work and for parents to make childrearing work. We generate the highest expectations of family life of any generation in human history, but provide the least guidance as to how to achieve success in our contemporary family forms. We struggle as a society over the most basic kinds of family support, such as unpaid leave for caring for babies and sick family members. And we have barely begun to face our joint responsibility to help families learn the skills for parenting, partnership, and intimacy that most of us expect of family life. No wonder that the odds of a happy lifetime marriage are probably no more than one in four—half of new couples divorce and another quarter are probably not very happy.

The second way that we collectively create Entropic Families is by putting up barriers to sustaining family rituals. Cars, televisions, busy work schedules, consumerism, and a host of other forces propel family members along fast-moving, diverging tracks. Family meals become casualties of soccer practice, violin lessons, work demands, and the lure of a favorite television rerun. Tired parents lack energy to focus the family on reconnecting at the end of the workday. The Christmas holidays appear before family plans are in place, and vacations are patched together at the last minute.

In Entropic Families, there is no less love, no less desire for meaning and connection than in Intentional Families. But their members gradually drift apart because they lack the infusions of bonding, intimacy, and community that only well-maintained family rituals can give. In the end, most families that are not intentional will follow the currents of entropy toward less closeness than they had hoped for when they started their family journey; the forces pulling on families are just too strong in the modern world. Ultimately, we must decide either to steer or go where the river takes us. The key to successful steering is to be intentional about our family rituals.

FAMILY RITUALS

When you recall your favorite memories of childhood, probably they center around family rituals such as bedtime, an annual vacation, Thanksgiving, Christmas, or the weekly Sabbath meal. Your worst memories might also be connected with these family rituals. Interestingly, many family researchers and family therapists have learned only recently how significant a component family rituals are to the glue that holds families together.[3] Previously, most researchers and therapists emphasized *talk:* how couples communicate, how parents verbally praise and discipline children. But as important as talking is, what professionals weren't considering was how we *enact* our family relationships.

Family rituals are repeated and coordinated activities that have significance for the family.[4] To be a ritual, the activity has to have *meaning* or *significance;* otherwise, it is a routine but not a ritual. For example, most families' bathroom activities are routines rather than rituals because they do not have much symbolic importance, although such an activity can become a ritual. For example, one of my clients and his new wife took a shower together every morning, which became a ritual for them. To be a ritual, then, the activity must also be *repeated;* an occasional, unplanned trip to a cabin would not make for a family ritual, whereas an annual trip that family members look forward to would. Finally, a ritual activity must be *coordinated;* a meal that each person fixes and eats alone would not qualify as a family ritual, whereas a meal that everyone gathers deliberately together to eat would, if done regularly and with meaning.

A goal of this book is to show you how to transform some family routines into family rituals. Family rituals give us four important things:

Predictability. The sense of regularity and order that families require, especially those with children. Knowing that the father will talk to his child and read a story every night makes bedtime something to look forward to and savor. If bedtime talks and stories have to be negotiated every night—if there is no predictability—then the ritual loses its power.

Connection. The bedtime ritual may be the primary one-to-one time shared between a father and his child. For couples, bedtime rituals may also be an important opportunity to connect emotionally and perhaps sexually after a busy, distracted day. Couples who value rituals of connection generally make sure they coordinate their evening plans so as to go to bed together. Those who generally go to bed at different times are apt to lose connection over time, unless they have strong alternative rituals of connection.

Identity. A sense of who belongs to the family and what is special about the family. You may know who your core family members are by who is invited to the Thanksgiving meal; including nonrelatives in core family rituals makes them "family," too. Families who take interesting vacations together acquire the self-image of a fun-loving family. They will say "We are campers" or "We are hikers." For some couples, shopping for antiques becomes a ritual outing that helps form a couple identity as antique lovers.

A way to enact values. Values demonstrate what we believe and hold dear. Religious rituals are a good example, as is a family volunteering together for community work; or ensuring that the children join in regular family visits to a grandparent in a nursing home, thereby teaching that it is important to honor and support this elderly family member.[5]

Types of Family Rituals

Family rituals by definition involve more than one family member, but not all family rituals necessarily involve the whole family. Some rituals involve just two members;

say, a married couple going out to dinner or a parent reading to a child. Some involve subgroups, as when my father took my sister and me to Philadelphia Phillies baseball games. Some involve the larger extended family, such as family reunions and holiday rituals. Others include close friends of the family, and still others, a larger community such as a church or synagogue or a volunteer group to support the local children's museum. It is important to think of the different combinations of participants in family rituals. Successful Intentional Families learn to ritualize everything from pairs to communities.[6]

I like to classify family rituals by the *function* they play for families; that is, by the needs they serve. Thus, there are rituals for connection or bonding, rituals for showing love to individual family members, and rituals that bind the family to the larger community.

Connection rituals offer everyday opportunities for family bonding, such as family meals, morning and bedtime routines, and the comings and goings of family members to and from work and school. They also involve family outings, from small trips to the ice cream store to major family vacations. The goal is a sense of family bonding.

Love rituals focus on developing one-to-one intimacy and making individual family members feel special. They can be subdivided into couple rituals and special-person rituals. Examples of couple love rituals are anniversaries, Valentine's Day, "dating," and sexual relations. Special-person rituals generally center around birthdays, Mother's Day, and Father's Day.

Community rituals have a more public dimension than connection and love rituals. They include major family events such as weddings and funerals that link families to their communities, as well as religious activities in churches, synagogues, or mosques. In addition, community rituals include conscious efforts to connect with a wider social network than the family, to both give and gain support. Too much writing about family life has ignored the public face of families and concentrated narrowly on the internal hearth and home. The healthiest families give to their communities and receive support back in good measure.

Thanksgiving and Christmas have evolved into a special category of family ritual, involving all three functions of rituals: connection, love, and community. They are the grand rituals of the calendar year for the majority of American families, Christian and non-Christian alike. And for many people, holiday rituals hold both the fondest and most depressing memories of childhood.

Historians have learned recently that community rituals, not "home" rituals, formed the linchpin of family life in the era of the Institutional Family. Before the mid-nineteenth century in Europe and America, family rituals hardly existed as we know of them today. Ritual activities occurred mostly in community settings such as churches and public commons, not inside the family itself. Families had daily routines, of course, but apparently they did not regard them as significant sources of family connection. They ate meals, but they did not think of family dinners as a special time separate from other times. Indeed, families prior to the late nineteenth century did not dwell much on their interior life. Christmas was celebrated with community festivals, not with family rituals of celebration and gift-giving. Families did not have birthday parties, and couples did not celebrate anniversaries. It was only with the passing of the Institutional Family and the gradual emergence of the Psychological Family after the Industrial Revolution that families began to think of themselves as separate from their communities and in need of special family rituals. As their urban environment grew more alien and as fathers went into the workforce away from home, families began to cultivate their inner world through special rituals. When communities broke up, families had to become intentional about their own rituals.[7]

There is no universal yardstick for measuring family rituals for all of our diverse contemporary families. Remarried families have different needs from first-married families, as do single-parent families from two-parent families. Different ethnic traditions require different degrees of flexibility or structure in family rituals. Some families are tied closely to their ethnic origins and to their extended families, and some have more independent lifestyles. Some families have young children, some have adolescents, and some have no children. Some families are experiencing peaceful periods in their life, and thus feel free to be creative with their rituals, while others are undergoing tremendous stress and need to just hang on to what they have. There is no ritual formula that applies to all this diversity. Indeed, the idea of the Intentional Family is encourage families to use their own values, histories, religions, and cultures to consciously plan their life together and in community.

TAMING TIME AND TECHNOLOGY

Becoming a ritualizing Intentional Family means learning to manage the two principal drains on the energy of most American families: time demands outside the home and electronic technology inside the home.

Now that most mothers are employed, and fathers are working as much or more than ever, there is a net decrease in the amount of time parents have to spend with their children and with each other. Add to that the fact that jobs for teenagers are plentiful, and many of them are also employed during family dinner hours and on weekends. And middle-class families in particular now spend a huge amount of time driving their children to various lessons and practices, on top of attending their games and events. If time is the raw material of family rituals, we are suffering from its shortage. Many American families feel starved for time.[8]

How can we become more intentional about family life in the face of this time shortage? Let's say you are already an overwhelmed single parent, or a married person who barely has time to talk to your spouse. Will thinking about enhancing your family rituals just serve to make you feel even more guilty than you already do? Two general strategies will be exemplified throughout this book. First is to make better use of the time you already spend on family activities. You have to feed your children, so start with improving the quality of those feeding rituals, without lengthening the time. You have to put your kids to bed; work on making it more pleasurable. You probably have birthday parties, holiday celebrations, and countless other family activities. You can enhance their quality while not adding to their number or extending their time requirements.

Disconnecting the Wires

The second general strategy is to experiment with carving out time from another activity that occupies more than its fair share of your attention. I recommend taming technology. We live in an era of the wired American family. The average American family has 2.5 television sets, and the average American spends over four hours per day watching television. That means television watching consumes half of our nonsleep, nonwork time. You can't tell me there is no surplus family ritual time to be carved out there! Add in CD players, telephones, and, increasingly, computers and the Internet. When we are in our cars, there is the radio and tape player. When we are out for walks, there are head phones. When we are running errands, more of us talk on cellular phones. We are always interruptible and distractible, two conditions that work against family rituals and intentional family life.[9]

Believe me, I am not a Luddite, rejecting all modern technology. When my daughter was in Europe, the telephone and e-mail kept us in contact. And television watching can be a relaxing way for family members to unwind. But, for many of us, electronic technology is the pet that has taken over the house. That's the bad news. The good news is that taming it even a little, such as by turning off the television during meals, can free up time for family rituals. We trained our dog to stay out of our bedrooms, and we banned television from there as well. No one, including the dog, has suffered for it.

The idea behind the Intentional Family is that families can decide for themselves, based on their own traditions, values, and circumstances, how best to ritualize their lives. Most families have some rituals they enjoy, some they don't enjoy but feel stuck with, and some they could benefit from creating or refurbishing. As you read this book, I encourage you to develop an agenda of current rituals you might want to remodel and new ones you might want to try. But hold off on trying anything new on your family until you read the last chapter, where I discuss specific strategies for creating and modifying family rituals. Moving too quickly or unilaterally in the domain of family rituals is sure to result in your family members saying "No way!" to your creative ideas. Changing family rituals requires sensitivity, tact, timing, and diplomatic skills—the very talents necessary to survive as an Intentional Family in an era of both unprecedented confusion and opportunity for families.

NOTES

1. See Steven Mintz and Susan Kellogg, *Domestic Revolutions: A Social History of American Family Life* (New York: The Free Press), 1988, pp. 107–131.
2. For background on changes in family norms from the Psychological Family to the Pluralistic Family in the twentieth century, see William J. Doherty, "Private Lives, Public Values," *Psychology Today*, 25 (May–June, 1990), pp. 32–37, 82; and Judith Stacey, *Brave New Families: Stories of Domestic Upheaval in Late Twentieth-Century America* (New York: Basic Books), 1990.
3. For academic and clinical background on family rituals, see James H. S. Bossard and Eleanor S. Boll, *Ritual in Family Living* (Philadelphia: University of Pennsylvania Press), 1950; Evan Imber-Black, Janine Roberts, and Richard Whiting (eds.), *Rituals in Families and Family Therapy* (New York: W.W. Norton), 1988; Evan Imber-Black and Janine Roberts, *Rituals for Our Times* (New York: Harper-Collins), 1992; Mara Selvini Palazzoli, Luigi Boscolo, Gianfranco Cecchin, Giuliana Prata, "Family Rituals: A Powerful Tool in Family Therapy," *Family Process* 16 (1977): pp. 445–454; Steven J. Wolin and Linda A. Bennett, "Family Rituals," *Family Process* 23 (1984), pp. 401–420.
4. This definition is my version of Wolin and Bennett's (1984) definition of a family ritual: "a symbolic form of communication that, owing to the satisfaction that family members experience through its repetition, is acted out in a systematic fashion over time." "Family Rituals," *Family Process*, 23 (1984), p. 401.
5. See Wolin and Bennett, "Family Rituals," *Family Process* 23 (1984), pp. 401–420; Evan Imber-Black, "Ritual Themes in Families and Family Therapy," in Imber-Black, Roberts, and Whiting, pp. 47–83.
6. The popular author Robert Fulghum has written about family and community rituals. However, he also refers to certain individual activities, such as personal morning routines, as rituals. I am using the term ritual in the more traditional social science sense to refer only to social, not private activities. See Robert Fulghum, *From Beginning to End: The Rituals of Our Lives* (New York: Viking), 1995.
7. See John R. Gillis, "Ritualization of Middle-Class Family Life in Nineteenth-Century Britain," *International Journal of Politics, Culture, and Society* 3 (1989): pp. 213–235; John Gillis, "Making Time for Family: The Invention of Family Time(s) and the Reinvention of Family History," *Journal of Family History* 21 (1996): pp. 4–21; Penne L. Restad, *Christmas in America: A History* (New York: Oxford University Press), 1995.
8. For data on parents' spending less time with children, see Joseph Pleck, "Paternal Involvement: Levels, Sources, and Consequences," in Michael E. Lamb (ed.), *The Role of the Father in Child Development.* Third edition. (Hillsdale, New Jersey: Erlbaum), 1996; for documentation of the amount of time spent working, see Juliet B. Schor, *The Overworked American* (New York: Basic Books), 1991.
9. George Gallup Jr., and Frank Newport, "Gallup Survey Finds More Viewers Are Getting Pickier," *Minneapolis-St. Paul Star Tribune,* October 7, 1990, pp. 1F, 7F.

THE AMERICAN FAMILY

New research about an old institution challenges the conventional wisdom that the family today is worse off than in the past. Essay by Stephanie Coontz

As the century comes to an end, many observers fear for the future of America's families. Our divorce rate is the highest in the world, and the percentage of unmarried women is significantly higher than in 1960. Educated women are having fewer babies, while immigrant children flood the schools, demanding to be taught in their native language. Harvard University reports that only 4 percent of its applicants can write a proper sentence.

There's an epidemic of sexually transmitted diseases among men. Many streets in urban neighborhoods are littered with cocaine vials. Youths call heroin "happy dust." Even in small towns, people have easy access to addictive drugs, and drug abuse by middle-class wives is skyrocketing. Police see 16-year-old killers, 12-year-old prostitutes, and gang members as young as 11.

DAHLSTROM COLLECTION/TIME INC.

c. 1890 A couple and their six children sit for a family portrait. With smaller families today, mothers spend twice as much time with each kid.

America at the end of the 1990s? No, America at the end of the 1890s.

The litany of complaints may sound familiar, but the truth is that many things were worse at the start of this century than they are today. Then, thousands of children worked full-time in mines, mills and sweatshops. Most workers labored 10 hours a day, often six days a week, which left them little time or energy for family life. Race riots were more frequent and more deadly than those experienced by recent generations. Women couldn't vote, and their wages were so low that many turned to prostitution.

In 1900 a white child had one chance in three of losing a brother or sister before age 15, and a black child had a fifty-fifty chance of seeing a sibling die. Children's-aid groups reported widespread abuse and neglect by parents.

Things were worse at the turn of the last century than they are today. Most workers labored 10 hours a day, six days a week, leaving little time for family life.

From *Life* magazine, November 1999, pp. 79, 90, 92, 94. © 1999 by Time, Inc. Magazine Company. Reprinted by permission.

LEWIS HINE/CULVER PICTURES

1915 An Italian immigrant family gathers around the dinner table in an apartment on the East Side of New York City. Today, most families still eat together—but often out.

states by literacy tests that were not administered to whites. Individuals who didn't follow the rigid gender and sexual rules of the day were ostracized.

Leave It to Beaver did not reflect the real-life experience of most American families. While many moved into the middle class during the 1950s, poverty remained more wide-spread than in the worst of our last three recessions. More children went hungry, and poverty rates for the elderly were more than twice as high as today's.

Even in the white middle class, not every woman was as serenely happy with her lot as June Cleaver was on TV. Housewives of the 1950s may have been less rushed than to-day's working mothers, but they were more likely to suffer anxiety and depression. In many states, women couldn't serve on juries or get loans or credit cards in their own names.

And not every kid was as wholesome as Beaver Cleaver, whose mischievous antics could be handled by Dad at the dinner table. In 1955 alone, Congress discussed 200 bills aimed at curbing juvenile delinquency. Three years later, LIFE reported that urban teachers were being terror-ized by their students. The drugs that were so freely avail-able in 1900 had been outlawed, but many children grew up in families ravaged by alcohol and barbiturate abuse.

Rates of unwed childbearing tripled between 1940 and 1958, but most Americans didn't notice because unwed mothers generally left town, gave their babies up for adop-tion and returned home as if nothing had happened. Trou-bled youths were encouraged to drop out of high school. Mentally handicapped children were warehoused in institu-tions like the Home for Idiotic and Imbecilic Children in Kansas, where a woman whose sister had lived there for most of the 1950s once took me. Wives routinely told poll-sters that being disparaged or ignored by their husbands was a normal part of a happier than-average marriage.

Denial extended to other areas of life as well. In the early 1900s, doctors refused to believe that the cases of

Men who deserted or divorced their wives rarely paid child support. And only 6 percent of the children gradu-ated from high school, compared with 88 percent today.

Why do so many people think American families are facing worse problems now than in the past? Partly it's because we compare the complex and diverse families of the 1990s with the seemingly more standard-issue ones of the 1950s, a unique decade when every long-term trend of the 20th century was temporarily reversed. In the 1950s, for the first time in 100 years, the divorce rate fell while marriage and fertility rates soared, crating a boom in nuclear-family living. The percentage of foreign-born individuals in the country decreased. And the debates over social and cultural issues that had divided Americans for 150 years were silenced, suggesting a national consensus on family values and norms.

Some nostalgia for the 1950s is understandable: Life looked pretty good in comparison with the hardship of the Great Depression and World War II. The GI Bill gave a generation of young fathers a college education and a subsidized mortgage on a new house. For the first time, a majority of men could support a family and buy a home without pooling their earnings with those of other family members. Many Americans built a stable family life on these foundations.

But much nostalgia for the 1950s is a result of selective amnesia—the same process that makes childhood memo-ries of summer vacations grow sunnier with each passing year. The superficial sameness of 1950s family life was achieved through censorship, coercion and discrimination. People with unconventional beliefs faced governmental investigation and arbitrary firings. African Americans and Mexican Americans were prevented from voting in some

Many of our worries today reflect how much better we want to be, not how much better we used to be.

15

gonorrhea and syphilis they saw in young girls could have been caused by sexual abuse. Instead, they reasoned, girls could get these diseases from toilet seats, a myth that terrified generations of mothers and daughters. In the 1950s, psychiatrists dismissed incest reports as Oedipal fantasies on the part of children.

Spousal rape was legal throughout the period and wife beating was not taken seriously by authorities. Much of what we now label child abuse was accepted as a normal part of parental discipline. Physicians saw no reason to question parents who claimed that their child's broken bones had been caused by a fall from a tree.

There are plenty of stresses in modern family life, but one reason they seem worse is that we no longer sweep them under the rug. Another is that we have higher expectations of parenting and marriage. That's a good thing. We're right to be concerned about inattentive parents, conflicted marriages, antisocial values, teen violence and child abuse. But we need to realize that many of our worries reflect how much better we *want* to be, not how much better we *used* to be.

Fathers in intact families are spending more time with their children than at any other point in the past 100 years. Although the number of hours the average woman spends at home with her children has declined since the early 1900s, there has been a decrease in the number of children per family and an increase in individual attention to each child. As a result, mothers today, including working moms, spend almost twice as much time with each child as mothers did in the 1920s. People who raised children in the 1940s and 1950s typically report that their own adult children and grandchildren communicate far better with their kids and spend more time helping with homework than they did—even as they complain that other parents today are doing a worse job than in the past.

Despite the rise in youth violence from the 1960s to the early 1990s, America's children are also safer now than they've ever been. An infant was four times more

likely to die in the 1950s than today. A parent then was three times more likely than a modern one to preside at the funeral of a child under the age of 15, and 27 percent more likely to lose an older teen to death.

If we look back over the last millennium, we can see that families have always been diverse and in flux. In each period, families have solved one set of problems only to face a new array of challenges. What works for a family in one economic and cultural setting doesn't work for a family in another. What's helpful at one stage of a family's life may be destructive at the next stage. If there is one

MARGARET BOURKE-WHITE

American Mirror

1937: The Hahn family sits in the living room of a working-class Muncie home, which rents for $10 a month. Class distinctions have eroded over 60 years.

Muncie, Ind. (pop. 67,476), calls itself America's Hometown. But to generations of sociologists it is better known as America's Middletown—the most studied place in the 20th century American landscape. "Muncie has nothing extraordinary about it," says University of Virginia professor Theodore Caplow, which is why, for the past 75 years, researchers have gone there to observe the typical American family. Muncie's averageness first drew sociologists Robert and Helen Lynd in 1924. They returned in 1935 (their follow-up study was featured in a LIFE photo essay by Margaret Bourke-White). And in 1976, armed with the Lynds' original questionnaires, Caplow launched yet another survey of the town's citizens.

Caplow discovered that family life in Muncie was much healthier in the 1970s than in the 1920s. No only were husbands and wives communicating more, but unlike married couples in the 1920s, they were also shopping, eating out, exercising and going to movies and concerts together. More than 90 percent of Muncie's couples characterized their marriages as "happy" or "very happy."

In 1929 the Lynds had described partnerships of a drearier kind, "marked by sober accommodation of each partner to his share in the joint undertaking of children, paying off the mortgage and generally 'getting on.' "

Caplow's five-year study, which inspired a six-part PBS series, found that even though more moms were working outside the home, two thirds of them spent at least two hours a day with their children; in 1924 fewer than half did. In 1924 most children expected their mothers to be good cooks and housekeepers, and wanted their fathers to spend time with them and respect their opinions. Fifty years later, expectations of fathers were unchanged, but children wanted the same—time and respect—from their mothers.

This year, Caplow went back to survey the town again. The results (and another TV documentary) won't be released until December 2000.

—Sora Song

MARK KAUFFMAN

1955 A family poses in Seattle. Husbands today are doing more housework.

lesson to be drawn from the last millennium of family history, it's that families are always having to play catch-up with a changing world.

Take the issue of working mothers. Families in which mothers spend as much time earning a living as they do raising children are nothing new. They were the norm throughout most of the last two millennia. In the 19th century, married women in the United States began a withdrawal from the workforce, but for most families this was made possible only by sending their children out to work instead. When child labor was abolished, married women began reentering the workforce in ever large numbers.

For a few decades, the decline in child labor was greater than the growth of women's employment. The result was an aberration: the male-breadwinner family. In the 1920s, for the first time, a bare majority of American children grew up in families where the husband provided all the income, the wife stayed home full-time, and they and their siblings went to school instead of work. During the 1950s, almost two thirds of children grew up in such families, an all-time high. Yet that same decade saw an acceleration of workforce participation by wives and mothers that soon made the dual-earner family the norm, a trend not likely to be reversed in the next century.

What's new is not that women make half their families' living, but that for the first time they have substantial control over their own income, along with the social freedom to remain single or to leave an unsatisfactory marriage. Also new is the declining proportion of their lives that people devote to rearing children, both because they have fewer kids and because they are living longer. Until about 1940, the typical marriage was broken by the death of

one partner within a few years after the last child left home. Today, couples can look forward to spending more than two decades together after the children leave.

The growing length of time partners spend with only each other for company has made many individuals less willing to put up with an unhappy marriage, while women's economic independence makes it less essential for them to do so. It is no wonder that divorce has risen steadily since 1900. Disregarding a spurt in 1946, a dip in the 1950s and another peak around 1980, the divorce rate is just where you'd expect to find it, based on the rate of increase from 1900 to 1950. Today, 40 percent of all marriages will end in divorce before a couple's 40th anniversary. Yet despite this high divorce rate, expanded life expectancies mean that more couples are reaching that anniversary than ever before.

Families and individuals in contemporary America have more life choices that in the past. That makes it easier for some to consider dangerous or unpopular options. But it also makes success easier for many families that never would have had a chance before—interracial, gay or lesbian, and single-mother families, for example. And it expands horizons for most families.

Women's new options are good not just for themselves but for their children. While some people say that women who choose to work are selfish, it turns out that maternal self-sacrifice is not good for children. Kids do better when their mothers are happy with their lives, whether their satisfaction comes from being a full-time homemaker or from having a job.

Largely because of women's new roles at work, men are doing more at home. Although most men still do less housework than their wives, the gap has been halved since the 1960s. Today, 49 percent of couples say they share childcare equally, compared with 25 percent of 1985.

Men's greater involvement at home is good for their relationships with their parents, and also good for their children. Hands-on fathers make better parents than men who let their wives do all the nurturing and childcare: They raise sons who are more expressive and daughters who are more likely to do well in school, especially in math and science.

In 1900, life expectancy was 47 years, and only 4 percent of the population was 65 or older. Today, life expectancy is 76 years, and by 2025, about 20 percent of Americans will be 65 or older. For the first time, a generation of adults must plan for the needs of both their parents and their children. Most Americans are responding with remarkable grace. One in four households gives the

The biggest problem is not that our families have changed too much but that our institutions have changed too little.

equivalent of a full day a week or more in unpaid care to an aging relative, and more than half say they expect to do so in the next 10 years. Older people are less likely to be impoverished or incapacitated by illness than in the past, and they have more opportunity to develop a relationship with their grandchildren.

Even some of the choices that worry us the most are turning out to be manageable. Divorce rates are likely to remain high, but more non-custodial parents are staying in touch with their children. Child-support receipts are up. And a lower proportion of kids from divorced families are exhibiting problems than in earlier decades. Stepfamilies are learning to maximize children's access to supportive adults rather than cutting them off from one side of the family.

Out-of-wedlock births are also high, however, and this will probably continue because the age of first marriage for women has risen to an all-time high of 25, almost five years above what it was in the 1950s. Women who marry at an older age are less likely to divorce, but they have more years when they are at risk—or at choice—for a nonmarital birth.

Nevertheless, births to teenagers have fallen from 50 percent of all nonmarital births in the late 1970s to just 30 percent today. A growing proportion of women who have a nonmarital birth are in their twenties and thirties and usually have more economic and educational resources than unwed mothers of the past. While two involved parents are generally better than one, a mother's personal maturity, along with her educational and eco-nomic status, is a better predictor of how well her child will turn out than her marital status. We should no longer assume that children raised by single parents face debilitating disadvantages.

As we begin to understand the range of sizes, shapes and colors that today's families come in, we find that the differences *within* family types are more important than the differences *between* them. No particular family form guarantees success, and no particular form is doomed to fail. How a family functions on the inside is more important than how it looks from the outside.

The biggest problem facing most families as this century draws to a close is not that our families have changed too much but that our institutions have changed too little. America's work policies are 50 years out of date, designed for a time when most moms weren't in the workforce and most dads didn't understand the joys of being involved in childcare. Our school schedules are 150 years out of date, designed for a time when kids needed to be home to help with the milking and haying. And many political leaders feel they have to decide whether to help parents stay home longer with their kids or invest in better childcare, preschool and afterschool programs, when most industrialized nations have long since learned it's possible to do both.

So America's social institutions have some Y2K bugs to iron out. But for the most part, our families are ready for the next millennium.

The Family: What Do We Really Want?

Michael Rustin

HOW SHOULD democratic socialists think about the family and its role in modern society? The essential problem is to find alternatives to individualist and marketized conceptions of social life. Solutions to this problem are most commonly sought in the political sphere. I want to argue that we cannot afford to neglect the sphere of the household, the informal sector, and relations of kinship and their chosen equivalents.

There are only a limited number of ways or organizing relations among human beings in society. The dominant one nowadays is the markets—the exchange of commodities and services by individuals (or entities behaving as if they were individuals) acting from self-interest. A second way is by political decision, enacted into law, and implemented through law—following organizations, often bureaucracies, sometimes professionals or enterprises acting under instruction from a government, or paid to carry out its wishes. Such legislated compliance may be undertaken under a democratic mandate or not. States were powerful in Europe long before democracy was the normal means of legitimating their power, and they still retain, as Ulrich Beck has pointed out, many attributes of their authoritarian heritage. Indeed, some might see democratic decision making as only the top-dressing, framing and to some degree giving a general steer to structures that remain for the most part more hierarchical than they are democratic.

And third, there is the form of relationship that depends on gifts, barter, or submergence of the interests of the self under that of some larger entity. Families are one of the principal entities of this kind, but there are also friendships, voluntary associations, churches, even political associations, which may be founded on similar principles.

Within families, gift and barter are ways of arranging cooperation between members of the same generation (spouses or long-standing partners who combine their different resources, energies, and talents for their mutual benefit), but more particularly between different generations. Parents make many "gifts" of their time, energy, and devotion to their children. In their turn, children make similar gifts to their parents, especially when the latter become needy or infirm. The greater part of caring for aged and ill who remain at home falls to family members, especially, of course, to women. Families are one of the principal means through which the obligations of one generation to another are recognized and enacted. Families are the primary locus of identification between generations.

Since it represents so substantial an alternative to commodification, individualism, and alienation, one might expect democratic socialists to be sympathetic to the family as a form of life. Marx famously described the family as a haven in a heartless world. Socialists have often used family relationship as a metaphor for the social relationships they wish to see, for example in the identification of fellow workers as "brothers" or "sisters" or in the ideas of community, mutual care, and responsibility that sustained the postwar project of the welfare state in Britain. The family has provided a rhetorical lexicon of norms with which socialists or progressives were supposed to identify. I remember a remarkable speech by Mario Cuomo to the Democratic convention many years ago that revolved around the ideal of America as an inclusive family.

Of course, matters are not so simple. Families have never existed in a free space, as a kind of voluntarist, cooperative alternative to the regimes of political hierarchy or market exchange. Their forms of relationship and domination were, and are, structured by law. Their members were subject to differential opportunities and pressures to engage in market exchange. They existed within a cultural and normative order in which the institutions of religion had, and continue to have, an important role.

The effects of these various structures were to impose on the supposedly voluntary order of the family extremely constraining and unequal features. Women and children were even in the last century to a considerable degree the property of their fathers or husbands, who had legal license to control or punish them with violence. Men were more free to exchange their labor in the market than women, who in some social groups were confined to virtual captivity at home. Men were politically enfranchised long before women. Far from a setting in which voluntary cooperation for mutual benefit was the norm, families were often a setting of domination and subordination—of one gender over another and of one generation over another.

Given this inherited situation, it is not surprising that in the modern period the family has been subjected to a deep critique. Women in particular have organized and campaigned to weaken the constraints exercised in the name of family values but, as they saw it, largely in the interests of men. Political battles about divorce and abortion have been an important aspect of this. Members of both sexes, but perhaps especially women, have also voted with their feet, avoiding the constraining relationship of the family or removing themselves from it when it became intolerable. Thus, especially in northern Europe and North America, rates of divorce, and of cohabitation before or instead of marriage, have risen substantially, to the point that in Britain about one in three marriages is likely to end in divorce and in the United States one in two. Young people too have exercised their freedom to live independently. Whereas in Italy, France, and Spain, it remains normal for young men and women to live with their parents throughout their studies and until they marry, in Britain, America, and Scandinavia it has become common for young people to live in small communities of their own generation, on university campuses or in shared apartments.

This widespread exit from the family, and the wish of individuals to live more of their lives outside its constraints, generates demands that its functions be picked up by other agencies and forms of organization. Women have sought a new balance between the part of their lives spent within the family, and the part they spend in the labor market. Demands have been made that government agencies take on the responsibilities that families no longer meet. There are thus demands for more and earlier child care, and for public provision of residential care for old and infirm people. My own mother-in-law, aged ninety-two and very infirm, enjoys the assistance of no fewer than four paid, caring caretakers, employed indirectly by the local authority, visiting her in her sheltered housing in an inner London borough at different times of the day or week and giving her various kinds of help, with getting up, shopping, cleaning, laundry, and so on, in return for a small financial contribution from her. This despite the fact that she has two grown-up daughters living within fifteen minutes of her and a son less than an hour away. She gets a great deal of help from her family too, but the point is that the public system provides impressive services.

"THE FAMILY" is still evaluated by many on the left in terms of the degree to which it impinges on the individual rights of its members. Claims made in terms of "family values" are critically reinter-preted as claims that enforce the covert domination of men over women. In Britain, concerns over the well-being of children are often formulated in terms of children's rights as individuals, even in terms of their implicit claims against their parents for injuries done to them. The common solution is to punish oppressive family members and remove the ill-treated children to hypothetical substitute families, found through procedures of fostering or adoption. It is unclear, however, whether the punitive, rights-based approach that has developed over recent years in England in response to anxieties about child abuse is in fact as helpful to children as a system of family law that gives priority to support for the family, such as is found in France.

There are of course many ways in which families confer unequal powers and responsibilities on men and women. It is commonly the case that the more burdens the state or society assigns to the family (to look after children, the ill, or the old), the less freedom women will have. But it is also true that the case for greater equality between the sexes is often made more as a demand for individual freedom, for stronger rights of exit *for women too*, than for more equal forms of partnership within freely chosen relationships. The culture of individualism has a large role in this, all the more so because the alternative "anti-individualist" model, the idea of the social or welfare state, has been under such persistent attack.

The question I want to raise is whether the support and strengthening of the family, and of other forms of relationship and cooperation that depend on mutual identification, gift, and barter, is a proper object of public policy. Should democratic socialists in particular still have a commitment to this idea, on grounds related to their traditional antipathy to individualist market relations and coercive political relations, as dominant forms of social life? I want to argue that they should have, and that they can do so in ways that nevertheless defend an equal division of rights and powers between men and women.

Stein Ringen, in a recent pamphlet and book that are in part valuable, in part misguided, has pointed out that the family is a very important locus of production, as well as of more readily recognized consumption. The standard of living, or goods of life, that citizens enjoy are substantially generated or enhanced by labor performed in the home or by family members working for one another outside the home.* They clean, shop, cook, drive, mend, build, garden, nurse, and perform many other services for one another. Most commodities and machines are inert and useless objects unless labor is invested in creating value out of them. Ringen points out that cooperation between family members is a highly efficient way of increasing the value gained

---

*Stein Ringen, *The Family in Question* (*Demos*, 1998) and *Citizens, families and reform* (Oxford University Press, 1997).

from such commodities or from the returns from labor in the market place. Cooking a meal for four does not take four times the work of cooking a meal for one. Two people do not need to occupy twice the living space of a single person in order to gain equivalent benefit from it. A garden maintained by one person can be enjoyed by many. A car can be driven by one person but may comfortably transport five. Ringen argues that the standard of living as measured by GNP grossly underestimates its real value because it does not include the value-added from the informal family or friendship economy.

He also deploys this argument to explain the dissatisfaction many feel at the failure of rising incomes (where they have them) to generate an increased sense of well-being. He argues that this is not because people do not understand their own interests or have unrealistic or greedy aspirations, but because the gains made at the level of monetary income are in reality often being paid for by real losses in the informal economy. Working a fifty-hour week generates more money, but it means there is less time available to produce "goods" in the informal sector—through the "work" of playing with the children, making a garden, coaching a local children's soccer team, or producing a play with an amateur theater company. One could add to this the work of conversation, or attending to the needs of other people, or educating oneself, too. The situation must be especially painful in the United States, where enforced workaholism—long working hours, short holidays—is reported to be more rife than in Europe, but the British position is certainly worsening for those with employment.

The schema of production and consumption, though they dominate our current view of the economy, are ideological constructions that mystify the real economic process. This schema makes work seem mainly a sacrifice that we undertake in order to earn the money to be able to consume the products of other people's work. But in reality, most consumption is merely the location of another labor process. The labor of consumption (cooking, gardening, travelling, home maintenance, child care) involves effort, and is by no means wholly painful, but its most significant feature is that it is undertaken in a context of gift and barter relationships, not for monetary exchange. And on the other side of the production/consumption divide, much work in the market has its intrinsic satisfactions, which are deeply missed by those who cannot enjoy them, for example the satisfactions derived from cooperation, mutual recognition, and the deployment of human capacities and energies. Those who rightly demand jobs as an output of economic policy are not merely asking for the means of generating income, but for the underpinnings of a whole way of life.

Ringen's argument is that just as it seems quite proper for society, through its elected governments, to support and sustain the formal economy (by providing infrastructure, an educated workforce, security, rules, insurance), so governments should also be prepared deliberately to support families as a site of production and as a generator of social and individual well-being. He argues that our present economy undervalues, or indeed entirely fails to recognize, the work that is done in these settings, and far from giving it support colludes with the interests of capital in undermining and draining it of human resources.

I F THE "opportunity costs" of bringing up a child or caring for an aged relative or friend are high, because of the superior rewards available from the market, then individuals will reduce their commitments to these tasks. If these activities are socially recognized and paid for (by child allowances, ore allowances to support the care of the infirm), then individuals will make different decisions, not in every case but for the most part. The system of taxes and benefits, and of course the organization of labor and other markets, selectively rewards and sanctions different kinds of activity. Ringen's explanation of declining family size, and even more important of declining commitment to work within families, is that the opportunity costs of this work in contrast to paid work has changed in a way too favorable to the latter.

This has happened in parts as a consequence of women's newly won freedom to enter the labor market and find gainful employment in it. The new freedom seems to be the effect of economic as well as political and cultural changes, as the growth of the service and information economies has reduced the comparative advantages men had in the preceding productive regimes of agriculture and industry. Opportunity costs have changed because women now have many choices, where formerly they had few. This is of course a positive development, and there should be no regression to the situation where choice was not available to them.

But the fact that work in the market is materially rewarded is not a good reason why work outside should not be. It should be possible to recognize many spheres of work in the informal sector, especially those involving care across generations, and to ensure that they are materially rewarded on a gender-neutral basis. This is what child allowances, paid maternity leave, allowances for the care of the disabled, set out to do. Paid holidays, educational leave, and even provisions for retirement come into this category, if one thinks of all of these, as one realistically should, as occasions for productive life-enhancing work in the non-monetary sector, as well as of relief from the regimes of work that are organized through the market.

One of the chief scandals of the Blair government in Britain has been the "welfare to work" legislation targeted at unemployed single mothers, which requires them to retain or re-enter the labor market as a condition for receiving benefits. This requirement was imposed irrespective of the age of their children, even though it is obvious that whereas children of four or five can be expected to spend time at school (and in the care of the state of other formal agencies) younger infants might well not do so, either by their own or their parents' preference. It is entirely reasonable to regard the time parents spend caring for such young children as no less a form of work than the time they might spend at the supermarket checkout counter or cooking school meals: it deserves just as much material reward. It is a paradox of the diminution of family responsibilities for the care of children or the old, on grounds of gender equality, that its outcome is that many women who might prefer to care for their own children or relatives in domestic settings end up caring for strangers in the employ of the government or of private agencies. Individuals of both sexes should be free to choose what they do, but not in these conditions, which reward one choice, and penalize another.

As always, the advocacy of personal liberty can mask as well as represent real interests. Whose interest is served by the emergence of a situation in which people become incapable of preparing a good meal, but depend instead on ready-made meals purchased in supermarkets or bought from take-out restaurants? Well, on the one hand, there are the interests of busy women or men, who are spared the work of cooking and washing up and can spend their time in different ways, most likely, especially in workaholic America, at their places of employment. But on the other hand, we see the interests of the capitalists (who may include you and me), who invest in the supermarkets and take-out chains, and who need an attenuated domestic economy in order to create this new marketplace for their goods.

How far should the state intervene not materially but legally to support the formation and maintenance of families? Does it matter that fewer people marry, that divorce is in effect obtainable on demand, that individuals may easily shrug off any responsibility they might have for the support of their children or parents? Is there a justifiable way of giving legal and normative support to lasting relationships and obligations, while not improperly infringing individual problems?

The Thatcher government tried, disastrously, to enforce parental obligations for the upkeep of teenage children aged sixteen through eighteen by denying the latter unemployment benefits and making them materially dependent on their parents. This imposed severe strain on many families of the young unemployed, both materially and in the visible withdrawal of public assistance for the parental function. The increased incidence of homelessness among the young, so visible in city streets in Britain, was in part a consequence of this punitive and counterproductive attempt to enforce family solidarity. These are very complex issues. We have become so much captured by libertarian values, and so (rightly) suspicious of

authoritarian moralism—one of New Labour's least likeable habits of mind—that it has become difficult to justify more solidaristic approaches in case they bring with them the coercion of individuals.

Ringen's solution is to regard marriages as binding contracts in which both partners and children have a legal and "democratic" stake—as if the family were a miniature republic. But this imports a conception of rational self-interest and contractual exchange into a sphere whose essence seems to be more open ended and unspecified so far as the precise shape of mutual gifts and obligations is concerned. Here, if anywhere, is a sphere where complex and not simple forms of equality should apply. Nor does resort by government to moral persuasion and re-education in family values seem a feasible or desirable remedy to the individualization brought about by the market. Some New Labour writers argue that the power of moral guidance is one of the chief levers available to modernizing governments, and this view is echoed in the speeches of Tony Blair. In this respect, however, New Labour seems to be latently authoritarian. It is moralistic in face of the symptoms of declining social solidarity, but blind to their prime causes in the deregulated markets that its main policy agendas support.

Perhaps the best way forward is to look to the state to provide support to family and other lasting relationships, not only through the financial incentives provided for individuals, but also in the resources that it can mobilize to sustain systems of social support. Most people probably prefer to maintain lasting ties to and responsibilities for family members and long-standing friends and neighbors if they can do so without unacceptable costs. The task for the state therefore is to keep these costs to individuals at an acceptable level, to provide services that are supportive and respectful of personal ties, and to organize mediatory arrangements that assist in the negotiation of difficulties, including the facilitation of "exit" where this is most appropriate or is deeply desired.

There are many ways in which this supportive conception has evolved as an enhancement of previously more impersonal and usurpatory social services. Encouragement of parents to stay with children in the hospital, hospices the encourage the presence of relatives, obstetric delivery rooms that welcome fathers, counseling services provided in circumstances of marital conflict, public-housing allocation policies that recognize the need for family members to remain near one another, encouragement of reflection concerning decisions about abortion, are all examples. A new conception of "Active Welfare" (the theme of a special issue of *Soundings* magazine, Spring 1998) needs to be worked out, in which priority is given to the enabling of participative and self-managed forms of welfare delivery.

It is hard to see how democratic socialists, properly critical of markets and capitalism as the dominant

3. Family: What Do We Really Want?

form of social relationship, and also of the state as an all-pervasive substitute for this, can neglect the sphere of the family, and of its informal cognates of friendship and voluntary association, as an essential dimension of the good society. This is especially the case if, as socialists, we are also sensitive to the natural and necessary emotional dimension of human lives.

Recognition of the place of the emotions in the ordering of social life is crucial to arguments about the relevance of the family to democratic socialism. The rationalism of the Enlightenment tradition, both in its liberal and Marxist versions, has tended to disregard the affective dimension of human existence. Consideration of what we really want from the family requires us to bring this back into the picture. It is a paradox of feminism that it deserves the main credit for reclaiming this area of experience as relevant to politics, while having also been highly critical of the institution that has hith-

erto been the primary location of intimate life—namely, the family. The development of a convincing socialist way of imagining our society depends on working through these dilemmas.

MICHAEL RUSTIN is a professor of sociology at the University of East London. He is co-editor of *Soundings* magazine. He recently co-edited and contributed to *Welfare and Culture in Europe*.

Unit Selections

4. **Boys Will Be Boys,** Barbara Kantrowitz and Claudia Kalb
5. **Sex Differences in the Brain,** Doreen Kimura
6. **Flirting Fascination,** Joann Ellison Rodgers
7. **What's Your Love Story?** Robert J. Sternberg
8. **Protecting Against Unintended Pregnancy: A Guide to Contraceptive Choices,** Tamar Nordenberg
9. **The Brave New World of Parenting,** Jessica Snyder Sachs
10. **How Old Is Too Old to Have a Baby?** Judith Newman
11. **Shaped by Life in the Womb,** Sharon Begley
12. **The Cost of Children,** Phillip J. Longman
13. **Our Babies, Ourselves,** Meredith F. Small

Key Points to Consider

❖ What do you think is the role of flirtation in the formation of relationships? What is the biological function of flirtation?

❖ What do you look for in a mate? Would you be willing to settle for less? Why or why not? Do you think you follow a story line in your relationships? What can be done to change your story line, if you have one?

❖ Have you thought about your own use of contraceptives? How would you advise a friend if he or she came to you and asked about the most appropriate contraceptive to use?

❖ Do you see children as a part of your life? Why or why not? At what age do you think one should stop considering having a child? What should be the determining factor?

❖ What is the nature of fetal development? What can be done to increase the likelihood of having a healthy child?

❖ How do children enrich a relationship? What are the drawbacks of having children? What are the responsibilities associated with parenthood? If you do have children, how do you think it will affect you and your relationship with your partner? What are your attitudes and beliefs about parenthood?

 **Links** **www.dushkin.com/online/**

These sites are annotated on pages 4 and 5.

By and large, humans are social animals, and as such, we seek out meaningful connections with other humans. John Bowlby, Mary Ainsworth, and others have proposed that this drive toward connection is biologically based and is at the core of what it means to be human. However it plays out in childhood and adulthood, the need for connection, to love and be loved, is a powerful force moving us to establish and maintain close relationships. At the same time, our biology influences the way in which we relate to each other and the way in which we create and maintain relationships.

As we explore various possibilities, we engage in the complex business of relationship building. In this business, many processes occur simultaneously: Messages are sent and received; differences are negotiated; assumptions and expectations are or are not met. The ultimate goals are closeness and continuity.

How we feel about others and what we see as essential to these relationships play an important role in our establishing and maintaining relationships. In this unit, we look at factors that underlie the establishment of relationships as well as the beginning stages of relationships.

The first subsection explores gender differences and their influences in relationships and on how we relate to the world. The first article, "Boys Will Be Boys," explores the results of a growing interest in the essential nature of boys. Among the topics discussed are parental responsibilities and techniques for recognizing unique characteristics of boys and ways of socializing them toward healthy relationships in childhood and beyond. "Sex Differences in the Brain" addresses the biological differences between male and female brains and their impact on relationship building and maintenance.

The second subsection takes a broad look at factors that influence the building of meaningful relationships and at the beginning stages of adult relationships. The first essay, "Flirting Fascination," describes biological explanations for flirtatious behavior. We form relationships in the context of stories, and in "What's Your Love Story?" Robert Sternberg describes 12 stories he has identified that act as guides for the formation, maintenance, and end of love relationships.

In the third subsection, important aspects of adult relationships are explored: sexuality and pregnancy. Particular attention is given to the idea of

responsibility to oneself and others in acting out our sexuality. "Protecting Against Unintended Pregnancy" is a fact-filled guide to the selection of a contraceptive.   The next article, "The Brave New World of Parenting," explores the results of successful efforts to overcome infertility and the problems that parents may face once they have had a child through extraordinary means.

In the final subsection, the creation of a new generation and the costs and joys of doing so are explored. "How Old Is Too Old to Have a Baby?" looks at a growing phenomenon—that of people deciding to become parents at older and older ages. "Shaped by Life in the Womb" looks at the nature of fetal and infant development. Readers of "The Cost of Children" may find themselves amazed at the high cost of rearing a child. Cross-cultural variations in maternal attitudes and beliefs are presented in "Our Babies, Ourselves."

Boys will be Boys

Developmental research has been focused on girls; now it's their brothers' turn. Boys need help, too, but first they need to be understood.

BY BARBARA KANTROWITZ AND CLAUDIA KALB

IT WAS A CLASSIC MARS-VENUS ENCOUNTER. Only in this case, the woman was from Harvard and the man—well, boy—was a 4-year-old at a suburban Boston nursery school. Graduate student Judy Chu was in his classroom last fall to gather observations for her doctoral dissertation on human development. His greeting was startling: he held up his finger as if it were a gun and pretended to shoot her. "I felt bad," Chu recalls. "I felt as if he didn't like me." Months later and much more boy-savvy, Chu has a different interpretation: the gunplay wasn't hostile—it was just a way for him to say hello. "They don't mean it to have harsh consequences. It's a way for them to connect."

Researchers like Chu are discovering new meaning in lots of things boys have done for ages. In fact, they're dissecting just about every aspect of the developing male psyche and creating a hot new field of inquiry: the study of boys. They're also producing a slew of books with titles like "Real Boys: Rescuing Our Sons From the Myths of Boyhood" and "Raising Cain: Protecting the Emotional Life of Boys" that will hit the stores in the next few months.

What some researchers are finding is that boys and girls really are from two different planets. But since the two sexes have to live together here on Earth, they should be raised with special consideration for their distinct needs. Boys and girls have different "crisis points," experts say, stages in their emotional and social development where things can go very wrong. Until recently, girls got all the attention. But boys need help, too. They're much more likely than girls to have discipline problems at school and to be diagnosed with attention deficit disorder (ADD). Boys far outnumber girls in special-education classes. They're also more likely to commit violent crimes and end up in jail. Consider the headlines: Jonesboro, Ark.; Paducah, Ky.; Pearl, Miss. In all these school shootings, the perpetrators were young adolescent boys.

Even normal boy behavior has come to be considered pathological in the wake of the feminist movement. An abundance of physical energy and the urge to conquer—these are normal male characteristics, and in an earlier age they were good things, even essential to survival. "If Huck Finn or Tom Sawyer were alive today," says Michael Gurian, author of "The Wonder of Boys," "we'd say they had ADD or a conduct disorder." He says one of the new insights we're gaining about boys is a very old one: boys will be boys. "They are who they are," says Gurian, "and we need to love them for who they are. Let's not try to rewire them."

Indirectly, boys are benefiting from all the research done on girls, especially the landmark work by Harvard University's Carol Gilligan. Her 1982 book, "In a Different Voice: Psychological Theory and Women's Development," inspired Take Our Daughters to Work Day, along with best-selling spinoffs like Mary Pipher's "Reviving Ophelia." The traditional, unisex way of looking at child development was profoundly flawed, Gilligan says: "It was like having a one-dimensional perspective on a two-dimensional scene." At Harvard, where she chairs the gender-studies department, Gilligan is now supervising work on males, including Chu's project. Other researchers are studying mental illness and violence in boys.

While girls' horizons have been expanding, boys' have narrowed, confined to rigid ideas of acceptable male behavior no matter how hard their parents tried to avoid stereotypes. The macho ideal still rules. "We gave boys dolls and they used them as guns," says Gurian. "For 15 years, all we heard was that [gender differences] were all about socialization. Parents who raised their kids through that period said in the end, 'That's not true. Boys and girls can be awfully different.' I think we're awakening to the biological realities and the sociological realities."

But what exactly is the essential nature of boys? Even as infants, boys and girls behave differently. A recent study at Children's Hospital in Boston found that boy babies are more emotionally expressive; girls are more reflective. (That means boy babies tend to cry when they're unhappy; girl babies suck their thumbs.) This could indicate that girls

The Wonder (and Worry) Years

There may be no such thing as *child* development anymore. Instead, researchers are now studying each gender's development separately and discovering that boys and girls face very different sorts of challenges. Here is a rough guide to the major phases in their development.

Boys

0–3 years At birth, boys have brains that are 5% larger than girls' (size doesn't affect intelligence) and proportionately larger bodies—disparities that increase with age.

4–6 years The start of school is a tough time as boys must curb aggressive impulses. They lag behind girls in reading skills, and hyperactivity may be a problem.

Age 1	2	3	4	5	6	7

Girls

0–3 years Girls are born with a higher proportion of nerve cells to process information. More brain regions are involved in language production and recognition.

4–6 years Girls are well suited to school. They are calm, get along with others, pick up on social cues, and reading and writing come easily to them.

are innately more able to control their emotions. Boys have higher levels of testosterone and lower levels of the neurotransmitter serotonin, which inhibits aggression and impulsivity. That may help explain why more males than females carry through with suicide, become alcoholics and are diagnosed with ADD.

The developmental research on the impact of these physiological differences is still in the embryonic stage, but psychologists are drawing some interesting comparisons between girls and boys (chart). For girls, the first crisis point often comes in early adolescence. Until then, Gilligan and others found, girls have an enormous capacity for establishing relationships and interpreting emotions. But in their early teens, girls clamp down, squash their emotions, blunt their insight. Their self-esteem plummets. The first crisis point for boys comes much earlier, researchers now say. "There's an outbreak of symptoms at age 5, 6, 7, just like you see in girls at 11, 12, 13," says Gilligan. Problems at this age include bed-wetting and separation anxiety. "They don't have the language or experience" to articulate it fully, she says, "but the feelings are no less intense." That's why Gilligan's student Chu is studying preschoolers. For girls at this age, Chu says, hugging a parent goodbye "is almost a nonissue." But little boys, who display a great deal of tenderness, soon begin to bury it with "big boy" behavior to avoid being called sissies. "When their parents drop them off, they want to be close and want to be held, but not in front of other people," says Chu. "Even as early as 4, they're already aware of those masculine stereotypes and are negotiating their way around them."

It's a phenomenon that parents, especially mothers, know well. One morning last month, Lori Dube, a 37-year-old mother of three from Evanston, Ill., visited her oldest son, Abe, almost 5, at his nursery school, where he was having lunch with his friends. She kissed him, prompting another boy to comment scornfully: "Do you know what your mom just did? She kissed you!" Dube acknowledges, with some sadness, that she'll have to be more sensitive to Abe's new reactions to future public displays of affection. "Even if he loves it, he's getting these messages that it's not good."

There's a struggle—a desire and need for warmth on the one hand and a pull toward independence on the other. Boys like Abe are going through what psychologists long ago declared an integral part of growing up: individualization and disconnection from parents, especially mothers. But now some researchers think that process is too abrupt. When boys repress normal feelings like love because of social pressure, says William Pollack, head of the Center for Men at Boston's McLean Hospital and author of the forthcoming "Real Boys," "they've lost contact with the genuine nature of who they are and what they feel. Boys are in a silent crisis. The only time we notice it is when they pull the trigger."

No one is saying that acting like Rambo in nursery school leads directly to tragedies like Jonesboro. But researchers do think that boys who are forced to shut down positive emotions are left with only one socially acceptable outlet: anger. The cultural ideals boys are exposed to in movies and on TV still emphasize traditional masculine roles—warrior, rogue, adventurer—with heavy doses of violence. For every Mr. Mom, there are a dozen Terminators. "The feminist movement has done a great job of convincing people that a woman can be nurturing and a mother and a tough trial lawyer at the same time," says Dan Kindlon, an assistant professor of psychiatry at Harvard Medical School. "But we haven't done that as much with men. We're afraid that if they're too soft, that's all they can be."

And the demands placed on boys in the early years of elementary school can increase their overall stress levels. Scientists have known for years that boys and girls develop physically and intellectually at very different rates (time-line). Boys' fine motor skills—the ability to hold a pencil, for example—are usually considerably behind girls. They often learn to read later. At the same time, they're much more active—not the best combination for academic advancement. "Boys feel like school is a game rigged against them," says Michael Thompson, co-author with Kindlon of "Raising Cain." "The things at which they excel—gross motor skills, visual and spatial skills, their exuberance—do not find as good a reception in school" as the things girls excel at. Boys (and girls) are also in academic programs at much younger ages than they used to be, increasing the chances that males will be forced to sit still before they are ready. The result, for many boys, is frustration, says Thompson: "By fourth grade, they're saying the teachers like girls better."

A second crisis point for boys occurs around the same time their sisters are stumbling, in early adolescence. By then, say Thompson and Kindlon, boys go one step further in their drive to be "real guys." They partake in a "culture of cruelty," enforcing male stereotypes on one another. "Anything tender, anything compassionate or too artistic is labeled gay," says Thompson. "The homophobia of boys in the 11, 12, 13 range is a stronger force than gravity."

Boys who refuse to fit the mold suffer. Glo Wellman of the California Parenting Institute in Santa Rosa has three sons, 22, 19 and 12. One of her boys, she says, is a "nontypical boy: he's very sensitive and caring and creative and artistic." Not surprisingly, he had the most difficulty growing up, she says. "We've got a long way to go to help boys . . . to have a sense that they can be anything they want to be."

In later adolescence, the once affectionate toddler has been replaced by a sulky stranger who often acts as though torture would be preferable to a brief exchange of words with Mom or Dad. Parents have to try even harder to keep in touch. Boys want and need the attention, but often just don't know how to ask for it. In a recent national poll, teenagers named their parents as their No. 1 heroes. Researchers say a strong parental bond is the most important protection against everything from smoking to suicide.

For San Francisco Chronicle columnist Adnir Lara, that message sank in when she was traveling to New York a few years ago with her son, then 15. She sat next to a woman who told her that until recently she

7-10 years While good at gross motor skills, boys trail girls in finer control. Many of the best students but also nearly all of the poorest ones are boys.

	8	9	10

7-10 years Very good years for girls. On average, they outperform boys at school, excelling in verbal skills while holding their own in math.

11-13 years A mixed bag. Dropout rates begin to climb, but good students start pulling ahead of girls in math skills and catching up some in verbal ones.

	11	12	13

11-13 years The start of puberty and girls' most vulnerable time. Many experience depression; as many as 15% may try to kill themselves.

14-16 years Entering adolescence, boys hit another rough patch. Indulging in drugs, alcohol and aggressive behavior are common forms of rebellion.

	14	15	16

14-16 years Eating disorders are a major concern. Although anorexia can manifest itself as early as 8, it typically afflicts girls starting at 11 or 12; bulimia at 15.

SOURCES: DR. MICHAEL THOMPSON, BARNEY BRAWER. RESEARCH BY BILL VOURVOULIAS —NEWSWEEK

Trouble Spots: Where Boys Run Into Problems

Not all boys are the same, of course, but most rebel in predictable patterns and with predictable weapons: underachievement, aggression and drug and alcohol use. While taking chances is an important aspect of the growth process, it can lead to real trouble.

When Johnny Can't Read

Girls have reading disorders nearly as often as boys, but are able to overcome them. Disability rates, as identified by:

CLINICAL TESTS		SCHOOLS	
Boys	8.7%	Boys	13.6%
Girls	6.9%	Girls	3.2%

SOURCE: DR. SALLY SHAYWITZ, CONN. LONGITUDINAL STUDY

Suicidal Impulses

While girls are much more likely to try to kill themselves, boys are likelier to die from their attempts.

SUICIDE ATTEMPTS*		SUICIDE FATALITIES	
Boys	3,000	Boys	260
Girls	23,000	Girls	77

1995, AGES 5–14. *NEWSWEEK ESTIMATE. SOURCES: NCHS, CDC

Binge Drinking

Boys binge more on alcohol. Those who had five or more drinks in a row in the last two weeks:

1997, BY GRADE

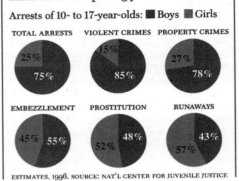

40%
30
20
10

Boys
Girls

8th   10th   12th

SOURCE: MONITORING THE FUTURE STUDY

Aggression That Turns to Violence

Boys get arrested three times as often as girls, but for some nonviolent crimes the numbers are surprisingly even.

Arrests of 10- to 17-year-olds: ■ Boys ■ Girls

TOTAL ARRESTS	VIOLENT CRIMES	PROPERTY CRIMES
25% / 75%	15% / 85%	27% / 78%

EMBEZZLEMENT	PROSTITUTION	RUNAWAYS
45% / 55%	52% / 48%	57% / 43%

ESTIMATES, 1996. SOURCE: NAT'L CENTER FOR JUVENILE JUSTICE

Eating Disorders

Boys can also have eating disorders. Kids who used laxatives or vomited to lose weight:

1995, BY GRADE

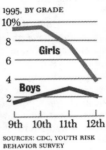

10%
8
6
4
2

Girls
Boys

9th   10th   11th   12th

SOURCES: CDC, YOUTH RISK BEHAVIOR SURVEY

---

would have had to change seats because she would not have been able to bear the pain of seeing a teenage son and mother together. The woman's son was 17 when his girlfriend dumped him; he went into the garage and killed himself. "This story made me aware that with a boy especially, you have to keep talking because they don't come and talk to you," she says. Lara's son is now 17; she also has a 19-year-old daughter. "My daughter stalked me. She followed me from room to room. She was yelling, but she was in touch. Boys don't do that. They leave the room and you don't know what they're feeling." Her son is now 6 feet 3. "He's a man. There are barriers. You have to reach through that and remember to ruffle his hair."

With the high rate of divorce, many boys are growing up without any adult men in their lives at all. Don Elium, coauthor of the best-selling 1992 book "Raising a Son," says that with troubled boys, there's often a common theme: distant, uninvolved fathers, and mothers who have taken on more responsibility to fill the gap. That was the case with Raymundo Infante Jr., a 16-year-old high-school junior, who lives with his mother, Mildred, 38, a hospital administrative assistant in Chicago, and his sister, Vanessa, 19. His parents divorced when he was a baby and he had little contact with his father until a year ago. The hurt built up—in sixth grade, Raymundo was so depressed that he told a classmate he wanted to kill himself. The classmate told the teacher, who told a counselor, and Raymundo saw a psychiatrist for a year. "I felt that I just wasn't good enough, or he just didn't want me," Raymundo says.

Last year Raymundo finally confronted his dad, who works two jobs—in an office and on a construction crew—and accused him of caring more about work than about his son. Now the two spend time together on weekends and sometimes go shopping, but there is still a huge gap of lost years.

Black boys are especially vulnerable, since they are more likely than whites to grow up in homes without fathers. They're often on their own much sooner than whites. Black leaders are looking for alternatives. In Atlanta, the Rev. Tim McDonald's First Iconium Baptist Church just chartered a Boy Scout troop. "Gangs are so prevalent because guys want to belong to something," says McDonald. "We've got to give them something positive to belong to." Black educators like Chicagoan Jawanza Kunjufu think mentoring programs will overcome the bias against academic success as "too white." Some cities are also experimenting with all-boy classrooms in predominantly black schools.

Researchers hope that in the next few years, they'll come up with strategies that will help boys the way the work of Gilligan and others helped girls. In the meantime, experts say, there are some guidelines. Parents can channel their sons' energy into constructive activities, like team sports. They should also look for "teachable moments" to encourage qualities such as empathy. When Diane Fisher, a Cincinnati-area psychologist, hears her 8- and 10-year-old boys talking about "finishing somebody," she knows she has mistakenly rented a violent videogame. She pulls the plug and tells them: "In our

house, killing people is not entertainment, even if it's just pretend."

Parents can also teach by example. New Yorkers Dana and Frank Minaya say they've never disciplined their 16-year-old son Walter in anger. They insist on resolving all disputes calmly and reasonably, without yelling. If there is a problem, they call an official family meeting "and we never leave without a big hug," says Frank. Walter tries to be open with his parents. "I don't want to miss out on any advice," he says.

Most of all, wise parents of boys should go with the flow. Cindy Lang, 36, a full-time mother in Woodside, Calif., is continually amazed by the relentless energy of her sons, Roger Lloyd, 12, and Chris, 9. "You accept the fact that they're going to involve themselves in risky behavior, like skateboarding down a flight of stairs. As a girl, I certainly wasn't skateboarding down a flight of stairs." Just last week, she got a phone call from school telling her that Roger Lloyd was in the emergency room because he had fallen backward while playing basketball and school officials thought he might have a concussion. He's fine now, but she's prepared for the next emergency: "I have a cell phone so I can be on alert." Boys will be boys. And we have to let them.

With KAREN SPRINGEN in Chicago, PATRICIA KING in San Francisco, PAT WINGERT in Washington, VERN E. SMITH in Atlanta and ELIZABETH ANGELL in New York by Doreen Kimura

Sex Differences in the Brain

Men and women display patterns of behavioral and cognitive differences that reflect varying hormonal influences on brain development

Men and women differ not only in their physical attributes and reproductive function but also in many other characteristics, including the way they solve intellectual problems. For the past few decades, it has been ideologically fashionable to insist that these behavioral differences are minimal and are the consequence of variations in experience during development before and after adolescence. Evidence accumulated more recently, however, suggests that the effects of sex hormones on brain organization occur so early in life that from the start the environment is acting on differently wired brains in boys and girls. Such effects make evaluating the role of experience, independent of physiological predisposition, a difficult if not dubious task. The biological bases of sex differences in brain and behavior have become much better known through increasing numbers of behavioral, neurological and endoctinological studies.

We know, for instance, from observations of both humans and nonhumans that males are more aggressive than females, that young males engage in more rough-and-tumble play than females and that females are more nurturing. We also know that in general males are better at a variety of spatial or navigational tasks. How do these and other sex differences come about? Much of our information and many of our ideas about how sexual differentiation takes place derive from research on animals. From such investigations, it appears that perhaps the most important factor in the differentiation of males and females is the level of exposure to various sex hormones early in life.

In most mammals, including humans, the developing organism has the potential to be male or female. Producing a male, however, is a complex process. When a Y chromosome is present, testes, or male gonads, form. This development is the critical first step toward becoming a male. When no Y chromosome is present, ovaries form.

Testes produce male hormones, or androgens (testosterone chief among them), which are responsible not only for transformation of the genitals into male organs but also for organization of corresponding male behaviors early in life. As with genital formation, the intrinsic tendency that occurs in the absence of masculinizing hormonal influence, according to seminal studies by Robert W. Goy of the University of Wisconsin, is to develop female genital structures and behavior. Female anatomy and probably most behavior associated with females are thus the default modes in the absence of androgens.

If a rodent with functional male genitals is deprived of androgens immediately after birth (either by castration or by the administration of a compound that blocks androgens), male sexual behavior, such as mounting, will be reduced, and more female sexual behavior, such as lordosis (arching of the back when receptive to coitus), will be expressed. Similarly, if androgens are administered to a female directly after birth, she will display more male sexual behavior and less female behavior in adulthood. These lifelong effects of early exposure to sex hormones are characterized as "organizational" because they appear to alter brain function permanently during a critical period in prenatal or early postnatal development. Administering the same sex hormones at later stages or in the adult has no such effect.

Not all the behaviors that categorize males are organized at the same time, however. Organization by androgens of the male-typical behaviors of mounting and of rough-and-tumble play, for example, occur at different times prenatally in rhesus monkeys.

The area in the brain that regulates female and male reproductive behavior is the hypothalamus. This tiny structure at the base of the brain connects to the pituitary, the master endocrine gland. It has been shown that a region of the hypothalamus is visibly larger in male rats than in females and that this size difference is under hormonal control. Scientists have also found parallel sex differences in a clump of nerve cells in the human brain—parts of the interstitial nucleus of the anterior hypothalamus—that is larger in men than in women. Even sexual orientation and gender identity have been related to anatomical variation in the hypothalamus. In 1991, while at the Salk Institute for Biological Studies in San Diego, Simon Levay reported that one of the interstitial nuclei of the anterior hypothalamus that is usually larger in human males than in females is smaller in homosexual than in heterosexual men. Other researchers, Jiang-Ning Zhou of the Netherlands Institute of Brain Research and his colleagues there and at Free University in Amsterdam, observed another part of the hypothalamus to be smaller in male-to-female transsexuals than in a male control group. These findings are consistent with suggestions that sexual orientation and gender identity have a significant biological component.

Hormones and Intellect

What of differences in intellectual function between men and women? Major sex differences in function seem to lie in patterns of ability rather than in overall level of intelligence (measured as IQ), although some researchers, such as Richard Lynn of the University of Ulster in Northern Ireland, have argued that there exists a small IQ difference favoring human males. Differences in intellectual pattern refer to the fact that people have different intellectual strengths. For example, some people are especially good at using words, whereas others are better at dealing with external stimuli, such as identifying an object in a different orientation. Individuals may have the same overall intelligence but differing abilities.

Sex differences in problem solving have been systematically studied in adults in laboratory situations. On average, men perform better than women at certain spatial tasks. In particular, men seem to have an advantage in tests that require the subject to imagine rotating an object or manipulating it in some other way. They also outperform women in mathematical reasoning tests and in navigating their way through a route. Further, men exhibit more accuracy in tests of target-directed motor skills—that is, in guiding or intercepting projectiles.

Women, on average, excel on tests that measure recall of words and on tests that challenge the person to find words that begin with a specific letter or fulfill some other constraint. They also tend to be better than men at rapidly identifying matching items and performing certain precision manual tasks, such as placing pegs in designated holes on a board.

In examining the nature of sex differences in navigating routes, one study found that men completed a computer simulation of a maze or labyrinth task more quickly and with fewer errors than women did. Another study by different researchers used a path on a tabletop map to measure route learning. Their results showed that although men learned the route in fewer trials and with fewer errors, women remembered more of the landmarks, such as pictures of different types of buildings, than men did. These results and others suggest that women tend to use landmarks as a strategy to orient themselves in everyday life more than men do.

Other findings seemed also to point to female superiority in landmark memory. Researchers tested the ability of individuals to recall objects and their locations within a confined space—such as in a room or on a tabletop. In these studies, women were better able to remember whether items had changed places or not. Other investigators found that women were superior at a memory task where they had to remember the locations of pictures on cards that were turned over in pairs. At this kind of object location, in contrast to other spatial tasks, women appeared to have the advantage.

It is important to keep in mind that some of the average sex differences in cognition vary from slight to quite large and that men and women overlap enormously on many cognitive tests that show average differences. For example, whereas women perform better than men in both verbal memory (recalling words from lists or paragraphs) and verbal fluency (finding words that begin with a specific letter), there was a large difference in memory ability but only a small disparity for the fluency tasks. On the whole, variation between men and women tends to be smaller than deviations within each sex, but very large differences between the groups do exist —in men's high level of visual-spatial targeting ability, for one.

Although it used to be thought that sex differences in problem solving did not appear until puberty, the accumulated evidence now suggests that some cognitive and skill differences are present much earlier. For example, researchers have found that three- and four-year-old boys were better at targeting and mentally rotating figures within a clock face than girls of the same age were. Prepubescent girls, however, excelled at recalling lists of words.

Male and female rodents have also been found to solve problems differently. Christina L. Williams of Duke University has shown that female rats have a greater tendency to use landmarks in spatial learning tasks, as it appears women do. In Williams's experiment, female rats used landmark cues, such as pictures on the wall, in preference to

Problem-Solving Tasks Favoring
Men

Men tend to perform better than women on certain spatial tasks. They do well on tests that involve mentally rotating an object or manipulating it in some fashion, such as imagining turning this three-dimensional object

or determining where the holes punched in a folded piece of paper will fall when the paper is unfolded:

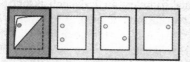

Men also are more accurate than women at target-directed motor skills, such as guiding or intercepting projectiles:

They do better at matching lines with identical slopes:

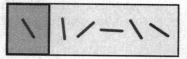

And men tend to do better than women on tests of mathematical reasoning:

 | 1,100 | If only 60 percent of seedlings will survive, how many must be planted to obtain 660 trees? |

Problem-Solving Tasks Favoring
Women

Women tend to perform better than men on tests of perceptual speed in which subjects must rapidly identify matching items—for example, pairing the house on the far left with its twin:

In addition, women remember whether an object, or a series of objects, has been displaced:

When read a story, paragraph or a list of unrelated words, women demonstrate better recall:

 Dog, shadow, hamburger, cloud, flower, eyelash, pencil, paper, water, light, fork, road, building....

Women do better on precision manual tasks—that is, those involving fine-motor coordination—such as placing the pegs in holes on a board:

And women do better than men on mathematical calculation tests:

| 77 | $14 \times 3 - 17 + 52$ |
| 43 | $2 (15 + 3) + 12 - \frac{15}{3}$ |

DOREEN KIMURA AND JOHN MENGEL

geometric cues: angles and the shape of the room, for instance. If no landmarks were available, however, females used the geometric cues. In contrast, males did not use land-marks at all, preferring geometric cues almost exclusively.

Williams also found that hormonal manipulation during the critical period could alter these behaviors.

Depriving newborn males of sex hormones by castrating them or administering hormones to newborn females resulted in a complete reversal of sex-typed behaviors in the adult animals. Treated males behaved like females and treated females like males.

Structural differences may parallel behavioral ones. Lucia F. Jacobs, then at the University of Pittsburgh, discovered that the hippocampus—a region thought to be involved in spatial learning in both birds and mammals–is larger in several male species of rodents than in females. At present, there are insufficient data on possible sex differences in hippocampal size in human subjects.

One of the most compelling areas of evidence for hormonally influenced sex differences in humans comes from studies of girls exposed to excess androgens in the prenatal or neonatal stage. The production of abnormally large quantities of adrenal androgens can occur because of a genetic defect in a condition called congenital adrenal hyperplasia (CAH). Before the 1970s a similar condition also unexpectedly appeared in the offspring of pregnant women who took various synthetic steroids. Although the consequent masculinization of the genitals can be corrected by surgery and drug therapy can stop the overproduction of androgens, the effects of prenatal exposure on the brain cannot be reversed.

Sheri A. Berenbaum of Southern Illinois University at Carbondale and Melissa Hines of the University of California at Los Angeles observed the play behavior of CAH girls and compared it with that of their male and female siblings. Given a choice of transportation and construction toys, dolls and kitchen supplies, or books and board games, the CAH girls preferred the more typically masculine toys—for example, they played with cars for the same amount of time that boys did. Both the CAH girls and the boys differed from unaffected girls in their patterns of choice. Berenbaum also found that CAH girls had greater

TESTOSTERONE LEVELS can affect performance on some tests (see boxes for example of tests). Women with high levels of testosterone perform better on spatial tasks (top) than women with low levels do, but men with low levels outperform men with high levels. One a mathematical reasoning test (middle), low testosterone corresponds to better performance in men; in women there is no such relation. On a test of perceptual speed in which women usually excel (bottom), no relation is found between testosterone and performance.

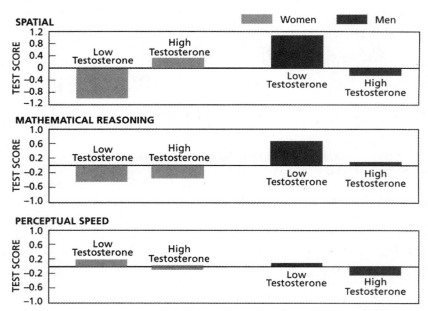

DOREEN KIMURA

interest in male-typical activities and careers. Because there is every reason to think parents would be at least as likely to encourage feminine preferences in their CAH daughters as in their unaffected daughters, these findings suggest that these preferences were actually altered in some way by the early hormonal environment.

Other researchers also found that spatial abilities that are typically better in males are enhanced in CAH girls. But the reverse was reported in one study of CAH-affected boys–they performed worse than unaffected boys on the spatial tests males usually excel at.

Such studies suggest that although levels of androgen relate to spatial ability, it is not simply the case that the higher the levels, the better the spatial scores. Rather studies point to some optimal level of androgen (in the low male range) for maximal spatial ability. This finding may also be true with men and mathematical reasoning; low-androgen men tested higher. There was no obvious correlation between hormone levels and women's math scores, however.

These findings are relevant to the suggestion by Camilla P. Benbow of Iowa State University that high mathematical ability has a significant biological determinant. Benbow and her colleagues have reported consistent sex differences in mathematical reasoning ability that favor males. In mathematically talented youth, the differences were especially sharp at the upper end of the distribution, where males outnumbered females 13 to one. Benbow argues that these differences are not readily explained by socialization.

It is important to keep in mind that the relation between natural hormone levels and problem solving is based on correlational data. Although some form of connection between the two measures exists, we do not necessarily know how the association is determined nor what its causal basis is. We also know little at present about the relation between adult levels of hormones and those in early life, when abilities appear to become organized in the nervous system.

Hormonal Highs and Lows

One of the most intriguing findings in adults is that cognitive patterns may remain sensitive to hormonal fluctuations throughout life. Elizabeth Hampson of the University of Western Ontario showed that women's performances at certain tasks changed throughout the menstrual cycle as levels of estrogen varied. High levels of the hormone were associated not only with relatively depressed spatial ability but also with enhanced speech and manual skill tasks. In addition, I have observed seasonal fluctuations in spatial ability in men: their performance improves in the spring, when testosterone levels are lower. Whether these hormonally

linked fluctuations in intellectual ability represent useful evolutionary adaptations or merely highs and lows of an average test level remains to be seen through further research endeavors.

A long history of studying people with damage to one half of their brain indicates that in most people the left hemisphere of the brain is critical for speech and the right for certain perceptual and spatial functions. Researchers studying sex differences have widely assumed that the right and left hemispheres of the brain are more asymmetrically organized for speech and spatial functions in men than in women.

This belief rests on several lines of research. Parts of the corpus callosum, a major neural system connecting the two hemispheres, as well as another connector, the anterior commissure, appear to be larger in women, which may permit better communication between hemispheres. Perceptual techniques that measure brain asymmetry in normal-functioning people sometimes show smaller asymmetries in women than in men, and damage to one brain hemisphere sometimes has a lesser effect in women than the comparable injury in men does. My own data on patients with damage to one hemisphere of the brain suggest that

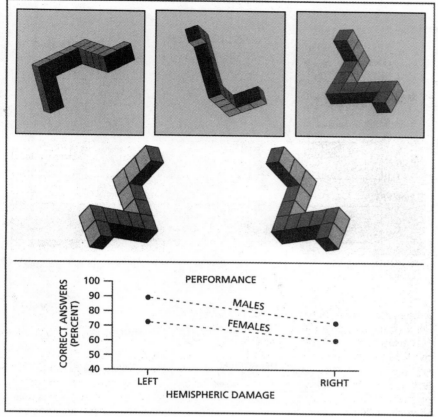

DOREEN KIMURA

RIGHT HEMISPHERIC DAMAGE affects spatial ability to the same degree in both sexes (graph at bottom), suggesting that women and men rely equally on that hemisphere for certain spatial tasks. In one test of spatial-rotation performance, photographs of a three-dimensional object must be matched to one of two mirror images of the same object.

for functions such as basic speech and spatial ability, there are no major sex differences in hemispheric asymmetry, although there may be such disparities in certain more abstract abilities, such as defining words.

If the known overall differences between men and women in spatial ability were related to differing dependence on the right brain hemisphere for such functions, then damage to that hemisphere might be expected to have a more devastating effect on spatial performance in men. My laboratory has studied the ability of patients with damage to one hemisphere of the brain to visualize the rotation of certain objects. As expected, for both sexes, those with damage to the right hemisphere got lower scores on these tests than those with damage to the left hemisphere did. Also, as anticipated, women did less well than

men on this test. Damage to the right hemisphere, however, had no greater effect on men than on women.

The results of this study and others suggest that the normal differences between men and women on rotational and line orientation tasks need not be the result of different degrees of dependence on the right hemisphere. Some other brain systems may be mediating the higher performance by men.

Another brain difference between the sexes has been shown for speech and certain manual functions. Women incur aphasia (impairment of the power to produce and understand speech) more often after anterior damage than after posterior damage to the brain. In men, posterior damage more often affects speech. A similar pattern is seen in apraxia, difficulty in selecting appropriate hand movements, such as

showing how to manipulate a particular object or copying the movements of the experimenter. Women seldom experience apraxia after left posterior damage, whereas men often do.

Men also incur aphasia from left hemisphere damage more often than women do. One explanation suggests that restricted damage within a hemisphere after a stroke more often affects the posterior region of the left hemisphere. Because men rely more on this region for speech than women do, they are more likely to be affected. We do not yet understand the effects on cognitive differences of such divergent patterns of speech and manual functions.

Although my laboratory has not found evidence of sex differences in functional brain asymmetry with regard to basic speech, movement or spatial-rotation abilities, we have found slight differences in some verbal skills. Scores on a vocabulary test and on a verbal fluency test, for instance, were slightly affected by damage to either hemisphere in women, but such scores were affected only by left hemisphere damage in men. These findings suggest that when using some more abstract verbal skills, women do use their hemispheres more equally than men do. But we have not found this to be true for all word-related tasks; for example, verbal memory appears to depend just as much on the left hemisphere in women as in men.

In recent years, new techniques for assessing the brain's activity—including functional magnetic resonance imaging (fMRI) and positron emission tomography (PET), when used during various problem-solving activities—have shown promise for providing more information about how brain function may vary among normal, healthy individuals. The research using these two techniques has so far yielded interesting, yet at times seemingly conflicting, results.

Some research has shown greater differences in activity between the hemispheres of men than of women during certain language tasks, such as judging if two words rhyme and cre-

APHASIA, or speech disorders, occur most often in women when damage is sustained in the anterior of the brain. In men, they occur more frequently when damage is in the posterior region. The data presented at the right derive from one set of patients.

INCIDENCE OF APHASIA

■ FEMALES
▨ MALES

65%
29%
MOTOR CORTEX
60%
12%
VISUAL CORTEX
ANTERIOR
POSTERIOR
LEFT HEMISPHERE

JARED SCHNEIDMAN

ating past tenses of verbs. Other research has failed to find sex differences in functional asymmetry. The different results may be attributed in part to different language tasks being used in the various studies, perhaps showing that the sexes may differ in brain organization for some language tasks but not for others.

The varying results may also reflect the complexity of these techniques. The brain is always active to some degree. So for any activity, such as reading aloud, the comparison activity—here, reading silently—is intended to be very similar. We then "subtract" the brain pattern that occurs during silent reading to find the brain pattern present while reading aloud. Yet such methods require dubious assumptions about what the subject is doing during either activity. In addition, the more complex the activity, the more difficult it is to know what is actually being measured after subtracting the comparison activity.

Looking Back

To understand human behavior—how men and women differ from one another, for instance–we must look beyond the demands of modern life. Our brains are essentially like those of our ancestors of 50,000 and more years ago, and we can gain some insight into sex differences by studying the differing roles men and women have played in evolutionary history. Men were responsible for hunting and scavenging, defending the group against predators and enemies, and shaping and using weapons. Women gathered food near the home base, tended the home, prepared food and clothing, and cared for small children. Such specialization would put different selection pressures on men and women.

Any behavioral differences between individuals or groups must somehow be mediated by the brain. Sex differences have been reported in brain structure and organization, and studies have been done on the role of sex hormones in influencing human behavior. But questions remain regarding how hormones act on human brain systems to produce the sex differences we described, such as in play behavior or in cognitive patterns.

The information we have from laboratory animals helps to guide our explanations, but ultimately these hypotheses must be tested on people. Refinements in brain-imaging techniques, when used in conjunction with our knowledge of hormonal influences and with continuing studies on the behavioral deficits after damage to various brain regions, should provide insight into some of these questions.

The Author

DOREEN KIMURA studies the neural and hormonal basis of human intellectual functions. She is professor of psychology at Simon Fraser University. Until recently, she was professor of psychology and honorary lecturer in the department of clinical neurological sciences at the University of Western Ontario. Kimura is a fellow of the Royal Society of Canada.

Further Reading

SEX ON THE BRAIN; THE BIOLOGICAL DIFFERENCES BETWEEN MEN AND WOMEN. Deborah Blum. Viking Press, 1997.

THE TROUBLE WITH TESTOSTERONE; AND OTHER ESSAYS ON THE BIOLOGY OF THE HUMAN PREDICAMENT. Robert M. Sapolsky. Scribner, 1997.

SEX AND COGNITION. Doreen Kimura. MIT Press, 1999.

EXACTLY how do we signal our amorous interest and intent in each other?

FLIRTING Fascination

It's been trivialized, even demonized, but the coquettish behavior indulged in by men and women alike is actually a vital silent language exchanging critical—and startling—information about our general health and reproductive fitness.

By Joann Ellison Rodgers

She was," he proclaimed, "so extraordinarily beautiful that I nearly laughed out loud. She . . . [was] famine, fire, destruction and plague . . . the only true begetter. Her breasts were apocalyptic, they would topple empires before they withered . . . her body was a miracle of construction . . . She was unquestionably gorgeous. She was lavish. She was a dark, unyielding largesse. She was, in short, too bloody much. . . . Those huge violet blue eyes . . . had an odd glint. . . . Aeons passed, civilizations came and went while these cosmic headlights examined my flawed personality. Every pockmark on my face became a crater of the moon."

So Richard Burton described his first sight of a 19-year-old Elizabeth Taylor. He didn't record what happened next, but a growing cadre of scientists would bet their lab coats and research budgets that sometime after that breath-catching, gut-gripping moment of instant mutual awareness, Liz tossed her hair, swayed her hips, arched her feet, giggled, gazed wide-eyed, flicked her tongue over her lips and extended that apocalyptic chest, and that Dick, for his part, arched his back, stretched his pecs, imperceptibly swayed his pelvis in a tame Elvis performance, swaggered, laughed loudly, tugged

his tie and clasped the back of his neck, which had the thoroughly engaging effect of stiffening his stance and puffing his chest.

What eventually got these two strangers from across the fabled crowded room to each other's side was what does it for all of us—in a word, flirtation, the capacity to automatically turn our actions into sexual semaphores signaling interest in the opposite sex as predictably and instinctively as peacocks fan their tails, codfish thrust their pelvic fins or mice twitch their noses and tilt their backs to draw in the object of their attention.

Long trivialized and even demonized, flirtation is gaining new respectability thanks to a spate of provocative studies of animal and human behavior in many parts of the world. The capacity of men and women to flirt and to be receptive to flirting turns out to be a remarkable set of behaviors embedded deep in our psyches. Every come-

WE SIGNAL our interest in the OPPOSITE SEX as instinctively as PEACOCKS flare their TAILS or FISH their FINS.

hither look sent and every sidelong glance received are mutually understood signals of such transcendent history and beguiling sophistication that only now are they beginning to yield clues to the psychological and biological wisdom they encode.

This much is clear so far: flirting is nature's solution to the problem every creature faces in a world full of potential mates—how to choose the right one. We all need a partner who is not merely fertile but genetically different as well as healthy enough to promise viable offspring, provide some kind of help in the hard job of parenting and offer some social compatibility.

Our animal and human ancestors needed a means of quickly and safely judging the value of potential mates without "going all the way" and risking pregnancy with every possible candidate they encountered. Flirting achieved that end, offering a relatively risk-free set of signals with which to sample the field, try out sexual wares and exchange vital information about candidates' general health and reproductive fitness.

Flirting is a negotiation process that takes place after there has been some initial attraction," observes Steven W. Gangestad, Ph.D., an evolutionary psychologist at the University of New Mexico in Albuquerque who is currently studying how people choose their mates. "Two people have to share with each other the information that they are attracted, and then test each other" on an array of attributes. Simply announcing, 'I'm attracted to you, are you attracted to me?' doesn't work so well. "It works much better to reveal this and have it revealed to you in smaller doses," explains Gangestad. "The flirting then becomes something that enhances the attraction."

It is an axiom of science that traits and behaviors crucial to survival—such as anything to do with attraction and sex—require, and get, a lot of an animal's resources. All mammals and most animals (including birds, fish, even fruit flies) engage in complicated and energy-intensive plots and plans for attracting others to the business of sex. That is, they flirt.

From nature's standpoint, the goal of life is the survival of our DNA. Sex is the way most animals gain the flexibility to healthfully sort and mix their genes. Getting sex, in turn, is wholly dependent on attracting attention and being attracted. And flirting is the way a person focuses the attention of a specific member of the opposite sex. If our ancestors hadn't done it well enough, we wouldn't be around to discuss it now.

SCIENCE has calculated just how CURVY a woman has to be to GARNER male appreciation.

A silent language of elaborate visual and other gestures, flirting is "spoken" by intellect-driven people as well as instinct-driven animals. The very universality of flirting, preserved through evolutionary history from insects to man, suggests that a flirting plan is wired into us, and that it has been embedded in our genes and in our brain's operating system the same way and for the same reasons that every other sexual trait has been—by trial and error, with conservation of what works best.

Like any other language, flirting may be deployed in ways subtle or coarse, adolescent or suave. Nevertheless, it has evolved just like pheasant spurs and lion manes: to advertise ourselves to the opposite sex.

Flirtation first emerged as a subject of serious scrutiny a scant 30 years ago. Irenäus Eibl-Eibesfeldt, now honorary director of the Ludwig-Boltzmann Institute for Urban Ethology in Vienna, was already familiar with the widespread dances and prances of mate-seeking animals. Then he discovered that people in dozens of cultures, from the South Sea islands to the Far East, Western Europe, Africa and South America, similarly engage in a fairly fixed repertoire of gestures to test sexual availability and interest.

Having devised a special camera that allowed him to point the lens in one direction while actually photographing in another, he "caught" couples on film during their flirtations, and discovered, for one thing, that women, from primitives who have no written language to those who read *Cosmo* and *Marie Claire,* use nonverbal signals that are startlingly alike. On Eibl-Eibesfeldt's screen flickered identical flirtation messages: a female smiling at a male, then arching her brows to make her eyes wide, quickly lowering her lids and, tucking her chin slightly down and coyly to the side, averting her gaze, followed within seconds, almost on cue, by putting her hands on or near her mouth and giggling.

Regardless of language, socioeconomic status or religious upbringing, couples who continued flirting placed a palm up on the table or knees, reassuring the prospective partner of harmlessness. They shrugged their shoulders, signifying helplessness. Women exaggeratedly extended their neck, a sign of vulnerability and submissiveness.

FLIRTING is self PROMOTION—but nature DEMANDS a certain amount of TRUTH in advertising.

For Eibl-Eibesfeldt, these gestures represented primal behaviors driven by the old parts of our brain's evolutionary memory. A woman presenting her extended neck to a man she wants is not much different, his work suggested, than a gray female wolf's submissiveness to a dominant male she's after.

Since then, researchers have turned up the intensity, looking, for example, at compressed bouts of flirting and courtship in their natural habitat–hotel bars and cocktail lounges. From observations at a Hyatt hotel cocktail lounge, researchers documented a set of signals that whisks a just-met man and woman from barroom to bedroom. Her giggles and soft laughs were followed by hair twirling and head-tossing; he countered with body arching, leaning back in the chair and placing his arms behind head, not unlike a pigeon puffing his chest.

If all went well, a couple would invariably progress from touching themselves to touching each other. The first tentative contacts could be termed "lint-picking." She would lift an imaginary mote from his lapel; he would brush a real or imaginary crumb from her lips. Their heads moved closer, their hands pressed out in front of them on the table, their fingers inches from each other's, playing with salt shakers or utensils. Whoops! An "accidental" finger touch, then perhaps some digital "dirty dancing," more touching and leaning in cheek to cheek. By body language alone, the investigators could predict which pairs would ride up the elevators together.

Social psychologist Timothy Perper, Ph.D., an independent scholar and writer based in Philadelphia, and anthropologist David Givens, Ph.D., spent months in dimly lit lounges documenting these flirtation rituals. Like the ear wiggles, nose flicks and back arches that signal "come hither" in rodents, the women smiled, gazed, swayed, giggled, licked their lips, and aided and abetted by the wearing of high heels, they swayed their backs, forcing their buttocks to tilt out and up and their chests to thrust forward.

The men arched, stretched, swiveled, and made grand gestures of whipping out lighters and lighting up cigarettes. They'd point their chins in the air with a cigarette dangling in their mouth, then loop their arms in a wide arc to put the lighter away. Their swaggers, bursts of laughter and grandiose gestures were an urban pantomime of the prancing and preening indulged in by male baboons and gorillas in the wild. Man or monkey, the signals all said, "Look at me, trust me, I'm powerful, but I won't hurt you." And "I don't want anything much . . . yet."

The sequence FLIRTATION takes is ALWAYS the same; LOOK, talk, touch, kiss, do the DEED.

All the silent swaying, leaning, smiling, bobbing and gazing eventually brought a pair into full frontal alignment. Face to face, they indulged in simultaneous touching of everything from eyeglasses to fingertips to crossed legs. Says Perper, "This kind of sequence–attention, recognition, dancing, synchronization–is fundamental to courtship. From the Song of Songs until today, the sequence is the same: look, talk, touch, kiss, do the deed."

The fact that flirting is a largely nonexplicit drama doesn't mean that important information isn't being delivered in those silent signals. By swaying her hips, or emphasizing them in a form-fitting dress, a flirtatious woman is riveting attention on her pelvis, suggesting its ample capacity for bearing a child. By arching her brows and exaggerating her gaze, her eyes appear large in her face, the way a child's eyes do, advertising, along

with giggles, her youth and "submissiveness." By drawing her tongue along her lips, she compels attention to what many biologists believe are facial echoes of vaginal lips, transmitting sexual maturity and her interest in sex. By coyly averting her gaze and playing "hard to get," she communicates her unwillingness to give sex to just anyone or to someone who will love her and leave her.

For his part, by extending a strong chin and jaw, expanding and showing off pectoral muscles and a hairy chest, flashing money, laughing loudly or resonantly, smiling, and doing all these things without accosting a woman, a man signals his ability to protect offspring, his resources and the testosterone-driven vitality of his sperm as well as the tamer side of him that is willing to stick around, after the sex, for fatherhood. It's the behavioral equivalent of "I'll respect you in the morning."

I can't tell you why I was attracted to her the instant she walked into my office," recalls a 32-year-old screenwriter. "It was chemistry. We both flirted and we both knew it would lead nowhere. I'm happily married." The statement is almost stupefyingly commonplace, but also instructive. Each of us "turns on" not to mankind or womankind but to a particular member of the opposite sex. Certain stances, personal styles, gestures, intimations of emotional compatibility, perhaps even odors, automatically arouse our interest because they not only instantly advertise genetic fitness but they match the template of Desired Mate we all carry in our mind's eye.

As with Dick and Liz, or any couple, the rational, thinking part of their brains got them to the place where girl met boy; they had the event on their calendars, planned what they would wear, arranged for transportation. But in that first meeting, their capacity to react with their instinct and hearts, not their heads, overrode their cognitive brains. Otherwise, they might not have had the nerve to look at each other.

The rational brain is always on the lookout for dangers, for complexities, for reasons to act or not act. If every time man and woman met they immediately considered all the possible risks and vulnerabilities they might face if they mated or had children, they'd run screaming from the room.

The instant of ATTRACTION in fact MIMICS a kind of BRAIN DAMAGE.

It's no secret that the brain's emotionally loaded limbic system sometimes operates independently of the more rational neocortex, such as in the face of danger, when the fight-or-flight response is activated. Similarly, when the matter is sex—another situation on which survival depends— we also react without even a neural nod to the neocortex. Instead, the flirtational operating system appears to kick in without conscious consent. If, at the moment they had met, Dick and Liz had stopped to consider all the possible outcomes of a relationship, they both would have been old before they got close enough to speak.

The moment of attraction, in fact, mimics a kind of brain damage. At the University of Iowa, where he is professor and head of neurology, Antonio Damasio, M.D., has found that people with damage to the connection between their limbic structures and the higher brain are smart and rational—but unable to make decisions. They bring commitment phobia to a whole new level. In attraction, we don't stop and think, we react, operating on a "gut" feeling, with butterflies, giddiness, sweaty palms and flushed faces brought on by the reactivity of the emotional brain. We suspend intellect at least long enough to propel us to the next step in the mating game—flirtation.

Somewhere beyond flirtation, as a relationship progresses, courtship gets under way, and with it, intellectual processes resume. Two adults can then evaluate potential mates more rationally, think things over and decide whether to love, honor and cherish. But at the moment of attraction and flirtation, bodies, minds and sense are temporarily hostage to the more ancient parts of the brain, the impulsive parts that humans share with animals.

If flirting is a form of self promotion, nature demands a certain amount of truth in advertising. "For a signaling system to convey something meaningful about a desirable attribute, there has to be some honesty," explains Gangestad, "so that if you don't have the attribute you can't fake it." Just as the extravagant colors of birds that figure so prominently in their flirting rituals proclaim the health of animals so plumed, humans have some signals that can't be faked.

Waist-hip ratio is likely one of them. It's no secret that men snap to attention and even go dry at the mouth at the sight of a shapely woman. Science has now calculated just how curvy a woman has to be to garner such appreciation: the waist must measure no more than 60 to 70% of her hip circumference. It is a visual signal that not only figures powerfully in attraction, but is a moving force in flirtation. And unless steel-boned corsets stage a comeback, it is an attribute that just can't be put into play unless it is real.

In simplest terms, says Gangestad, waist-hip ratio is an honest indicator of health. Studies have shown that hourglass-shaped women are less likely than other women to get diabetes and cardiac disease. They are also most likely to bear children, as hips take their shape at puberty from the feminizing hormone estrogen.

"The literature shows that women with a 0.7 waist-hip ratio have a sex-typical hormone profile in the relationship of estrogen to testosterone, and that women with a straighter torso, meaning a waist-hip ratio closer to 1:1, indeed have lower fertility," Gangestad reports. "It appears that males have evolved to pay attention to this cue that ancestrally was related to fertility."

The virtually visceral responsiveness to physical features in flirtation may also be as good a guarantee as one can get that a potential partner shapes up on a hidden but crucial aspect of health: immunity to disease. Scientists know that the testosterone that gives men jutting jaws, prominent noses and big brows, and, to a lesser extent, the estrogen that gives women soft features and curving hips, also suppresses the ability to fight disease. But looks have their own logic, and bodies and faces that are exemplars of their gender signal that their bearer has biological power to spare; after all, he or she has survived despite the hormonal "handicap."

Take the case of such elaborate male ornamentation as peacock tails and stag antlers. In the 1980s, evolutionary biologists William Hamilton and Marlena Zuk linked such features to inborn resistance to disease parasites. Antlers and tail feathers are known to be attractive to females of their species and are major machinery of flirtation. But developing and maintaining such extravagant equipment is costly, taking huge nutritional resources and even slowing the animals down, making them more vulnerable to predators.

The only animals that can afford such ornamentation are those with tip-top constitutions. So, like big bones, big horns, big tails and big spurs in animals, jutting jaws are honest markers for a healthy immune system. Scientists point out that such features are in fact respected by other men as well as attractive to women. Studies show that tall, square-jawed men achieve higher ranks in the military than do those with weak chins, and that taller men are over-represented in boardrooms as well as bedrooms.

Whatever specific physical features men and women are primed to respond to, they all have a quality in common—symmetry That is, attributes deemed attractive have an outward appearance of evenness and right-left balance. Unlike the color and condition of tail feathers, symmetry serves not so much as an honest marker of current health status, but as a signal of a general capacity to be healthy. Symmetry, says Gangestad, is "a footprint left by your whole developmental history." It alone explains why Elizabeth Taylor, Denzel Washington and Queen Nefertiti are universally recognized as beautiful—and full of sex appeal.

Women prefer men with symmetrical features, and they prefer them at a very specific time—when they are most fertile.

"Bilateral symmetry is a hot topic these days," beams Albert Thornhill, a biologist at the University of New Mexico and a pioneer in the study of symmetry in attraction and flirtation. He and Gangestad believe it is a marker of "developmental precision," the extent to which a genetic blueprint is realized in the flesh despite all the environmental and other perturbations that tend to throw development off course.

Recent studies conducted by the two demonstrate not only that women prefer symmetrical men, they prefer them at a very specific time—when they are most fertile. "We found that female preferences change across the menstrual cycle," Gangestad reports. "We think the finding says something

about the way female mate preferences are designed. Because the preference for male symmetry is specific to the time of ovulation, when women are most likely to conceive, we think women are choosing a mate who is going to provide better genes for healthy babies. It's an indirect benefit, rather than a direct or material benefit to the female herself."

In their study, 52 women rated the attractiveness of 42 men—by their smell. Each of the men slept in one T-shirt for two nights, after which the women were given a whiff of it. Prior to the smell test, all the men had undergone careful calipered measurement of 10 features, from ear width to finger length. Those whose body features were the most symmetrical were the ones whose smells were most preferred, but only among women who were in the ovulatory phase of their menstrual cycle. At other times in their cycle, women had no preference either for symmetrical or asymmetrical males.

The preference for symmetry is not limited to humans. Thornhill first stumbled upon symmetry two decades ago, during experiments with scorpion flies in Australia, Japan and Europe. He noticed that females chose particular male flies on the basis of the level and quality of "nuptial gifts," nutrients passed to the female during courtship and mating.

"That was the first inkling I had that insects were very sophisticated about their mating strategies," Thornhill recalls. But the more time he spent recording the sexual lives of scorpion flies, the more he realized that the females were selecting partners long before they sampled any gifts, and they were reckoning by the symmetry of the males' wings. "I discovered that males and females with the most symmetrical wings had the most mating success and that by using wing symmetry, I—and presumably the fly—could predict reproductive fitness better than scent or any other factor."

Since then, Thornhill and colleagues around the world have conducted more than 20 separate tests of

symmetry of everything from eyes, ears and nostrils to limbs, wrists and fingers. Even if they never speak a word or get closer than a photograph, women view symmetrical men as more dominant, powerful, richer and better sex and marriage material. And symmetrical men view themselves the same way! Men, for their part, rate symmetrical women as more fertile, more attractive, healthier and better sex and marriage material, too—just as such women see themselves as having a competitive edge in the mating sweepstakes.

Flirtation, it turns out, is most successful among the most symmetrical. Men's bodily symmetry matches up with the number of lifetime sex partners they report having. Symmetrical men also engage in more infidelity in their romantic relationships—"extra-pair copulations" in the language of the lab. And they get to sex more quickly after meeting a romantic partner compared to asymmetrical men. They lose their virginity earlier in life, too.

When women flirt with symmetrical men, what their instincts are reading might once have been banned in Boston. Male symmetry is also shorthand for female sexual satisfaction. Gangestad and Thornhill surveyed 86 couples in 1995 and found that symmetrical men "fire off more female copulatory orgasms than asymmetrical men." Women with symmetrical partners were more than twice as likely to climax during intercourse. Thrills are only a short-term payoff, however; female orgasm is really a shill for fertilization, pulling sperm from the vagina into the cervix.

Successful as symmetrical men are at flirtation, it's only their presumably better genes that women really want. Women definitely do not prefer symmetrical men for long-term relationships. There's a definite downside to getting someone with really good DNA. Symmetry, Gangestad explains, affords those men who possess it to take a dastardly mating strategy. His studies show that symmetrical men invest less in any one romantic relationship—less time, less attention, less money. And less fidelity. They're too busy spreading around their symmetry. "They also tend to sexualize other women more," Gangestad reports. "It may be that males who can have the most access without giving a lot of investment take advantage of that."

A guy who will stick around and help out with parenting is on most women's wish list of qualities in a mate, Gangestad concedes. "I wouldn't exclude the possibility that men have been doing some direct parental care for some time, and so a preference for that might also have an evolutionary basis." But also on a woman's wish list from an evolutionary standpoint would be someone who is going to provide good genes for healthy babies. Unfortunately, says the Albuquerque researcher, "what can and does happen in a mating market is that those things don't all come in the same package."

Although the signals and semaphores of flirting are largely devoid of explicit content, the style with which one flirts can be downright revelatory. "*How* a person flirts honestly reveals some important qualities about an individual," says Gangestad. Symmetry isn't everything; there are signals of more subtle skills.

In some species, the females watch the males fight each other and then choose the one who can hold the central territory. But we humans are more differently evolved creatures with more complex lives in which our higher faculties presumably contribute something to success, whether it's surviving in primitive equatorial caves or sophisticated urban ones.

Enter creativity, humor and intelligence. Deployed in flirting, they disclose more about an individual person than all the antlers do about leching animals. "They are likely saying something important about our very viability," says Gangestad. "When we can engage in humor and creativity, they

act as an honest signal that we've got a reasonably well put together nervous system. They may indicate there's some developmental integrity underneath our brain." And a certain ability to withstand whatever challenges life throws a person's way.

Symmetrical men give women more orgasms, but they also are more likely to be unfaithful to their partners.

What's more, our basic social ability to "read" another's facial gestures and emotional expressions acts as a fact-checking system in flirtation. It enables us to glimpse the tone of a prospective mate's inner life and to check for the presence or absence of psychological weakness. And in fact, women are pretty good at doping out information about such important attributes—even when they get very little time to make a judgment.

In a recent set of studies, Gangestad and a colleague extracted one-minute segments from more extensive videotaped interviews with men not in committed relationships. The brief segments were then shown to women who were asked to rate the men on a variety of characteristics, including how attractive they'd be in a pair relationship. The women were able to make judgments about each man's intelligence, ability to be caring and how nice he seemed. They also paid attention to another set of characteristics—how effective a man was likely to be with other males, how socially influential he was.

The men who were rated most attractive for long-term relationships scored high on both sets of charac-

teristics. But what may be most notable about the study was that women's observations, from a mere snippet of videotape, were remarkably accurate. They correlated closely with the men's ratings of their own personality.

After two people share the information that they are attracted, then, through the way they flirt, they may unwittingly let on more about themselves. "It becomes a testing ground as well as an information-revealing process," says Gangestad.

Thus, while we appear to be pre-programmed with an urge to wile or wiggle our way onto another's mental radar screen, we also seem psychologically constituted to pay rapt attention to looks and actions intended to be sexually appealing. Otherwise, neither Liz and Dick nor any two contenders would have a reliable, safe or peaceful means of communicating attraction and getting to the more durable business of courtship, mating and commitment to the offspring that will carry our DNA into the next generation.

JOANN RODGERS wishes that people were less squeamish about sex. "It's unfortunate," she says, since "sex is the most important aspect of the survival of our species," a view she espouses both in her upcoming book on the natural science of sex and in her article on flirting. Especially tragic, she says, "is how difficult it is to find funding for sex research in this P.C. era." Director of media relations at the Johns Hopkins Medical Institutions in Baltimore, Maryland, Rodgers has also written on medicine and life science for numerous magazines. She is a former President of the National Association of Science Writers.

What's Your Love Story?

In your relationship, are you a cop, a comedian, a prince or a martyr? *Robert J. Sternberg, Ph.D.,* **reveals how you can use your "love story" to find your perfect match.**

Relationships can be as unpredictable as the most suspense-filled mystery novel. Why do some couples live happily ever after, while others are as star-crossed as Romeo and Juliet? Why do we often seem destined to relive the same romantic mistakes over and over, following the same script with different people in different places, as if the fate of our relationships, from courtship to demise, were written at birth?

Perhaps because, in essence, it is. As much as psychologists have attempted to explain the mysteries of love through scientific laws and theories, it turns out that the best mirrors of the romantic experience may be *Wuthering Heights,* *Casablanca* and *General Hospital.* At some level, lay people recognize what many psychologists don't: that the love between two people follows a story. If we want to understand love, we have to understand the stories that dictate our beliefs and expectations of love. These stories, which we start to write as children, predict the patterns of our romantic experiences time and time again. Luckily, we can learn to rewrite them.

I came up with the theory of love as a story because I was dissatisfied—not only with other people's work on love, but also with my own. I had initially proposed a triangular theory of love, suggesting that it comprises three elements: intimacy, passion and commitment. Different loving relationships have different combinations of these elements. Complete love requires all three elements. But the theory leaves an important question unanswered: what makes a person the kind of lover they are? And what attracts them to other lovers? I had to dig deeper to understand the love's origins. I found them in stories.

My research, which incorporates studies performed over the past decade with hundreds of couples in Connecticut, as well as ongoing studies, has shown that people describe love in many ways. This description reveals their love story. For example, someone who strongly agrees with the statement "I believe close relationships are like good partnerships" tells a business story; someone who says they end up with partners who scare them—or that they like intimidating their partner—enacts a horror story.

Couples usually start out being physically attracted and having similar interests and values. But eventually, they may notice something missing in the relationship. That something is usually story compatibility. A couple whose stories don't match is like two characters on one stage acting out different plays—they may look right at first glance, but there is an underlying lack of coordination to their interaction.

This is why couples that seem likely to thrive often do not, and couples that seem unlikely to survive sometimes do. Two people may have similar outlooks, but if one longs to be rescued like Julia Roberts in *Pretty Woman* and the other wants a partnership like the lawyers on the television show *The Practice,* the relationship may not go very far. In contrast, two people with a war story like the bickering spouses in *Who's Afraid of Virginia Woolf* may seem wildly incompatible to their friends, but their shared need for combat may be what keeps their love alive.

More than anything, the key to compatibility with a romantic partner is whether our stories match. To change the pattern of our relation-

ships, we must become conscious of our love stories, seek people with compatible tales, and replot conclusions that aren't working for us.

The Beginning of the Story

We start forming our ideas about love soon after birth, based on our inborn personality, our early experiences and our observations of our parents' relationships, as well as depictions of romance in movies, television and books. We then seek to live out these conceptions of love ourselves.

Based on interviews I conducted in the 1990s, asking college students to write about their romantic ideals and expectations, I have identified at least 25 common stories which people use to describe love. (There are probably many more.)

Some stories are far more popular than others. In 1995, one of my students, Laurie Lynch, and I identified some of the most common tales by asking people to rate, on a scale of one to seven, the extent to which a group of statements characterized their relationships. Their highest-ranked statements indicated their personal love story. Among the most popular were the travel story ("I believe that beginning a relationship is like starting a new journey that promises to be both exciting and challenging"), the gardening story ("I believe any relationship that is left unattended will not survive") and the humor story ("I think taking a relationship too seriously can spoil it"). Among the least popular were the horror story ("I find it exciting when I feel my partner is somewhat frightened of me," or "I tend to end up with people who frighten me"), the collectibles story ("I like dating different partners simultaneously; each partner should fit a particular need") and the autocratic government story ("I think it is more efficient if one person takes control of the important decisions in a relationship").

Another study of 43 couples, conducted with Mahzad Hojji, Ph.D., in 1996, showed that women prefer the travel story more than men, who pre-

fer the art ("Physical attractiveness is the most essential characteristic I look for in a partner"), collectibles and pornography ("It is very important to be able to gratify all my partner's sexual desires and whims," or "I can never be happy with a partner who is not very adventurous in his or her sex life") stories. Men also prefer the sacrifice story ("I believe sacrifice is a key part of true love"). Originally, we had expected the opposite. Then we realized that the men reported sacrificing things that women did consider significant offerings.

No one story guarantees success, our study showed. But some stories seem to predict doom more than others: the business, collectibles, government, horror, mystery, police ("I believe it is necessary to watch your partner's every move" or "My partner often calls me several times a day to ask what I am doing"), recovery ("I often find myself helping people get their life back in order" or "I need someone to help me recover from my painful past"), science fiction ("I often find myself attracted to individuals who have unusual and strange characteristics") and theater stories ("I think my relationships are like plays" or "I often find myself attracted to partners who play different roles").

How Stories Spin Our Relationships

When you talk to two people who have just split up, their breakup stories often sound like depictions of two completely different relationships. In a sense they are. Each partner has his or her own story to tell.

Most important to a healthy, happy relationship is that both partners have compatible stories—that is, compatible expectations. Indeed, a 1998 study conducted with Mahzad Hojjat, Ph.D., and Michael Barnes, Ph.D., indicated that the more similar couples' stories were, the happier they were together.

Stories tend to be compatible if they are complementary roles in a single story, such as prince and princess, or if the stories are similar enough that they can be merged into a new and unified story. For example, a fantasy story can merge with a gardening story because one can nourish, or garden, a relationship while dreaming of being rescued by a knight on a white steed. A fantasy and a business story are unlikely to blend, however, because they represent such different ideals–fate-bound princes and princesses don't work at romance!

Of course, story compatibility isn't the only ingredient in a successful relationship. Sometimes, our favorite story can be hazardous to our well-being. People often try to make dangerous or unsatisfying stories come true. Thus, someone who has, say, a horror or recovery story may try to turn a healthy relationship into a Nightmare on Elm Street. People complain that they keep ending up with the same kind of bad partner, that they are unlucky in love. In reality, luck has nothing to do with it: They are subconsciously finding people to play out their love stories, or foisting their stories on the people they meet.

Making Happy Endings

Treating problems in relationships by changing our behaviors and habits ul-timately won't work because crisis comes from the story we're playing out. Unless we change our stories, we're treating symptoms rather than causes. If we're dissatisfied with our partner, we should look not at his or her faults, but at how he or she fits into our expectations.

To figure out what we want, we need to consider all of our past relationships, and we should ask ourselves what attributes characterized the people to whom we felt most attracted, and what attributes characterized the people in whom we eventually lost interest. We also need to see which romantic tale we aim to tell–and whether or not it has the potential to lead to a "happily ever after" scenario (see box, "Find Your Love Story").

Once we understand the ideas and beliefs behind the stories we accept as our own, we can do some replot-ting. We can ask ourselves what we like and don't like about our current story, what hasn't been working in our relationships, and how we would like to change it. How can we rewrite the scenario? This may involve changing stories, or transforming an existing story to make it more practical. For example, horror stories may be fantasized during sexual or other activity, rather than actually physically played out.

We can change our story by experimenting with new and different plots. Sometimes, psychotherapy can help us to move from perilous stories (such as a horror story) to more promising ones (such as a travel story). Once we've recognized our story–or learned to live a healthy one of our choosing–we can begin to recognize elements of that story in potential mates. Love mirrors stories because it is a story itself. The difference is that we are the authors, and can write ourselves a happy ending.

Robert J. Sternberg is IBM Professor of Psychology and Education in the department of psychology at Yale University.

READ MORE ABOUT IT

Love Is a Story, Robert J. Sternberg, Ph.D. (Oxford University Press, 1998)

A Natural History of Love, Diane Ackerman (Random House, 1994)

Find Your Love Story

Adapted from *Love Is a Story* by Robert J. Sternberg, Ph.D.

Rate each statement on a scale from 1 to 9, 1 meaning that it doesn't characterize your romantic relationships at all, 9 meaning that it describes them extremely well. Then average your scores for each story. In general, averaged scores of 7 to 9 are high, indicating a strong attraction to a story, and 1 to 3 are low, indicating little or no interest in the story. Moderate scores of 4 to 6 indicate some interest, but probably not enough to generate or keep a romantic interest. Next, evaluate your own love story. (There are 12 listed here; see the book for more.)

STORY #1

1. I enjoy making sacrifices for the sake of my partner.
2. I believe sacrifice is a key part of true love.
3. I often compromise my own comfort to satisfy my partner's needs.
Score:__

The **sacrifice story** can lead to happy relationships when both partners are content in the roles they are playing, particularly when they both make sacrifices. It is likely to cause friction when partners feel compelled to make sacrifices. Research suggests that relationships of all kinds are happiest when they are roughly equitable. The greatest risk in a sacrifice story is that the give-and-take will become too out of bal-ance, with one partner always being the giver or receiver.

STORY #2

Officer:

1. I believe that you need to keep a close eye on your partner.
2. I believe it is foolish to trust your partner completely.
3. I would never trust my partner to work closely with a person of the opposite sex. **Score:__**

Suspect:

1. My partner often calls me several times a day to ask exactly what I am doing.
2. My partner needs to know everything that I do.

3. My partner gets very upset if I don't let him or her know exactly where I have been. **Score:__**

Police stories do not have very favorable prognoses because they can completely detach from reality. The police story may offer some people the feeling of being cared for. People who are very insecure relish the attention that they get as a "suspect," that they are unable to receive in any other way. But they can end up paying a steep price. As the plot thickens, the suspect first begins to lose freedom, then dignity, and then any kind of self-respect. Eventually, the person's mental and even physical well-being may be threatened.

STORY #3

1. I believe that, in a good relationship, partners change and grow together.
2. I believe love is a constant process of discovery and growth.
3. I believe that beginning a relationship is like starting a new journey that promises to be both exciting and challenging. **Score:__**

Travel stories that last beyond a very short period of time generally have a favorable prognosis, because if the travelers can agree on a destination and path, they are already a long way toward success. If they can't, they often find out quite quickly that they want different things from the relationship and split up. Travel relationships tend to be dynamic and focus on the future. The greatest risk is that over time one or both partners will change the destination or path they desire. When people speak of growing apart, they often mean that the paths they wish to take are no longer the same. In such cases, the relationship is likely to become increasingly unhappy, or even dissolve completely.

STORY #4

Object:
1. The truth is that I don't mind being treated as a sex toy by my partner.
2. It is very important to me to gratify my partner's sexual desires and whims, even if people might view them as debasing.

3. I like it when my partner wants me to try new and unusual, and even painful, sexual techniques. **Score:__**

Subject:
1. The most important thing to me in my relationship is for my partner to be an excellent sex toy, doing anything I desire.
2. I can never be happy with a partner who is not very adventurous in sex.
3. The truth is that I like a partner who feels like a sex object. **Score:__**

There are no obvious advantages to the **pornography story.** The disadvantages are quite clear, however. First, the excitement people attain is through degradation of themselves and others. Second, the need to debase and be debased is likely to keep escalating. Third, once one adopts the story, it may be difficult to adopt another story. Fourth, the story can become physically as well as psychologically dangerous. And finally, no matter how one tries, it is difficult to turn the story into one that's good for psychological or physical well-being.

STORY #5

Terrorizer:
1. I often make sure that my partner knows that I am in charge, even if it makes him or her scared of me.
2. I actually find it exciting when I feel my partner is somewhat frightened of me.
3. I sometimes do things that scare my partner, because I think it is actually good for a relationship to have one partner slightly frightened of the other. **Score:__**

Victim:
1. I believe it is somewhat exciting to be slightly scared of your partner.
2. I find it arousing when my partner creates a sense of fear in me.
3. I tend to end up with people who sometimes frighten me. **Score:__**

The **horror story** probably is the least advantageous of the stories. To some, it may be exciting. But the forms of terror needed to sustain the excitement tend to get out of control and to put their participants, and even sometimes those around them, at both psychological and

physical risk. Those who discover that they have this story or are in a relationship that is enacting it would be well-advised to seek counseling, and perhaps even police protection.

STORY #6

Co-dependent:
1. I often end up with people who are facing a specific problem, and I find myself helping them get their life back in order.
2. I enjoy being involved in relationships in which my partner needs my help to get over some problem.
3. I often find myself with partners who need my help to recover from their past. **Score:__**

Person in recovery:
1. I need someone who will help me recover from my painful past.
2. I believe that a relationship can save me from a life that is crumbling around me.
3. I need help getting over my past. **Score:__**

The main advantage to the **recovery story** is that the co-dependent may really help the other partner to recover, so long as the other partner has genuinely made the decision to recover. Many of us know individuals who sought to reform their partners, only to experience total frustration when their partners made little or no effort to reform. At the same time, the co-dependent is someone who needs to feel he or she is helping someone, and gains this feeling of making a difference to someone through the relationship. The problem: Others can assist in recovery, but the decision to recover can only be made by the person in need of recovery. As a result, recovery stories can assist in, but not produce, actual recovery.

STORY #7

1. I believe a good relationship is attainable only if you spend time and energy to care for it, just as you tend a garden.
2. I believe relationships need to be nourished constantly to help weather the ups and downs of life.
3. I believe the secret to a successful relationship is the care that partners take of each other and of their love. **Score:__**

The biggest advantage of a **garden story** is its recognition of the importance of nurture. No other story involves this amount of care and attention. The biggest potential disadvantage is that a lack of spontaneity or boredom may develop. People in garden stories are not immune to the lure of extramarital relationships, for example, and may get involved in them to generate excitement, even if they still highly value their primary relationship. In getting involved in other relationships, however, they are putting the primary relationship at risk. Another potential disadvantage is that of smothering—that the attention becomes too much. Just as one can overwater a flower, one can overattend a relationship. Sometimes it's best to let things be and allow nature to take its course.

STORY #8

1. I believe that close relationships are partnerships.
2. I believe that in a romantic relationship, just as in a job, both partners should perform their duties and responsibilities according to their "job description."
3. Whenever I consider having a relationship with someone, I always consider the financial implications of the relationship as well. **Score:__**

A **business story** has several potential advantages, not the least of which is that the bills are more likely to get paid than in other types of relationships. That's because someone is always minding the store. Another potential advantage is that the roles tend to be more dearly defined than in other relationships. The partners are also in a good position to "get ahead" in terms of whatever it is that they want. One potential disadvantage occurs if only one of the two partners sees their relationship as a business story. The other partner may quickly become bored and look for interest and excitement outside the marriage. The story can also turn sour if the distribution of authority does not satisfy one or both partners. If the partners cannot work out mutually compatible roles, they may find themselves spending a lot of time fighting for position. It is impor-tant to maintain the option of flexibility.

STORY #9

1. I think fairy tales about relationships can come true.
2. I do believe that there is someone out there for me who is my perfect match.
3. I like my relationships to be ones in which I view my partner as something like a prince or princess in days of yore. **Score:__**

The **fantasy story** can be a powerful one. The individual may feel swept up in the emotion of the search for the perfect partner or of developing the perfect relationship with an existing partner. It is probably no coincidence that in literature most fantasy stories take place before or outside of marriage: Fantasies are hard to maintain when one has to pay the bills, pack the children off to school and resolve marital fights. To maintain the happy feeling of the fantasy, therefore, one has to ignore, to some extent, the mundane aspects of life. The potential disadvantages of the fantasy relationship are quite plain. The greatest is the possibility for disillusionment when one partner discovers that no one could fulfill the fantastic expectations that have been created. This can lead partners to feel dissatisfied with relationships that most others would view as quite successful. If a couple can create a fantasy story based on realistic rather than idealistic ideals, they have the potential for success; if they want to be characters in a myth, chances are that's exactly what they'll get: a myth.

STORY #10

1. I think it is more interesting to argue than to compromise.
2. I think frequent arguments help bring conflictive issues into the open and keep the relationship healthy.
3. I actually like to fight with my partner. **Score:__**

The **war story** is advantageous in a relationship only when both partners clearly share it and want the same thing. In these cases, threats of divorce and worse may be common, but neither partner would seriously dream of leaving: They're both having too much fun, in their own way. The major disadvantage, of course, is that the story often isn't shared, leading to intense and sustained conflict that can leave the partner without the war story feeling devastated much of the time. People can find themselves in a warring relationship without either of them having war as a preferred story. In such cases, the constant fighting may make both partners miserable. If the war continues in such a context, there is no joy in it for either partner.

STORY #11

Audience:
1. I like a partner who is willing to think about the funny side of our conflicts.
2. I think taking a relationship too seriously can spoil it; that's why I like partners who have a sense of humor.
3. I like a partner who makes me laugh whenever we are facing a tense situation in our relationship. **Score:__**

Comedian:
1. I admit that I sometimes try to use humor to avoid facing a problem in my relationship.
2. I like to use humor when I have a conflict with my partner because I believe there is a humorous side to any conflict.
3. When I disagree with my partner, I often try to make a joke out of it. **Score:__**

The **humor story** can have one enormous advantage: Most situations do have a lighter side, and people with this story are likely to see it. When things in a relationship become tense, sometimes nothing works better than a little humor, especially if it comes from within the relationship. Humor stories also allow relationships to be creative and dynamic. But the humor story also has some potential disadvantages. Probably the greatest one is the risk of using humor to deflect important issues: A serious conversation that needs to take place keeps getting put off with jokes. Humor can also be used to be cruel in a passive-aggressive way. When humor is used as a means of demeaning a person to protect the comedian from responsibility ("I was only joking"), a relationship is bound to be imperiled. Thus, moderate amounts are good for a relationship, but excessive amounts can be deleterious.

STORY #12

1. I think it is okay to have multiple partners who fulfill my different needs.
2. I sometimes like to think about how many people I could potentially date all at the same time.

3. I tend and like to have multiple intimate partners at once, each fulfilling somewhat different roles.
Score:__

There are a few advantages to a **collection story**. For one thing, the collector generally cares about the collectible's physical well-being, as appearance is much of what makes a collection shine. The collector also finds a way of meeting multiple needs. Usually those needs will be met in parallel—by having several intimate relationships at the same time—but a collector may also enter into serial monogamous relationships, where each successive relationship meets needs that

the last relationship did not meet. In a society that values monogamy, collection stories work best if they do not become serious or if individuals in the collection are each viewed in different lights, such as friendship or intellectual stimulation. The disadvantages of this story become most obvious when people are trying to form serious relationships. The collector may find it difficult to establish intimacy, or anything approaching a complete relationship and commitment toward a single individual. Collections can also become expensive, time-consuming, and in some cases illegal (as when an individual enters into multiple marriages simultaneously).

Protecting Against
Unintended Pregnancy
A Guide To Contraceptive Choices

by Tamar Nordenberg

> *I am 20 and have never gone to see a doctor about birth control.*
> *My boyfriend and I have been going together for a couple of years and have*
> *been using condoms. So far, everything is fine. Are condoms alone safe enough,*
> *or is something else safe besides the Pill? I do not want to go on the Pill.*
> **—Letter to the Kinsey Institute for Research in Sex, Gender, and Reproduction**

This young woman is not alone in her uncertainty about contraceptive options. A 1995 report by the National Academy of Sciences' Institute of Medicine, *The Best Intentions: Unintended Pregnancy and the Well-being of Children and Families,* attributed the high rate of unintended pregnancies in the United States, in part, to Americans' lack of knowledge about contraception. About 6 of every 10 pregnancies in the United States are unplanned, according to the report.

Being informed about the pros and cons of various contraceptives is important not only for preventing unintended pregnancies but also for reducing the risk of illness or death from sexually transmitted diseases (STDs), including AIDS.

The Food and Drug Administration has approved a number of birth control methods, ranging from over-the-counter male and female condoms and vaginal spermicides to doctor-

1994 by Photodisc, Inc.

From *FDA Consumer,* April 1997, pp. 20-26. Reprinted by permission of *FDA Consumer,* the magazine of the U.S. Food and Drug Administration.

prescribed birth control pills, diaphragms, intrauterine devices (IUDs), injected hormones, and hormonal implants. Other contraceptive options include fertility awareness and voluntary surgical sterilization.

"On the whole, the contraceptive choices that Americans have are very safe and effective," says Dennis Barbour, president of the Association of Reproductive Health Professionals, "but a method that is very good for one woman may be lousy for another."

The choice of birth control depends on factors such as a person's health, frequency of sexual activity, number of partners, and desire to have children in the future. Effectiveness rates, based on statistical estimates, are another key consideration (see "Birth Control Guide"). FDA is developing a more consumer-friendly table to be added to the labeling of all contraceptive drugs and devices.

Barrier Methods

• *Male condom.* The male condom is a sheath placed over the erect penis before penetration, preventing pregnancy by blocking the passage of sperm.

A condom can be used only once. Some have spermicide added, usually nonoxynol-9 in the United States, to kill sperm. Spermicide has not been scientifically shown to provide additional contraceptive protection over the condom alone. Because they act

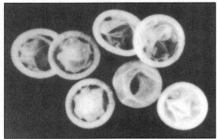

Photos from Planned Parenthood Federation

as a mechanical barrier, condoms prevent direct vaginal contact with semen, infectious genital secretions, and genital lesions and discharges.

Most condoms are made from latex rubber, while a small percentage

are made from lamb intestines (sometimes called "lambskin" condoms). Condoms made from polyurethane have been marketed in the United States since 1994.

Except for abstinence, latex condoms are the most effective method for reducing the risk of infection from the viruses that cause AIDS, other HIV-related illnesses, and other STDs.

Some condoms are prelubricated. These lubricants don't provide more birth control or STD protection. Non-oil-based lubricants, such as water or KY jelly, can be used with latex or lambskin condoms, but oil-based lubricants, such as petroleum jelly (Vaseline), lotions, or massage or baby oil, should not be used because they can weaken the material.

• *Female condom.* The Reality Female Condom, approved by FDA in April 1993, consists of a lubricated polyurethane sheath shaped similarly to the male condom. The closed end, which has a flexible ring, is inserted

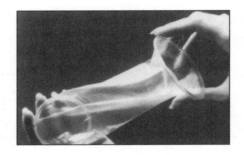

into the vagina, while the open end remains outside, partially covering the labia.

The female condom, like the male condom, is available without a prescription and is intended for one-time use. It should not be used together with a male condom because they may not both stay in place.

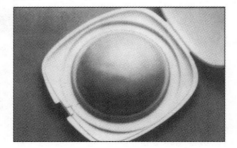

• *Diaphragm.* Available by prescription only and sized by a health professional to achieve a proper fit, the diaphragm has a dual mechanism to prevent pregnancy. A dome-shaped rubber disk with a flexible rim covers the cervix so sperm can't reach the uterus, while a spermicide applied to the diaphragm before insertion kills sperm.

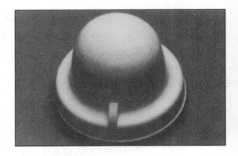

The diaphragm protects for six hours. For intercourse after the six-hour period, or for repeated intercourse within this period, fresh spermicide should be placed in the vagina with the diaphragm still in place. The diaphragm should be left in place for at least six hours after the last intercourse but not for longer than a total of 24 hours because of the risk of toxic shock syndrome (TSS), a rare but potentially fatal infection. Symptoms of TSS include sudden fever, stomach upset, sunburn-like rash, and a drop in blood pressure.

• *Cervical cap.* The cap is a soft rubber cup with a round rim, sized by a health professional to fit snugly around the cervix. It is available by prescription only and, like the diaphragm, is used with spermicide.

It protects for 48 hours and for multiple acts of intercourse within this time. Wearing it for more than 48 hours is not recommended because of the risk, though low, of TSS. Also, with prolonged use of two or more days, the cap may cause an unpleasant vaginal odor or discharge in some women.

• *Sponge.* The vaginal contraceptive sponge has not been available since the sole manufacturer, Whitehall Laboratories of Madison, N.J., voluntarily stopped selling it in 1995. It remains an approved product and could be marketed again.

The sponge, a donut-shaped polyurethane device containing the spermicide nonoxynol-9, is inserted into the vagina to cover the cervix. A woven polyester loop is designed to ease removal.

The sponge protects for up to 24 hours and for multiple acts of intercourse within this time. It should be left in place for at least six hours after intercourse but should be removed no more than 30 hours after insertion because of the risk, though low, of TSS.

Vaginal Spermicides Alone

Vaginal spermicides are available in foam, cream, jelly, film, suppository, or tablet forms. All types contain a sperm-killing chemical.

Studies have not produced definitive data on the efficacy of spermicides alone, but according to the authors of *Contraceptive Technology*, a leading resource for contraceptive information, the failure rate for typical users may be 21 percent per year.

Package instructions must be carefully followed because some spermicide products require the couple to wait 10 minutes or more after inserting the spermicide before having sex. One dose of spermicide is usually effective for one hour. For repeated intercourse, additional spermicide must be applied. And after intercourse, the spermicide has to remain in place for at least six to eight hours to ensure that all sperm are killed. The woman should not douche or rinse the vagina during this time.

Hormonal Methods

• *Combined oral contraceptives.* Typically called "the pill," combined oral contraceptives have been on the market for more than 35 years and are the most popular form of reversible birth control in the United States. This form of birth control suppresses ovulation (the monthly release of an egg from the ovaries) by the combined actions of the hormones estrogen and progestin.

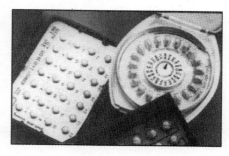

If a woman remembers to take the pill every day as directed, she has an extremely low chance of becoming pregnant in a year. But the pill's effectiveness may be reduced if the woman is taking some medications, such as certain antibiotics.

Besides preventing pregnancy, the pill offers additional benefits. As stated in the labeling, the pill can make periods more regular. It also has a protective effect against pelvic inflammatory disease, an infection of the fallopian tubes or uterus that is a major cause of infertility in women, and against ovarian and endometrial cancers.

The decision whether to take the pill should be made in consultation with a health professional. Birth control pills are safe for most women—safer even than delivering a baby—but they carry some risks.

Current low-dose pills have fewer risks associated with them than earlier versions. But women who smoke—especially those over 35—and women with certain medical conditions, such as a history of blood clots or breast or endometrial cancer, may be advised against taking the pill. The pill may contribute to cardiovascular disease, including high blood pressure, blood clots, and blockage of the arteries.

One of the biggest questions has been whether the pill increases the risk of breast cancer in past and current pill users. An international study published in the September 1996 journal *Contraception* concluded that women's risk of breast cancer 10 years after going off birth control pills was no higher than that of women who had never used the pill. During pill use and for the first 10 years after stopping the pill, women's risk of breast cancer was only slightly higher in pill users than non-pill users.

Side effects of the pill, which often subside after a few months' use, include nausea, headache, breast tenderness, weight gain, irregular bleeding, and depression.

Doctors sometimes prescribe higher doses of combined oral contraceptives for use as "morning after" pills to be taken within 72 hours of unprotected intercourse to prevent the possibly fertilized egg from reaching the uterus. In a Feb. 25, 1997, *Federal Register* notice, FDA stated its conclusion that, on the basis of current scientific evidence, certain oral contraceptives are safe and effective for this use.

• *Minipills.* Although taken daily like combined oral contraceptives, minipills contain only the hormone progestin and no estrogen. They work by reducing and thickening cervical mucus to prevent sperm from reaching the egg. They also keep the uterine lining from thickening, which prevents a fertilized egg from implanting in the uterus. These pills are generally less effective than combined oral contraceptives.

Minipills can decrease menstrual bleeding and cramps, as well as the risk of endometrial and ovarian cancer and pelvic inflammatory disease. Because they contain no estrogen, minipills don't present the risk of blood clots associated with estrogen in combined pills. They are a good option for women who can't take estrogen because they are breast-feeding or because estrogen-containing products cause them to have severe headaches or high blood pressure.

Side effects of minipills include menstrual cycle changes, weight gain, and breast tenderness.

• *Injectable progestins.* Depo-Provera, approved by FDA in 1992, is injected by a health professional into the buttocks or arm muscle every three months. Depo-Provera prevents pregnancy in three ways: It inhibits ovulation, changes the cervical mucus to help prevent sperm from reaching the egg, and changes the uterine lining to prevent the fertilized egg from implanting in the uterus. The progestin injection is extremely effective in preventing pregnancy, in large part because it requires little effort for the woman to comply: She simply has to get an injection by a doctor once every three months.

The benefits are similar to those of the minipill and another progestin-only contraceptive, Norplant. Side effects are also similar and can include irregular or missed periods, weight gain, and breast tenderness.

(See "Depo-Provera: The Quarterly Contraceptive" in the March 1993 *FDA Consumer.*)

• *Implantable progestins.* Norplant, approved by FDA in 1990, and the newer Norplant 2, approved in 1996, are the third type of progestin-only contraceptive. Made up of matchstick-sized rubber rods, this contraceptive is surgically implanted under the skin of the upper arm, where it steadily releases the contraceptive steroid levonorgestrel.

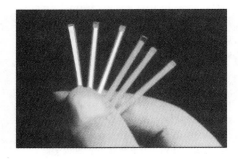

The six-rod Norplant provides protection for up to five years (or until it is removed), while the two-rod Norplant 2 protects for up to three years.

Norplant failures are rare, but are higher with increased body weight.

Some women may experience inflammation or infection at the site of the implant. Other side effects include menstrual cycle changes, weight gain, and breast tenderness.

Intrauterine Devices

An IUD is a T-shaped device inserted into the uterus by a health-care professional. Two types of IUDs are available in the United States: the Paragard CopperT 380A and the Progestasert Progesterone T. The Paragard IUD can remain in place for 10 years, while the Progestasert IUD must be replaced every year.

It's not entirely clear how IUDs prevent pregnancy. They seem to prevent sperm and eggs from meeting by either immobilizing the sperm on their way to the fallopian tubes or changing the uterine lining so the fertilized egg cannot implant in it.

IUDs have one of the lowest failure rates of any contraceptive method. "In the population for which the IUD is appropriate—for those in a mutually monogamous, stable relationship who aren't at a high risk of infection—the IUD is a very safe and very effective method of contraception," says Lisa Rarick, M.D., director of FDA's division of reproductive and urologic drug products.

The IUD's image suffered when the Dalkon Shield IUD was taken off the market in 1975. This IUD was associated with a high incidence of pelvic infections and infertility, and some deaths. Today, serious complications from IUDs are rare, although IUD users may be at increased risk of developing pelvic inflammatory disease. Other side effects can include perforation of the uterus, abnormal bleeding, and cramps. Complications occur most often during and immediately after insertion.

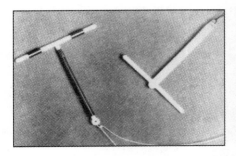

Traditional Methods

• *Fertility awareness.* Also known as natural family planning or periodic abstinence, fertility awareness entails not having sexual intercourse on the days of a woman's menstrual cycle when she could become pregnant or using a barrier method of birth control on those days.

Because a sperm may live in the female's reproductive tract for up to seven days and the egg remains fertile for about 24 hours, a woman can get pregnant within a substantial window of time—from seven days before ovulation to three days after. Methods

to approximate when a woman is fertile are usually based on the menstrual cycle, changes in cervical mucus, or changes in body temperature.

"Natural family planning can work," Rarick says, "but it takes an extremely motivated couple to use the method effectively."

• *Withdrawal.* In this method, also called *coitus interruptus,* the man withdraws his penis from the vagina before ejaculation. Fertilization is prevented because the sperm don't enter the vagina.

Effectiveness depends on the male's ability to withdraw before ejaculation. Also, withdrawal doesn't provide protection from STDs, including HIV.

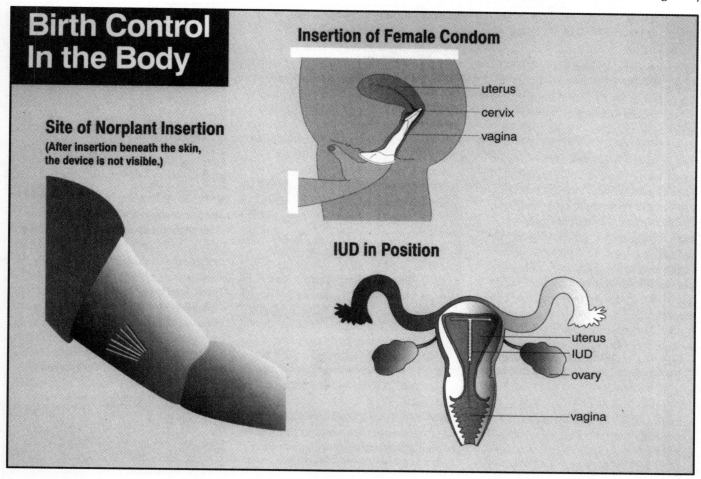

Birth Control In the Body

Site of Norplant Insertion
(After insertion beneath the skin, the device is not visible.)

Insertion of Female Condom

- uterus
- cervix
- vagina

IUD in Position

- uterus
- IUD
- ovary
- vagina

Birth Control Guide

Efficacy rates in this chart are based on Contraceptive Technology (16th edition, 1994). They are yearly estimates of effectiveness in typical use, which refers to a method's reliability in real life, when people don't always use a method properly. For comparison, about 85 percent of sexually active women using no contraception would be expected to become pregnant in a year.

This chart is a summary; it is not intended to be used alone. All product labeling should be followed carefully, and a health-care professional should be consulted for some methods.

Type	Estimated Effectiveness	Some Risks[d]	Protection from Sexually Transmitted Diseases (STDs)	Convenience	Availability
Male Condom	88%[a]	Irritation and allergic reactions (less likely with polyurethane)	Except for abstinence, latex condoms are the best protection against STDs, including herpes and AIDS.	Applied immediately before intercourse; used only once and discarded.	Nonprescription
Female Condom	79%	Irritation and allergic reactions	May give some STD protection; not as effective as latex condom.	Applied immediately before intercourse; used only once and discarded.	Nonprescription

(continued)

Type	Estimated Effectiveness	Some Risks[d]	Protection from Sexually Transmitted Diseases (STDs)	Convenience	Availability
Diaphragm with Spermicide	82%	Irritation and allergic reactions, urinary tract infection	Protects against cervical infection; spermicide may give some protection against chlamydia and gonorrhea; otherwise unknown.	Inserted before intercourse and left in place at least six hours after; can be left in place for 24 hours, with additional spermicide for repeated intercourse.	Prescription
Cervical Cap with Spermicide	64–82%[b]	Irritation and allergic reactions, abnormal Pap test	Spermicide may give some protection against chlamydia and gonorrhea; otherwise unknown.	May be difficult to insert; can remain in place for 48 hours without reapplying spermicide for repeated intercourse.	Prescription
Sponge with Spermicide (not currently marketed)	64–82%[b]	Irritation and allergic reactions, difficulty in removal	Spermicide may give some protection against chlamydia and gonorrhea; otherwise unknown.	Inserted before intercourse and protects for 24 hours without additional spermicide; must be left in place for at least six hours after intercourse; must be removed within 30 hours of insertion; used only once and discarded.	Nonprescription; not currently marketed.
Spermicides Alone	79%	Irritation and allergic reactions	May give some protection against chlamydia and gonorrhea; otherwise unknown.	Instructions vary: usually applied no more than one hour before intercourse and left in place at least six to eight hours after.	Nonprescription
Oral Contraceptives— combined pill	Over 99%[c]	Dizziness; nausea; changes in menstruation, mood, and weight; rarely, cardiovascular disease, including high blood pressure, blood clots, heart attack, and strokes	None, except some protection against pelvic inflammatory disease.	Must be taken on daily schedule, regardless of frequency of intercourse.	Prescription
Oral Contraceptives— progestin-only minipill	Over 99%[c]	Ectopic pregnancy, irregular bleeding, weight gain, breast tenderness	None, except some protection against pelvic inflammatory disease.	Must be taken on daily schedule, regardless of frequency of intercourse.	Prescription
Injection (Depo-Provera)	Over 99%	Irregular bleeding, weight gain, breast tenderness, headaches	None	One injection every three months	Prescription
Implant (Norplant)	Over 99%	Irregular bleeding, weight gain, breast tenderness, headaches, difficulty in removal	None	Implanted by health-care provider—minor outpatient surgical procedure; effective for up to five years.	Prescription
IUD (Intrauterine Device)	98–99%	Cramps, bleeding, pelvic inflammatory disease, infertility, perforation of uterus	None	After insertion by physician, can remain in place for up to one or 10 years, depending on type.	Prescription
Periodic Abstinence	About 80% (varies, based on method)	None	None	Requires frequent monitoring of body functions (for example, body temperature for one method).	Instructions from health-care provider

(continued)

Type	Estimated Effectiveness	Some Risks[d]	Protection from Sexually Transmitted Diseases (STDs)	Convenience	Availability
Surgical Sterilization —female or male	Over 99%	Pain, bleeding, infection, other minor postsurgical complications	None	One-time surgical procedure	Surgery

a Effectiveness rate for polyurethane condoms has not been established.
b Less effective for women who have had a baby because the birth process stretches the vagina and cervix, making it more difficult to achieve a proper fit.
c Based on perfect use, when the woman takes the pill every day as directed.

Infectious diseases can be transmitted by direct contact with surface lesions and by pre-ejaculatory fluid.

Surgical Sterilization

Surgical sterilization is a contraceptive option intended for people who don't want children in the future. It is considered permanent because reversal requires major surgery that is often unsuccessful.

• *Female sterilization.* Female sterilization blocks the fallopian tubes so the egg can't travel to the uterus. Sterilization is done by various surgical techniques performed under general anesthesia.

Complications from these operations are rare and can include infection, hemorrhage, and problems related to the use of general anesthesia.

• *Male sterilization.* This procedure, called a vasectomy, involves sealing, tying or cutting a man's vas deferens, which otherwise would carry the sperm from the testicle to the penis.

Vasectomy involves a quick operation, usually under 30 minutes, with possible minor postsurgical complications, such as bleeding or infection.

Research continues on effective contraceptives that minimize side effects. One important research focus, according to FDA's Rarick, is the development of birth control methods that are both spermicidal and microbicidal to prevent not only pregnancy but also transmission of HIV and other STDs.

Tamar Nordenberg is a staff writer for FDA Consumer.

THE BRAVE NEW WORLD OF PARENTING

More and more couples who might never have
been able to conceive are now giving birth, thanks
to high-tech infertility treatments. But as parents,
they face unexpected emotional challenges

BY JESSICA SNYDER SACHS

LAURA BENCIVENGA GETS LIVID WHEN HER HUSBAND GRUMBLES
about their toddler waking them in the night. "He'll mutter
something under his breath, and I'll say, 'How can you
say that? We worked so hard for this,' " she says. "I guess
I don't feel we have the right to complain."

Infertility is a heartache shared by over five million
couples in this country. Thanks to advances in technology,
however, pregnancy and parenthood are now possible for
more than half of these families.

Possible, perhaps, but seldom easy. Infertility treatment
can involve years of powerful drugs, hormone injections,
and an alphabet soup of such invasive procedures as IVF
(in vitro fertilization), GIFT (gamete intrafallopian transfer), and ZIFT (zygote intrafallopian transfer). Many couple also grapple with difficult decisions about whether to
use donor sperm or eggs, or even a surrogate mother.

These high-tech routes to parenthood, collectively known as assisted reproductive technology (ART), often don't work, but they do result in more than 16,000 babies each year in the U.S. alone. Studies show that ART babies are as healthy as those conceived "the easy way." It's their parents who have the experts concerned.

"Infertility and years of aggressive treatment can leave wounds that don't entirely heal," says therapist Ellen Glazer, coauthor of *Choosing Assisted Reproductions: Social, Emotional, and Ethical Considerations* and the mother of two daughters, 14 and 17, one through adoption and the other with the help of fertility treatments. "You make promises to yourself like, If I'm ever a parent, I'll never complain, I'll always be patient, I'll never take my child for granted."

Such unrealistic expectations aren't restricted to the previously infertile, of course; nor are separation anxiety or worries about a baby's health or one's competence as a parent. But years of fertility treatments can dramatically inflate not only expectations but also insecurities and fears.

Midnight grumblings aside, Barrett Bencivenga, of Short Hills, New Jersey, admits to a painfully intense protectiveness for his 2½-year-old daughter, Caroline: "We're so lucky to have her, I feel I have to make sure nothing happens to her." When Caroline was learning to walk, Daddy became her shadow, his outstretched arms trying to keep gravity at bay. "At work, I find myself worrying about where she is and what she's doing," he says. Not just once in a while, but many times throughout the day. "I don't want to be stifling," he says. "I know she needs to explore her world."

Acknowledging such feelings can be tremendously helpful, according to infertility and adoption educator Patricia Irwin-Johnston, author of *Taking Charge of Infertility.* "Parents who have worked through the medical as well as emotional ramifications of infertility, and who understand how their losses can continue to play a role in their lives, are among the best parents I know," she says.

THE ROYAL TREATMENT?

Six years ago, an article in *The New York Times Magazine* posed the question "What does it feel like being a $100,000 baby?" The assumption was that any child conceived at such great expense and effort was bound to be spoiled rotten and to fail the impossible task of justifying her cost in the eyes of her parents.

Michael and Pamela Stevinson, of Madera, California, confess to giving their in vitro twins anything they want. "When their second birthday came around, our house had more toys than Toys 'R' Us," says their mom.

Once-infertile couples need to free themselves of the self-imposed obligation to be superparents

Adding fuel to the Stevinsons' overindulgence is the fact that they underwent a procedure called fetal reduction. Like hundreds of other couples who've used in vitro fertilization, they had agreed to the implantation of multiple embryos, four of which took. Eighteen weeks into the pregnancy, specialists urged reducing the pregnancy to twins to improve the odds of healthy births. (Quadruplets are more than 13 times likelier to die within the first year than single-birth children. Twins face five times the risk.) "Our joy came with a bittersweet reminder of

those we lost," says Pamela. "How can we help but overindulge?"

Still, most experts say that the stereotype of the spoiled "test-tube baby" is inaccurate. "We just don't find the His-Majesty-the-Baby stuff among the families we've studied," says Dorothy Greenfeld, director of psychological services at the Yale Center for Reproductive Medicine. "As a group, these children aren't any more spoiled than others."

Part of the reason may be that the long ordeal of infertility treatment inspires many parents to invest extra effort in disciplining their kids. "All those years of waiting gave us plenty of time to see how we didn't want our children to behave," says Pat Kotsakis, of Palatine, Illinois, now the mother of a 5-, a 7-, and a 9-year-old. "It bothered us to see other kids acting bratty and spoiled."

Still, discipline *can* involve an inner struggle, according to Tom and Margaret Potter, of Bridgewater, New Jersey. "Sometimes I feel guilty after raising my voice to my older daughter," says Margaret. "I think, How could I? She's such an incredible gift!" The Potters' two children—Sarah, 4, and Brooke, 1½—were born with the help of in vitro fertilization and a gestational surrogate. Margaret's uterus, but not her ovaries, had been removed due to cervical cancer.

"WHERE DID I COME FROM?"

Kids delight in hearing the story of their birth, but the telling can fluster a parent who has traveled the high-tech route to pregnancy.

Making the project easier are two helpful guidebooks: *The Long-Awaited Stork: A Guide to Parenting After Infertility,* by therapist Ellen Glazer (Jossey-Bass); and *Flight of the Stork: What Children Think (and When) About Sex and Family Building,* by family psychologist Anne Bernstein (Perspective Press).
IN THE BEGINNING Around age 3 or 4, according to Bernstein, kids become curious about where they came from. Their questions are a natural opportunity to broach the subject, but parents need to be careful not to overwhelm their children with technical details. "When conception involves the mother's egg and father's sperm, I see no need to tell the child how that egg and sperm got together," says Bernstein. "After all, if your child was conceived in bed, you wouldn't discuss sexual positions."
EXTRA EXPLANATIONS Kids born through sperm or egg donation need more information. Bernstein gives this example of what a parent might say:

"Babies grow in the mother's uterus. To start the baby, a woman's egg and a man's sperm must join together. But sometimes, when a woman and a man try to start a baby, a baby doesn't grow. There are lots of reasons why that can happen. Sometimes, the father's sperm/mother's egg isn't strong or healthy. If the man and woman really want to grow a baby, they may get sperm/eggs from a man/woman who wants to help."
CALMING WORDS Some kids may need reassurance that the donor was not a parent who rejected them:

Child: "Why didn't the man/woman who gave the sperm/eggs want to be my daddy/mommy?"

Parent: "This person didn't know you. He/she gave his sperm/egg because he/she wanted to help, not because he/she was ready to be a daddy/mommy."

"The concepts take time for children to assimilate," says Bernstein. "Encourage questions, and let them know you're open to their concerns without making them feel like they're different." —J.S.S.

GREAT EXPECTATIONS

Sometimes the long, arduous course of infertility treatment and waiting can result in parents who become demanding, as if their children have some kind of debt to pay, says Diane Clapp, a counselor with RESOLVE, a national infertility support and advocacy group. But by expecting brilliance or perfect behavior all the time, they place an unfair burden on the kids. "Such parents need to remember that the infertility treatment was something they did themselves," she says. Children should never have to carry any burden because of the mechanics of their conception.

More common are the overblown expectations that once-infertile parents place on *themselves*. "It's as if they don't feel deserving if they're anything less than perfect," says Glazer. Laura Bencivenga, for example, recalls her extreme dismay at Caroline's first diaper rash, which developed two weeks after she was born. "I felt totally incompetent, like I couldn't even put on a diaper right," she says. Fortunately, Bencivenga's sister assured her that such ailments are common and are not a reflection of a person's ability to raise a child. Experts advise parents like Bencivenga to try to free themselves of self-imposed obligations to be superparents.

Also common is the assumption that child rearing will be nothing but a joy, says Clapp. Parents may fantasize about how perfect life will be when their baby finally arrives. Then, when the reality of midnight crying and endless diapers finally hits, normal feelings of resentment can stir up guilt.

Previously infertile parents need to give themselves permission occasionally to resent the day-to-day drudgery and strain of parenthood—and even to complain, the way other parents do, says Clapp.

A IS FOR ANXIETY

Infertility can shake a person's self-confidence to the core. "Many of the couples I see had been very successful in their lives," says Judith Kottick, counseling coordinator for the department of reproductive medicine at Saint Barnabas Medical Center, in Livingston, New Jersey. "Then infertility hit them and shattered their rosy view. Many struggle with feelings that they're somehow incapable and that they were never meant to be parents." Admits Laura Bencivenga: The experience of infertility has never left me. I still second-guess myself on everything that has to do with being a parent."

Some parents who've been through a series of infertility treatments become overanxious about their baby's health. Janet Moller (not her real name), of Boston, confesses to steering her 9-month-old son clear of playgroups and crowded restaurants, where germs may abound. "The prospect of any-

Some expectant parents feel so vulnerable that they refuse to embrace the pregnancy or birth for fear of tempting fate

thing happening to this baby is too terrible to imagine," she says. After eight years of trying, Moller and her husband had a child with the help of a surrogate, who donated her egg and also carried the baby to term. "It's as if years of miscarriages and failed attempts at pregnancy have robbed these parents of their naïveté that things will be okay," says Judith Lewis, Ph.D., a nurse researcher at Virginia Commonwealth University. "They expect things to go wrong."

It may be no surprise, then, that midnight finds more than a few such parents checking to make sure their baby is still breathing. "I know all parents do it occasionally," says Margo Rush, of Shelton, Connecticut. "But I do it a lot more than most." Rush's son, Jonathan (now 20 months), was born after five miscarriages and four years of infertility treatment. "I think it's still in the back of my mind that I might lose him, that this is too good to be true."

After two years of infertility treatment and a heart-wrenching experience with fetal reduction, Michael Stevinson found himself afraid to hold his newborn twins, Douglas and Michelle. "He never talked about it," says his wife, Pamela. "But I know he was scared to get attached, afraid that they might die too."

In a recent study of previously infertile mothers, Lewis found that 90 percent brought babies home to nurseries so sparsely furnished, some didn't even have a crib. She calls it "vulnerable parent syndrome." It's as if these parents fear they'd be tempting fate if they let themselves embrace the reality of pregnancy and birth.

In many cases, feelings of fear and denial begin to subside in the first days or weeks after birth. Occasionally, Lewis says, they linger longer.

For some, a feeling of impending doom magnifies separation anxiety. "Other parents tend to look back on their childless days with an easy fondness," says Glazer. "They look forward to having time to themselves again, if only for an occasional night out.

But for infertile couples, revisiting the feeling of being 'without child' can be terribly painful."

Glazer encourages such parents to be patient with themselves. "There will be times when it will feel easier to let go and others when you'll need to hold on," she says. "It's part of a process that will go on for years."

TOO MUCH TOO SOON?

Infertile couples sometimes feel compelled to jump back on the treatment treadmill soon after their baby's arrival, before it's too late to conceive again. Within seven months of giving birth, Laura Bencivenga, then 41, was back on fertility drugs and preparing for another cycle of in vitro fertilization. She was almost relieved when her doctors told her that her ovaries were no longer responding. "I knew I didn't want to put my body and my family through this anymore," she says with resignation.

There are no easy answers to the question of when new parents should resume infertility treatment, but experts advise that they give themselves a hefty dose of compassion. "Realize that you may be emotionally exhausted from your first go-around with new parenthood," says Clapp. Parents should weigh the importance of rushing back into treatment against the need to savor their baby and recoup their inner strength. What can help: close friends and family, or even a secondary infertility support group through a local chapter of RESOLVE or an infertility clinic.

WHEN DONOR MAKES THREE

Over 300,000 children in this country have been born through donor insemination. And though not as common, babies born through egg donation are rapidly increasing in number, from a few hundred per year in the 1980s to several thousand annually today.

Since one parent will lack genetic ties to the child, counselors at fertility clinics urge prospective parents to carefully explore their feelings before pursuing this route to conception. Still, they shouldn't be surprised if certain issues resurface after birth, says Anne Bernstein, Ph.D., a psychologist in Berkeley, California. Sometimes the parent without a genetic link ends up feeling less legitimate than the other, and retreats emotionally.

Many parents worry that a child born through the help of a donor may feel stigmatized or may someday reject them as "real" parents. For these and other reasons, parents may choose not to reveal that the conception was donor-aided, even to their own child.

But psychologists caution about the effects of such secrecy. "There will be times when the child will pick up that something

MINDING YOUR MARRIAGE

Infertility treatment can take a terrible toll on a couple's sex life. Feelings of failure can taint the intimacy and passion between partners. Years of scheduled intercourse can wear down their sense of spontaneity and fun. And the stigma of infertility can warp a woman's image of herself, says Judith Lewis, Ph.D., of Virginia Commonwealth University's School of Nursing.

Men commonly suffer sexual dysfunction after infertility treatment. Though seldom required to undergo invasive surgical procedures, men can be affected by the cold, mechanical nature of supplying sperm for in vitro fertilization into a cup.

And the transition to parenthood—a stress on any marriage—can add further strain.

Experts emphasize that talking about your feelings is essential, giving each other some room to grumble, as well as lots of love and support.

Make an effort to revive dating too. "Within a few months after the birth, you need to get out, just the two of you," says Peter Kaplan, M.D., a clinical instructor of psychiatry at the New York University School of Medicine.

"Now that you're launched as a family," says therapist Ellen Glazer, "it's time to begin reexperiencing the pleasure and passion that were part of your relationship and inspired you to have a family." —J. S. S.

is wrong," says Bernstein. "It may be a pinched expression when someone tells the parent, 'Oh, he looks just like you,' or an awkward silence when the pediatrician asks about family medical history."

Like many mental health workers, Bernstein urges parents to be open with their children. "The question is, do you want to spring this potentially mind-blowing information on a child when he's a teenager, or introduce it naturally, early on, as part of the story of his birth?"

For better or worse, secrecy isn't an option for the thousands of single women who

become mothers through donor insemination. Linda Gerhart, of Plano, Texas, is already anticipating the day when 9-month-old Brandon asks, "Where's Daddy?" Among the things that Gerhart will share with her son is an audiotape of his biological father, in which he talks about himself and the altruistic reasons that he chose to become a sperm donor.

"It would be dishonest to say that I didn't want my genes to be carried on, that I didn't want my children to look like me, be like me," admits Mark Sullivan (not his real

name), of suburban Maryland. His and his wife's two children, 3 and 5, were conceived through donor insemination.

Sullivan feels comfortable as a father today, he says, because he acknowledged his loss. "There's a residue of sadness," he says. "But I know that I'm not less of a father." He and his wife have formed a support group for parents of children conceived with donor sperm or eggs. "Now, as we tell the kids the story of their birth, we can point out friends born in a similar way."

Janet Moller and her husband have chosen to stay in contact with the egg donor, who also carried their son to term. (Janet has legally adopted the child.) "He will know that he's special because he has two mommies who love him," she says. He will also know that he has a half-brother by his birth mom. "If and how a relationship evolves remains to be seen," she says.

Whatever the circumstances of their birth, what kids need most is a sense of confidence. "Both parents and children need to come to believe that they are entitled to and deserving of one another and that they belong together," says Irwin-Johnston. The biggest gift moms and dads can give their children, she adds, is to fully embrace their wonderful new role as parents.

Contributing editor JESSICA SNYDER SACHS *is a science and health writer and the former editor of* Science Digest.

How Old Is Too Old to Have a Baby?

Fertility technology is advancing at such an astonishing pace that couples who fail to have children in their forties could realistically wait until their sixties to try again

BY JUDITH NEWMAN

TO BECOME A FATHER at 52 is unusual. To become a mother at 52 is to defy nature. Alan and Deirdre, both 52, don't want to let many of their friends and colleagues in on their secret yet, in case something goes wrong. But they are doing everything in their power to have a baby. They have the money, and they have the will. Deirdre, a trim, athletic researcher at a medical school in Connecticut, has three adult children from a previous marriage; Alan, a college English professor, has never had kids. "I always wanted children," he says. "Three years ago, when I found this woman I loved who was my own age, I thought, 'Well, that's one dream I'll have to relinquish.'"

Deirdre had already gone through menopause. By supplying the correct amounts of estrogen and progesterone via hormone therapy, it is relatively easy to make the uterus of a post-menopausal woman hospitable to a fetus. But even then, the chance of a woman Deirdre's age getting pregnant with her own eggs is nonexistent. So doctors suggested the couple consider implanting a donor egg fertilized with Alan's sperm. Egg donation is no longer considered cutting-edge medicine, but using the procedure to impregnate a woman over 50 is. Still,

Alan and Deirdre were overjoyed. "I thought, 'Isn't science great?'" Alan says.

In a few weeks, Machelle Seibel, a reproductive endocrinologist at the Fertility Center of New England, will mix the eggs of a much younger woman with Alan's sperm and introduce the resulting embryos to Deirdre's uterus. Her chances of giving birth will then rocket from less than 1 percent to 50 percent. "I would have considered doing this even if I hadn't remarried," Deirdre says with a lopsided grin. "The idea of having another child at this stage is compelling."

Not that Deirdre and Alan are unaware of the problems of being older parents. They worry about how they'll function with little sleep—"although I needed a lot of sleep even when I was in college," Alan says—and they are concerned that they might not be around to see their child come of age. If Deirdre gets pregnant, they plan to move to the Midwest to be near Alan's four brothers and sisters. "As a hedge against possible early death, we want our child to be surrounded by as much family as possible," Alan says.

Deirdre's three children, all in their twenties, are trying to be supportive. But

they're skeptical. "Independently they came to me and said they thought it would be weird to be their age and have parents in their late seventies," Deirdre says. "But I look at it like this: Our definition of 'family' has expanded. Now there are gay and adoptive and single-parent families who've used assisted technology. So although an 'older-parent family' is what we'll be, it's only one of several variations."

Twenty-two years after the world's first test-tube baby was conceived through in vitro fertilization, science is giving men and women—at least those who can afford the steep medical fees—increasing flexibility to alter the seasons of their lives. Infertility treatments once considered revolutionary are now commonplace: If a man has a low sperm count, sperm cells can be retrieved from a testicle for direct injection into an egg's cytoplasm. If the shell of an egg has hardened because of age, doctors can hatch it in the lab and then implant it on the uterine wall. If a woman has stopped producing eggs, she can avail herself of drugs to induce ovulation, as well as donor eggs or donor embryos. These days, the science of assisted reproductive technology is advancing at such a rapid rate that laboratory researchers say it will soon be medically possible for even a centenarian to give birth. But such tinkering with the biological clock begs a commonsense question: How old is too old to have a baby? And this seemingly straightforward question trickles into a cascade of other questions: How old is too old for parents? For children? For society?

When it comes to treating women for infertility, the American Society for Reproductive Medicine would like to draw its line in the sand at menopause. "Around 50, that's when reproductive processes have physiologically stopped, and therefore the intervention and treatment by physicians should also stop," says Robert Stillman, a former member of the society's board of directors. "Infertility is a medical disorder, affected by the reproductive life span. Just as we wouldn't consider inducing a prepubescent individual to conceive—although we could—we shouldn't induce pregnancy in someone who's gone through menopause."

In recent years, an increasing number of women have chosen to spend more time building a career, or looking for the right mate, before having children. Some have been shocked to belatedly discover there is no denying a fact of nature. Without any scientific intervention, childbearing is out of the question for most women by the time they reach their early forties. Between the ages of 35 and 40, fertility tapers off, and after 43 it pretty much plummets off the cliff. That is because something about the aging process upsets the process of meiosis, the nuclear division of the ovum or sperm in which chromosomes are reduced to half their original number. Sex cells do not divide properly, and there are too many or too few chromosomes in the egg or sperm. For women in their mid-forties, there is a dramatic increase in the risk that their eggs will have the wrong number of chromosomes after ovulation. Hence the difficulty in getting, and staying, pregnant. And unlike a man, whose sperm supply is constantly renewing itself, a woman is born with all the eggs she'll ever have. In fact, ovaries start aging before a woman's birth. A 20-week-old fetus has about 7 million eggs. Eighteen weeks later, at birth, that number has been decimated to less than 2 million. Even though the eggs remain unused throughout childhood, by puberty the egg supply has dropped to 400,000—less than

Double Trouble

Since the advent of in vitro fertilization two decades ago, there has been an explosion in the number of multiple births, particularly among women over 40. Statistics released last September by the Centers for Disease Control reveal a 52 percent increase overall in twin births between 1980 and 1997. Among women between 40 and 44, the increase in the number of twins born was 63 percent, and among women between 45 and 49 it was a staggering 1,000 percent. The ages of the mothers had less effect on the health or survival of the infants than the pregnancy complications generally associated with multiple births. For example, the risk of a very low birth weight is eight times higher for twins than for single births. The ultimate impact of multiple births on the lives of older parents is immeasurable. "Keeping up with two kids instead of one is a real challenge," says Machelle Seibel. "The increase in energy required is exponential rather than additive."

6 percent of what the child started with. By menopause, the egg larder is close to empty.

Even when an older mother manages to get pregnant, she and her baby face additional medical hurdles. With mothers over 35, there is a greater risk of hypertension and diabetes for themselves, and likely a greater risk of juvenile diabetes for the children. A 1995 Swedish study found that women born to mothers age 45 or older had a slightly higher chance of developing breast cancer than women born to younger mothers. Most well known is the increased risk of certain chromosomal abnormalities such as Down's syndrome, in which there is an extra set of genes in each cell.

Studies suggest that being the child of an older father also carries risk. Because older sperm tend to have more chromosomal mutations—ranging in seriousness from harmless to lethal—there is among older fathers a higher rate of kids born with certain rare tumors, neural-tube defects, congenital cataracts, and upper limb defects. Curiously, there's also a higher rate of homosexual children born to older dads.

While men experience some decline in the number of sperm, motility, and morphology—the number of normal sperm—after age 40, it's generally not enough to prevent them from becoming fathers. There are typically 150 to 300 million sperm released in one ejaculation. Even if the number drops by 50 percent, there are still pretty good odds there will be some keepers.

And now, technology has advanced to the point where even men with extremely poor sperm quality can father

children. With intracytoplasmic sperm injection, an embryologist can inject a single sperm into the cytoplasm of an egg with a microscopic needle while bypassing the normal cascade of chemical reactions necessary for fertilization. The procedure, which has only been around since 1992, is a primary reason for the speed-of-light development of fertility treatment for aging would-be parents—because it's not only sperm that can be injected into the egg. The processes of microinjection and micromanipulation of egg and sperm are making a wider array of new treatments possible.

For example, embryologist Jacques Cohen, scientific director at the Institute for Reproductive Medicine and Science of Saint Barnabas in Livingston, New Jersey, has developed a procedure called cytoplasmic transfer that shows promise for assisting women approaching their early forties who either can't get pregnant through in vitro fertilization or have embryos of such poor quality they don't survive. Doctors take the cytoplasm of a youthful and healthy egg—containing not the DNA but the proteins and enzymes for healthy cell growth—and inject it into the problematic egg to boost its quality. Possible health risks with the procedure have not yet been conclusively studied and there are troubling ethical questions. (See box "Can a Baby Have Three Parents?") But out of 26 attempts, the technique has resulted in 12 live births.

Jamie Grifo, director of New York University's reproductive endocrinology unit, is further refining another technique to assist women between 42 and 45, whose chances of having a child with their own eggs hover around 5 per-

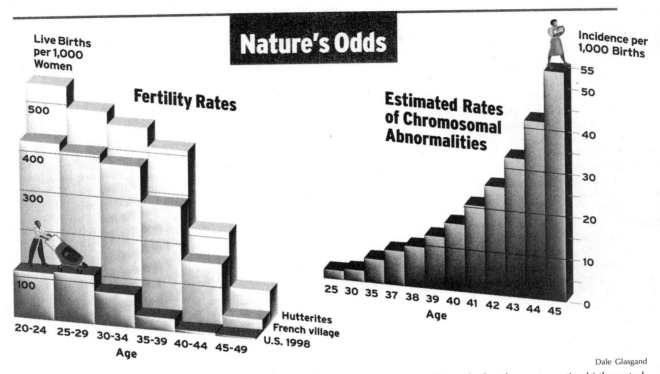

Dale Glasgand

LEFT: Contemporary birth records of the Hutterites, a religious sect in the western U.S. and Canada that does not practice birth control, and seventeenth-century birth records from a French village reveal a similar pattern: Natural fertility rates among women drop off precipitously around age 40. The latest available overall birthrates for U.S. women follow the same downward trend but are lower across the board because of the prevalence of birth control and a tendency of women to marry later in life. RIGHT: Statistics indicate that the risk of women having children with chromosomal abnormalities, including Down's syndrome, rises steadily from 2.1 per thousand births at age 25 to 53.7 per thousand births at age 45.

cent. He takes an older woman's egg and extracts the nucleus, which contains the DNA. Then he removes the nucleus from the donor egg of a much younger woman and in its place microinjects the genetic material of the older woman. The procedure, attempted on two women last year, resulted in fertilized embryos but not babies. Grifo and his team went back to the lab, perfecting the process on mice. The result: baby mice.

Grifo's groundbreaking work could provide the answer women like Alison Carlson are looking for. Carlson is a golden girl: blond, sunny, a former professional tennis coach in San Francisco. When she got married last year to a younger man and started trying to get pregnant at 42, she assumed she'd succeed quickly. "I was an athlete," she says. "I felt the normal rules wouldn't apply to me." At first it seemed she would be right. In her initial round of in vitro fertilization, Carlson produced an impressive 27 eggs, and 25 were fertilized: "I was a champ." She got pregnant but quickly miscarried. Forty-five percent of women over 40 do, usually

because of chromosomal abnormalities in their eggs. "Suddenly I felt like I should buy one of these T-shirts that say 'I Can't Believe I Forgot to Have Children.' " Carlson says that when she tried again, she failed to get pregnant at all.

Intellectuallly, Carlson knows the problem is age, but emotionally she cannot accept it. Like so many men and women over 40 who begin fertility treatments, she feels pressure to keep trying. "I'm embarrassed because, first, I felt I was being so arrogant," she says. "Like, here we all are, a bunch of baby boomers who went to college in the second wave of feminism, dedicated to having important careers before having babies, and then paying gobs of money so science can give us what we want. I'm appalled at my own sense of entitlement."

Given the anguish many aging baby boomers now experience trying to get pregnant, it's hard to fathom that the future holds no less than the end of infertility. Doctors recently discovered how to freeze a woman's eggs when she's young and then thaw them when she's ready to get pregnant. A woman could

finish college and graduate school, launch a career, and then start a family with eggs she parked on ice at age 18.

Banking individual eggs is just the beginning. Recently Kutluk Oktay, the chief of reproductive endocrinology and infertility at New York Methodist Hospital in Brooklyn, has been experimenting with freezing and transplanting swatches of ovarian tissue. Each bit of tissue contains thousands of immature follicle eggs. While individual, already-developed eggs die easily when frozen, immature follicle eggs embedded in the ovarian tissue fare a lot better. Oktay has already tried the technique on a 30-year-old dancer from Arizona who'd had her first ovary removed at 17 because of cysts but had the foresight to have her second ovary frozen. Last fall, Oktay sewed 80 small pieces of the tissue back into her pelvis and revived her menstrual cycle. The woman is not trying to conceive. But Oktay's colleague, Roger Gosden, now reproductive biology research director of McGill University's Royal Victoria Hospital in Montreal, has removed the ovaries of sheep, frozen them, thawed them, sutured them back in the sheep—and gotten lambs aplenty.

Of course cryopreservation will not help those whose eggs are already sitting on the porch in little rocking chairs. But researchers have found ways to keep old eggs alive. Jon Tilly, the director of the Vincent Center for Reproductive Biology at Massachusetts General Hospital in Boston, has been studying genetically altered mice to better understand the process of apoptosis, or natural cell death. Cells are programmed to die: Fifty or sixty genes, maybe more, regulate their expiration. One specifically involved in the death of immature eggs in the ovaries is known as the bax gene. When Tilly and his researchers studied mice that lacked the bax gene, they found that 24-month-old females—the equivalent of 80- to 100-year-old humans—still have functioning, estrogen-producing ovaries. "We were pretty amazed," says Tilly. "And the bax gene has a precise counterpart in humans that appears to be responsible for the decimation of eggs during menopause." Silencing of one of the "cell death" genes may be the first step in finding treatments to help woman delay menopause or avoid the health problems—osteoporosis, heart disease—associated with the cessation of estrogen production. Tilly also believes that in the not-wildly-distant future the ability to suppress the bax gene in women's ovaries may prolong their fertility too. He is quick to add, however, that even though the old female mice with newly viable eggs were allowed to cavort with young, studly mice, they did not produce offspring. This is because older mice lose the capacity to excrete adequate levels of two hormones: one that stimulates egg follicles to grow and mature and another that causes the ripened egg to be released from the ovary into the reproductive tract.

Another approach to ending infertility involves beating the numbers game. What if a woman had an unlimited number of eggs? This may someday be possible if researchers can get somatic cells—that is, cells from anywhere in the body—to act like sex cells. Normal cells are diploid, with 46 chromosomes—23 from one's father and 23 from one's mother. The gonads (testicles and ovaries) divide the chromosomes to create haploid cells, namely spermatozoa and eggs. As the eggs age, most suffer from aneuploidy, the uneven division

Can a Baby Have Three Parents?

One new fertility treatment called cytoplasmic transfer involves taking a younger woman's "egg white," which contains the proteins and enzymes necessary for proper growth, and microinjecting it into the egg of an older woman. The idea is to restore healthy components to the older woman's egg, making fertilization and pregnancy more likely. The problem, says Machelle Seibel, is that mitochondria—tiny football-shaped structures in the cytoplasm that are the energy powerhouses of a cell—also contain some DNA. And scientists know that there are a number of inherited mitochondrial DNA diseases, resulting in health problems that range from the mild to the fatal. (Problems as varied as sudden infant death syndrome and Alzheimer's are thought to stem from genetic defects in the mitochondria.) Theoretically, the young woman giving her cytoplasm becomes the third parent, capable of passing along some genetic information, including her family diseases. "I don't think this component of the procedure is completely appreciated by the providers or the receivers," says Seibel. "Cytoplasmic transfer may be fine, but its safety is unproven. This makes me a little uncomfortable."

of the chromosomes. Anything other than 23 sets of chromosomes makes the egg either entirely unviable, or viable but resulting in abnormalities like Down's syndrome. It is not that the eggs, in their undeveloped state, are abnormal; it's that something about the machinery of meiosis—the chromosomal division at ovulation—goes awry as women age. The key to fixing this problem is to make faux eggs—normal body cells that behave like eggs by undergoing meiosis. Thus, anyone 18 to 100 would have an unlimited supply of easily harvested "sex cells."

This is exactly what Cohen and some other researchers are working on now. Bioethicists balk, because the process sounds like a kissing cousin to cloning. But it's not. The resulting cell has half its mother's chromosomes and, when united with sperm, could be expected to create a bona fide, half-his, half-hers human. The catch is that the parents could theoretically be 100 or more years old. "This is going to involve some major discussions about what's clinically acceptable and what's socially acceptable," Cohen says.

Of course, even if they have all the financial resources in the world, most couples past the age of retirement probably won't want to start raising children. "This won't be some huge public policy issue," says Arthur Caplan, director of the University of Pennsylvania's Center for Bioethics. "It's not like you'll see all these people running from nursing homes to birthing centers." But, Caplan adds, the very fact that 50-year-old

mothers and fathers could become relatively commonplace raises another issue. "One of the ethical questions becomes: What's in the best interest of the child? And the answer is simple: It's good not to be an orphan. A good, loving environment requires one parent. So if a father is 20 and a mother 80, that's not a problem. If the father is 60 and the mother 40, well, one should think about the implications of depriving a child of grandparents. It's not morally reprehensible, but it's an issue. Now, if both parents are in their sixties"—as was the case in 1996 with Arceli Keh, the 63-year-old Filipino who gave birth after lying about her age to her fertility specialists in California—"that's a problem."

Contemplating their own untimely demise won't deter truly determined older parent wanna-bes, like Eileen and Charles Volz of Millbury, Massachusetts. Eileen, a certified public accountant, was 42 and had just married Charles, a digital commerce executive, in 1992 when she was diagnosed with breast cancer. Radiation and chemotherapy put her into immediate menopause, but she overcame the cancer. Four years passed before she and her husband heard about egg donation. "People thought we were a little nuts," says Charles Volz. "I mean, I already had three children, and she had survived breast cancer—why should we tempt fate?"

One look at their son, C.J., answers the question. On her first try at Machelle Seibel's clinic, she got pregnant with a donor egg and had C.J. at 48. "I never for a moment felt he wasn't mine,"

Eileen says. "Genetics is the smallest part of being a mother."

Eileen Volz is now 50; her husband is 48. They tried a second round of egg donation, which failed, but they are contemplating a third. Sure they'll be collecting Social Security by the time C.J. is ready to head off to college. But Charles Volz speaks for older parents everywhere when he offers this Pollyannaish view of his midlife adventure: "It's not a problem at all. Hey, I'm going to live forever."

Perhaps the biggest question for science and society will not be answered for a number of years, until the first generation of children born to older parents through assisted reproductive technology enters their teenage years: What happens when children nature did

not intend to create become adults? Already there are some troubling questions about the 20,000 children conceived throughout the world by intracytoplasmic sperm injection. Aggressively injecting a sperm into an egg manually has been found to change a whole sequence of molecular events in fertilization; for example, the DNA packaged in the head of the sperm unravels more slowly than in normal fertilization, throwing off the timing of the process. Scientists worry that although there hasn't been an obvious increase in birth defects so far, sex chromosome abnormalities may show up when the children reach puberty. One 1998 study in Belgium showed that of 1,082 prenatal tests on intracytoplasmic sperm injection pregnancies, one in

120 had sex chromosome abnormalities, as compared to a general population figure of one in 500 pregnancies.

"Fertility is a unique field in some respects," says Massachusetts General's Jon Tilly. "In most fields of scientific inquiry, most of the problems are worked out in animal models. But here, technology is moving so fast, and people are so desperate for answers, that work on humans is paralleling work on animals. That may turn out to be good, because we are accelerating the application of our knowledge. But it may be bad, because we don't know what's safe. We don't know about unforeseen problems. There may be reasons the body is not designed to be reproducing after its early forties."

SHAPED BY LIFE IN THE WOMB

Scientists used to think that adult illnesses like diabetes, obesity, cardiovascular disease and breast cancer were the result of either unhealthy living or bad genes. No longer. Startling new research suggests that these conditions may have their roots before birth.

BY SHARON BEGLEY

When John Carter was born, 73 years ago, the doctor in the town of Ware just north of London wasn't sure if the little guy would make it: he weighed a mere 3.4 pounds. "They laid me on a hot-water bottle, wrapped me in cotton soaked in cod-liver oil and gave me brandy through the nib of a fountain pen," Carter says. "Surviving was rather a miracle." But the little boy grew to manhood, landing a job as a warehouseman and enjoying normal health—until his early 50s. That's when a physical discovered that Carter had sky-high blood pressure. Another test found that he had adult-onset diabetes.

Carter had no reason to suspect it, but his illnesses may not stem from the usual culprits: genetic defects, unhealthy living or environmental toxics. Cutting-edge research suggests instead that the roots of both his high blood pressure and his diabetes stretch back decades—to his life in the womb. Scientists now think that conditions during gestation, ranging from the torrent of hormones that flow from Mom to how well the placenta delivers nutrients to the tiny limbs and organs, shape the health of the adult that fetus becomes. "Recent research" says Dr. Peter Nathanaielsz of Cornell University, whose new book "Life in the Womb" ex-

plores this science, "provides compelling proof that the health we enjoy throughout our lives is determined to a large extent by the conditions in which we developed, [conditions that] can program how our liver, heart, kidneys and especially our brain function." It is no exaggeration to call these findings a revolution in the making. The discovery of how conditions in the womb influence the risk of adult disease casts doubt on how much genes contribute to disease (because what scientists classify as a genetic influence may instead reflect gestational conditions) and suggests that adult illnesses long blamed on years of living dangerously (like dining on pizza and cupcakes) instead reflect "fetal programming." "Two years ago no one was even thinking about this," says Dr. Matthew Gillman of Harvard Medical School. "But now what we are seeing is nothing short of a new paradigm in public health."

What is so startling is that the findings go far beyond the widespread recognition that conditions during gestation shape the health of the newborn. We've known for a while that alcohol reaching the fetus can lead to mental retardation and heart defects and that the stew of toxins in tobacco can cause upper-respiratory-tract and ear infections. But these compounds work by more or less

poisoning the baby. The result is often a child who, at birth or soon after, has detectable problems. The new findings are dramatically different. First of all, the gestational conditions scientists are talking about fall far short of toxic. They are, instead, paragons of subtlety. They are conditions that reprogram the fetus's physiology so that, for instance, the child's (and eventually the adult's) metabolism turns just about everything she eats into body fat. This is the woman who needn't bother actually eating the french fries; she might as well just insert them directly into her hips. Second, unlike the toxic influences whose effects on a fetus are apparent immediately, the effects of fetal programming often show up only decades later. The nine-pound bouncing girl will be perfectly healthy for decades. But the same influences that gave her layers of baby fat—"growth factors" like estrogen's crossing the placenta from Mom—prime her mammary tissue so that exposure to estrogen after puberty gives her breast cancer at 46.

There is one thing the findings do not mean. While they may tempt you to blame Mom for even more of your ills, or make you feel powerless against a fate that was set before you cried your first cry, forget it: how you live your life outside the womb still matters. Since the conditions in which the

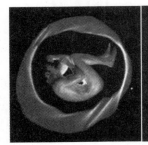

EARLY WIRING: The growth factors that give a newborn baby fat may prime her mammary tissue, making her more susceptible to breast cancer in her 40s.

PHOTO ILLUSTRATION BY JOSEPH PLUCHINO

fetus develops influence adult health, learning what those conditions are (through measurements of length, weight, girth and head size at birth) tells you what extra risks you carry with you into the world. And that suggests ways to keep these risks from becoming reality. If as a newborn your abdomen was unusually small, for instance, then your liver may be too small to clear cholesterol from your bloodstream as well as it should, and you may have an extra risk of elevated cholesterol at the age of 50. So scrutinize those baby pictures: if your tummy was scrawny compared with the rest of chubby-cheeked you, be careful about controlling your cholesterol levels.

The discovery of fetal programming might never have happened if Dr. David Barker of England's University of Southampton had not noticed, in 1984, some maps that did not seem to make sense. They displayed measures of health throughout England and Wales. Barker saw that neonatal mortality in the early 1900s was high in the same regions where deaths from heart disease were high.

Ominous signs: *Michels's study of thousands of American women finds a link between a girl's birth weight and her risk of breast cancer at a relatively young age*

That was odd. In general, infant mortality rises in pockets of poverty; heart disease is supposedly a disease of affluence (butter, meat and all that). They shouldn't go together. Barker wondered whether the search for the cause of heart disease should begin in the womb. To embark on his quest, he needed birth records, and lots of them, going back decades, to link conditions at the beginning of life with the health of the adults he would study. Lending a hand, Britain's Medical Research Council hired an Oxford University historian to scour the country for such records. During a two-year hunt, the historian found records in archives, lofts, sheds, garages, boiler rooms and even flooded basements—but the best records were in Hertfordshire. There, the "lady inspector of midwives" had recorded the weight of every baby born in the shire (including John Carter) from 1911 to 1945. Barker had his data.

Soon Barker and his colleagues had their "Aha!" moment. Studying 13,249 men born in Hertfordshire and Sheffield, Barker found

A Tragic But Telling Legacy

Doctors are using a horror of war to learn more about the long-term effects of nutrition on fetal development

YOU COULDN'T DESIGN a grimmer experiment. A Nazi blockade of the western Netherlands in September 1944 and an early winter triggered a famine that lasted until the spring of 1945. By January, daily rations in the cities were down to 750 calories, half of what they had been earlier in the war; they would eventually fall below 500 calories. City dwellers were forced into the country to scavenge for food, including tulip bulbs. The "Hunger Winter" had killed 20,000

people by Liberation Day on May 5, 1945, scarring an entire populace—including, scientists later found, generations yet unborn. In the 1960s, husband-and-wife researchers Zena Stein and Mervyn Susser realized that, horrific as it was, the Dutch Hunger Winter offered unprecedented clues to the effects of prenatal nutrition.

Stein and Susser discovered that fetuses exposed to the famine early in gestation, when organs form, had an increased risk of central-nervous-

system defects like spina bifida, in which the brain or spine is not fully developed. Other scientists found that a fetus starved early in development during the famine was at high risk for adult obesity. Two decades later, Stein and Susser's son, Ezra Susser, went further. Now a pioneering epidemiologist at Columbia University, Susser examined psychiatric evaluations of adults who were Hunger Winter babies to study the theory that schizophrenia was the result of a

defect in neural development. Susser and Hans Hoek in the Netherlands discovered that fetuses who received poor nutrition early in gestation were twice as likely to develop schizophrenia in adulthood as fetuses whose mothers had an adequate diet. Susser is now looking for links between prenatal nutrition and other mental illnesses. It's a sad but revealing legacy of that season of devastation.

JOHN DAVENPORT

Tragic Echoes: *Children relied on relief programs; infants suffered later in life*

The Roots of Health

Disorders such as heart disease and diabetes are not only the result of unhealthy habits or bad genes. The new science of "fetal programming" suggests that as pregnancy progresses, each month in the womb shapes your health for life.

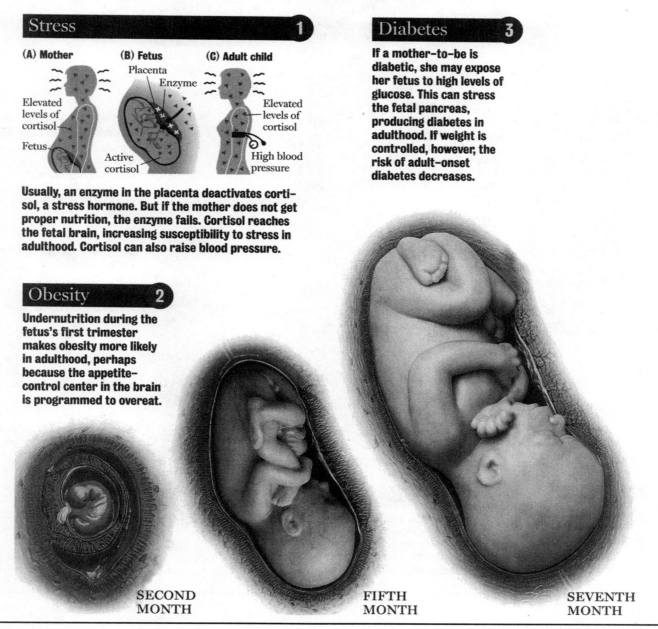

Stress 1

(A) Mother

Elevated levels of cortisol

Fetus

(B) Fetus

Placenta

Enzyme

Active cortisol

(C) Adult child

Elevated levels of cortisol

High blood pressure

Usually, an enzyme in the placenta deactivates cortisol, a stress hormone. But if the mother does not get proper nutrition, the enzyme fails. Cortisol reaches the fetal brain, increasing susceptibility to stress in adulthood. Cortisol can also raise blood pressure.

Obesity 2

Undernutrition during the fetus's first trimester makes obesity more likely in adulthood, perhaps because the appetite-control center in the brain is programmed to overeat.

Diabetes 3

If a mother-to-be is diabetic, she may expose her fetus to high levels of glucose. This can stress the fetal pancreas, producing diabetes in adulthood. If weight is controlled, however, the risk of adult-onset diabetes decreases.

SECOND MONTH

FIFTH MONTH

SEVENTH MONTH

---

that a man who weighed less than 5.5 pounds at birth has a 50 percent greater chance of dying of heart disease than a man with a higher birth weight, even accounting for socioeconomic differences and other heart risks. "Death rates from both stroke and coronary heart disease tended to be highest in men whose birth weight had been low," says Barker, especially when it was low compared with their length or head size (an indication that the baby's growth was

stunted). Using other birth records from India, Barker found the same link in a 1996 study. Again, low birth weight predicted coronary heart disease, especially in the middle-aged: 11 percent of 42- to 62-year-olds who weighed 5.5 pounds or less at birth got it, compared with 3 percent of those born chubbier. The link between low birth weight and cardiovascular disease is now one of the strongest in the whole field of fetal programming, holding across continents as well as

genders. Researchers led by Dr. Janet Rich-Edwards of Harvard reported, in 1997, that of 70,297 American women studied, those born weighing less than 5.5 pounds had a 23 percent higher risk of cardiovascular disease than women born heftier.

But it is not smallness per se that causes heart disease decades later. Instead, what seems to happen is that the same suboptimal conditions in the womb that stunt a baby's growth also saddle it with risk factors that

(continued)

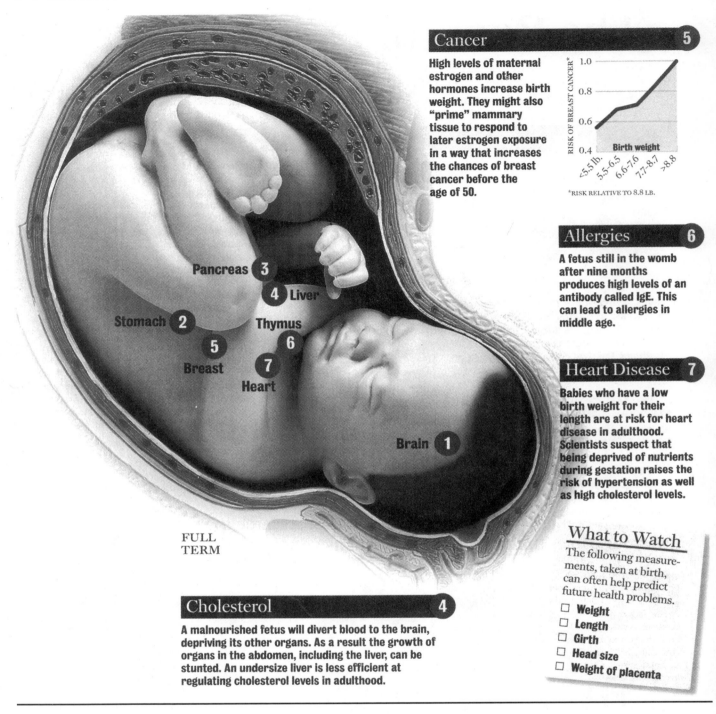

Cancer 5

High levels of maternal estrogen and other hormones increase birth weight. They might also "prime" mammary tissue to respond to later estrogen exposure in a way that increases the chances of breast cancer before the age of 50.

RISK OF BREAST CANCER

1.0
0.8
0.6
0.4

Birth weight

<5.5 lb. 5.5-6.5 6.6-7.6 7.7-8.7 >8.8

*RISK RELATIVE TO 8.8 LB.

Allergies 6

A fetus still in the womb after nine months produces high levels of an antibody called IgE. This can lead to allergies in middle age.

Heart Disease 7

Babies who have a low birth weight for their length are at risk for heart disease in adulthood. Scientists suspect that being deprived of nutrients during gestation raises the risk of hypertension as well as high cholesterol levels.

Pancreas 3
Liver 4
Stomach 2
Thymus
Breast 5
6
Heart 7
Brain 1

FULL TERM

Cholesterol 4

A malnourished fetus will divert blood to the brain, depriving its other organs. As a result the growth of organs in the abdomen, including the liver, can be stunted. An undersize liver is less efficient at regulating cholesterol levels in adulthood.

What to Watch

The following measurements, taken at birth, can often help predict future health problems.

☐ Weight
☐ Length
☐ Girth
☐ Head size
☐ Weight of placenta

lead to heart disease. "Birth weight is a proxy for something," says Rich-Edwards. "It's a marker for a complex set of factors that influence both growth in the womb and susceptibility to disease later on." Scientists have some suspects. Nathanielsz suggests it may be as simple as having undersized kidneys: these organs help regulate blood pressure, but if they are not up to the task, the result can be hypertension, a leading cause of heart disease. Or, animal studies have shown that if a fetus does not receive adequate protein, then an enzyme in the placenta

loses its punch and can no longer disarm harmful hormones trying to sneak into the fetus. One such hormone is cortisol. Cortisol raises blood pressure, as you are reminded every time stress makes your veins bulge. In the fetus, cortisol seems to raise the set point for blood pressure—irreversibly. "You are talking about hard-wiring the system," says Jonathan Seckl of the University of Edinburgh.

The discoveries are drawing throngs of excited scientists. A year ago the Society for Epidemiologic Research half-filled a small room at its annual meeting for a session on

fetal programming. This spring the same subject packed a whole lecture hall. "This whole topic is just now catching fire," says Rich-Edwards. The surge in interest reflects the lengthening list of diseases that scientists are tracing back to the womb. The National Institutes of Health held a conference in January on the link between conditions in the womb and breast cancer; in September, another NIH confab examined the link to cardiovascular disease, kidney disease and other ills. A conference at Harvard will explore the topic in November.

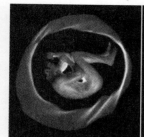

HARD WIRED: A fetus's response to conditions inside the uterus produces permanent physiological changes. But there's still plenty you can fix later.

The breast-cancer link is one of the most surprising. The very existence of the disease is bad enough. What terrifies women is that it strikes so many who have no known risk factors—such as age, close relatives with the disease or not bearing a child before 30. Dr. Karin Michels of the Harvard School of Public Health has identified one overlooked cause. After collecting health data from tens of thousands of nurses, Michels and colleagues reported in 1997 that women who had weighed about 5.5 pounds at birth had half the risk of breast cancer compared with women who had weighed about 9 pounds at birth. That was especially true of breast cancers in women 50 or younger. "There is increasing evidence," says Michels, "that breast cancer may originate before birth."

A very high birth weight may be a marker for uterine influences that "prime" mammary tissue for cancer. Growth factors, living up to their name, make a fetus larger. Such factors include insulin, leptin and estrogen. If the mother has high levels of these substances (being obese raises levels of estrogen, for instance), and if they reach her fetus, the hormones may do more than act like Miracle-Gro on backyard tomatoes: they may alter nascent mammary tissue in such a way that it responds to estrogen during puberty by becoming malignant. This is no reason to starve your girl fetus—stunted fetal growth leads to other problems. But it does suggest that if you were a pudgy newborn you might want to be extra vigilant about breast exams.

The same message emerges from the other links that scientists are turning up. Weight and other traits at birth may offer a map of where your personal disease land mines are buried:

■ Cholesterol: The smaller the abdomen at birth, the higher the cholesterol level in adulthood. What may happen is that if the mother is poorly nourished or if a problem with the placenta keeps the fetus from receiving adequate nutrition, then the fetus switches into emergency mode: it shunts blood to the brain, the most vital organ, at the expense of organs in the abdomen. That includes the liver, which plays a key role in regulating cholesterol levels. A smaller liver can't clear cholesterol as well as a hefty one. This suggests an answer to the longstanding puzzle of how some people can eat high-fat and cholesterol-laden diets with impunity:

Heart of the matter:
Barker's discovery that birth weight is linked to cardio-vascular disease in adulthood has launched a revolution in public health

these lucky folks were programmed as fetuses to process fat and cholesterol as efficiently as a sewage-treatment plant. The others have defective treatment plants. "When a fetus adapts to conditions in the womb," says Southampton's Barker, "that adaptation tends to be permanent."

■ Obesity: This was the first trait suspected of reflecting life in the womb. In World War II, the Nazis tried to starve the population of western Holland from September 1944 until the following May (sidebar). Men who were fetuses during all or part of the period showed a telling pattern. If their mothers were starving during the first trimester—from March to May 1945—but got adequate food later, the men were born heavier, longer and with larger heads than babies in normal periods. As adults, they were more likely to be obese. If their mothers went hungry only in the final trimester—if the boys were born in November 1944, say—the men usually stayed svelte. What may happen is this: if food is scarce during the first trimester, the fetus develops a so-called thrifty phenotype. Its metabolism is set so that every available calorie sticks. Or, the availability or scarcity of food may affect the appetite centers in the fetal brain. In that case, undernutrition early in fetal life could dial up the appetite controls to the setting "eat whatever's around: you never know when famine will hit." An abundance of food early keeps the dial at "no need to pig out." Fetuses undernourished later in gestation may develop fewer fat cells (it is in the later months that

most cells are added). That makes it harder to become fat after birth.

■ Diabetes: Being skinny at birth puts an individual at high risk for diabetes in middle age, finds David Leon of the London School of Hygiene and Tropical Medicine. The effect is powerful: diabetes is three times more common in 60-year-old men who, as newborns, were in the bottom fifth on a scale of plumpness (technically, it's birth weight divided by length cubed) than in more rotund babies. "One explanation is that inadequate nutrition programs the fetus to develop a thrifty metabolism," says Leon. "That includes insulin resistance, so the body saves and marshals existing glucose stores." When this metabolism meets junk food, the body is flooded with glucose and becomes diabetic. But diabetes is a prime example of how life in the womb is not an immutable sentence. Although thinness at birth raises the risk of developing diabetes in middle age, finds Leon, that risk is much reduced if you stay thin.

■ Brain: Research on how life in the womb influences the brain is only beginning. But already there are hints, from both animal and human research, that something is going on. In a 1997 paper, biologists reported on a study of people with asymmetries in traits like feet, fingers, ears and elbows. IQs were lower in asymmetric people by about as much (percentage-wise) as their measurements deviate from perfect symmetry. Some sort of stress during fetal development probably causes asymmetries, suggests Randy Thornhill of the University of New Mexico. The same stress may cause imperfections in the developing nervous system, leading to less efficient neurons for sensing, remembering and thinking. Here, too, asymmetry is a marker for something going wrong in the womb. Thornhill estimates that between 17 and 50 percent of IQ differences reflect in utero causes.

The new science of fetal programming suggests that we may have gone overboard in ascribing traits to genes. "Programming," concludes Nathanielsz, "is equally if not more important than our genes in determining how we perform mentally and physically." Consider one of the standard ways that scientists assess how much of a trait reflects genetic influences and how much reflects environment: they compare twins. If identical twins share a trait more than other

What Moms Can Do Now

If you're pregnant, take advantage of the latest research to give your babies the best start. They'll thank you later.

OF COURSE THOSE nine months matter. Doctors now say that from the moment the sperm and egg fuse, conditions in your body determine how healthy your baby will be as an adult. Pediatricians can estimate risk for diseases by measuring length, weight, girth and head size at birth. Visit an obstetrician who's up on the latest research before you get pregnant and follow these guidelines:

Preconception care: A doctor can help you avoid medicines that harm embryos. Tell your obstetrician about any diseases or conditions you have that might complicate the pregnancy. If you're diabetic, make sure to take your insulin. To prevent neural-tube defects such as spina bifida, get at least 400 micrograms of folic acid a day from foods like leafy green vegetables and orange juice.

Meal plan: Eat about 300 extra calories a day during pregnancy. Snack or eat small meals throughout the day if you can't take large amounts of food. Your baby needs nutrients to grow normally, and you can't make up for lost calories by eating more later on.

The right stuff: Eat lots of carbohydrates, but don't skimp on fruits, vegetables, low-fat dairy products and lean meats. These foods contain protein, vitamins and minerals that build your baby's blood, bones and muscles.

Weight gain: Try to put on about 25 to 35 pounds if your weight is normal (more if you're on the thin side and less if you're fat). Focus on gaining weight, not watching calories. Your baby needs the extra nutrition to develop properly.

Drugs: Ask your doctor about any medications you take. Anticonvulsants and the acne drug Accutane can cause birth defects. Some antidepressants and painkillers may affect the baby, but don't stop taking them without consulting a doctor. Cocaine can kill a fetus, and babies born addicted to narcotics will suffer withdrawal after birth.

Caffeine: Your blood volume doubles during pregnancy, so a java overdose will dehydrate you when you need water most. Some research has linked excessive doses of caffeine to low birth weight, so limit yourself to a couple of cups a day.

Exercise: Staying in shape may ease labor and speed recovery after delivery. But don't exercise to exhaustion, and stay away from sports that expose your belly to trauma. Swimming and walking should be high on your list.

Stress: Reduce it. Both chronic and sudden, intense stress may increase the risk of premature labor by raising your levels of cortisol, a stress hormone. Try cutting back on work hours or joining a yoga class. And remember to get enough sleep.

Seat belts: Use them; your uterus and amniotic fluid prevent seat belts from injuring the fetus. Wear the lap belt below your belly, and adjust the shoulder strap so it rests between your breasts.

Alcohol: Doctors urge temperance during pregnancy. Excessive alcohol causes facial and heart defects, mental retardation and behavioral problems.

Smoking: Kick the habit now. Smoking contributes to 25 percent of cases of low birth weight and can cause miscarriage and premature birth.

STDs: Get tested. Untreated chlamydia, HIV, gonorrhea, syphilis and herpes cause a wide range of complications during pregnancy and childbirth.

ERIKA CHECK

siblings do, the trait is deemed to be largely under genetic control. But twins share something besides genes: a womb. Some of the concordance attributed to shared genes might instead reflect a shared uterine environment. The womb may have another effect. Merely *having* a gene is not enough to express the associated trait. The genes must be turned on to exert an effect, otherwise they are silent—just as having a collection of CDs doesn't mean that your home is filled with music unless you play them. In the womb, a flood of stress hormones may actually turn off genes associated with the stress response; the response becomes less effective, which is another way of saying this child is at risk of growing into an adult who can't handle stress. "The script written on the genes is altered by . . . the environment in the womb," says Nathanielsz.

As fetal programming becomes better understood, it may even resurrect the long-discredited theory known as Lamarckism. This idea holds that traits acquired by an organism during its lifetime can be passed on to children—that if a woman spends the 10 years before pregnancy whipping herself into a bodybuilder physique, her baby will emerge ready to pump iron. Modern genetics showed that inheritance does not work that way. But according to fetal programming, some traits a mother acquires can indeed be visited on her child. If she becomes diabetic, then she floods her fetus with glucose; waves on glucose may overwhelm the developing pancreas so that fetal cells that secrete insulin become exhausted. As a result, the child, too, becomes diabetic in adulthood. When this child becomes pregnant, she too, floods her fetus with glucose, stressing its pancreas and priming it for adult-onset diabetes. This baby will develop diabetes because of something that happened two generations before—a kind of grandmother effect.

In "Brave New World," Aldous Huxley describes how workers at the Central London Hatchery, where fetuses grow in special broths, adjust the ingredients of the amniotic soup depending on which kind of child they need. Children destined to work in chemical factories are treated so they can tolerate lead and cadmium; those destined to pilot rockets are constantly rotated so that they learn to enjoy being upside-down. The quest for the secrets of fetal programming won't yield up such simple recipes. But it is already showing that the seeds of health are planted even before you draw your first breath, and that the nine short months of life in the womb shape your health as long as you live.

With WILLIAM UNDERHILL
in London

THE COST OF CHILDREN

Of course they're cute. But have you any idea how much one will set you back? A hardheaded inquiry

BY PHILLIP J. LONGMAN

To examine in coldly economic terms a parent's decision to have children is widely thought to be in bad taste. A child, after all, isn't precisely akin to a consumer product such as a dishwasher, a house, a car, or a personal computer—any one of which, of course, is cheaper to acquire and usually easier to return. A child is a font of love, hope for the future, continuation of one's bloodline, and various other intangible pleasures, and it is these sentimental considerations (along with some earthier imperatives) that prevail when parents bring a child into this world.

But let's face it: Children don't come free. Indeed, their cost is rising. According to one government calculation, the direct cost of raising a child to age 18 has risen by 20 percent since 1960 (adjusted for inflation and changes in family size). And this calculation doesn't take into account the forgone wages that result from a parent taking time off to raise children—an economic cost that has skyrocketed during the last generation as women have entered the work force in unprecedented numbers. "It's become much more expensive to raise children while the economic returns to parents have diminished," notes feminist economist Shirley Burggraf. "The family can't survive on romance."

Knowing the real cost of children is critical to a host of financial questions, such as how much house one can afford, how much one should be saving for college tuition, and how much one must earn to have a larger family. To help answer such questions, *U.S. News* has undertaken to identify and add up as best it can all the costs of raising a child from birth to college graduation. (For the purposes of this calculation, we're assuming these children will pay for any advanced degrees they may want out of their own pockets.)

Our starting point is data from the United States Department of Agriculture, which every year publishes estimates of how much families in different income brackets spend on raising children to age 18. To these calculations we have added the cost of a college education and wages forgone because of the rigors of child-rearing. (There's plenty we haven't counted: soccer camp, cello lessons, SAT prep., and other extra-cost options.) What we've found is that the typical child in a middle-income family requires a 22-year investment of just over $1.45 million. That's a pretty steep price tag in a country where the median income for families with children is just $41,000. The child's unit cost rises to $2.78 million for the top-third income bracket and drops to $761,871 for the bottom-third income bracket.

Tut tut, you say. Surely this is another case of newsmagazine hyperbole. All right, then, let's take it from the top:

■ **Acquisition costs.** In most cases, conceiving a child biologically is gloriously cost free. But not for all: An estimated 6.1 percent of women ages 15–24, and 11.2 percent of women ages 25–34, suffer from what health statisticians refer to as "impaired fecundity." Serving this huge market are some 300 infertility clinics nationwide that performed 59,142 treatment "cycles" in 1995, according to a recently released study by the Centers for Disease Control and Prevention. The cost of treatments–only 19 percent of which actually produced a take-home baby–averaged around $8,000 a try. It's not uncommon for infertile couples to spend $50,000 or more in pursuit of pregnancy. Though most insurance policies will pay for some form of infertility treatment, insurers are cutting back rapidly in the total bills they'll cover. For the purposes of our tally, we'll ignore fertility treatments, but this can be a significant cost.

For most people, the meter starts running with pregnancy. Costs vary dramatically from hospital to hospital, from region to region, and according to how complicated the pregnancy is. Out-of-pocket costs, obviously, will also vary depending on how much health insurance you have. But here's an idea of what your bills might be.

For an uneventful normal pregnancy, 12 prenatal care visits are usually recommended–the cost of which varies according to one's insurance plan. According to HCIA Inc., a Baltimore health care information company, the cost to insured patients of a normal delivery in a hospital averages about $2,800. (Twins are cheaper on a per-head basis: typical total delivery cost: $4,115.)

For parents without insurance, direct costs are clearly much higher. According to a 1994 study, the cost of an uncomplicated "normal" delivery averages $6,400 nationally. Caesarean delivery costs an average of $11,000, and more complicated births may range up to $400,000. Premature babies requiring neonatal intensive care will cost $1,000 to $2,500 for every day they stay in the hospital. Though most people can count on insurance to cover a majority of such costs, there are many people who can't. According to a report issued in March by the U.S. government's Agency for Health Care Policy and Research, 17 percent of Hispanic children, 12.6 percent of black children, and 6 percent of white ones lack any health in-

surance coverage whatsoever, including coverage by Medicaid or other public programs.

An alternative path to acquiring a child is through adoption. Of the roughly 30,000 adoptions of healthy infants in the United States each year, most involve expenses of $10,000 to $15,000. These include the cost of paying for a social worker to perform a "home study" to vouchsafe the adoptive parents' suitability, agency fees, travel expenses (many adoptions these days cross national boundaries), medical and sometimes living expenses for the birth mother, and legal fees. Offsetting these costs for parents who adopt is a new $5,000 federal tax credit. Since most people don't adopt, these costs, too, are excluded from *U.S. News*'s tally.

THREADS.
To clothe a child to age 18 costs **$22,063.** And yes, girls cost 18 percent more than boys.

■ **Child care.** The Department of Agriculture calculates that the middle-class parents of a 3-to-5-year-old spend just over $1,260 a year on average for child care. (According to the Census Bureau, fully 56 percent of American families with children use paid child care.) Wealthier families are more likely to opt for the pricier nanny. Irish Nanny Services of Dublin advertises Irish nannies "with good moral standards" who are "renowned for their expertise with children." The price for U.S. parents begins at $250 per week; plus 1.5 paid holidays for every month

worked; plus a nonrefundable finder's fee equal to 10 percent of the yearly salary payable upfront.

The average cost for all families using child care is $74.15 a week, or about 7.5 percent of average pretax family income, which is roughly equal to most workers' employee-contribution rate for Social Security. The rate is much steeper, of course, at the low end of the income scale; families making less than $1,200 a month who use day care spend an average 25.1 percent of their income on day-care expenses.

■ **Food.** Middle-class families spend an average $990 a year feeding a child under 2. (Breast-feeding helps: One serving of infant formula can cost as much as $3.29.) As kids get bigger, so do their appetites: Feeding a middle-class 15-year-old currently costs $1,920 a year on average. A middle-class only child born in 1997 can be expected to consume a total of $54,795 in food by age 18.

■ **Housing.** The bigger your family, the bigger the house you need. Families with children also often pay a premium to live in safe, leafy neighborhoods with good schools. USDA estimates that the average middle-class, husband-wife family with one child will spend, on a per capita basis, an additional $97,549 to provide the child with shelter.

■ **Transportation.** Priced a minivan lately? The added transportation cost of having one middle-class child totals $46,345, according to the USDA. This does not include the cost of commuting to jobs parents must hold in order to support their children. Predictably, as children get older, the cost of driving them around grows. Parents with teenagers spend over 70 percent more on transportation than families with infants. Just the cost of providing teenage drivers with auto insurance can run into the thousands.

■ **Health care.** Obviously, this cost varies tremendously, depending largely on the health of the child. The lifetime health costs of a child born with cerebral palsy, for instance, average $503,000; with Down's syndrome, $451,000; and with spina bifida,

$294,000, according to the March of Dimes.

Again, out-of-pocket costs for health care will depend largely on whether the parents have good (or any) health insurance. In 1996, nearly 11 million American children, or 15.4 percent of the population under 18, had none. Deductibles, copayments, and specific coverages also vary widely even among those with insurance. Taking all these variables into account, and including the cost of insurance, the USDA estimates that the average cost of keeping a middle-class child born in 1997 healthy to age 18 will be more than $20,757.

■ **Clothing.** Even after allowing for hand-me-downs and gifts from doting grandparents, keeping an only child properly dressed to age 18 will cost an average total of $22,063, according to the USDA. Predictably, in this realm, daughters cost more than sons: According to the Bureau of Labor Statistics, husband-wife families with children spend nearly 18 percent more on girls' clothes than on those for boys.

■ **Primary and secondary education.** Fully 89 percent of all school-age kids in the United States attend public schools. Public education costs American society more than $293 billion per year, but for the purposes of this tally, we'll exclude taxes (which, after all, are paid by parents and non-parents alike) and consider public education to be free.

For the roughly 5 million grade-school students now enrolled in private schools, costs vary widely. About 50 percent of these students attend parochial schools, where tuition averaged $1,934 in 1993–94, the last school year for which data are available. By contrast, parents earning over $125,000 a year who send a child to the elite Deerfield Academy in Deerfield, Mass., and who manage to qualify for financial aid, are expected to contribute $10,600 a year in tuition. Overall, the U.S. Department of Education reports, private-school tuition in 1993–94 averaged $2,200 a year in elementary schools and $5,500 in secondary schools, with

schools for children who are handicapped or have "special needs" charging an average $15,189. These costs have been rising quickly. Reflecting increasing demand, the average tuition of private schools increased by more than double the overall rate of inflation between 1990 and 1996.

■ **Toys and other miscellaneous expenses.** The USDA doesn't break out spending on toys by income group or the age of children. But for all husband-and-wife families with children, the average amount spent on pets, toys, and playground equipment in 1995 was $485.

TUMBLES.
Children are usually quite healthy, but they'll still run you **$20,757** to keep fit till age 18.

What do all these bills come to? USDA calculates that a typical middle-class, husband-wife family will spend a total of $301,183 to raise an only child born in 1997 to age 18 (table, "Cost of children born in 1997). More affluent parents (with income over $59,700 a year) will spend an average of $437,869 on an only child. The average figure for lower-income families (with income below $35,500 a year) is $221,750.

Certain economies of scale are available to larger families. As family size increases, food costs per person go down the most. (Just feed everyone stew.) Per capita housing and transportation costs also decrease, but not by as much. All told, for middle-class families, the marginal cost of raising a second child will be approximately 24

percent less than the cost of a single child. The marginal unit cost continues to drop for each successive child.

Now let's consider two costs the USDA calculation leaves out. The first is college. From the start of the 1990s through September of 1997, average tuition at the nation's colleges increased by more than 75 percent, while overall prices in the economy inflated by little more than 26 percent. Common sense would suggest that this rate of tuition inflation cannot possibly sustain itself over the long term, especially if real family income remains flat or grows only slowly. Sooner or later, some combination of new technology and organizational reform will surely render higher education less costly. Still, who would have imagined that the price of a college education would ever have risen to where it is today? With an undergraduate education becoming ever more necessary to guarantee a middle-class lifestyle, perhaps its price will rise even faster in the future. Given these imponderables, we'll assume college costs will continue to rise at the average annual rate of the 1990s, or 7.45 percent, and that the cost of room, board, and books grows at 5 percent, which is the annual inflation rate of the past 20 years.

Now, let's do some illustrative arithmetic. Say you had a child in September 1997. Let's forget straight off about sending him to Harvard or Princeton, or any other private college, and aim for a top state school, the University of Michigan–Ann Arbor. Tuition, fees, plus room and board for in-state students there currently amount to $11,694 a year. Under the inflation assumptions described above, it turns out you'll need a total of $157,831 to see a child born last year through graduation at Ann Arbor (assuming you are a Michigan resident; tuition is more than three times higher for out-of-state residents).

Ok, now let's figure out how to pay for that tuition. Assuming an average annual 7 percent total return on savings, you'll have put away more than $319 each month, starting on your child's date

Cost of children born in 1997

Higher income (one-child family; 1997 before-tax family income: more than $59,700)

Age	Housing	Food	Transportation	Clothing	Health care	Day care and education	Misc.	College (Princeton)	Forgone wages	Total for year
0	$5,915	$1,624	$1,885	$719	$744	$2,120	$1,860		$44,650	**$59,518**
1	$6,211	$1,706	$1,979	$755	$781	$2,226	$1,953		$48,669	**$64,279**
2	$6,521	$1,791	$2,078	$793	$820	$2,338	$2,051		$53,049	**$69,440**
3	$6,804	$2,124	$2,139	$818	$833	$2,670	$2,168		$57,823	**$75,379**
4	$7,144	$2,231	$2,246	$859	$874	$2,803	$2,276		$63,027	**$81,461**
5	$7,501	$2,342	$2,358	$902	$918	$2,944	$2,390		$41,047	**$60,402**
6	$7,760	$2,974	$2,675	$1,030	$1,097	$2,127	$2,576		$45,847	**$66,087**
7	$8,148	$3,123	$2,809	$1,082	$1,152	$2,233	$2,704		$52,033	**$73,285**
8	$8,556	$3,279	$2,950	$1,136	$1,209	$2,345	$2,840		$57,900	**$80,214**
9	$8,599	$4,001	$3,232	$1,308	$1,366	$1,712	$3,039		$65,315	**$88,572**
10	$9,029	$4,201	$3,393	$1,373	$1,434	$1,798	$3,191		$72,460	**$96,880**
11	$9,480	$4,411	$3,563	$1,442	$1,506	$1,888	$3,351		$64,402	**$90,042**
12	$10,444	$4,855	$3,986	$2,494	$1,581	$1,537	$3,897		$72,230	**$101,024**
13	$10,966	$5,097	$4,185	$2,619	$1,660	$1,613	$4,092		$82,517	**$112,750**
14	$11,514	$5,352	$4,395	$2,750	$1,743	$1,694	$4,296		$92,118	**$123,863**
15	$11,008	$5,929	$5,620	$2,629	$1,933	$3,119	$3,944		$104,460	**$138,642**
16	$11,558	$6,226	$5,901	$2,761	$2,030	$3,275	$4,141		$116,188	**$152,080**
17	$12,136	$6,537	$6,196	$2,899	$2,132	$3,439	$4,348		$130,979	**$168,665**
18								$103,574	$145,257	**$248,831**
19								$110,831	$140,766	**$251,597**
20								$118,605	$156,987	**$275,592**
21								$126,935	$177,732	**$304,667**
Total	$159,294	$67,805	$61,589	$28,370	$23,813	$41,881	$55,117	$459,945	$1,885,454	**$2,783,268**

Middle income (one-child family; 1997 before-tax family income: $35,500 to $59,700)

Age	Housing	Food	Transportation	Clothing	Health care	Day care and education	Misc.	College (Univ. of Michigan)	Forgone wages	Total for year
0	$3,720	$1,228	$1,352	$546	$645	$1,401	$1,104		$23,600	**$33,594**
1	$3,906	$1,289	$1,419	$573	$677	$1,471	$1,159		$25,724	**$36,218**
2	$4,101	$1,353	$1,490	$602	$711	$1,545	$1,217		$28,039	**$39,058**
3	$4,263	$1,636	$1,522	$617	$718	$1,809	$1,306		$30,563	**$42,434**
4	$4,476	$1,718	$1,598	$648	$754	$1,899	$1,372		$33,313	**$45,778**
5	$4,700	$1,804	$1,678	$681	$791	$1,994	$1,440		$21,695	**$34,783**
6	$4,819	$2,426	$1,961	$798	$947	$1,346	$1,579		$24,233	**$38,108**
7	$5,060	$2,547	$2,059	$838	$995	$1,413	$1,658		$27,502	**$42,072**
8	$5,313	$2,675	$2,162	$879	$1,044	$1,484	$1,740		$30,603	**$45,901**
9	$5,194	$3,289	$2,405	$1,020	$1,193	$1,020	$1,885		$34,523	**$50,527**

(continued on next page)

of birth, to have enough money on hand to pay for four years of college as each semester's tuition bill comes due. If you wait until the child is in kindergarten to start saving, your monthly savings requirement will jump to $524. If you wait until the child reaches freshman year of high school, the number will jump to $1,957 a month.

Or here's another way to look at the challenge. Take a middle-class fam-

Age	Housing	Food	Transportation	Clothing	Health care	Day care and education	Misc.	College (Univ. of Michigan)	Forgone wages	Total for year
10	$5,454	$3,454	$2,525	$1,071	$1,252	$1,071	$1,979		$38,299	**$55,104**
11	$5,726	$3,627	$2,651	$1,124	$1,315	$1,124	$2,078		$34,040	**$51,685**
12	$6,502	$3,852	$3,029	$1,982	$1,381	$868	$2,539		$38,178	**$58,331**
13	$6,828	$4,045	$3,180	$2,081	$1,450	$912	$2,666		$43,615	**$64,776**
14	$7,169	$4,247	$3,339	$2,185	$1,522	$957	$2,799		$48,690	**$70,908**
15	$6,445	$4,950	$4,434	$2,037	$1,701	$1,701	$2,372		$55,213	**$78,852**
16	$6,767	$5,197	$4,656	$2,138	$1,786	$1,786	$2,490		$61,412	**$86,233**
17	$7,105	$5,457	$4,888	$2,245	$1,876	$1,876	$2,615		$69,230	**$95,292**
18								$35,821	$76,777	**$112,598**
19								$38,140	$74,402	**$112,543**
20								$40,614	$82,976	**$123,591**
21								$43,255	$93,941	**$137,196**
Total	**$97,549**	**$54,795**	**$46,345**	**$22,063**	**$20,757**	**$25,678**	**$33,996**	**$157,832**	**$996,567**	**$1,455,581**

Lower income (one-child family; 1997 before-tax family income: less than $35,500)

Age	Housing	Food	Transportation	Clothing	Health care	Day care and education	Misc.	College (Florida A&M)	Forgone wages	Total for year
0	$2,753	$1,029	$905	$459	$496	$856	$719		$11,050	**$18,267**
1	$2,890	$1,081	$950	$482	$521	$898	$755		$12,045	**$19,622**
2	$3,035	$1,135	$998	$506	$547	$943	$793		$13,129	**$21,085**
3	$3,144	$1,321	$1,005	$517	$545	$1,120	$847		$14,310	**$22,808**
4	$3,301	$1,387	$1,055	$543	$573	$1,176	$889		$15,598	**$24,521**
5	$3,466	$1,456	$1,108	$570	$601	$1,234	$934		$10,158	**$19,527**
6	$3,523	$1,977	$1,363	$681	$731	$764	$1,047		$11,346	**$21,433**
7	$3,699	$2,076	$1,431	$715	$768	$803	$1,099		$12,877	**$23,468**
8	$3,884	$2,180	$1,502	$751	$806	$843	$1,154		$14,329	**$25,450**
9	$3,674	$2,732	$1,712	$866	$923	$539	$1,270		$16,164	**$27,879**
10	$3,858	$2,868	$1,798	$909	$970	$566	$1,333		$17,932	**$30,233**
11	$4,051	$3,012	$1,888	$954	$1,018	$594	$1,400		$15,938	**$28,854**
12	$4,743	$3,318	$2,227	$1,692	$1,069	$445	$1,826		$17,876	**$33,196**
13	$4,980	$3,484	$2,338	$1,777	$1,122	$468	$1,917		$20,421	**$36,508**
14	$5,229	$3,658	$2,455	$1,866	$1,178	$491	$2,013		$22,797	**$39,689**
15	$4,434	$4,150	$3,480	$1,727	$1,315	$851	$1,547		$25,852	**$43,355**
16	$4,656	$4,358	$3,654	$1,814	$1,380	$893	$1,624		$28,754	**$47,133**
17	$4,888	$4,576	$3,837	$1,904	$51,449	$938	$1,705		$32,415	**$51,713**
18								$16,783	$35,948	**$52,731**
19								$17,802	$34,837	**$52,639**
20								$18,886	$38,851	**$57,737**
21								$20,038	$43,985	**$64,023**
Total	**$70,208**	**$45,797**	**$33,705**	**$18,732**	**$16,013**	**$14,421**	**$22,873**	**$73,508**	**$466,613**	**$761,871**

Note: Numbers may not add up because of rounding

ily earning, say, $47,200 in 1998. Assume that inflation will average 5 percent over the next 18 years and that this family's income will grow 4 percent above inflation. Assume finally that this family will earn a 7 percent annual average return on its savings. Now suppose this family had a new child last year, and the parents want to prefund the likely cost of sending this child to a top-rank state school. What percent of family income do they need to put away each year toward the child's college expenses? Answer: about 4 percent.

So far, this accounting puts the cost of raising and educating a middle-class, only child at roughly $459,014 ($301,183 in direct expenditures to age 18 plus $157,831 for college costs). Now suppose you're considering having a child and want to have enough money in the bank by the day the child is born to be able to cover all of his or her direct future costs to you. No one actually does this, of course, but as any chief financial officer knows, this is a useful way to calculate the real burden of long-term liabilities. Assume you can earn 7 percent on your investments after your child is born. In that case, you'll need to build a nest egg of $204,470 by delivery day. Assuming you want to raise your child with a middle-class standard of living, this is the approximate present value of your liabilities for future expenses related to that child.

Or, suppose you want to have a child 10 years from now and want to start a regular savings plan that will allow you just enough money by the child's date of birth to cover all future child-related expenses as they occur. What you need to start saving today is $1,181 a month. Again, nobody actually does this, but amortizing the cost of children in this way provides a useful benchmark in figuring how "affordable" children are. Could you "afford" to pay an extra $1,181 every month for the next 10 years servicing your credit-card debt? Failing to prefund future liabilities, such as the future cost of a child, is financially equivalent to borrowing. If your family income goes up substantially in the future, you may be able to afford your child-related "unfunded liabilities," but if it remains stagnant or grows only slowly, as real family income has for decades, then these unfunded liabilities will hurt.

A final expenditure to add to our tally is a bit more abstract but no less real: forgone family income. People who have children tend to have less time on their hands to make money.

Consider first the forgone income for an unwed teenage mother who rears her child alone. Researchers at the University of Michigan have compared the earning power, over 20 years, of women who did and did not have children out of wedlock as teenagers. Interestingly, at ages 19 and 20, women who had given birth to illegitimate children actually had slightly higher incomes on average than women who remained childless during their teenage years; this presumably reflected the effect of welfare payments, which can boost short-term income above what the average childless full-time student earns. But by age 21, unmarried women who refrained from having become pregnant as teenagers, or who had abortions, began to pull well ahead of those who did not. By age 29, women who did not have the burden of raising a child alone as teenagers could expect to have earned a total of $72,191 more than women who did carry this burden.

What does it cost a married woman to have children? The answer depends crucially on her opportunities. Obviously, a woman who gives up a career as a nurse's aide to have a baby does not forgo as much income as a woman who gives up a law partnership. But for both there is an "opportunity cost," which can be roughly estimated. As economist Burggraf points out in her recent book, *The Feminine Economy and Economic Man,* people tend to take marriage partners of similar educational backgrounds and aspirations (social scientists label this "assortive mating"). For example, college-educated men are 15 times more likely to marry college-educated women than are men who never completed high school. This means that the opportunity cost of either spouse taking time off to raise a child is often 50 percent of a family's potential income.

That's exactly the trade-off faced by Colette Hochstein and her husband, Michael Lingenfelter. Both are librarians who work extensively with computer-information retrieval systems. Her position is with the National Institutes of Health in Bethesda,

Md.; he works in the White House library. Together, they spend more money on day care for their 2-year-old daughter, Miranda—about 17 percent of their household income—than on any other expense except their mortgage. Yet since they both earn roughly the same salary, the only way to avoid paying for day care would be to sacrifice half their household income. If either of them were to quit work to take care of Miranda full time, says Hochstein, the economic cost would extend beyond Miranda's childhood years: "In this rapidly changing, high-tech time, there are few professions in which one could take even a year's leave of absence without falling seriously behind."

Given the career opportunities now available to women, virtually all parents face some opportunity cost in having children, and it usually adds up to serious money. Consider this hypothetical middle-class, husband-wife family. They met in college and soon after married. Two years into their marriage, they each were earning $23,600, but then came Junior. She immediately quit her job to stay home with the baby, causing their family income to fall by half. After their child reaches kindergarten, she hopes to begin working half time; by the time the child reaches age 11, she hopes to be able to boost her work hours to 30 a week. But remembering her own escapades while home alone during high school, she does not plan to return to full-time work until the child goes off to college.

What's the opportunity cost of these life choices? Assume, as the USDA does, that inflation averages 5 percent over her working life. Further assume that, because of her "mommy track," her average annual real wage increases come to 2 percent instead of a possible 4 percent she could have earned as a childless and fully committed full-time professional. In that event, she'll sacrifice $996,567 in forgone income over just the next 21 years. Adjusting for inflation, that's equal in today's dollars to roughly $548,563.

Where does this leave the total bill? Combine $996,567 in forgone wages with the USDA's estimates of a typical middle-class family's direct child-related expenses for an only child ($301,183); add in the likely cost of sending a child born last year to a first-rank, in-state public university ($157,831), and the total cost of one typical middle-class child born in 1997 comes in at $1,445,581. Even after adjusting for inflation, the cost of a middle-class child born last year is still $799,913 in today's dollars.

To be sure, parents also receive some direct subsidies for their child-care costs. Being able to claim a dependent is worth $2,650 in federal taxes due this year, for example. And under current law, families are eligible to take a tax credit for child-care expenses, with a maximum credit of $720 for one child in a low-income family and up to $1,440 for two or more children. President Clinton recently proposed making this credit more generous, so that a family of four making $35,000 and saddled with high child-care bills would no longer owe any federal income taxes. But even if Clinton's plan is approved, parents who stay home with their kids will continue to receive no compensation for their lost income, and even those taking the credits will find themselves far worse off financially, in most cases, than if they had decided to remain childless.

Given current economic incentives, it is hardly surprising that the "smartest" people in our society end up being those least likely to have children. Middle-aged women with graduate degrees are more than three times more likely to be childless than those who dropped out of high school. Similarly, two-income married-couple families earning over $75,000 are 70 percent more likely to be childless than those earning between $10,000 and $19,999. You don't have to be an economic materialist to see the financial reality behind these numbers. Highly educated, high-income people have a higher opportu-

nity cost, in the form of lost income, if they decide to have children.

Government policy makers are forever talking about the need for society to "invest" in today's youth, if for no other reason than to pay for the huge, largely socialized cost of supporting the growing ranks of the elderly. It's a noble goal, but at the individual family level, a child, financially speaking, looks more like a high-priced consumer item with no warranty. It's the decision to remain childless that offers the real investment opportunity.

TUMMIES. Feeding a middle-class 15-year-old costs **$1,920** a year on average. Hide the Cheez-Its!

Imagine a middle-class, college-age, sexually active woman who is contemplating whether to spend $5,000 to have her tubes tied so she'll never have to worry about getting pregnant. We've already seen how the cost of giving birth to just one child could easily exceed $1.4 million over the next 22 years. Even though many of those costs could be well down the road, a typical middle-class young woman paying $5,000 for such an operation could expect that "investment" to compound at a rate of fully 680 percent over the next 22 years alone. (The return on a vasectomy, which is even cheaper, would be much high-

er.) It will be a long time before anyone finds a deal that lucrative on Wall Street.

But wait a minute. Isn't this an absurd conclusion? Children aren't just a bundle of liabilities. If they were, the way for society to become richer would be for everyone to stop having kids, but of course that wouldn't work. Without a rising new generation of workers, there will be nobody around to assume our debts, and before long, even the store shelves will be empty. So why does our accounting suggest the opposite?

Because society's economic interests and those of parents as individuals don't perfectly coincide. The financial sacrifice a parent makes to have and raise children creates enormous wealth for society as a whole. But the modern reality is that everyone shares in much of that wealth regardless of what role he or she played in creating it. If, for example, you don't choose to have children, or you treat your children badly, you still won't have to give up any of your Social Security pension.

Historically, support in old age did depend, almost entirely, on how many children you had, and on how well your investment in them turned out. Even before parents grew old, they could usually count on their children to perform economically useful tasks around the farm or shop. This made children economic assets—from the point of view of both society at large and parents.

Now the economic returns of parenting mostly bypass parents, and a proper accounting has to reflect that. For economic man in the late 20th century, child-rearing has become a crummy financial bargain. Fortunately, as Mom always said, there's more to life than money.

Amy Graham contributed to this article.

Our Babies, Ourselves

By Meredith F. Small

During one of his many trips to Gusiiland in southwestern Kenya, anthropologist Robert LeVine tried an experiment: he showed a group of Gusii mothers a videotape of middle-class American women tending their babies. The Gusii mothers were appalled. Why does that mother ignore the cries of her unhappy baby during a simple diaper change? And how come that grandmother does nothing to soothe the screaming baby in her lap? These American women, the Gusii concluded, are clearly incompetent mothers. In response, the same charge might be leveled at the Gusii by American mothers. What mother hands over her tiny infant to a six-year-old sister and expects the older child to provide adequate care? And why don't those Gusii women spend more time talking to their babies, so that they will grow up smart?

Both culture—the traditional way of doing things in a particular society—and individual experience guide parents in their tasks. When a father chooses to pick up his newborn and not let it cry, when a mother decides to bottle-feed on a schedule rather than breast-feed on demand, when a couple bring the newborn into their bed at night, they are prompted by what they believe to be the best methods of caregiving.

For decades, anthropologists have been recording how children are raised in different societies. At first, the major goals were to describe parental roles and understand how child-rearing practices and rituals helped to generate adult per-

Gusii Survival Skills

By Robert A. LeVine

Farming peoples of subSaharan Africa have long faced the grim reality that many babies fail to survive, often succumbing to gastrointestinal diseases, malaria, or other infections. In the 1970s, when I lived among the Gusii in a small town in southwestern Kenya, infant mortality in that nation was on the decline but was still high—about eighty deaths per thousand live births during the first years, compared with about ten in the United States at that time and six to eight in Western Europe.

The Gusii grew corn, millet, and cash crops such as coffee and tea. Women handled the more routine tasks of cultivation, food processing, and trading, while men were supervisors or entrepreneurs. Many men worked at jobs outside the village, in urban centers or on plantations. The society was polygamous, with perhaps 10 percent of the men having two or more wives. A woman was expected to give birth every two years, from marriage to menopause, and the average married women bore about ten live children—one of the highest fertility rates in the world.

Nursing mothers slept alone with a new infant for fifteen months to insure its health. For the first three to six months, the Gusii mothers were especially vigilant for signs of ill health or slow growth, and they were quick to nurture unusually small or sick infants by feeding and holding them more often. Mothers whose newborns were deemed particularly at risk—including twins and those born prematurely—entered a ritual seclusion for several weeks, staying with their infants in a hut with a constant fire.

Mothers kept infants from crying in the early months by holding them constantly and being quick to comfort them. After three to six months—if the baby was growing normally—mothers began to entrust the baby to the care of other children (usually six to twelve years old) in order to pursue tasks that helped support the family. Fathers did not take care of infants, for this was not a traditional male activity.

Because they were so worried about their children's survival, Gusii parents did not explicitly strive to foster cognitive, social, and emotional development. These needs were not neglected, however, because from birth Gusii babies entered an active and responsive interpersonal environment, first with their mothers and young caregivers, and later as part of a group of children.

An Infant's Three Rs

By Sara Harkness and Charles M. Super

You are an American visitor spending a morning in a pleasant middle-class Dutch home to observe the normal routine of a mother and her six-month-old baby. The mother made sure you got there by 8:30 to witness the morning bath, an opportunity for playful interaction with the baby. The baby was then dressed in cozy warm clothes, her hair brushed and styled with a tiny curlicue atop her head. The mother gave her the midmorning bottle, then sang to her and played patty-cake for a few minutes before placing her in the playpen to entertain herself with a mobile while the mother attended to other things nearby. Now, about half an hour later, the baby is beginning to get fussy.

The mother watches for a minute, then offers a toy and turns away. The baby again begins to fuss. "Seems bored and in need of attention," you think. But the mother looks at the baby sympathetically and in a soothing voice says, "Oh, are you tired?" Without further ado she picks up the baby, carries her upstairs, tucks her into her crib, and pulls down the shades. To your surprise, the baby fusses for only a few more moments, then is quiet. The mother returns looking serene. "She needs plenty of sleep in order to grow," she explains. "When she doesn't have her nap or go to bed on time, we can always tell the difference—she's not so happy and playful."

Different patterns in infant sleep can be found in Western societies that seem quite similar to those of the United States. We discovered the "three R's" of Dutch child rearing—*rust* (rest), *regelmaat* (regularity) and *reinheid* (cleanliness)—while doing research on a sample of sixty families with infants or young children in a middle-class community near Leiden and Amsterdam, the sort of community typical of Dutch life styles in all but the big cities nowadays. At six months, the Dutch babies were sleeping more than a comparison group of American babies—a total of fifteen hours per day compared with thirteen hours for the Americans. While awake at home, the Dutch babies were more often left to play quietly in their playpens or infant seats. A daily ride in the baby carriage provided time for the baby to look around at the passing scene or to doze peacefully. If the mother needed to go out for a while without the baby, she could leave it alone in bed for a short period or time her outing with the baby's nap time and ask a neighbor to monitor with a "baby phone."

To understand how Dutch families manage to establish such a restful routine by the time their babies are six months old, we made a second research visit to the same community. We found that by two weeks of age, the Dutch babies were already sleeping more than same-age American babies. In fact, a dilemma for some Dutch parents was whether to wake the baby after eight hours, as instructed by the local health care providers, or let them sleep longer. The main method for establishing and maintaining this pattern was to create a calm, regular, and restful environment for the infant throughout the day.

Far from worrying about providing "adequate stimulation," these mothers were conscientious about avoiding overstimulation in the form of late family out-ings, disruptions in the regularity of eating and sleeping, or too many things to look at or listen to. Few parents were troubled by their babies' nighttime sleep routines. Babies's feeding schedules were structured following the guidelines of the local baby clinic (a national service). If a baby continued to wake up at night when feeding was no longer considered necessary, the mother (or father) would most commonly give it a pacifier and a little back rub to help it get back to sleep. Only in rare instances did parents find themselves forced to choose between letting the baby scream and allowing too much night waking.

Many aspects of Dutch society support the three Rs throughout infancy and childhood—for example, shopping is close to home, and families usually have neighbors and relatives nearby who are available to help out with child care. The small scale of neighborhoods and a network of bicycle paths provide local play sites and a safe way for children to get around easily on their own (no "soccer moms" are needed for daily transportation!). Work sites for both fathers and mothers are also generally close to home, and there are many flexible or part-time job arrangements.

National policies for health and other social benefits insure universal coverage regardless of one's employment status, and the principle of the "family wage" has prevailed in labor relations so that mothers of infants and young children rarely work more than part-time, if at all. In many ways, the three Rs of Dutch child rearing are just one aspect of a calm and unhurried life style for the whole family.

sonality. In the 1950s, for example, John and Beatrice Whiting, and their colleagues at Harvard, Yale, and Cornell Universities, launched a major comparative study of childhood, looking at six varied communities in different regions: Okinawa, the Philippines, northern India, Kenya, Mexico, and New England. They showed that communal expectations play a major role in setting parenting styles, which in turn play a part in shaping children to become accepted adults.

More recent work by anthropologists and child-development researchers has shown that parents readily accept their society's prevailing ideology on how babies should be treated, usually because it makes sense in their environmental or social circumstances. In the United States, for example, where individualism is valued, parents do not hold babies as much as in other cultures, and they place them in rooms of their own to sleep. Pediatricians and parents alike often say this fosters independence and self-reliance. Japanese parents, in contrast, believe that individuals should be well integrated into society, and so they "indulge" their babies: Japanese infants are held more often, not left to cry, and sleep with their parents. Efe parents in Congo believe even more in a communal life, and their infants are regularly nursed, held, and comforted by any number of group members, not just parents. Whether such practices help form the anticipated adult personality traits remains to be shown, however.

Recently, a group of anthropologists, child-development experts, and pediatricians have taken the cross-cultural approach in a new direction by investigating how differing parenting styles affect infant health and growth. Instead of emphasizing the development of adult personality, these researchers, who call themselves ethnopediatricians, focus

Doctor's Orders

By Edward Z. Tronick

In Boston, a pediatric resident is experiencing a vague sense of disquiet as she interviews a Puerto Rican mother who has brought her baby in for a checkup. When she is at work, the mother explains, the two older children, ages six and nine, take care of the two younger ones, a two-year-old and the three-month-old baby. Warning bells go off for the resident: young children cannot possibly be sensitive to the needs of babies and toddlers. And yet the baby is thriving; he is well over the ninetieth percentile in weight and height and is full of smiles.

The resident questions the mother in detail: How is the baby fed? Is the apartment safe for a two-year-old? The responses are all reassuring, but the resident nonetheless launches into a lecture on the importance of the mother to normal infant development. The mother falls silent, and the resident is now convinced that something is seriously wrong. And something is—the resident's model of child care.

The resident subscribes to what I call the "continuous care and contact" model of parenting, which demands a high level of contact, frequent feeding, and constant supervision, with almost all care provided by the mother. According to this model, a mother should also enhance cognitive development with play and verbal engagement. The pediatric resident is comfortable with this formula—she is not even conscious of it—because she was raised this way and treats her own child in the same manner. But at the Child Development Unit of Children's Hospital in Boston, which I direct, I want residents to abandon the idea that there is only one way to raise a child. Not to do so may interfere with patient care.

Many models of parenting are valid. Among Efe foragers of Congo's Ituri Forest, for example, a newborn is routinely cared for by several people. Babies are even nursed by many women. But few individuals ever play with the infant; as far as the Efe are concerned, the baby's job is to sleep.

In Peru, the Quechua swaddle their infants in a pouch of blankets that the mother, or a child caretaker, carries on her back. Inside the pouch, the infant cannot move, and its eyes are covered. Quechua babies are nursed in a perfunctory fashion, with three or four hours between feedings.

As I explain to novice pediatricians, such practices do not fit the continuous care and contact model; yet these babies grow up just fine. But my residents see these cultures as exotic, not relevant to the industrialized world. And so I follow up with examples closer to home: Dutch parents who leave an infant alone in order to go shopping, sometimes pinning the child's shirt to the bed to keep the baby on its back; or Japanese mothers who periodically wake a sleeping infant to teach the child who is in charge. The questions soon follow. "How could a mother leave her infant alone?" "Why would a parent ever want to wake up a sleeping baby?"

The data from cross-cultural studies indicate that child-care practices vary, and that these styles aim to make the child into a culturally appropriate adult. The Efe make future Efe. The resident makes future residents. A doctor who has a vague sense that something is wrong with how someone cares for a baby may first need to explore his or her own assumptions, the hidden "shoulds" that are based solely on tradition. Of course, pediatric residents must make sure children are cared for responsibly. I know I have helped residents broaden their views when their lectures on good mothering are replaced by such comments as "What a gorgeous baby! I can't imagine how you manage both work and three others at home!"

on the child as an organism. Ethnopediatricians see the human infant as a product of evolution, geared to enter a particular environment of care. What an infant actually gets is a compromise, as parents are pulled by their offspring's needs and pushed by social and personal expectations.

Compared with offspring of many other mammals, primate infants are dependent and vulnerable. Baby monkeys and apes stay close to the mother's body, clinging to her stomach or riding on her back, and nursing at will. They are protected in this way for many months, until they develop enough motor and cognitive skills to move about. Human infants are at the extreme: virtually helpless as newborns, they need twelve months just to learn to walk and years of social learning before they can function on their own.

Dependence during infancy is the price we pay for being hominids, members of the group of upright-walking primates that includes humans and their extinct relatives. Four million years ago, when our ancestors became bipedal, the hominid pelvis underwent a necessary renovation. At first, this new pelvic architecture presented no problem during birth because the early hominids, known as australopithecines, still had rather small brains, one-third the present size. But starting about 1.5 million years ago, human brain size ballooned. Hominid babies now had to twist and bend to pass through the birth canal, and more important, birth had to be triggered before the skull grew too big.

As a result, the human infant is born neurologically unfinished and unable to coordinate muscle movement. Natural selection has compensated for this by favoring a close adult-infant tie that lasts years and goes beyond meeting the needs of food and shelter. In a sense, the human baby is not isolated but is part of a physiologically and emotionally entwined dyad of infant and caregiver. The adult might be male or female, a birth or adoptive parent, as long as at least one person is attuned to the infant's needs.

The signs of this interrelationship are many. Through conditioning, a mother's breast milk often begins to flow at the sound of her own infant's cries, even before the nipple is stimulated. New mothers also easily recognize the cries (and smells) of their infants over those of other babies. For their part, newborns recognize their own mother's voice and prefer it over others. One experiment showed that a baby's heart rate quickly synchronizes with Mom's or Dad's, but not with that of a friendly stranger. Babies are also predisposed

The Crying Game

By Ronald G. Barr

All normal human infants cry, although they vary a great deal in how much. A mysterious and still unexplained phenomenon is that crying tends to increase in the first few weeks of life, peaks in the second or third month, and then decreases. Some babies in the United States cry so much during the peak period—often in excess of three hours a day—and seem so difficult to soothe that parents come to doubt their nurturing skills or begin to fear that their offspring is suffering from a painful disease. Some mothers discontinue nursing and switch to bottle-feeding because they believe their breast milk is insufficiently nutritious and that their infants are always hungry. In extreme cases, the crying may provoke physical abuse, sometimes even precipitating the infant's death.

A look at another culture, the !Kung San hunter-gatherers of southern Africa, provides us with an opportunity to see whether caregiving strategies have any effect on infant crying. Both the !Kung San and Western infants escalate their crying during the early weeks of life, with a similar peak at two or three months. A comparison of Dutch, American, and !Kung San infants shows that the number of individual crying episodes are virtually identical. What differs is their length: !Kung San infants cry about half as long as Western babies. This implies that caregiving can influence only some aspects of crying, such as duration.

What is particularly striking about child-rearing among the !Kung San is that infants are in constant contact with a caregiver; they are carried or held most of the time, are usually in an upright position, and are breast-fed about four times an hour for one to two minutes at a time. Furthermore, the mother almost always responds to the smallest cry or fret within ten seconds.

I believe that crying was adaptive for our ancestors. As seen in the contemporary !Kung San, crying probably elicited a quick response, and thus consisted of frequent but relatively short episodes. This pattern helped keep an adult close by to provide adequate nutrition as well as protection from predators. I have also argued that crying helped an infant forge a strong attachment with the mother and—because new pregnancies are delayed by the prolongation of frequent nursing—secure more of her caregiving resources.

In the United States, where the threat of predation has receded and adequate nutrition is usually available even without breast-feeding, crying may be less adaptive. In any case, caregiving in the United States may be viewed as a cultural experiment in which the infant is relatively more separated—and separable—from the mother, both in terms of frequency of contact and actual distance.

The Western strategy is advantageous when the mother's employment outside of the home and away from the baby is necessary to sustain family resources. But the trade-off seems to be an increase in the length of crying bouts.

to be socially engaged with caregivers. From birth, infants move their bodies in synchrony with adult speech and the general nature of language. Babies quickly recognize the arrangement of a human face—two eyes, a nose, and a mouth in the right place—over other more Picasso-like rearrangements. And mothers and infants will position themselves face-to-face when they lie down to sleep.

Babies and mothers seem to follow a typical pattern of play, a coordinated waltz that moves from attention to inattention and back again. This innate social connection was tested experimentally by Jeffrey Cohn and Edward Tronick in a series of three-minute laboratory experiments at the University of Massachusetts, in which they asked mothers to act depressed and not respond to baby's cues. When faced with a suddenly unresponsive mother, a baby repeatedly reaches out and flaps around, trying to catch her eye. When this tactic does not work, the baby gives up, turning away and going limp. And when the mother begins to respond again, it takes thirty seconds for the baby to reengage.

Given that human infants arrive in a state of dependency, ethnopediatricians have sought to define the care required to meet their physical, cognitive, and emotional needs. They assume there must be ways to treat babies that have proved adaptive over time and are therefore likely to be most appropriate. Surveys of parenting in different societies reveal broad patterns. In almost all cultures, infants sleep with their parents in the same room and most often in the same bed. At all other times, infants are usually carried. Caregivers also usually respond quickly to infant cries; mothers most often by offering the breast. Since most hunter-gatherer groups also follow this overall style, this is probably the ancestral pattern. If there is an exception to these generalizations, it is the industrialized West.

Nuances of caretaking, however, do vary with particular social situations. !Kung San mothers of Botswana usually carry their infants on gathering expeditions, while the forest-living Ache of Paraguay, also hunters and gatherers, usually leave infants in camp while they gather. Gusii mothers working in garden plots leave their babies in the care of older children, while working mothers in the West may turn to unrelated adults. Such choices have physiological or behavioral consequences for the infant. As parents navigate between infant needs and the constraints of making a life, they may face a series of trade-offs that set the caregiver-infant dyad at odds. The areas of greatest controversy are breast-feeding, crying, and sleep—the major preoccupations of babies and their parents.

Strapped to their mothers' sides or backs in traditional fashion, human infants have quick access to the breast. Easy access makes sense because of the nature of human milk. Compared with that of other mammals, primate milk is relatively low in fat and protein but high in carbohydrates. Such milk is biologically suitable if the infant can nurse on a frequent basis. Most Western babies are fed in a somewhat different way. At least half are bottle-fed from birth, while

When to Wean

By Katherine A. Dettwyler

Breast-feeding in humans is a biological process grounded in our mammalian ancestry. It is also an activity modified by social and cultural constraints, including a mother's everyday work schedule and a variety of beliefs about personal autonomy, the proper relationship between mother and child (or between mother and father), and infant health and nutrition. The same may be said of the termination of breast-feeding, or weaning.

In the United States, children are commonly bottle-fed from birth or weaned within a few months. But in some societies, children as old as four or five years may still be nursed. The American Academy of Pediatrics currently advises breast-feeding for a minimum of one year (this may be revised upward), and the World Health Organization recommends two years or more. Amid conflicting advice, many wonder how long breast-feeding should last to provide an infant with optimal nutrition and health.

Nonhuman primates and other mammals give us some clues as to what the "natural" age of weaning would be if humans were less bound by cultural norms. Compared with most other orders of placental mammals, primates (including humans) have longer life spans and spend more time at each life stage, such as gestation, infant dependency, and puberty. Within the primate order itself, the trend in longevity increases from smaller-bodied, smaller-brained, often solitary prosimians through the larger-bodied, larger-brained, and usually social apes and humans. Gestation, for instance, is eighteen weeks in lemurs, twenty-four weeks in macaques, thirty-three weeks in chimpanzees, and thirty-eight weeks in humans.

Studies of nonhuman primates offer a number of different means of estimating the natural time for human weaning. First, large-bodied primates wean their offspring some months after the young have quadrupled their birth weight. In modern humans, this weight milestone is passed at about two and a half to three years of age. Second, like many other mammals, primate offspring tend to be weaned when they have attained about one third of their adult weight; humans reach this level between four and seven years of age. Third, in all species studied so far, primates also wean their offspring at the time the first permanent molars erupt; this occurs at five and a half to six years in modern humans. Fourth, in chimpanzees and gorillas, breast-feeding usually lasts about six times the duration of gestation. On this basis, a human breast-feeding would be projected to continue for four and a half years.

Taken together, these and other projections suggest that somewhat more than two and a half years is the natural minimum age of weaning for humans and seven years the maximum age, well into childhood. The high end of this range, six to seven years, closely matches both the completion of human brain growth and the maturation of the child's immune system.

In many non-Western cultures, children are routinely nursed for three to five years. Incidentally, this practice inhibits ovulation in the mother, providing a natural mechanism of family planning. Even in the United States, a significant number of children are breast-fed beyond three years of age. While not all women are able or willing to nurse each of their children for many years, those who do should be encouraged and sup-ported. Health care professionals, family, friends, and nosy neighbors should be reassured that "extended" breast-feeding, for as long as seven years, appears physiologically normal and natural.

Substantial evidence is already available to suggest that curtailing the duration of breast-feeding far below two and a half years—when the human child has evolved to expect more—can be deleterious. Every study that includes the duration of breast-feeding as a variable shows that, on average, the longer a baby is nursed, the better its health and cognitive development. For example, breast-fed children have fewer allergies, fewer ear infections, and less diarrhea, and their risk for sudden infant death syndrome (a rare but devastating occurrence) is lower. Breast-fed children also have higher cognitive test scores and lower incidence of attention deficit hyperactivity disorder.

In many cases, specific biochemical constituents of breast milk have been identified that either protect directly against disease or help the child's body develop its own defense system. For example, in the case of many viral diseases, the baby brings the virus to the mother, and her gut-wall cells manufacture specific antibodies against the virus, which then travel to the mammary glands and go back to the baby. The docosahesanoic acid in breast milk may be responsible for improved cognitive and attention functions. And the infant's exposure to the hormones and cholesterol in the milk appears to condition the body, reducing the risk of heart disease and breast cancer in later years. These and other discoveries show that breast-feeding serves functions for which no simple substitute is available.

others are weaned from breast to bottle after only a few months. And most—whether nursed or bottle-fed—are fed at scheduled times, waiting hours between feedings. Long intervals in nursing disrupt the manufacture of breast milk, making it still lower in fat and thus less satisfying the next time the nipple is offered. And so crying over food and even the struggles of weaning result from the infant's unfulfilled expectations.

Sleep is also a major issue for new parents. In the West, babies are encouraged to sleep all through the night as soon as possible. And when infants do not do so, they merit the label "sleep problem" from both parents and pediatricians. But infants seem predisposed to sleep rather lightly, waking many times during the night. And while sleeping close to an adult allows infants to nurse more often and may have other beneficial effects, Westerners usually expect babies to sleep alone. This practice has roots in ecclesiastical laws enacted to protect against the smothering of infants by "lying over"—often a thinly disguised cover for infanticide—which was a concern in Europe beginning in the Middle Ages. Solitary sleep is reinforced by the rather recent notion of parental privacy. Western parents are also often convinced that solitary sleep will mold strong character.

Infants' care is shaped by tradition, fads, science, and folk wisdom. Cross-cultural and evolutionary studies provide a useful perspective for parents and pediatricians as they sift through the alternatives. Where these insights fail to guide us, however, important clues are provided by the floppy but interactive

Bedtime Story

By James J. McKenna

For as far back as you care to go, mothers have followed the protective and convenient practice of sleeping with their infants. Even now, for the vast majority of people across the globe, "cosleeping" and nighttime breast-feeding remain inseparable practices. Only in the past 200 years, and mostly in Western industrialized societies, have parents considered it normal and biologically appropriate for a mother and infant to sleep apart.

In the sleep laboratory at the University of California's Irvine School of Medicine, my colleagues and I observed mother-infant pairs as they slept both apart and together over three consecutive nights. Using a polygraph, we recorded the mother's and infant's heart rates, brain waves (EEGs), breathing, body temperature, and episodes of nursing. Infrared video photography simultaneously monitored their behavior.

We found that bed-sharing infants face their mothers for most of the night and that both mother and infants are highly responsive to each other's movements, wake more frequently, and spend more time in lighter stages of sleep than they do while sleeping alone. Bed-sharing infants nurse almost twice as often, and three times as long per bout, than they do when sleeping alone. But they rarely cry. Mothers who routinely sleep with their infants get at least as much sleep as mothers who sleep without them.

In addition to providing more nighttime nourishment and greater protection, sleeping with the mother supplies the infant with a steady stream of sensations of the mother's presence, including touch, smell, movement, and warmth. These stimuli can perhaps even compensate for the human infant's extreme neurological immaturity at birth.

Cosleeping might also turn out to give some babies protection from sudden infant death syndrome (SIDS), a heartbreaking and enigmatic killer. Cosleeping infants nurse more often, sleep more lightly, and have practice responding to maternal arousals. Arousal deficiencies are suspected in some SIDS deaths, and long periods in deep sleep may exacerbate this problem. Perhaps the physiological changes induced by cosleeping, especially when combined with nighttime breast-feeding, can benefit some infants by helping them sleep more lightly. At the same time, cosleeping makes it easier for a mother to detect and respond to an infant in crisis. Rethinking another sleeping practice has already shown a dramatic effect: In the United States, SIDS rates fell at least 30 percent after 1992, when the American Academy of Pediatrics recommended placing sleeping babies on their backs, rather than face down.

The effect of cosleeping on SIDS remains to be proved, so it would be premature to recommend it as the best arrangement for all families. The possible hazards of cosleeping must also be assessed. Is the environment otherwise safe, with appropriate bedding materials? Do the parents smoke? Do they use drugs or alcohol? (These appear to be the main factors in those rare cases in which a mother inadvertently smothers her child.) Since cosleeping was the ancestral condition, the future for our infants may well entail a borrowing back from ancient ways.

babies themselves. Grinning when we talk to them, crying in distress when left alone, sleeping best when close at heart, they teach us that growth is a cooperative venture.

A professor of anthropology at Cornell University, **Meredith F. Small** became interested in "ethnopediatrics" in 1995, after interviewing anthropologist James J. McKenna on the subject of infant sleep. Trained as a primate behaviorist, Small has observed female mating behavior in three species of macaque monkeys. She now writes about science for a general audience; her book *Our Babies, Ourselves* is published by Anchor Books/Doubleday (1998). Her previous contributions to *Natural History* include "These Animals Think, Therefore..." (August 1996) and "Read in the Bone" (June 1997).

RECOMMENDED READING

Parents' Cultural Belief Systems: Their Origins, Expressions, and Consequences, by Sara Harkness and Charles M. Super (Guilford Press, 1996)

Child Care and Culture: Lessons from Africa, by Robert A. LeVine et al. (Cambridge University Press, 1994)

Our Babies, Ourselves, by Meredith F. Small (Anchor Books/Doubleday, 1998)

Breastfeeding: Biocultural Perspectives, edited by Patricia Stuart-Macadam and Katherine A. Dettwyler (Aldine de Gruyler, 1995)

The Family Bed: An Age Old Concept in Childrearing, by Tine Thevenin (Avery Publishing Group, 1987)

Human Birth: An Evolutionary Perspective, by Wenda R. Trevathan (Aldine de Gruyler, 1987)

Six Cultures: Studies of Child Rearing, edited by Beatrice B. Whiting (John Wiley, 1963)

Unit 3

Key Points to Consider

❖ Is marriage necessary for a happy, fulfilling life? Why is or is that not so? When you think of a marriage, what do you picture? What are your expectations of your (future) spouse? What are your expectations of yourself? What and how much are you willing to give to your marriage? Who, in your opinion, should get married? How is your experience of committed relationships influenced by those you saw while growing up? How do those relationships affect your own willingness to enter a committed relationship?

❖ How should each spouse behave in a marriage? How are men's and women's roles the same or different?

❖ Do you believe that fathers and mothers should have different roles? How would you contrast the views of parents and children? Do they see their relationship in radically different ways? Just how influential are parents in their children's lives?

 **Links**   **www.dushkin.com/online/**

These sites are annotated on pages 4 and 5.

And they lived happily ever after. . . . The romantic image conjured up by this well-known final line from fairy tales is not reflective of the reality of family life and relationship maintenance. The belief that somehow love alone should carry us through is pervasive. In reality, maintaining a relationship takes dedication, hard work, and commitment.

We come into relationships, regardless of their nature, with fantasies about how things ought to be. Partners, spouses, parents, children, siblings, and others—all family members have at least some unrealistic expectations about each other. It is through the negotiation of their lives together that they come to work through these expectations and replace them with other, it is hoped, more realistic ones. By recognizing and acting on their own contribution to the family, members can set and attain realistic family goals. Tolerance and acceptance of differences can facilitate this process as can competent communication skills. Along the way, family members need to learn new skills and develop new habits of relating to each other. This will not be easy, and, try as they may, not everything will be controllable. Factors both inside and outside the family may impede their progress.

Even before one enters a marriage or other committed relationship, attitudes, standards, and beliefs influence our choices. Increasingly, choices include whether or not we should commit to such a relationship. From the start of a committed relationship, the expectations both partners have of their relationship have an impact, and the need to negotiate differences is a constant factor. Adding a child to the family affects the lives of parents in ways that they could previously only imagine. Feeling under siege, many parents struggle to know the right way to rear their children. These factors can all combine to make child rearing more difficult than it might otherwise have been. Other family relationships also evolve, and in our nuclear family–focused culture, it is possible to forget that family relationships extend beyond those between spouses and parents and children.

The initial subsection presents a number of aspects regarding marital and other committed relationships, decisions about entering such a relationship, and ways of balancing multiple and often competing roles played by today's couples, who hope to fulfill individual as well as joint needs. It is a difficult balancing act to cope with the expectations and pressures of work, home, children, and relational intimacy. "Flying Solo" explores changed views about women and marriage along

with the decisions women are now making about deferring or doing without marriage altogether. The next two articles explore issues regarding good marriages. In "The Science of a Good Marriage," the research done by John Gottman on what makes a good marriage is detailed. What is presented may surprise the reader, as some forms of good marriages contradict previously held ideas. This is complemented by the work reported on in "Will Your Marriage Last?" In the last article in this subsection, Olivia Mellan, in "Men, Women & Money," suggests ways in which couples can put money, an emotionally loaded topic, in its place.

The next subsection examines the parent/child relationship. The first article, "Father Love and Child Development: History and Current Evidence" offers a look at how father love affects child development as much as mother love. The next reading, "Do Parents Really Matter? Kid Stuff," looks at the parent-child relationship from the perspective of the child. The final article, "Family Matters," presents a supportive view of parental influence on the mental health of children, using data from a 13-year study conducted in Santa Domingo.

FLYING SOLO

More women are deciding that marriage is not inevitable, that they can lead a fulfilling life as a single. It's an empowering choice, but for many not an easy one

BY TAMALA M. EDWARDS

Jodie Hannaman grew up in Houston, a city as fond of formal weddings as of barbecues and rodeos. So it was saying something at Duschene Academy, her Roman Catholic girls' school, that Hannaman was chosen as Most Likely to Be Married First. But her teenage fantasies of buttercream frosting and silky bridesmaids dresses first began to crack with her high school sweetheart. He dated her for more than a decade before she finally got tired of waiting for a marriage proposal that was never going to come. There were other men after that, but it was Hannaman who repeatedly decided against a life built for two. Marriage, it began to dawn on her, wasn't an end in itself but rather something she wanted only if she found the right guy.

Now Hannaman, 32, spends 60 hours a week in her job as project manager for Chase Bank of Texas in Houston, in an office decorated with art-museum magnets and Cathy cartoons. She extends her business trips into the weekends for solo mini-vacations, enjoys the social whirl of the Junior League volunteer circuit, and has started looking for a house. While she would love a great romance that would lead to marriage,

■ Which best describes your attitude toward marriage?

	SINGLE WOMEN	SINGLE MEN
I would marry only if I find the right man/woman	66%	63%
I definitely want to get married	24%	27%
I don't plan to marry	8%	9%

■ Do you think you'll eventually find, and marry, your perfect mate?

	SINGLE WOMEN		SINGLE MEN
	78%	Yes	79%
	18%	No	15%

■ If you couldn't find the perfect mate, would you marry someone else?

	SINGLE WOMEN		SINGLE MEN
	34%	Yes	41%
	61%	No	54%

From a telephone poll of 465 never-married single adults between the ages of 18 and 49 years old (including 205 women and 260 men) taken for TIME/CNN on Aug. 9–10 by Yankelovich Partners Inc. Margin of error is ± 4.5%. "Not sures" omitted.

she no longer feels she has to apologize for being single. "I've finally matured enough

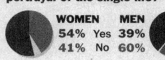

Is Sex *and the City* a realistic portrayal of the single life?

	WOMEN		MEN
Yes	54%		39%
No	41%		60%

Asked of women:

Do you have as much sex as the women in *Sex and the City*?

Yes	21%
No	73%

Which of the main characters do you most identify with?

Carrie, the introspective writer played by Sarah Jessica Parker ... 36%

Charlotte, the art dealer looking to get married 25%

Samantha, the blond who's out to have a good time 10%

Miranda, the redhead with hang-ups 9%

Don't identify with any 13%

Asked of 186 never-married single adults comprising 88 women and 98 men who watch the show. Sampling is ±7.2%

to acknowledge that there's more to life than being married," she says. "I'd like to get married and have kids, but something in the past few years has changed. I'm happier being single."

Hannaman might seem to have little in common with the four lead characters on TV's *Sex and the City*, single women who live the supafly life and discard men quicker than last season's bag and shoes —and look damn good doing it. Her sex life isn't nearly as colorful, for one thing. All of them, nevertheless, are part of a major societal shift: single women, once treated as virtual outcasts, have moved to the center of our social and cultural life. Unattached females—wisecracking, gutsy gals, not pathetic saps—are the heroine du jour in fiction, from Melissa

Bank's collection of stories, *The Girls' Guide to Hunting and Fishing,* to Helen Fielding's *Bridget Jones's Diary,* the publishing juggernaut that has spawned one sequel and will soon be a movie. The single woman is TV's It Girl as well, not just on *Sex and the City,* the smash HBO series in the midst of its third buzz-producing season, but also on a growing number of network shows focused on strong, career-minded single women, such as *Judging Amy* and *Providence.*

The single woman has come into her own. Not too long ago, she would live a temporary existence: a rented apartment shared with a girlfriend or two and a job she could easily ditch. Adult life—a house, a car, travel, children—only came with a husband.

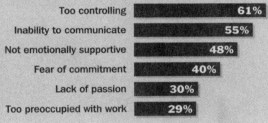

Would you consider raising a child on your own?

Answered YES:

SINGLE WOMEN 61%

SINGLE MEN 55%

Asked of single women: Which do you find a very serious fault in men's ability to relate to women?

Too controlling	61%
Inability to communicate	55%
Not emotionally supportive	48%
Fear of commitment	40%
Lack of passion	30%
Too preoccupied with work	29%

SEX AND THE CITY
Waiting for Prince Charming

To UNDERSTAND WHAT *Sex and the City* says about women, it helps to understand what it says about men. It's simple: men are dogs.

This is not necessarily an insult. *Sex* (Sundays, 9 p.m. E.T. on HBO, which is owned by TIME's parent company, Time Warner) likens even its finest men to man's best friend. Sex columnist Carrie (Sarah Jessica Parker) meets her lover Aidan—a shaggy, happy-go-lucky golden retriever of a guy—when his dog cheerfully buries his snout in her crotch. Lawyer Miranda (Cynthia Nixon), cohabiting with scruffy bartender Steve, agrees to buy a pooch with him, and it becomes a metaphor for their unworkable relationship. Husband-hunting Charlotte (Kristin Davis) learns to control her new fiancé with a hand on the wrist: Roll over, boy! Then there's Carrie's on-and-off-and-on squeeze Mr. Big (Chris Noth), a sexy, powerful (and married) alpha wolf.

Dogs are adorable—in theory. Take one in, though, and it can shed, stray, and worse. In its first two seasons *Sex* became a pop-culture icon for its astute

bedroom politics, for the saucy *Seinfeld* banter (laced with corny double entendres) of its glam foursome, but above all for recognizing that a woman can live well without being at either end of a man's leash.

Its exceptional third season, though has complicated the arch social comedy by experimenting with—*gasp!*—committed relationships. "What if Price Charming had never shown up?" Carrie asks. "Would Snow White have slept in that glass coffin forever? Or would she have eventually woken up, spit out the apple, got a job, a health-care package and a baby from her local neighborhood sperm bank?" Maybe. But this year our heroines are considering another option: settling down with Prince Almost-as-Charming. (All but Samantha—the deliciously vulpine Kim Cattrall—who episode after bed-hopping episode takes Manhattan like, well, a man.)

It proved these women's ability to cut deep that they've been called both "evil, emasculating harpies" (*USA Today*) and male fantasies. Sex is fantasy, but not that kind. The high-powered

Sexettes can afford Manolo Blahnik shoes, Le Bernardin dinners and swank Manhattan apartments. Their charmed circumstances would sweeten the solo life for a man or a woman.

But their conflicts are real and honest. *Sex* voids p.c. feminism and love-conquers-all romanticism. These over-30 women can read the New York *Times* wedding section—"the single women's sports pages"—with both envy and contempt for the 24-year-old brides nabbing investment bankers and ditching their careers. It also avoids pat sitcom solutions. When Miranda and Steve parted, he wasn't wackily written off but instead left as he showed up—a decent guy who proved wrong for her.

Love—or lust—in *Sex* is no '70s-style war between the sexes. It's a border negotiation over personal space, customs and autonomy. It's an accomplishment that *Sex* holds out the possibility of saying no to changing your life for a man. It is an equal one that it can also imagine, just maybe, saying yes.

—*By James Poniewozik*

Well, gone are the days. Forty-three million women are currently single—more than 40% of all adult females, up from about 30% in 1960. (The ranks of single men have grown at roughly the same rate.) If you separate out women of the most marriageable age, the numbers are even more head snapping: in 1963, 83% of women 25 to 55 were married; by 1997 that figure had dropped to 65%. "Are you kidding? An 18% to 20% point change? This is huge," says Linda Waite, a sociologist at the University of Chicago.

To be sure, the rise in single women encompasses some other important trends. An estimated 4 million of these unmarried women are cohabiting with their lovers, and a growing number are being more open about gay relationships. Nevertheless, single women as a group are wielding more and more clout. A Young and Rubicam study released earlier this summer labeled single women the yuppies of this decade, the blockbuster consumer group whose tastes will matter most to retailers and dictate our trends. The report found that nearly 60% of single women own their own home, buying them faster than single men; that single women fuel the home-renovation market; and that unmarried women are giving a big boost to the travel industry, making up half the adventure travelers and 2 out of 5 business travelers.

Equally important is the attitudinal change. The dictionary once defined a spinster as an unmarried woman above a certain age: 30. If you passed that milestone without a partner, your best hope was to be seen as an eccentric Auntie Mame; your worst fear was to grow old like Miss Havisham, locked in her cavernous mansion, bitter after being ditched at the altar. Not anymore. "We've ended the spinster era," says Philadelphia psychotherapist Diana Adile Kirschner, who has made single women a focus of her practice. "Women used to tell me about isolation, living alone, low level of activity, feeling different. Now there's family, lots of friends, they're less isolated and more integrated into social lives."

More confident, more self-sufficient, and more choosy than ever, women no longer see marriage as a matter of survival and acceptance. They feel free to start and end relationships at will—more like, say, men. In a Yankelovich poll for TIME and CNN, nearly 80% of men and women said they thought they would eventually find the perfect mate. But when asked, if they didn't find Mr. Perfect, whether they would marry someone else, only 34% of women said yes, in contrast to 41% of men. "Let's face it. You don't just want a man in your life," says author Bank, 39. "You only want a great man in your life."

Single by choice—it's an empowering statement for many women. Yet it's not a choice that all women arrive at easily or without some angst, and it raises a multitude of questions. Are women too unrealistic about marriage—so picky about men that they're denying themselves and society the benefits of marriage while they pursue an impossible ideal? Does the rejection of marriage by more women reflect a widening gender gap—as daughters of the women's movement discover that men, all too often, have a far less liberated view of the wife's role in marriage? Do the burgeoning ranks of single women mean an outbreak of *Sex and the City* promiscuity? And what about children? When a woman makes the empowering decision to rear a child on her own, what are the consequences, for mother and child?

SOCIETY, TO BE SURE, IS FAR MORE accepting of single women than it was even a few years ago. When Barbara Baldwin, the director of Planned Parenthood in Tennessee, divorced her husband in 1981, she needed her father's help before anyone would give the then 29-year-old single mother a car loan and a credit card. Beverley DeJulio, a divorced Chicago mother who hosts Handy Ma'am, a weekly home-improvement show on PBS, says she dreaded the hardware store for years, because salespeople kept asking, "Where's your husband?" And the Stone Age year when Anne Elizabeth, a Chicago artist, then 35, had to fight to not be listed as spinster on the mortgage application for her lakeside home? It was 1984.

Business has wised up. Now some auto manufacturers train salespeople to aim their pitches at women, going for the softer sell rather than the hard-nosed, macho wrangling of yesteryear. More than 100 travel companies have started to take women-only trekkers across deserts, up mountains and into volcanoes. Ace Hardware (where the slogan "Home of the Helpful Hardware Man" has been replaced by "Home of the Helpful Hardware Folks") now offers drills that are lighter with easy-grip handles, greenhouses full of flowers, and walls painted in pastels. They also run special seminars for women, who make up at least half their customers.

About a fifth of all home sales last year were to unmarried women, up from 10% in 1985. "Lenders don't presume single women can't make the mortgage anymore," says Mark Calabria, a senior economist at the National Association of Realtors. Orna Yaary, 42, a single mother and an interior designer, recalls that in the 1980s her single-women clients typically viewed their home as a temporary way station on the road to marriage. "It was like these single women with suitcases at the door, they wanted something but not anything permanent," says Yaary. Now she's decorating apartments for women like the 35-year-old investment banker who ordered built-in furniture and reconstructed the bathroom of her apartment. "She's doing what she wants. None of this attitude of 'I'll need to take it with me when I meet a guy.' "

Meanwhile, more single women—especially those watching their biological clocks run down—are resorting to solo pregnancies, sperm donors or adoption agencies. While the birthrate has fallen among teenagers, it has climbed 15% among unmarried thirtysomethings since 1990. In the TIME/CNN poll, fully 61% of single women ages 18 to 49 answered yes when asked whether they would consider rearing a child on their own.

Playwright Wendy Wasserstein recalls the clamor raised against her 1989 Pulitzer-prizewinning play, *The Heidi Chronicles,* because it concerns a woman who decides to have a baby alone. One female critic returned more than once to trash the play. "She said this was a cop-out, my saying women could be happy having a baby alone," the playwright says. Last year Wasserstein, still single at 49, gave birth to a daughter, Lucy Jane, conceived with the sperm of a friend she won't identify. "If I put Heidi out now, people would just say, 'Yeah, that's true,' " she says, shrugging.

AND WHILE MANY WOMEN WHO have embraced the single life are, like Wasserstein, well educated and economically independent, they cross social and class lines. Last year the National Marriage Project at Rutgers University released a report showing that the marriage rate among women had fallen one-third since 1970 and that young women had become more pessimistic about their chances of wedding. "The reality is that marriage is now the interlude and singlehood the state of affairs," says Barbara Dafoe Whitehead, a co-director of the center. For this summer's study, Whitehead chose to focus on blue-collar women in their 20s and expected more traditional attitudes. However, she found these women too were focused more on goals like college degrees, entrepreneurship and home ownership than on matrimony. "They wanted to be married, yet they were preparing as if that was not going to be the case," she says. "There was a sense they couldn't count on men and marriage."

The embrace of singlehood is, in some ways, a logical result of the expanding possibilities for women brought on by the women's movement. "Women get addicted to the possibilities of their lives, the idea that on any given day you have the freedom to do this or that," explains Melissa Roth, author of *On the Loose,* a chronicle of a year in the life of three thirtysomething women. And so, while still looking for love, many women today are slow to let go of their space and schedules for the daily compromises—and sacrifices—of marriage.

Debra DeLee, 52, who is divorced and the director of a nonprofit group in Washington, is so taken with her life—a gorgeous Capitol Hill town house, trips all over the world and a silver blue BMW roadster—that she's reluctant to change it even for the man of her dreams, Arnie Miller, 59, an executive recruiter who lives in Boston. "We talk about getting married, but this is so good right now," says DeLee, who ran the Democratic Convention in 1996. "Two minutes before he leaves, I think it's so hard to see him pick up and leave. But two minutes after he's gone, I think, *Ahh*, I've got my house back." Miller likes the arrangement too. "Why should this be off-putting? I'm high-powered too," he says. "We both like our space. And three days later, we're racing to be back together."

At the same time, there's been a change in attitude toward love and marriage. Previous generations of women made their barter as much around the need for male protection and financial help as affection. And if at some point the sizzle went south, well. . . . But women today have a very different wish list from their mother's. "My single friends have their own life and money to bring to the table," says Sarah Jessica Parker, the star of *Sex and the City*. "It's the same as the characters on the show: my friends are looking for a relationship as fulfilling, challenging and fun as the one they have with their girlfriends."

Yet there are doubtless few women who recognize much about the wild, bed-hopping lifestyle that *Sex and the City* portrays every week. Indeed, only a fifth of single women who watch the show said in the TIME/CNN poll that their life mirrors the show's sexcapades. Yet when asked what they miss most from not being married, 75% of women said companionship, and only 4% said sex. While surveys show married people generally have more sex than supposedly "swinging" singles, it's clear that living alone does not mean a life of abstinence. Experiences vary widely, from women who go through long periods without sexual relationships to others who have regular, casual flings. "You can easily take care of your needs," notes a D.C. single woman. Many women enjoy comfortable relationships with men that include sex but no hint of marriage—like the fiftysomething Nashville, Tenn., woman whose male friend comes to town for a handful of visits each year. "He's someone I know and trust," she says. "The sex is great, and we stay up till 4 a.m. talking."

One thing women find more real about *Sex and the City* is the parade of sorry guys whom Carrie and her friends encounter each week. It's hard to find a woman without at least one horror story of a guy like the one Bank used to date, who in the middle of a fight blurted out the reason for his resentment of her: "You have never cleaned my bathroom." Says Bank: "I hate to feel like someone wants to control me. And I've ended up with a lot of men who do."

Yet the choice to be single involves more than just rejecting the inevitable boors and slouches. More often, women speak of af-

■ **What would you miss most about not being married?**	**SINGLE WOMEN**	**SINGLE MEN**
Companionship	75%	80%
Financial security	11%	4%
Sex life	4%	7%
Ability to have children	4%	7%

fairs that lasted for months, if not years, with men they in many ways loved. But after much turmoil and tears, they ended things, deciding that being on their own was simply better than the alternative—being stuck with a man, and in a marriage, that didn't feel right.

"I totally adored him," says Lila Hicks, 32, a media producer, of the investment banker with whom she ended a seven-year romance not long ago, deciding life with him would be too limiting. "But I wasn't happy. I didn't think I could make him happy and retain my spirit, what makes me shine." Shawna Perry, an emergency-medicine doctor in Jacksonville, Fla., recently ended a 10-year relationship with a man whom she loves but feels is behind her in personal and professional growth. "His ups and downs were affecting our relationship and my security," she says. "I realized we were not building a life together and that this was not a good place to be considering marriage."

IN MANY CASES, WOMEN WHO choose the single life have looked at those around them and vowed not to make their mistakes. "My mother married her first boyfriend. All my relatives stayed in marriages that are really tough," says Pam Henneberry, 31, an accountant who lives in Manhattan. "When I looked at the unhappiness that was in my parents' marriage, I said, 'I can't do that.'" If Cynthia Rowe, 43, a Los Angeles-area store manager and divorcé, gets depressed, she thinks of her five closest girlfriends. "They are all just existing in their marriages," she says. "Two of them got married when they were young. Twenty years later, they had outgrown each other. One has not got over her husband's affair. Two friends aren't even sleeping in the same bedroom with their husband anymore. Their personal happiness is placed last, and their kids know they are miserable."

Some women, of course, have learned from their own life. "At 28, I was terrified of the world," says Mary Lou Parsons, a Raleigh, N.C., professional fund raiser, recalling her 1980 divorce. "I'd been raised a Southern woman, sheltered and protected by my family, then by my husband." In the ensuing 20 years she learned to raise her kids on her own—and how to start her own business, buy a town house, move to Alaska and

back and, most of all, relish life on her own. "I had to get beyond that thinking in a lot of women's minds that aloneness is not O.K. But now I find solitude exhilarating." Marcelle Clements, author of *The Improvised Woman: Single Women Reinventing the Single Life,* notes that there are many women, like Parsons, who were "taken by surprise. They were in relationships that broke up, hit what they thought was catastrophe, only to find that they were O.K., and [they] adopt an attitude that said, I'm fine, I don't need to be with anyone else."

Not surprisingly, many conservatives are disturbed at this growing acceptance of singlehood and its implied rejection of marriage. Danielle Crittenden, author of *What Our Mothers Didn't Tell Us,* argues that women have set themselves up for disappointment, putting off marriage until their 30s only to find themselves unskilled in the art of compatibility and surrounded by male peers looking over their Chardonnays at women in their 20s. "Modern people approach marriage like it's a Bosnia-Serbia negotiation. Marriage is no longer as attractive to men," she says. "No one's telling college girls it's easier to have kids in your 20s than in your 30s."

Women who have chosen the single life sometimes have their own qualms. Singlehood does not yield itself to a simple, blithe embrace. It's complicated, messy terrain because not needing a man is not the same as not wanting one. For all the laughs on *Sex and the City,* one can feel the ache that comes when yet another episode ends with the heart still a lonely hunter. And if you think being a single woman is all fun and games, just listen to star Parker, who is married to actor Matthew Broderick. Even as she's become a mascot for the feisty new single woman, Parker says she often stands on the set in her spike Jimmy Choo opentoes and see-through shirts, worried that she isn't being a good traditional wife. "I know he doesn't have his laundry done, that he hasn't had a hot meal in days," she says of her husband. "That stuff weighs on my mind." Parker regales single friends with tales of how boring married life is and how much luckier they are to have freedom and fun. Does she really believe it? "Well, no," she admits. "It's just a fun thing to say to make single people feel better."

Even women who generally reflect on their choices with assurance find themselves sometimes in the valley of what-ifs: What if I made the wrong choice to walk away? What if singlehood turns out to be not a temporary choice but an enforced state? "My sister knows that I'm good for a call every couple of·months just crying, 'What's wrong with me?' " says Henneberry. "I'm not willing to accept someone who's going to make me unhappy. But there are days when I have a physical need to go to sleep and wake up with someone there." Mary Mayotte, 49, has a successful bicoastal career as a public-speaking coach. But she admits the occasional pang of regret. "There was a point where I had men coming out of my ears," she says. "I don't think I was so nice to some of them. Every now and then I wonder if God is punishing me. Sometimes I look back and say, 'I wish I had made a different decision there.' "

Some feel women are on an impossible search for the perfect man, the one who not only makes you feel, as Julia Roberts said of meeting Benjamin Bratt, "hit in the head with a bat," but also better for it. "Marriage is not what it used to be, getting stability or economic help," says the National Marriage Project's Whitehead. "Marriage has become this spiritualized thing, with labels like 'best friend' and 'soul mate.' " Some sociologists say these lofty standards make sense at a time when the high divorce rate hisses in the background like Darth Vader. But others suggest the marriage pendulum has swung from the hollowly pragmatic to an unhealthy romantic ideal.

Michael Broder, a Philadelphia psychotherapist and author of *The Art of Living Single,* decries what he calls the "perfect-person problem," in which women refuse to engage unless they're immediately taken with a man, failing to give a relationship a chance to develop. "Few women can't tell you about someone they turned down, and I'm not talking about some grotesque monster," he says. "But there's the idea that there has to be this great· degree of passion to get involved, which isn't always functional. So you have people saying things like, 'If I can't have my soul mate, I'd rather be alone.' And after that, I say, 'Well, you got your second choice.' "

Single women are used to hearing this complaint, and most don't buy it. "Some in my family think I'm not stopping till I find perfection," says Henneberry. "I don't feel like that. I just want the one who makes me go, 'Finally.' " Harvard sociologist Carol Gilligan notes, "There's now a pressure to create relationships that both men and women want to be in, and that's great. This is revolutionary." Even Ellen Fein, co-author of the notorious 1996 dating guide *The Rules,* says her man-chasing disciples don't settle for just anyone. "Most of my clients have jobs; they can pay the rent; they can take themselves out to dinner," says Fein. "They want men to value them."

Many women can tell the story of a friend or relative who looked at her and said, "If you really wanted to be married, you'd be married." The comment can sometimes slap like a wet towel, in part because it is true and in part because of its implicit message: You could have compromised, perhaps settled, and been among the married. And so, the logic follows, you have no one to blame but yourself.

But these women have fought for years to be themselves—self-reliant, successful, clever, funny, willful, spirited—and for all the angst that the single life can bring, they're not willing to give it up for any arrangement that would stifle them. "It would be great if I found a relationship that allowed me to be as I am and added something to that," says documentary producer Pam Wolfe, 33, sitting in her one-bedroom condo in New York City. "But I'm not going to do anything to attract a person that means changing. I've worked long and hard to be myself."

—With reporting by Tammerlin Drummond/New York, Elizabeth Kaufman/Nashville, Anne Moffett/Washington, Jacqueline Savaiano/Los Angeles and Maggie Sieger/Chicago

The Science of a Good Marriage

Psychology is unlocking the secrets of happy couples.

BY BARBARA KANTROWITZ AND PAT WINGERT

THE MYTH OF MARRIAGE GOES LIKE this: somewhere out there is the perfect soul mate, the yin that meshes easily and effortlessly with your yang. And then there is the reality of marriage, which, as any spouse knows, is not unlike what Thomas Edison once said about genius: 1 percent inspiration and 99 percent perspiration. That sweaty part, the hard work of keeping a marriage healthy and strong, fascinates John Gottman. He's a psychologist at the University of Washington, and he has spent more than two decades trying to unravel the bewildering complex of emotions that binds two humans together for a year, a decade or even (if you're lucky) a lifetime.

Gottman, 56, comes to this endeavor with the best of qualifications: he's got the spirit of a scientist and the soul of a romantic. A survivor of one divorce, he's now happily married to fellow psychologist Julie Schwartz Gottman (they run couples workshops together). His daunting task is to quantify such intangibles as joy, contempt and tension. Ground zero for this research is the Family Research Laboratory on the Seattle campus (nicknamed the Love Lab). It consists of a series of nondescript offices equipped with video cameras and pulse, sweat and movement monitors to read the hearts and minds of hundreds of couples who have volunteered to be guinea pigs in longitudinal studies of the marital relationship. These volunteers have opened up their lives to the researchers, dissecting everything from the frequency of sex to who takes out

the garbage. The results form the basis of Gottman's new book, "The Seven Principles for Making Marriage Work," which he hopes will give spouses a scientific road map to happiness.

Among his unexpected conclusions: anger is not the most destructive emotion in a marriage, since both happy and miserable couples fight. Many popular therapies aim at defusing anger between spouses, but Gottman found that the real demons (he calls them "the Four Horsemen of the Apocalypse") are criticism, contempt, defensiveness and stonewalling. His research shows that the best way to keep these demons at bay is for couples to develop a "love map" of their spouse's dreams and fears. The happy couples all had such a deep understanding of their partner's psyche that they could navigate roadblocks without creating emotional gridlock.

Gottman's research also contradicts the Mars-Venus school of relationships, which holds that men and women come from two very different emotional worlds. According to his studies, gender differences may contribute to marital problems, but they don't cause them. Equal percentages of both men and women he interviewed said that the quality of the spousal friendship is the most important factor in marital satisfaction.

Gottman says he can predict, with more than 90 percent accuracy, which couples are likely to end up in divorce court. The first seven years are especially precarious; the average time for a divorce in this group is 5.2

years. The next danger point comes around 16 to 20 years into the marriage, with an average of 16.4 years. He describes one couple he first met as newlyweds: even then they began every discussion of their problems with sarcasm or criticism, what Gottman calls a "harsh start-up." Although they professed to be in love and committed to the relationship, Gottman correctly predicted that they were in trouble. Four years later they were headed for divorce, he says.

An unequal balance of power is also deadly to a marriage. Gottman found that a husband who doesn't share power with his wife has a much higher risk of damaging the relationship. Why are men singled out? Gottman says his data show that most wives, even those in unstable marriages, are likely to accept their husband's influence. It's the men who need to shape up, he says. The changes can be simple, like turning off the football game when she needs to talk. Gottman says the gesture proves he values "us" over "me."

Gottman's research is built on the work of many other scientists who have focused on emotion and human interaction. Early studies of marriage relied heavily on questionnaires filled out by couples, but these were often inaccurate. In the 1970s several psychology labs began using direct observation of couples to study marriage. A big boon was a relatively new tool for psychologists: videotape. Having a visual record that could be endlessly replayed made it much easier to study the emotional flow between spouses. In 1978 researchers Paul Ekman and Wallace Freisen devised a coding system for the human face (see, "Facing Your Problems") that eventually provided another way to measure interchange between spouses.

Although early studies focused on couples in trouble, Gottman thought it was also important to study couples whose marriages work; he thinks they're the real experts. The Love Lab volunteers are interviewed about the history of their marriage. They then talk in front of the cameras about subjects that cause conflict between them. One couple Gottman describes in the book, Tim and Kara, argued constantly about his friend Buddy, who often wound up spending the night on Tim and Kara's couch. The researchers take scenes like this and break down every second of interaction to create a statistical pattern of good and bad moments. How many times did she roll her eyes (a sign of contempt) when he spoke? How often did he fidget (indicating tension or stress)? The frequency of negative and positive expressions, combined with the data collected by the heart, sweat and other monitors, provides a multidimensional view of the relationship. (Tim and Kara ultimately decided Buddy could stay, only not as often.)

Gottman and other researchers see their work as a matter of public health. The average couple who seek help have been having problems for six years—long enough to have done serious damage to their relationship. That delay, Gottman says, is as dangerous as putting off regular mammograms. The United States has one of the highest divorce rates in the industrialized world, and studies have shown a direct correlation between marriage and well-being. Happily married people are healthier; even their immune systems work better than those of people who are unhappily married or divorced. Kids suffer as well; if their parents split, they're more likely to have emotional or school problems.

But going to a marriage counselor won't necessarily help. "Therapy is at an impasse," Gottman says, "because it is not based on solid empirical knowledge of what real couples do to keep their marriages happy and stable." In a 1995 Consumer Reports survey, marriage therapy ranked at the bottom of a poll of patient satisfaction with various psychotherapies. The magazine said part of the problem was that "almost anyone can hang out a shingle as a marriage counselor." Even credentialed therapists may use approaches that have no basis in research. Several recent studies have shown that many current treatments produce few long-term benefits for couples who seek help.

One example: the process called "active listening." It was originally used by therapists to objectively summarize the complaints of a patient and validate the way the patient is feeling. ("So, I'm hearing that you think your father always liked your sister

Know Your Spouse

Test the strength of your marriage in this relationship quiz prepared especially for NEWSWEEK by John Gottman.

TRUE/FALSE

1	I can name my partner's best friends	☐ ☐
2	I can tell you what stresses my partner is currently facing	☐ ☐
3	I know the names of some of the people who have been irritating my partner lately	☐ ☐
4	I can tell you some of my partner's life dreams	☐ ☐
5	I can tell you about my partner's basic philosophy of life	☐ ☐
6	I can list the relatives my partner likes the least	☐ ☐
7	I feel that my partner knows me pretty well	☐ ☐
8	When we are apart, I often think fondly of my partner	☐ ☐
9	I often touch or kiss my partner affectionately	☐ ☐
10	My partner really respects me	☐ ☐
11	There is fire and passion in this relationship	☐ ☐
12	Romance is definitely still a part of our relationship	☐ ☐
13	My partner appreciates the things I do in this relationship	☐ ☐
14	My partner generally likes my personality	☐ ☐
15	Our sex life is mostly satisfying	☐ ☐
16	At the end of the day my partner is glad to see me	☐ ☐
17	My partner is one of my best friends	☐ ☐
18	We just love talking to each other	☐ ☐
19	There is lots of give and take (both people have influence) in our discussions	☐ ☐
20	My partner listens respectfully, even when we disagree	☐ ☐
21	My partner is usually a great help as a problem solver	☐ ☐
22	We generally mesh well on basic values and goals in life	☐ ☐

Scoring: GIVE YOURSELF ONE POINT FOR EACH "TRUE" ANSWER. ABOVE 12: YOU HAVE A LOT OF STRENGTH IN YOUR RELATIONSHIP. CONGRATULATIONS. BELOW 12: YOUR RELATIONSHIP COULD STAND SOME IMPROVEMENT AND COULD PROBABLY BENEFIT FROM SOME WORK ON THE BASICS, SUCH AS IMPROVING COMMUNICATION.

better and you're hurt by that.") In recent years this technique has been modified for marital therapy—ineffectively, Gottman says. Even highly trained therapists would have a hard time stepping back in the middle of a fight and saying, "So, I'm hearing that you think I'm a fat, lazy slob."

Happily married couples have a very different way of relating to each other during disputes, Gottman found. The partners make frequent "repair attempts," reaching out to each other in an effort to prevent negativity from getting out of control in the midst of conflict. Humor is often part of a successful repair attempt. In his book, Gottman describes one couple arguing about the kind of

car to buy (she favors a minivan; he wants a snazzier Jeep). In the midst of yelling, the wife suddenly puts her hand on her hip and sticks out her tongue—mimicking their 4-year-old son. They both start laughing, and the tension is defused.

In happy unions, couples build what Gottman calls a "sound marital house" by working together and appreciating the best in each other. They learn to cope with the two kinds of problems that are part of every marriage: solvable conflicts and perpetual problems that may represent underlying conflicts and that can lead to emotional gridlock. Gottman says 69 percent of marital conflicts fall into the latter category. Happy spouses

Facing Your Problems

I N THE LAB, THE WAY A MARRIED COUPLE FIGHTS CAN OFTEN tell psychologists more than *what* they fight about. The expressions and underlying emotions displayed during a conflict may reveal the strength or weakness of the marriage. During a couple's 15-minute conversation—on a topic known to be a sore point—researchers at the University of Washington measure physiological responses (below) and facial expressions, which can reveal true feelings even when words don't. Videotapes also show how long the partners' emotional responses last—even the happiest of couples has fleeting moments of bad feeling, but if the negative indicators tend to endure, it can signal a marriage in trouble.

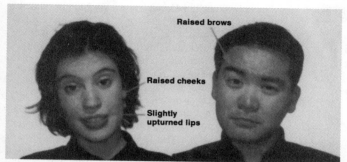

Interest: A calm voice and positive body language—leaning forward, for example—signal the genuine article. It's a real desire to hear a partner's opinion, not an attempt to influence.

Photos by Andrew Brusso.

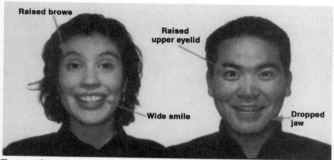

Surprise: A big smile, with popping eyes, indicates a positive surprise. Something unexpected but unpleasant yields the eye-pop only. Either way, a short-lived state.

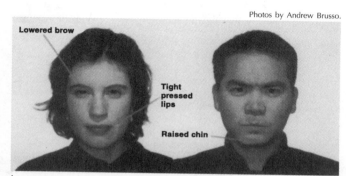

Anger: The tone is cold or loud, the wording staccato. But honest anger, an internal state, is different from contempt, directed at the spouse. A fake smile, without raised cheeks, may mask anger.

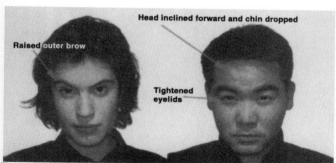

Domineering: A "low and slow" voice often signals that one partner is trying to force the other to his or her view. Ranges from lawyerly cross-examination to blatant threats.

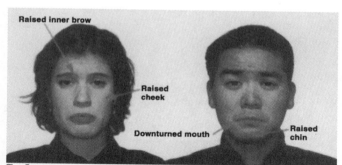

Sadness: Passivity and sulking can look like stonewalling or idsengaging from a fight, but sad people maintain more eye contact that stonewallers.

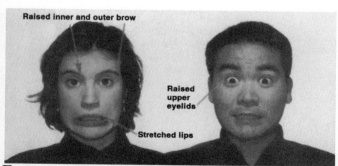

Fear: Outright fear is rare; a lower-grade version—tension— is more common. And a wife's tension, if pronounced, can be a predictor for divorce down the road.

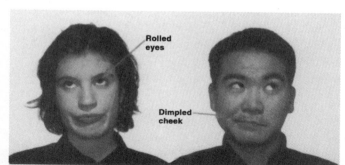

Contempt: If prolonged, this expression is a red alert. Especially when accompanied by sarcasm and insults, it suggests a marriage in serious trouble.

deal with these issues in a way that strengthens the marriage. One couple Gottman studied argued constantly about order in their household (she demanded neatness, and he couldn't care less). Over the years they managed to accommodate their differences, acknowledging that their affection for each other was more important than newspapers piled up in the corner of the living room.

As psychologists learn more about marriage, they have begun devising new approaches to therapy. Philip Cowan and Carolyn Pape-Cowan, a husband-and-wife team (married for 41 years) at the University of California, Berkeley, are looking at one of the most critical periods in a marriage: the birth of a first child. (Two thirds of couples experience a "precipitous drop" in marital satisfaction at this point, researchers say.) "Trying to take two people's dreams of a perfect family and make them one is quite a trick," Pape-Cowan says. The happiest couples were those who looked on their spouses as partners with whom they shared household and child-care duties. The Cowans say one way to help spouses get through the transition to parenting would be ongoing group sessions with other young families to provide the kind of support people used to get from their communities and extended families.

Inside the Love Lab

In the laboratory, video cameras record facial expressions. Motion-sensing jiggle-ometers register fidgeting, and a cluster of sensors reads physiological data.

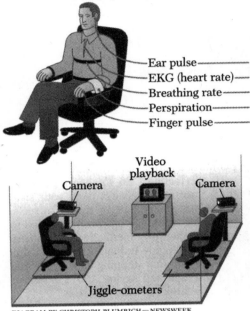

Ear pulse
EKG (heart rate)
Breathing rate
Perspiration
Finger pulse

Video playback
Camera   Camera
Jiggle-ometers

DIAGRAM BY CHRISTOPH BLUMRICH — NEWSWEEK

Two other researchers—Neil Jacobson at the University of Washington and Andrew Christensen at UCLA—have developed what they call "acceptance therapy" after studying the interactions of couples in conflict. The goal of their therapy is to help people learn to live with aspects of their spouse's characters that simply can't be changed. "People can love each other not just for what they have in common but for things that make them complementary," says Jacobson. "When we looked at a clinical sample of what predicted failure in traditional behavior therapy, what we came upon again and again was an inability to accept differences."

Despite all these advances in marital therapy, researchers still say they can't save all marriages—and in fact there are some that *shouldn't* be saved. Patterns of physical abuse, for example, are extremely difficult to alter, Gottman says. And there are cases where the differences between the spouses are so profound and long-standing that even the best therapy is futile. Gottman says one quick way to test whether a couple still has a chance is to ask what initially attracted them to each other. If they can recall those magic first moments (and smile when they talk about them), all is not lost. "We can still fan the embers," says Gottman. For all the rest of us, there's hope.

Will Your Marriage Last?

New studies show that the newlywed years can foretell the long-term outcome of almost every marriage. What do your newlywed years predict for you?

By Aviva Patz

What if I told you that there is a man in America who can predict, from the outset, whether or not your marriage will last? He doesn't need to hear you arguing; he doesn't need to know what you argue about. He doesn't even care whether you argue at all.

I was dubious, too, but I was curious enough to attend a lecture on the subject at the most recent American Psychological Association convention in Boston. Ted Huston, Ph.D., a professor of human ecology and psychology at the University of Texas at Austin, was showcasing the results of a long-term study of married couples that pierces the heart of social psychological science: the ability to forecast whether a husband and wife, two years after taking their vows, will stay together and whether they will be happy.

My press pass notwithstanding, I went to the seminar for reasons of my own. Fresh out of college I had gotten married—and burned. Some part of me was still reeling from three years of

waking up angry every morning, not wanting to go home after work, feeling lonely even as my then husband sat beside me. I went because I have recently remarried and just celebrated my one-year anniversary. Needless to say, I'd like to make this one work. So I scribbled furiously in my notebook, drinking in the graphs and charts—for psychology, for husbands and wives everywhere, but mostly for myself.

Huston, a pioneer in the psychology of relationships, launched the Processes of Adaptation in Intimate Relationships (the "PAIR Project") in 1981, in which he followed 168 couples—drawn from marriage license records in four counties in a rural and working-class area of Pennsylvania—from their wedding day through 13 years of marriage.

Through multiple interviews, Huston looked at the way partners related to one another during courtship, as newlyweds and through the early years of marriage. Were they "gaga?" Comfortable? Unsure? He measured their positive and negative feelings for each other and

BLISS OR BUST?
TAKE THE MARRIAGE QUIZ

Created for PSYCHOLOGY TODAY by Ted Huston, Ph.D., Shanna Smith, Sylvia Niehuis, Christopher Rasmussen and Paul Miller

Circle the answer that best describes your level of agreement with each of the following statements:

Part 1 Our Relationship As Newlyweds

1. As newlyweds, we were constantly touching, kissing, pledging our love or doing sweet things for one another.
Strongly disagree (1 pt.) Disagree (2 pts.) Agree (3 pts.) Strongly agree (4 pts.)

2. As newlyweds, how often did you express criticism, anger, annoyance, impatience or dissatisfaction to one another?
Often (1 pt.) Sometimes (2 pts.) Rarely (3 pts.) Almost never (4 pts.)

3. As newlyweds, my partner and I felt we belonged together; we were extremely close and deeply in love.
Disagree (1 pt.) Mildly agree (2 pts.) Agree (3 pts.) Strongly agree (4 pts.)

4. As a newlywed, I think one or both of us were confused about our feelings toward each other, or worried that we were not right for each other.
Strongly agree (1 pt.) Agree (2 pts.) Disagree (3 pts.) Strongly disagree (4 pts.)

Part 2 Our Relationship By Our Second Anniversary

1. By our second anniversary, we were disappointed that we touched, kissed, pledged our love or did sweet things for one another less often than we had as newlyweds.
Strongly disagree (1 pt.) Disagree (2 pts.) Agree (3 pts.) Strongly agree (4 pts.)

2. By our second anniversary, we expressed criticism, anger, annoyance, impatience or dissatisfaction a lot more than we had as newlyweds.
Strongly disagree (1 pt.) Disagree (2 pts.) Agree (3 pts.) Strongly agree (4 pts.)

3. By our second anniversary, we felt much less belonging and closeness with one another than we had before.
Disagree (1 pt.) Mildly agree (2 pts.) Agree (3 pts.) Strongly agree (4 pts.)

4. By our second anniversary, I felt much more confused or worried about the relationship than I did as a newlywed.
Strongly disagree (1 pt.) Disagree (2 pts.) Agree (3 pts.) Strongly agree (4 pts.)

Scoring: Add up the points that correspond to your answers in Part 1. If you scored between 4 and 8, place yourself in Group "A." If you scored between 9 and 16, place yourself in Group "B." Now add up the points that correspond to your answers in Part 2. If you scored between 4 and 8, place yourself in Group "C.' If you scored between 9 and 16, place yourself in Group "D.'

Your Results: Find the type of marriage first by considering your score in part 1 (either A or B) in combination with your score in part 2 (either C or D): If you scored A + C, read "Mixed Blessings"; If you scored A + D, read "Disengaging Duo"; If you scored B + C, read "A Fine Romance"; If you scored B + D, read "Disaffected Lovers."

Disaffected Lovers
The contrast between the giddiness you felt as newlyweds and how you felt later may cause disenchantment. While you and your spouse are still affectionate and in love, there are clouds behind the silver lining. You may bicker and disagree, which, combined with a loss of affection and love in your relationship, could give rise to the first serious doubts about your future together.

Food for Thought: Your relationship may be at risk for eventual divorce. But the pattern of decline early on does not have to continue. Ask yourself: Did we set ourselves up for disappointment with an overly romantic view of marriage? Did we assume it would require little effort to sustain? Did we take each other for granted? Did our disappointment lead to frustration and anger? Will continued bickering erode the love we have left?

A Fine Romance
You have a highly affectionate, loving and harmonious marriage. It may have lost a touch of its initial glow as the mundane realities of marriage have demanded more of your time. But you feel a certain sense of security in the marriage: The relationship's gifts you unwrapped as newlyweds continue to delight.

Food for Thought: You have the makings of a happy, stable marriage. The cohesive partnership you have maintained bodes well for its future. You will not always be happy—all marriages go through rough periods. But your ability to sustain a healthy marriage over the critical first two years suggests that you and your partner operate together like a thermostat in a home—when it's chilly, you identify the source of the draft and elimi-

Continued on next page

nate it, and when it's hot, you find ways to circulate cool air.

Mixed Blessings

Your marriage is less enchanting and filled with more conflict and ambivalence than Western society's romantic ideal, but it has changed little over its first two years, losing only a modicum of "good feeling." It seems to coast along, showing few signs that it will deteriorate further or become deeply distressed.

Food for Thought: This relationship may not be the romance you envisioned, but it just might serve you well. Many people in such relationships are content, finding their marriage a reassuringly stable foundation that allows them to devote their attention to career, children or other pursuits. Other people in these relationships are slightly dissatisfied, but stay married because the rewards outweigh the drawbacks. A few people may eventually leave such marriages in search of a "fine romance."

Disengaging Duo

You and your mate are not overly affectionate and frequently express displeasure with one another. In contrast to those in a marriage of "mixed blessings," the love you once felt diminished soon after the wedding, and you became more ambivalent about the relationship. You may already have a sense that your relationship is on shaky ground.

Food for Thought: Your relationship may be in immediate trouble. You may have married hoping that problems in the relationship would go away after the wedding, but they didn't. Ask yourself: Did I see our problems coming while we were dating? Did I think they would dissolve with marriage? What kinds of changes would I need to see in my partner in order to be happy? How likely are they to occur? How bad would things have to get before the marriage would no longer be worthwhile?

---

observed how those feelings changed over time. Are newlyweds who hug and kiss more likely than other couples to have a happy marriage, he wondered, or are they particularly susceptible to divorce if their romance dissipates? Are newlyweds who bicker destined to part ways?

Since one in two marriages ends in divorce in this country, there ought to be tons of research explaining why. But the existing literature provides only pieces of the larger puzzle.

Past research has led social scientists to believe that newlyweds begin their life together in romantic bliss, and can then be brought down by their inability to navigate the issues that inevitably crop up during the marriage. When Benjamin Karny and Thomas Bradbury did a comprehensive review of the literature in 1995, they confirmed studies such as those of John Gottman and Neil Jacobson, maintaining that the best predictors of divorce are interactive difficulties, such as frequent expressions of antagonism, lack of respect for each other's ideas and similar interpersonal issues.

But most of this research was done on couples who had been married a number of years, with many of them already well on their way to divorce. It came as no surprise, then, that researchers thought their hostility toward one another predicted the further demise of the relationship.

> ... the major distinguishing factor between those who divorced and those who remained married was the amount of change in the relationship over the first two years.

Huston's study was unique in that it looked at couples much earlier, when they were courting and during the initial years of marriage, thus providing the first complete picture of the earliest stages of distress. Its four main findings were quite surprising.

First, contrary to popular belief, Huston found that many newlyweds are far from blissfully in love. Second, couples whose marriages begin in romantic bliss are particularly divorce-prone because such intensity is too hard to maintain. Believe it or not, marriages that start out with less "Hollywood romance" usually have more promising futures. Accordingly, and this is the third major finding, spouses in lasting but lackluster marriages are not prone to divorce, as one might suspect; their marriages are less fulfilling to begin with, so there is no erosion of a Western-style romantic ideal. Lastly, and perhaps most importantly, it is the loss of love and affection, not the emergence of interpersonal issues, that sends couples journeying toward divorce.

By the end of Huston's study in 1994, the couples looked a lot like the rest of America, falling into four groups. They were either married and happy; married and unhappy; divorced early, within seven years; or divorced later, after seven years—and each category showed a distinct pattern.

Those who remained happily married were very "in love" and affec-

Believe it or not, marriages that start out with less 'Hollywood romance' usually have more promising futures.

tionate as newlyweds. They showed less ambivalence, expressed negative feelings less often and viewed their mate more positively than other couples. Most importantly, these feelings remained stable over time. By contrast, although many couples who divorced later were very affectionate as newlyweds, they gradually became less loving, more negative, and more critical of their spouse.

Indeed, Huston found that how well spouses got along as newlyweds affected their future, but the major distinguishing factor between those who divorced and those who remained married was the amount of change in the relationship over its first two years.

"The first two years are key–that's when the risk of divorce is particularly high," he says. "And the changes that take place during this time tell us a lot about where the marriage is headed."

What surprised Huston most was the nature of the changes that led to divorce: The experiences of the 56 participating couples who divorced showed that loss of initial levels of love and affection, rather than conflict, was the most salient predictor of distress and divorce. This loss sends the relationship into a downward spiral, leading to increased bickering and fighting, and to the collapse of the union.

"This ought to change the way we think about the early roots of what goes wrong in marriage," Huston said. "The dominant approach has been to work with couples to resolve conflict, but it should focus on pre-

serving the positive feelings. That's a very important take-home lesson."

"Huston's research fills an important gap in the literature by suggesting that there is more to a successful relationship than simply managing conflict," said Harry Reis, Ph.D., of the University of Rochester, a leading social psychologist.

"My own research speaks to 'loss of intimacy,' in the sense that when people first become close they feel a tremendous sense of validation from each other, like their partner is the only other person on earth who sees things as they do. That feeling sometimes fades, and when it does, it can take a heavy toll on the marriage."

Social science has a name for that fading dynamic–"disillusionment": Lovers initially put their best foot forward, ignoring each other's–and the relationship's–shortcomings. But after they tie the knot, hidden aspects of their personalities emerge, and idealized images give way to more realistic ones. This can lead to disappointment, loss of love and, ultimately, distress and divorce.

When Marriage Fails

The story of Peter and Suzie, participants in the PAIR Project, shows classic disillusionment. When they met, Suzie was 24, a new waitress at the golf course where Peter, then 26, played. He was "awed" by her beauty. After a month the two considered themselves an exclusive couple. Peter said Suzie "wasn't an airhead; she seemed kind of smart, and she's pretty." Suzie said Peter "cared a lot about me as a person, and was willing to overlook things."

By the time they strolled down the aisle on Valentine's Day in 1981, Peter and Suzie had dated only nine months, experiencing many ups and downs along the way.

Huston says couples are most vulnerable to disillusionment when their courtship is brief. In a whirlwind romance, it's easy to paint an unrealistically rosy picture of the relationship, one that cannot be sustained.

Sure enough, reality soon set in for Peter and Suzie. Within two years, Suzie was less satisfied with almost every aspect of their marriage. She expressed less affection for Peter and felt her love decline continuously. She considered him to have "contrary" traits, such as jealousy and possessiveness, and resented his propensity to find fault with her.

Peter, for his part, was disappointed that his wife did not become the flawless parent and homemaker he had envisioned.

Another danger sign for relationships is a courtship filled with drama and driven by external circumstances. For this pair, events related to Peter's jealousy propelled the relationship forward. He was the force behind their destroying letters and pictures from former lovers. It was a phone call between Suzie and an old flame that prompted him to bring up the idea of marriage in the first place. And it was a fit of jealousy–over Suzie's claiming to go shopping and then coming home suspiciously late–that convinced Peter he was ready to marry.

Theirs was a recipe for disaster: A short courtship, driven largely by Peter's jealousy, enabled the pair to ignore flaws in the relationship and in each other, setting them up for disappointment. That disappointment eroded their love and affection, which soured their perception of each other's personalities, creating feelings of ambivalence.

Ten years after saying "I do," the disaffected lovers were in the midst of divorce. When Suzie filed the papers, she cited as the primary reason a gradual loss of love.

O**ur culture is also to blame . . . for perpetuating the myth of storybook romance, which is more likely to doom a marriage than strengthen it.**

The parallels between Peter and Suzie's failed marriage and my own are striking: My courtship with my first husband was short, also about nine months. Like Peter, I had shallow criteria: This guy was cool; he had long hair, wore a leather jacket, played guitar and adored the same obscure band that I did.

When it came time to build a life together, however, we were clearly mismatched. I wanted a traditional family with children; he would have been happy living on a hippie commune. In college, when we wanted to move in together, we thought our parents would be more approving if we got engaged first. So we did, even though we weren't completely sold on the idea of marriage.

The road to divorce was paved early, by the end of the first year: I had said I wanted us to spend more time together; he accused me of trying to keep him from his hobbies, and told me, in so many words, to "get a life." Well I did, and, two years later, he wasn't in it.

When Marriage Succeeds

While the disillusionment model best describes those who divorce, Huston found that another model suits those who stay married, whether or not they are happy: The "enduring dynamics model," in which partners establish patterns of behavior early and maintain them over time, highlights

stability in the relationship—the feature that distinguishes those who remain together from those who eventually split up.

The major difference between the unhappily married couples and their happy counterparts is simply that they have a lower level of satisfaction across the board. Yet, oddly enough, this relative unhappiness by itself does not doom the marriage. "We have a whole group of people who are stable in unhappy marriages and not necessarily dissatisfied," Huston said. "It's just a different model of marriage. It's not that they're happy about their marriage, it's just that the discontent doesn't spill over and spoil the rest of their lives."

And while all married couples eventually lose a bit of that honeymoon euphoria, Huston notes, those who remain married don't consider this a crushing blow, but rather a natural transition from "romantic relationship" to "working partnership." And when conflict does arise, they diffuse it with various constructive coping mechanisms.

Nancy and John, participants in Huston's study, are a shining example of happy, healthy balance. They met in February 1978 and were immediately attracted to each other. John said Nancy was "fun to be with" and he "could take her anywhere." Nancy said John always complimented her and liked to do things she enjoyed, things "other guys wouldn't do."

During their courtship, they spent a lot of time together, going to dances at their high school and hanging out with friends. They became comfortable with each other and began to openly disclose their opinions and feelings, realizing they had a lot in common and really enjoyed each other's company.

John paid many surprise visits to Nancy and bought her a number of gifts. Toward the end of the summer, John gave Nancy a charm necklace with a "genuine diamond." She recalls his saying: "This isn't your ring, honey, but you're going to get one." And she did. The two married on Jan. 17, 1981, nearly three years after they began dating.

The prognosis for this relationship is good. Nancy and John have a "fine romance"—a solid foundation of love and affection, built on honesty and intimacy. A three-year courtship enabled them to paint realistic portraits of one another, lessening the chances of a rude awakening after marriage.

In 1994, when they were last interviewed, Nancy and John were highly satisfied with their marriage. They were very compatible, disagreeing only about politics. Both felt they strongly benefited from the marriage and said they had no desire to leave.

W**hen the seminar ends, I can't get to a pay phone fast enough. After two rings, the phone is answered. He's there, of course. Dependable. Predictable. That's one of the things that first set my husband apart. At the close of one date, he'd lock in the next. "Can I see you tomorrow for lunch?" "Will you have dinner with me next week?"

Unlike the fantasy-quality of my first marriage, I felt a deep sense of comfort and companionship with him, and did not harbor outrageous expectations. We exchanged vows three and a half years later, in August 1998.

There at the convention center, I try to tell my husband about Huston's study, about the critical first few years, about "enduring dynamics." It all comes out in a jumble.

"You're saying we have a good marriage, that we're not going to get divorced?" he asks.

"Yes," I say breathlessly, relieved of the burden of explanation.

"Well I'm glad to hear that," he says, "but I wasn't really worried."

Sometimes I wonder: Knowing what I know now, could I have saved my first marriage? Probably not. Huston's research suggests that the harbingers of disaster were present even before my wedding day.

And he blames our culture. Unlike many other world cultures, he says, Western society makes marriage the key adult relationship, which puts a lot of pressure on people to marry. "People feel they have to find a way to get there and one way is to force it, even if it only works for the time being," he says.

Our culture is also to blame, Huston says, for perpetuating the myth of storybook romance, which is more likely to doom a marriage than strengthen it. He has few kind words for Hollywood, which brings us unrealistic, unsustainable passion.

So if your new romance starts to resemble a movie script, try to remember: The audience never sees what happens after the credits roll.

Aviva Patz is the executive editor of PSYCHOLOGY TODAY.

READ MORE ABOUT IT

When Love Dies: The Process of Marital Disaffection, Karen Kayser, Ph.D. (Guildford Press, 1993)

Fighting For Your Marriage: Positive Steps For Preventing Divorce and Preserving A Lasting Love, H. Markman, S. Stanley and S. Blumberg (Jossey-Bass, 1994)

MEN, WOMEN, & MONEY

MONEY IS SUCH AN **EMOTIONALLY** LOADED TOPIC THAT FEW **COUPLES** DISCUSS IT DIRECTLY. **YET** IT, MORE THAN **SEX**, IS WHAT **DRIVES** PARTNERS **APART**. PSYCHOTHERAPIST **OLIVIA MELLAN** SHOWS **HOW** TO PUT **MONEY** IN ITS PLACE.

FOR MOST PEOPLE, MONEY IS never just money, a tool to accomplish some of life's goals. It is love, power, happiness, security, control, dependency, independence, freedom and more. Money is so loaded a symbol that to unload it—and I believe it must be unloaded to live in a fully rational and balanced relationship to money—reaches deep into the human psyche. Usually, when the button of money is pressed, deeper issues emerge that have long been neglected. As a result, money matters are a perfect vehicle for awareness and growth.

Most people relate to money much as they relate to a person—in an ongoing and complex way that taps deep-seated emotions. When two individuals form an enduring relationship with each other, money is always a partner, too. In these liberated times, couples discuss many things before marriage, but the meaning of money is not one of them. Money is still a taboo topic. Often, the silence is a shield for the shame, guilt and anxiety people feel about their own ways with money. I, for one, would not want to tell a date that I'm an overspender.

Many individuals have a troubled relationship with money. Then, when they get into a couple relationship, money matters get explosive. Other people may have no problem with money individually; the trouble starts after they're in the relationship.

IN TWO DECADES as a psychotherapist specializing in resolving money conflicts, I have observed that couples usually polarize around money. Partners tend to assume defense styles, or personalities, in relation to money that are direct opposites to each other. I call it Mellan's Law: If opposites don't attract right off the bat, then they will create each other eventually.

Commonly, a hoarder marries a spender. The United States is in fact a nation of overspenders. We live in a market economy and we are led to believe that we are good citizens to the degree that we go out and spend. Because of our community breakdown and spiritual alienation, many people feel a core emptiness that they try to fill up with Things. If we're not overspending, we're typically worrying about money or compulsively hoarding it.

We grow up in families where nobody talks about money. Most people will immediately protest: "Not true. My family talked about money all the time." When I ask, "How did you talk?" they reply, "My father worried about not having enough, and he yelled at my mother for spending too much."

The fact remains that people do not grow up with educational or philosophic conversations about what money is and isn't, what it can and can't do. We don't examine the societal messages telling us that gratification lies in spending or that keeping up with the

OPPOSITES ATTRACT. HOARDERS TYPICALLY PAIR WITH SPENDERS, AND WORRIERS JOIN WITH AVOIDERS.

Joneses is important. Information-based money discussions are so taboo that we usually reach adulthood without a realistic sense of our family's finances.

I ONCE MET A MAN who had no idea that he grew up in a wealthy family. He said, "We had a family restaurant and my mother was always worrying about how we were at the edge of doom. As a child I developed a stammer from all that money anxiety. As an adolescent, I worked day and night to keep the restaurant afloat. Years later, my mother was talking about the good old days when we were making so much money in the restaurant business. I started screaming at her about all the money anxiety I carried. I was outraged that it wasn't even based on a real threat. When I stopped screaming, I noticed that my stammer was gone."

And it never returned. That's a therapist's dream story: one catharsis, no symptom. But it does show how money carries a huge emotional load.

As a result of the money taboo, I grew up as most kids do: imitating my parents' way of handling money without being aware of it. My father, affected by the Depression, worried out loud about money. My mother was a shopaholic, expressing love by buying me and herself clothes. She'd hide the purchases behind a living room chair until my father was in a good mood. As an adult, whenever I felt either depressed or particularly happy, I too would go out and shop. And even if I bought everything at a thrift store, I'd hide all the items behind a chair until my husband was in a good mood. Actually, I alternated between shopping and worrying about money.

Some people do the opposite. They typically say, "My father was a hoarder and a worrier. I hated the way he made me account for every penny of my allowance. I made a vow to myself that I'd never be like that." Such people, however, are any-thing but free of the parental attitude; their behavior is still defined by it.

In addition to irrational attitudes and beliefs about money that we internalize from our families of origin, we carry our own emotionally-charged memories of money from childhood. I remember being in a barbershop with my father when I was six, and some kid asked his father for a quarter. The father said no. The kid started to sob uncontrollably. I remember being so gripped by the child's sense of deprivation, I made a vow right then that I was never going to feel deprived like that. If you tell yourself at six that you're never going to feel deprived, you have the makings of a chronic overspender.

COUPLES POLARIZED over money engage in a balancing dance of opposites. Two spenders who come together will fight each other for the superspender role; the other, as a defense, will learn to hoard because someone has to set limits. When it comes to defense styles, there's always a pursuer (or clinger) and a withdrawer. With two withdrawers, one will become the superwithdrawer. The other will become a pursuer, because if they both withdrew there would be no connection at all.

An equally common polarity is the worrier and avoider. Avoiders don't focus on the details of their money life, such as whether they have enough money or how much interest they're paying on their credit cards; they just spend. A worrier will turn a mate into an avoider just as a way of escaping the avalanche of worry. And an avoider will turn a mate into a worrier. Two partners couldn't both avoid forever; somebody will eventually get concerned and take on the worrier role. Doubling the trouble, hoarders are usually worriers and spenders are usually avoiders.

As with all polar personality styles, hoarders and spenders live in different universes marked by opposing beliefs. What feels good to one feels horrible to the other. When not spending, a hoarder feels virtuous, in control. A spender when not spending feels anx-

---

DOING **WHAT DOESN'T** COME **NATURALLY**

GROWTH, CREATIVITY, INTIMACY AND FLEXIBILITY come from doing what is not automatic. For a hoarder, spending money on one's self or a loved one for immediate pleasure changes the pattern. For a spender, it's saving or investing money, or going on a slow, choreographed binge. Breaking habits doesn't happen all at once; it's a slow process. For example, I can't say, "Don't worry!" to a worrier. But I can say, "Pick one hour to worry, write down your worries for that time and give up worrying for the rest of the day."

PARTNERS CAN BEGIN to change their ingrained habits by taking the following steps:

- Do what doesn't come naturally once a week. Eventually you and your partner will have moved enough toward some middle ground that you are not locked into your roles.
- While practicing a new behavior, write down how it feels in order to monitor your progress.
- Reward yourself for that new behavior.—*O.M.*

PLANNERS OFTEN FIND THEMSELVES TIED TO DREAMERS, AND MONEY MONKS GET TOGETHER WITH DEDICATED AMASSERS.

ious and deprived. Indeed, spenders can't tolerate the word "budget"; financial planners have to draw up a "spending plan."

Other money personalities include planners, who are detail-oriented, and dreamers, who are global visionaries. In addition, there are money monks, often ex-hippies, political activists or spiritual souls, who feel that money corrupts and it's better to not have too much. Sometimes they marry money amassers, who believe that the guy with the most money wins. Amassers are not hoarders; they don't simply save, they invest to make their money grow. They save, spend and invest.

WHAT MAKES EACH OF the personality types is the operation of internal belief systems, what I call money myths—all the money messages, vows and emotional memories acquired from the family of origin, the peer group, the culture at large and filtered through a person's intrinsic temperament. Many spenders, for example, don't give away just money; they are effusive with feelings, words, everything. Hoarders are typically taciturn and withholding. Even in therapy, they have to be encouraged to open up.

Here is the ironic part. The longer couples are married, the more they lock into polarized roles. Then they attack each other for their differences, projecting onto the other attitudes about every other spender or hoarder

they have encountered in their life. They fail to acknowledge the positive aspects of their partner's personality type and of the balancing dance itself.

The failure of people to explore their money personalities leads to deep misunderstanding and hurt. Take the case of a man who views money as security. He does not believe in spending a great deal on gifts; he believes in saving. He's married to a woman who believes that money is both love and happiness; she's a spender. They are about to celebrate a major anniversary. He spends days in record stores searching for the song they danced to when they were dating in the '60s, "their song." When she gets his gift, she thinks he's chintzy and is insulted. He's inconsolably hurt. She, meanwhile, has bought him an expensive gift.

Money issues rarely manifest themselves openly in relationships. Instead, couples fight over what money represents. And while money issues can rear their head anytime; there are specific transition periods in relationships that force them to the surface: tax time, starting a family and buying a house. Couples may complain, "We can't agree on where we want to live." Or, "He wants to go on vacation and I want to save our money for retirement." Or, "She keeps indulging the children, getting them everything they want, and I don't think that's good for the kids."

In addition to money personalities, there are male-female differences in approaches to money that haunt many relationships. It could be said that some differences reflect men as hunters and women as gatherers. In his theater piece *Defending the Caveman*, Rob Becker describes men: they go out and buy a shirt, wear it until it dies, then go out and kill another shirt. Women, in contrast, gather. They shop for this for next Christmas for their niece and for that for their son-in-law.

OTHER PERVASIVE MONEY differences exist between the genders. First, men and women have differences of personal boundaries because

CONVERSING WITH CASH

HOW DO YOU TURN YOUR consciousness to an area that's usually in the dark? When a couple comes in fighting about money, I first have them clarify their own personal history and private relationship with money before turning to the dynamic between them.

I want people to see what money symbolizes to them. Then they can "unload" the symbol.

As an exercise at home, I ask each to engage in a dialogue with their Money, and not share the conversation until they come back. The goal is to see what money symbolizes for each person, and to recognize that money is just a tool to accomplish certain of life's goals.

In the dialogue, imagine your money is being interviewed on *Oprah*. Ask how it thinks the relationship between you two is going, how it feels about the way you treat it.

Perhaps Money will reply, "You know, you're squeezing me so tight, I can't breathe. You need to let go a little." Or, "You throw me around, but you don't treat me with respect. You need to pay more attention to me." Either speak into a tape recorder or write the conversation down on paper.

After this dialogue, draw on at least three voices in your head—mother, father and any other figure—and have them comment on what has transpired. Finally, consider what God, a Higher Power or inner wisdom might say.

Either Money or God, or both, will help you see the direction you need to move in to achieve money harmony.

Occasionally, a couple is unable to have a dialogue with Money. I then ask them to write down all their childhood memories and associations relating to money and start there.—*O.M.*

they are both raised largely by women. Men have to psychologically separate more rigidly from women because of the sex difference; women do not have to separate so rigidly, and therefore can afford less distinct boundaries.

MEN THINK NOTHING OF CHOOSING THE FAMILY CAR BY THEMSELVES, WHILE WOMEN THINK IT SHOULD BE A TEAM EFFORT.

Second, men are raised to see the world as hierarchical and competitive. There's always a one-up and one-down position, a winner and a loser. Women see the world as cooperative and democratic; they share. In addition, they are allowed—even encouraged—to be needy and vulnerable, while men are discouraged from such display.

The boundary and hierarchical differences between men and women lead to clashes around money decisionmaking. Men think nothing of going out alone and buying a big-screen TV, or even the family car or com-

puter, then coming home and saying, "Hi honey. I have a new car." She says, "Why didn't you consult me? I thought we were a team." And he says, "Are you my mother? Do I have to ask your permission?"

Because of their more rigid boundaries, men think of themselves as islands and withdraw when facing difficulties of intimacy. They don't see themselves as part of a team. And, of course, men and women are raised to believe different things about the way they should actually handle money. Despite many social changes, men are still bred to believe they will be good at dealing with money—although nobody tells them how to do it. In that way, money is like sex; they're just supposed to know. Women are raised to believe they won't be good at it and, if they're lucky, some man will take care of the details of money and investing.

One of the major financial houses recently canvassed high school students and asked how good they were about math and money The boys said, "We're pretty good." The girls said, "We're not very good." In fact, they both knew the same amount about money; but their confidence levels were vastly different.

Moreover, when men make money in the stock market, they

credit their own cleverness. When they lose money, they blame the incompetence of their advisors or bad luck. When women make money in the market, they credit the cleverness of their advisors, good luck or even the stars. When they lose money, they blame themselves.

This explanatory style is literally and figuratively depressing. In addition, women are still paid three-quarters of what men are paid for the same job. These events conspire to reduce women's confidence—and inspire "bag-lady" nightmares. Because of the forced dependency on men to make decisions about money, women fear being out on the street with nothing.

When men make more money than their spouse, they believe their superior earnings entitle them to greater power in decision-making. By contrast, women who make more than their mates almost always desire democratic decision-making. As a woman and a therapist, I have a definite bias towards shared decision-making and shared power. It is the only arrangement that works. I prefer to think of men's sense of money not as an entitlement but as a defense against the terrible provider-burden they carry.

Men are trained to believe that money equals power and that power is

8 TIPS TO TALKING ABOUT MONEY

NEVER TRY TO NEGOTIATE about money before airing your feelings; otherwise, negotiations will always break down.

1 Find a non-stressful time when money is not a loaded issue (not tax season, please) and when the kids are not around. Agree on some ground rules: no interrupting each other; no long tirades; after one person shares a difficult piece of information, the partner will try to mirror it back before responding.
2 Take turns sharing your childhood messages about money. How did your parents save it, spend it, talk about it? How did they deal with allowances? What specific money messages did you get and how might they be affecting you today?
3 Share your old hurts, resentments and fears about money.

4 Mention your concerns and fears about your partner's money style. Then acknowledge what you admire about their methods and what you secretly envy. Hoarders secretly admire spenders' capacity to enjoy life in the present, while spenders secretly envy hoarders' ability to set limits, to budget and delay gratification. But typically they won't tell each other because they're afraid it confers license to continue in that style. In reality, positive statements help to make partners feel safe enough to give up the negative aspects of their behavior.
5 Talk about your goals for the future, short- and long-term.
6 Share your hopes and dreams.
7 Consider making a shared budget or a spending plan together by merging the hopes and the goals that have come up on your list more than once.
8 Set a time to have the next money talk. Aim for weekly conversations in the beginning, then monthly ones.—O.M.

TYPICALLY MEN WANT TO MERGE ALL THE COUPLE'S MONEY WHILE WOMEN WANT TO KEEP AT LEAST SOME MONEY SEPARATE.

the path to respect. However, power and control are not compatible with intimacy. Relationships succeed only when both partners are willing to display their vulnerabilities to each other. It's important for men to know that failing to share power cheats them of the intimacy and love they want.

ANOTHER IMPORTANT difference between men and women concerns their interests in merging their money. Typically, men want to merge all the couple's money—while maintaining primary decision-making power. Women want to keep at least some money separate.

The fight goes like this:

HE: "Why do you want separate money? You must not trust me. Are you planning to file for a divorce?"

SHE: "Why do you want to merge all of our money? It must be that you want to control me."

There may be truth in both positions. Still, experience has led me to see a very positive, and probably unconscious, longing in both views, and it has to do with the challenge of intimacy. Merging, getting connected

and staying connected, is more difficult for men. At the first sign of conflict, it's easy for them to withdraw.

I believe that men's desire to merge the family money is a loving expression of the desire for intimacy and connection. Perhaps it is even a safeguard against their withdrawing. I have come to see that women want separate money as a loving expression of their need for healthy autonomy. Their biggest challenge in relationships is not losing themselves; it's holding on to their own sense of self.

Neither his demand for merged money nor her desire for separate funds is a position taken up against the spouse—although that is how partners tend to see it. When couples understand this, their new perspective has the power to transform their entire relationship.

American culture, I believe, makes a big mistake in pressuring married couples to merge all their money. It is in fact unwise for couples to merge money right away. Since couples don't talk about money before they marry, you don't know if you're tying yourself to an overspender in debt or a worrier who could drive you crazy.

Couples can merge some of their common assets for joint expenses, savings and investing and keep the rest separate. That definitely averts some kinds of conflicts. Your partner doesn't get to comment on how you spend your money. I've always kept a portion of money apart because I knew I was an overspender and I didn't want to mess up the family finances or credit rating.

Alternatively, couples could merge some money and only the woman could have separate funds. Solutions do not have to be symmetrical to work well. They just have to appeal

to the deeper needs of both partners. The difficulty is in making clear to the other what your own needs are.

MONEY ISSUES ARE different from other problems in relationships. They're harder to talk about and harder to resolve because of our extensive cultural conditioning. The most important thing in couples communication is empathy, or putting yourself in your partner's place. It is almost always more important to be heard and understood than to have a partner agree with what you say

Spouses who start talking genuinely about what they like about each other's money style create an atmosphere of safety and nondefensiveness. Once such a way of talking about money is established and once couples understand the positive intent of the partner, they can then work out a solution to almost any problem, a solution that best fits their own unique needs.

OLIVIA MELLAN, a therapist specializing in women's issues, found her true calling when a friend noted that money was the last taboo, discussed even less than sex and childhood trauma. "I felt like someone had hit me with a thunderbolt," she recalls. After giving a 1982 workshop on the topic with her perceptive pal, men, women and money "took over half my work and my life," she says. Mellan is in private practice with the Washington Therapy Guild and resides in Washington D.C. Her latest book, *Overcoming Overspending* (Walker) has just been released in paperback; her next, on women's myths about money, will be published next year.

Father Love and Child Development: History and Current Evidence

Abstract

Six types of studies show that father love sometimes explains as much or more of the variation in specific child and adult outcomes as does mother love. Sometimes, however, only father love is statistically associated with specific aspects of offsprings' development and adjustment, after controlling for the influence of mother love. Recognition of these facts was clouded historically by the cultural construction of fatherhood and fathering in America.

Keywords

father love; paternal acceptance; parental acceptance-rejection theory

Ronald P. Rohner[1]

Center for the Study of Parental Acceptance and Rejection, School of Family Studies, University of Connecticut, Storrs, Connecticut

Research in every major ethnic group of America (Rohner, 1998b), in dozens of nations internationally, and with several hundred societies in two major cross-cultural surveys (Rohner 1975, 1986, 1998c; Rohner & Chaki-Sircar, 1988) suggests that children and adults everywhere—regardless of differences in race, ethnicity, gender, or culture—tend to respond in essentially the same way when they experience themselves to be loved or unloved by their parents. The overwhelming bulk of research dealing with parental acceptance and rejection concentrates on mothers' behavior, however. Until recently, the possible influence of father love has been largely ignored. Here, I concentrate on evidence

showing the influence of fathers' love-related behaviors—or simply, *father love*—in relation to the social, emotional, and cognitive development and functioning of children, adolescents, and adult offspring. Moreover, I focus primarily, but not exclusively, on families for which information is available about both fathers and mothers—or about youths' perceptions of both their fathers' and mothers' parenting. My principal objective is to identify evidence about the relative contribution to offspring development of father love vis-à-vis mother love.

I define father love in terms of paternal acceptance and rejection as construed in parental acceptance-rejection theory (Rohner, 1986, in press). Paternal

acceptance includes such feelings and behaviors (or children's perceptions of such feelings and behaviors) as paternal nurturance, warmth, affection, support, comfort, and concern. Paternal rejection, on the other hand, is defined as the real or perceived absence or withdrawal of these feelings and behaviors. Rejection includes such feelings as coldness, indifference, and hostility toward the child. Paternal rejection may be expressed behaviorally as a lack of affection toward the child, as physical or verbal aggression, or as neglect. Paternal rejection may also be experienced in the form of undifferentiated rejection; that is, there may be situations in which individuals feel that their fathers (or significant male

From *Current Directions in Psychological Science,* October 1998, pp. 157-161. © 1998 by Ronald P. Rohner and the American Psychological Society. Reprinted by permission of Blackwell Publishers.

caregivers) do not really care about, want, or love them, even though there may not be observable behavioral indicators showing that the fathers are neglecting, unaffectionate, or aggressive toward them. Mother love (maternal acceptance-rejection) is defined in the same way.

FATHERHOOD AND MOTHERHOOD ARE CULTURAL CONSTRUCTIONS

The widely held cultural construction of fatherhood in America—especially prior to the 1970s—has two strands. Historically, the first strand asserted that fathers are ineffective, often incompetent, and maybe even biologically unsuited to the job of child-rearing. (The maternal counterpoint to this is that women are genetically endowed for child care.) The second strand asserted that fathers' influence on child development is unimportant, or at the very most peripheral or indirect. (The maternal counterpoint here is that mother love and competent maternal care provide everything that children need for normal, healthy development.) Because researchers internalized these cultural beliefs as their own personal beliefs, fathers were essentially ignored by mainstream behavioral science until late in the 20th century. The 1970s through the 1990s, however, have seen a revolution in recognizing fathers and the influence of their love on child development. Three interrelated lines of influence I have discussed elsewhere (Rohner, 1998a) seem to account for this revolution. The net effect of these influences has been to draw attention to the fact that father love sometimes explains a unique, independent portion of the variation in specific child outcomes, over and above the portion explained by mother love. In fact, a few recent studies suggest that father love is the sole significant predictor of specific outcomes, after removing the influence of mother love.

STUDIES SHOWING THE INFLUENCE OF FATHER LOVE

Six types of studies (discussed at greater length in Rohner, 1998a) demonstrate a strong association between father love and aspects of offspring development.

Studies Looking Exclusively at Variations in the Influence of Father Love

Many of the studies looking exclusively at the influence of variations in father love deal with one of two topics: gender role development, especially of sons, and father involvement. Studies of gender role development emerged prominently in the 1940s and continued through the 1970s. Commonly, researchers assessed the masculinity of fathers and of sons, and then correlated the two sets of scores. Many psychologists were surprised at first to discover that no consistent results emerged from this research. But when they examined the quality of the father-son relationship, they found that if the relationship between masculine fathers and their sons was warm and loving, the boys were indeed more masculine. Later, however, researchers found that the masculinity of fathers per se did not seem to make much difference because "boys seemed to conform to the sex-role standards of their culture when their relationships with their fathers were warm, regardless of how 'masculine' the fathers were" (Lamb, 1997, p. 9).

Paternal involvement is the second domain in which there has been a substantial amount of research on the influence of variations in father love. Many studies have concluded that children with highly involved fathers, in relation to children with less involved fathers, tend to be more cognitively and socially competent, less inclined toward gender stereotyping, more empathic, psychologically better adjusted, and the like. But "caring for" children is not necessarily the same thing as "caring about" them. And a closer examination of these studies suggests that it was not the simple fact of paternal engagement (i.e., direct interaction with the child), availability, or responsibility for child care that was associated with these positive outcomes. Rather, it appears that the quality of the father-child relationship—especially of father love—makes the greatest difference (Lamb, 1997; Veneziano & Rohner, 1998).

Father Love Is as Important as Mother Love

The great majority of studies in this category deal with one or a combination of the following four issues among children, adolescents, and young adults: (a) personality and psychological adjustment problems, including issues of self-concept and self-esteem, emotional

stability, and aggression; (b) conduct problems, especially in school; (c) cognitive and academic performance issues; and (d) psychopathology. Recent studies employing multivariate analyses have allowed researchers to conclude that fathers' and mothers' behaviors are sometimes each associated significantly and uniquely with these outcomes. The work of Young, Miller, Norton, and Hill (1995) is one of these studies. These authors employed a national sample of 640 12- to 16-year-olds living in two-parent families. They found that perceived paternal love and caring was as predictive of sons' and daughters' life satisfaction—including their sense of well-being—as was maternal love and caring.

Father Love Predicts Specific Outcomes Better Than Mother Love

As complex statistical procedures have become more commonplace in the 1980s and 1990s, it has also become more common to discover that the influence of father love explains a unique, independent portion of the variation in specific child and adult outcomes, over and above the portion of variation explained by mother love. Studies drawing this conclusion tend to deal with one or more of the following four issues among children, adolescents, and young adults: (a) personality and psychological adjustment problems, (b) conduct problems, (c) delinquency, and (d) psychopathology. For example, evidence is mounting that fathers may be especially salient in the development of such forms of psychopathology as substance abuse (drug and alcohol use and abuse), depression and depressed emotion, and behavior problems, including conduct disorder and externalizing behaviors (including aggression toward people and animals, property destruction, deceitfulness, and theft) (Rohner, 1998c). Fathers are also being increasingly implicated in the etiology of borderline personality disorder (a pervasive pattern of emotional and behavioral instability, especially in interpersonal relationships and in self-image) and borderline personality organization (a less severe form of borderline personality disorder) (Fowler, 1990; Rohner & Brothers, in press).

Father love appears to be uniquely associated not just with behavioral and psychological problems, however, but also with health and well-being. Amato (1994), for example, found in a national sample that perceived closeness to fathers made a significant contribution—over and above the contribution made by perceived closeness to mothers—to adult sons' and daughters' happiness, life satisfaction, and low psychological distress (i.e., to overall psychological well-being).

Father Love Is the Sole Significant Predictor of Specific Outcomes

In the 1990s, a handful of studies using a variety of multivariate statistics have concluded that father love is the sole significant predictor of specific child outcomes, after removing the influences of mother love. Most of these studies have dealt with psychological and behavioral problems of adolescents. For example, Cole and McPherson (1993) concluded that father-child conflict but not mother-child conflict (in each case, after the influence of the other was statistically controlled) was positively associated with depressive symptoms in adolescents. Moreover, father-adolescent cohesion was positively associated with the absence of depressive symptoms in adolescents. These results are consistent with Barrera and Garrison-Jones's (1992) conclusion that adolescents' satisfaction with fathers' support was related to a lowered incidence of depressive symptoms, whereas satisfaction with mothers' support was not. Barnett, Marshall, and Pleck (1992), too, found that when measures of the quality of both mother-son and father-son relationships were entered simultaneously into a regression equation, only the father-son relationship was related significantly to adult sons' psychological distress (a summed measure of anxiety and depression).

Father Love Moderates the Influence of Mother Love

A small but growing number of studies have concluded that fathers' behavior moderates and is moderated by (i.e., interacts with) other influences within the family. Apparently, however, only one study so far has addressed the issue of whether mother love has different effects on specific child outcomes depending on the level of father love. This study, by Forehand and Nousiainen (1993), found that when mothers were low in acceptance, fathers' acceptance scores had no significant impact on youths' cognitive competence. But when mothers were high in acceptance, fathers' acceptance scores made a dramatic difference: Fathers with low acceptance scores tended to have children with poorer cognitive competence, whereas highly accepting fathers tended to have children with substantially better cognitive competence.

Paternal Versus Maternal Parenting Is Sometimes Associated With Different Outcomes for Sons, Daughters, or Both

Many of the studies in this category were published in the 1950s and 1960s, and even earlier. Many of them may be criticized on methodological and conceptual grounds. Nonetheless, evidence suggests that serious research questions should be raised in the future about the possibility that associations between love-related parenting and child outcomes may depend on the gender of the parent and of the child. Three different kinds of studies tend to be found in this category.

First, some research shows that one pattern of paternal love-related behavior and a different pattern of maternal love-related behavior may be associated with a single outcome in sons, daughters, or both. For example, Barber and Thomas (1986) found that daughters' self-esteem was best predicted by their mothers' general support (e.g., praise and approval) but by their fathers' physical affection. Sons' self-esteem, however, was best predicted by their mothers' companionship (e.g., shared activities) and by their fathers' sustained contact (e.g., picking up the boys for safety or for fun).

Second, other research in this category shows that a single pattern of paternal love-related behavior may be associated with one outcome for sons and a different outcome for daughters. For example, Jordan, Radin, and Epstein (1975) found that paternal nurturance was positively associated with boys' but not girls' performance on an IQ test. Finally, the third type of research in this category shows that the influence of a single pattern of paternal love-related behaviors may be more strongly associated with a given outcome for one gender of offspring than for the other. For example, Eisman (1981) reported that fathers' love and acceptance correlated more highly with daughters' than with sons' self-concept.

DISCUSSION

The data reported here are but a minuscule part of a larger body of work showing that father love is heavily implicated not only in children's and adults' psychological well-being and health, but also in an array of psychological and behavioral problems. This evidence punctuates the need to include fathers (and other significant males, when appropriate) as well as mothers in future research, and then to analyze separately the data for possible father and mother

effects. It is only by separating data in this way that behavioral scientists can discern when and under what conditions paternal and maternal factors have similar or different effects on specific outcomes for children. This recommendation explicitly contradicts a call sometimes seen in published research to merge data about fathers' and mothers' parenting behaviors.

Finally, it is important to note several problems and limitations in the existing research on father love. For example, even though it seems unmistakably clear that father love makes an important contribution to offsprings' development and psychological functioning, it is not at all clear what generative mechanisms produce these contributions. In particular, it is unclear why father love is sometimes more strongly associated with specific offspring outcomes than is mother love. And it is unclear why patterns of paternal versus maternal parenting may be associated with different outcomes for sons, daughters, or children of both genders. It remains for future research to inquire directly about these issues. Until then, we can know only that father love is often as influential as mother love—and sometimes more so.

Note

1. Address correspondence to Ronald P. Rohner, Center for the Study of Parental Acceptance and Rejection, School of Family Studies, University of Connecticut, Storrs, CT 06269–2058; e-mail: rohner@uconnvm.uconn.edu or http://vm.uconn.edu/~rohner.

References

Amato, P. R. (1994). Father-child relations, mother-child relations and offspring psychological well-being in adulthood. *Journal of Marriage and the Family, 56,* 1031–1042.

Barber, B. & Thomas, D. (1986). Dimensions of fathers' and mothers' supportive behavior: A case for physical affection. *Journal of Marriage and the Family, 48,* 783–794.

Barnett, R. C., Marshall, N. L., & Pleck, J. H. (1992). Adult son-parent relationships and the associations with sons' psychological distress. *Journal of Family Issues, 13,* 505–525.

Barrera, M., Jr., & Garrison-Jones, C. (1992). Family and peer social support as specific correlates of adolescent depressive symptoms. *Journal of Abnormal Child Psychology, 20,* 1–16.

Cole, D., & McPherson, A. E. (1993). Relation of family subsystems to adolescent depression: Implementing a new family assessment strategy. *Journal of Family Psychology, 7,* 119–133.

Eisman, E. M. (1981). Sex-role characteristics of the parent, parental acceptance of the child and child self-concept. (Doctoral dissertation, California School of Professional Psychology at Los Angeles, 1981). *Dissertation Abstracts International, 24,* 2062.

Forehand, R., & Nousiainen, S. (1993). Maternal and paternal parenting: Critical dimensions in adolescent functioning. *Journal of Family Psychology, 7,* 213–221.

Fowler, S. D. (1990). *Paternal effects on severity of borderline psychopathology.* Unpublished doctoral dissertation, University of Texas, Austin.

Jordan, B., Radin, N., & Epstein, A. (1975). Paternal behavior and intellectual functioning in preschool boys and girls. *Developmental Psychology, 11,* 407–408.

Lamb, M. E. (1997). Fathers and child development: An introductory overview and guide. In M. E. Lamb (Ed.), *The role of the father in child development* (pp. 1–18). New York: John Wiley & Sons.

Rohner, R. P. (1975). *They love me, they love me not: A worldwide study of the effects of parental acceptance and rejection.* New Haven, CT: HRAF Press.

Rohner, R. P. (1986). *The warmth dimension: Foundations of parental acceptance-rejection theory.* Newbury Park, CA: SAGE.

Rohner, R. P. (1998a). *The importance of father love: History and contemporary evidence.* Manuscript submitted for publication.

Rohner, R. P. (1998b). *Parental acceptance-rejection bibliography* [On-line]. Available: http://vm.unconn.edu/~rohner

Rohner, R. P. (1998c). *Worldwide mental health correlates of parental acceptance-rejection: Review of cross-cultural and intracultural evidence.* Manuscript submitted for publication.

Rohner, R. P. (in press). Acceptance and rejection. In D. Levinson, J. Ponzetti, & P. Jorgensen (Eds.), *Encyclopedia of human emotions.* New York: MacMillan.

Rohner, R. P., & Brothers, S. A. (in press). Perceived parental rejection, psychological maladjustment, and borderline personality disorder. *Journal of Emotional Abuse.*

Rohner, R. P., & Chaki-Sircar, M. (1988). *Women and children in a Bengali village.* Hanover, NH: University Press of New England.

Veneziano, R. A., & Rohner, R. P. (1998). Perceived paternal warmth, paternal involvement, and youths' psychological adjustment in a rural, biracial southern community. *Journal of Marriage and the Family, 60,* 335–343.

Young, M. H., Miller, B. E., Norton, M. C., & Hill, J. E. (1995). The effect of parental supportive behaviors on life satisfaction of adolescent offspring. *Journal of Marriage and the Family, 57,* 813–822.

Recommended Reading

Biller, H. B. (1993). *Fathers and families: Paternal factors in child development.* Westport, CT: Auburn House.

Booth, A., & Crouter, A. C. (Eds.). (1998). *Men in families: When do they get involved? What difference does it make?* Mahwah, NJ: Erlbaum.

Lamb, M. E. (Ed.). (1997). *The role of the father in child development.* New York: John Wiley & Sons.

Rohner, R. P. (1986). (See References)

Do Parents Really Matter?

Once, parents were given all the credit—and all the blame—for how their children turned out. Then researchers told us that heredity determines who we are. The latest take: parents can work with their children's innate tendencies to rear happy, healthy kids. It's a message many parents will find reassuring—but it may make others very nervous.

By Annie Murphy Paul

David Reiss, M.D., didn't want to believe it. The George Washington University psychiatrist had worked for more than 12 years on a study of adolescent development—just completed—and its conclusions were a surprise, to say the least. "I'm talking to you seven or eight years after the initial results came out, so I can sound very calm and collected now," says Reiss. "But I was shocked." This, even though other scientists had previously reached similar conclusions in many smaller-scale studies. "We knew about those results, but we didn't believe it," says Reiss, speaking of himself and one of his collaborators, E. Mavis Heatherington, Ph.D. "Now we've done the research ourselves, so . . ." He sighs. "We're not ever going to believe it, but we're going to have to act as if we do."

What Reiss and his colleagues discovered, in one of the longest and most thorough studies of child development ever attempted, was that parents appear to have relatively little effect on how children turn out, once genetic influences are accounted for. "The original objective was to look for environmental differences," says Reiss. "We didn't find many." Instead, it seems that genetic influences are largely responsible for how "adjusted" kids are: how well they do in school, how they get along with their peers, whether they engage in dangerous or delinquent behavior. "If you follow the study's implications through to the end, it's a radical revision of contemporary theories of child development," says Reiss. "I can't even describe what a paradigm shift it is."

The way heredity shapes who we are is less like one-way dictation and more like spirited rounds of call and response.

The only member of the research team who wasn't surprised by the results, Reiss recalls, was Robert Plomin, Ph.D., a researcher at the Institute of Psychiatry in London. Plomin is a behavioral geneticist, and he and others in his field have been saying for years what Reiss has just begun to accept: genes have a much greater influence on our personalities than previously thought, and parenting much less. The work of behavioral geneticists has been the focus of considerable controversy among psychologists, but it has been mostly ignored by parents, despite ample attention from the media. That may be because such coverage has rarely described just how genes are thought to wield their purported influence. Behavioral geneticists don't claim that genes are blueprints that depict every detail of our personality and behavior; rather, they propose that heredity reveals itself through complex interactions with the environment. Their theories are far more subtle, and more persuasive, than the simple idea of heredity as destiny. It is by participating in these very interactions, some scientists now say, that parents exert their own considerable influence—and they can learn to exert even more.

NATURE MEETS NURTURE

As behavioral geneticists understand it, the way heredity shapes who we are is less like one-way dictation and more like spirited rounds of call and response, with each

phrase spoken by heredity summoning an answer from the environment. Scientists' unwieldy name for this exchange is "evocative gene-environment correlations," so called because people's genetic makeup is thought to bring forth particular reactions from others, which in turn influence their personalities. A baby with a sunny disposition will receive more affection than one who is difficult; an attractive child will be smiled at more often than a homely one. And the qualities that prompt such responses from parents are likely to elicit more of the same from others, so that over time a self-image is created and confirmed in others' eyes.

Even as genes are calling forth particular reactions, they're also reaching out for particular kinds of experience. That's because each person's DNA codes for a certain type of nervous system: one that feels alarm at new situations, one that craves strong sensations, or one that is sluggish and slow to react. Given an array of opportunities, some researchers say, children will pick the ones that are most suited to their "genotype," or genetic endowment. As they grow older, they have more chances to choose—friends, interests, jobs, spouses—decisions that both reflect and define personality.

In order for genes and environment to interact in this way, they need to be in constant conversation, back and forth. Since parents usually raise the children to whom they have passed on their genes, that's rarely a problem: they are likely to share and perhaps appreciate the qualities of their offspring. And the environment they provide their children with may further support their natural abilities: highly literate parents might give birth to an equally verbal child, then raise her in a house full of books. Developmental psychologists call this fortunate match "goodness of fit." But problems may arise if nurture and nature aren't on speaking terms—if a child's environment doesn't permit or encourage expression of his natural tendencies. That may happen when children's abilities don't match their parents' expectations; when their genetically-influenced temperament clashes with that of their parents; or when their environment offers them few opportunities to express themselves constructively, as is often the case with children who grow up in severe poverty. Research has shown that a poor person-to-environment match can lead to decreased motivation, diminished mental health, and rebellious or antisocial behavior.

The dialogue between genes and environment becomes more complicated when a sibling adds another voice. Although siblings share an average of 50 percent of their genes, the half that is different—and the kaleidoscopic ways that genes can combine—leads their genotypes to ask different

questions and get different answers from what would seem to be the same environment. In fact, siblings create individual environments of their own by seeking out different experiences and by evoking different responses from parents, friends, and others. Like the proverbial blind men touching the leg, the trunk, or the tail of an elephant, they "see" different parts of the same animal. "Our studies show that parents do indeed treat their children differently, but that they are in large measure responding to differences that are already there," says Robert Plomin. "Family environment does have an effect on personality development, but not in the way we've always thought. It's the experiences that siblings *don't* share that matter, not the ones they do."

KIDS IN CHARGE?

One intriguing implication of behavioral genetic research is that children are in many ways driving their own development, through the choices they make, the reactions they elicit, even the friends they pick (see "The Power of Peers"). But parents are crucial collaborators in that process, and that means that their role in shaping their children may actually be larger than it first appears. *How* a parent responds to a child's genetically-influenced characteristics may make all the difference in how those traits are expressed, says David Reiss. In his formulation, the parent-child relationship acts as a sort of translator of genetic influence: the genotype provides the basic plot, but parenting gives it tone and inflection, accent and emphasis. He calls this conception of gene-environment correlation "the relationship code," and says that it returns to parents some of the influence his study would seem to give to genes. "Our data actually give the role of parents a real boost—but it's saying that the story doesn't necessarily start with the parent," says Reiss. "It starts with the kid, and then the parent picks up on it."

To Reiss, parents' role as interpreters of the language of heredity holds out an exciting possibility. "If you could intervene with parents and get them to respond differently to troublesome behavior, you might be able to offset much of the genetic influence" on those traits, he says. In other words, if genes become behavior by way of the environment, then changing the environment might change the expression of the genes. Although such intervention studies are years away from fruition, small-scale research and clinical experience are pointing the way toward working with children's hereditary strengths and weaknesses. Stanley Greenspan, M.D., a pediatric psychiatrist at George Washington Medical School and author of *The Growth*

THE **POWER**
OF **peers**

IT'S A WORLD OUT OF A FANCIFUL children's book: a place where parents and teachers don't matter, where the company of other kids is most meaningful, where nothing much would change if we left children in their homes and schools "but switched all the parents around." That doesn't describe an imagined never-never land, however, but the environment that every one of us grows up in, contends Judith Rich Harris. The maverick writer and theoretician believes that peers, not parents, determine our personalities, and her unorthodox views have made the very real world of psychology sit up and take notice.

Harris, who is unaffiliated with any university or institution, laid out her radical theory in a 1995 *Psychological Review* paper, which was later cited as one of the year's outstanding articles by the American Psychological Association. Like

behavioral geneticists, Harris believes that heredity is a force to be reckoned with. But she sees another powerful force at work: group socialization, or the shaping of one's character by one's peers.

Central to this theory is the idea that behavior is "context-specific": we act in specific ways in specific circumstances. "Children today live in two different worlds: home and the world outside the home," says Harris. "There is little overlap between these two worlds, and the rules for how to behave in them are quite different." Displays of emotion, for example, are often accepted by parents but discouraged by teachers or friends. Rewards and punishments are different too. At home, children may be scolded for their failures and praised for their successes; outside the home, they may be ridiculed when they make a mistake or ignored when they behave appropriately.

As children grow older and peer influence grows stronger, says Harris, they come to prefer the ways of peers over those of their parents. She like to use language as an example: the children of immigrants, she notes, will readily learn to speak the language of the new country without an accent.

They may continue to speak in their parents' tongue when at home, but over time the language of their peers will become their "native" language. Adopting the ways of their contemporaries makes sense, says Harris, because children will live among them, and not among older adults, for the greater part of their lives. "Parents are past, peers are future," she says.

It's evolutionarily adaptive, too. "Humans were designed to live not in nuclear families, but in larger groups," observes Harris. "The individuals who became our ancestors succeeded partly

of the Mind, is actively applying the discoveries of genetics to parenting. "Genes do create certain general tendencies, but parents can work with these by tailoring their actions to the nervous system of the child," says Greenspan. He believes that the responses children "naturally" elicit may not

----

The exact same temperament that might predispose a kid to become a criminal can also make for a hot test pilot.

----

be in their best interests—but that parents can consciously and deliberately give them the ones that are. "You have to pay attention to what you're doing intuitively, and make sure that is what the kids really need," he says.

A baby with a sluggish temperament, for example, won't respond as readily to his parents' advances as a child with a more active nervous system. Disappointed at their offsprings' lack of engagement, parents may respond with dwindling interest and attention. Left to his own devices, the baby may become even more withdrawn, failing to make crucial connections and to master developmental challenges. But if the parents resist their inclinations, and engage the baby with special enthusiasm, Greenspan has found that the child will change his own behavior in response. The same principle of working against the grain of a child's genotype applies to those who are especially active or oversensitive, suggests Greenspan, comparing the process to a right-handed baseball player who practices throwing with his left hand. "It feels funny at first, but gradually you build up strength in an area in which you would naturally be weak," he says.

Of course, honing a right-handed pitch is important, too. Parents can improve on their children's hereditary strengths by encouraging their tendency to seek out experiences in tune with their genes. "Parents should think of themselves as resource providers," says Plomin. "Expose the child to a lot of things, see what they like, what

they're good at, and go with that." By offering opportunities congenial to children's genetic constitutions, parents are in a sense improving their "goodness of fit" with the environment.

WILL YOUR KID GO TO YALE—OR TO JAIL?

For those traits that could easily become either assets or liabilities, parenting may be especially critical to the outcome. "The same temperament that can make for a criminal can also make for a hot test pilot or astronaut," says David Lykken, Ph.D., a behavioral geneticist at the University of Minnesota. "That kind of little boy—aggressive, fearless, impulsive—is hard to handle. It's easy for parents to give up and let him run wild, or turn up the heat and the punishment and thereby alienate him and lose all control. But properly handled, this can be the kid who grows up to break the sound barrier." Lykken believes that especially firm, conscientious, and responsive parents can make the difference—but not all behavioral geneticists agree. David Rowe, Ph.D., a University of Arizona psychologist and author of *The Limits of Family Influence,* claims that "much of the effort of 'superparents' may be wasted, if not because they had the ability to get along with the other members." The group continues to influence us in a number of ways: we identify ourselves with it, and change our behavior to conform to its norms. We define our group by contrasting it with other groups, and seek to distinguish our group by our actions and appearance. Within the group, we compare ourselves to others and jockey for higher status. We may receive labels from our peers, and strive to live up (or down) to them. Finally, we may be most lastingly affected by peers by being rejected by them. People who were rejected as children often report longterm self-esteem problems, poor social skills, and increased rates of psychopathology.

Our personalities become less flexible as we grow older, says Harris, so

that "the language and personality acquired in childhood and adolescent peer groups persist, with little modification, for the remainder of the life span." It's a startling conclusion, but Harris claims that her greatest challenge lies not in persuading people that peers matter, but in convincing them that parents don't. She calls the belief in parents' enduring importance "the nurture assumption," and her forthcoming book by that title will argue that it's simply a myth of modern culture. She doesn't deny that children need the care and protection of parents, and acknowledges that mothers and fathers can influence things like religious affiliation and choice of career. But, she maintains, "parental behaviors have no effect on the psychological characteristics their children will have as adults."

In fact, she says, "probably the most important way that parents can influence their children is by determining who their peers are. The immigrants who move their children to another country have provided them with a completely different set of peers. But a less dramatic shift—simply deciding which neighborhood to live in—can also make a difference." From one area to another, she notes, there are substantial variations in the rates of delinquency, truancy, and teen pregnancy—problems parents can try to avoid by surrounding their offspring with suitable friends. Beyond that, however, children will make their own choices. "It's pretty easy to control the social life of a three-year-old," says Harris. "But once the kids are past age 10 or 12, all bets are off."

—A.M.P.

counter-productive." And as for exposing children to a variety of experiences, Rowe thinks that this can give genetically talented children the chance they need, "but not many children have that much potential. This may not be so in Lake Wobegon [where every child is "above average"], but it is true in the rest of the world."

But with an optimism worthy of Garrison Keillor, advocates of parental influence insist that genes aren't the end of the story "The old idea is that you tried to live up to a potential that was set by genes," says Greenspan. "The new idea is that environment helps create potential." His view is supported by recent research that suggests a baby is born with only basic neural "wir-

ing" in place, wiring whose connections are then elaborated by experience. Both sides will have to await the next chapter of genetic research, which may reveal even more complicated interactions between the worlds within and without. In the long-running debate between genes and the environment, neither one has yet had the last word.

FAMILY MATTERS

THE NEW BUZZ IN PSYCHOLOGY IS THAT PEERS ARE MORE IMPORTANT IN SHAPING A CHILD'S PERSONALITY THAN PARENTS ARE. BUT A 13-YEAR STUDY IN DOMINICA, OF ALL PLACES, SAYS HOME LIFE IS GROUND ZERO FOR MENTAL HEALTH

BY MEREDITH F. SMALL

LOPING THROUGH THE VILLAGE OF BWA Mawego, on the Caribbean island of Dominica, Mark Flinn looks and acts like a slimmer, bespectacled Al Gore stumping on the campaign trail. He stops at each house to chat. He shakes hands, touches shoulders. He asks parents about their children in lilting Creole and talks of his own three young boys back home. At the University of Missouri, where Flinn teaches anthropology, he is an admittedly aloof and distant colleague. But here in Bwa Mawego, everyone knows everything about everybody—"If you talk about someone and you don't see them soon," one villager says, "they are either in jail or in the cemetery"—and that suits Flinn just fine. In fact, his research depends on it. As Flinn makes his way up the crest of a ravine on a winding dirt road, he runs into two boys, aged 10 and 7, on their way to school. The boys have on the requisite brown shorts and pale yellow shirts and carry book bags. "Have time to spit?" Flinn asks.

Flinn gives each boy a stick of Wrigley's spearmint gum, and they chew and spit into plastic cups. Next, an elderly matriarch named Evelyn comes up the road and lends a hand. Moving like a veteran lab assistant, she takes a plastic pipette, deftly sucks up five milliliters of saliva from one of the boys' cups, and transfers the saliva to a labeled tube. Finally, Flinn turns to the boys and asks them how things are at home. "When did you get up? Did anybody fall this morning? Did you sleep at your grandmother's or at home?"

The whole sequence, described in that way, sounds faintly absurd. Yet every action here has a reasonable purpose, and Flinn's lines are hardly non sequiturs. He is studying the relationship between stress and health in children, and two of the best ways to gauge stress are by asking personal questions and by measuring a hormone called cortisol, found in saliva. Since 1988, Flinn has collected more than 25,000 saliva samples from 287 children in this village—an average of 96 samples per child. He has tracked the children's growth and measured their immunoglobulin levels to see if their immune systems are healthy. He has checked their health records and sent out an as-

sistant to see who's sick. Perhaps most important, he has watched, listened, and asked questions. The result is a year-by-year, day-by-day, and sometimes even hour-by-hour glimpse of these children's lives. It's also a compelling rebuttal to one of the most widely publicized new theories in developmental psychology.

According to that theory, propounded by psychologist Judith Harris in her controversial 1998 book *The Nurture Assumption,* parents have relatively little power to shape a child's character. Studies of identical twins raised apart since birth have proved "beyond a shadow of a doubt that heredity is responsible for a sizable portion of the variations if people's personalities." Harris writes. At the same time, she points to a number of studies that seemed to suggest that the rest of a child's personality is shaped more by peers than by parents. How else—to take one example—could the children of non-English-speaking immigrants speak perfect English?

After generations of child-centered parenting books, Harris's argument immediately captured the media spotlight, perhaps mostly because it lets parents off the hook. If *The Nurture Assumption* is right, parents can all relax, put their kids in day care, and stop worrying that a little scolding will damage them for life. As an article in *The New Yorker* put it: "In some key sense, parents don't much matter."

Flinn's work makes an altogether different point—one as unfashionable as it is reasonable. His thousands of data points can be grouped into any number of constellations, but one pattern shines through all the others: Families matter more than anything else in a child's life. When a family has problems, it sends stress hormones coursing through a child's system. When family members get along, or have numerous relatives to call on, they can shelter a child from the worst social upheavals in the outside world. Emotionally and physiologically, family life is ground zero for a child's health.

BWA MAWEGO IS THE PERFECT SETTING for such research. (For the sake of privacy, the names of the village and all villagers have been changed.) Life is lived in the open here, making it far easier to meet people and follow them around, and many incidental sources of stress are naturally filtered out. There is no traffic, no rat race, no threat of war. The forest is fragrant with bay leaf bushes, the winding paths littered with ripe mangoes, the houses clustered in picturesque hamlets overlooking the sea. Of course, poverty, poor roads, and exposure to the elements take their own toll, but local people—some 700 of them, all of mixed African, Carib, and European descent—are unlikely to blame their stress on their surroundings.

Take Kristen, a 4-year-old in town. Every morning she wakes up to a billion-dollar view: Her house is built on stilts, on a volcanic cliff overlooking the Atlantic. In the front yard, clean laundry hangs on the trees that dot the hard-packed mud, chickens run about, and a soft Caribbean breeze wafts the smell of roasting coffee beans across the porch. With her large brown eyes, sweet smile, and quiet manner, Kristen is a child anyone would want to hug, and lots of people do—her mother, grandparents, and a multitude of relatives all live within walking distance.

Yet Kristen's life has its share of stress. Before she was born, her mother, Julianne, was single and going to high school in the city. When Julianne became pregnant, she had to move back home and hasn't worked since. Although Robbie, a nice guy and an old friend of Julianne's, has since become a kind of stepfather to Kristen, Julianne still worries about the opportunities she missed by not getting an education. In Bwa Mawego, as in most places, life can be tough for a single mother. And today Kristen has a cold.

Flinn sees no coincidence there. "In the village, illness among children increases more than twofold following significant stress," he says. "About 30 percent of the children in the village have the current cold, even though most of them have been exposed to the pathogen. So why are only certain ones sick? In the West we think it is mostly contact—send your child to preschool and expect them to get sick. But I am convinced that resistance is more important than contact frequency."

The reason is as complex biologically as it is emotionally. When a person is in trouble, Flinn explains, the brain automatically sends signals to the sympathetic nervous system, initiating a "fight or flight" response. First adrenaline and then cortisol are secreted by the adrenal glands, revving up the body and the sustaining the energy flow to different systems. The lungs pump faster and the heart starts to race; blood pressure rises, charging up the muscles and sharpening the mind; the stomach gets jumpy and the rush of endorphins numbs the body. At the same time, the appetite, libido, and immune system shut down, and the energy they would normally consume is diverted to muscles that will help the body fight the immediate threat.

The payoff for Flinn's 13-year study is a startlingly intimate view of childhood and its discontents

---

This is all well and good—unless the perceived threat persists. In that case, adrenaline washes out of the body quickly, but cortisol may linger for days, weeks, or even years, keeping the immune system and other important functions depressed. Children are especially vulnerable to stress. Their bodies are "nothing other than a long-term building project," says Robert Sapolsky, a stress researcher at Stanford University. Yet chronic stress is "constantly telling them, 'Don't fix stuff now, do it tomorrow, do it tomorrow.'" In the long term, too much cortisol can slow down a child's growth, brain development, and sexual maturation. In the short term, it can make a child prone to upper-respiratory infections and diarrhea, diseases that are often fatal at that age.

Stress can make you sick.

THANKS TO CORTISOL, MEASURING stress is as easy as a lab test or two. But only patient, detailed, long-term work like Flinn's can untangle its myriad causes. Hormone levels differ from child to child, Flinn says, and they fluctuate naturally over the course of a day. "The old dogma was that if you got a sample once a day, collected between 8 to 10 a.m., that was enough. But I've found that controlling for time of day is not enough. If you have a tough kid who is habituated to the mundane, giving a saliva sample in a lab would be a bore. You need to know what happened to this kid the day before: Is he burned out? What are his reserves? What's the context?"

Taking repeated measurements, as Flinn does, is expensive, complicated, and time-consuming. But the payoff is a startlingly intimate view of childhood and its discontents. One summer, for instance, Flinn took samples from a group of cousins, aged 3 to 8, who were playing house. Valerie and Kathy decided to be the parents, and they made Jane the child—a role of lowly status. Jane wasn't happy being the child. Worse, she felt betrayed: Valerie was *her* best friend. Why had she sided with Kathy? So Jane organized the other children into a game of jump rope, ruining Valerie and Kathy's plans.

A ruckus ensued. Kathy, still playing parent, told Jane she was being disobedient and threatened to beat her; Jane and her jump-rope partner swung the rope and hit Kathy in the face by mistake. Soon the children were yelling and their mothers were running over and accusations were flying. Kathy even threw a rock in Jane's direction as they parted.

If children's personalities are largely shaped by their peers, this should have been a traumatic event. Harris cites an informal study by sociologist Anne-Marie Ambert, of York University in Ontario, in which 37 percent of the students in a class blamed their most depressing experience on peers, while only 9 percent blamed it on parents. As evidence of peer influence, she also notes that siblings grow up to be very different adults; that adopted children are more like their biological parents than their adopted parents in terms of such traits as criminality; and that adolescents from poor neighborhoods are more likely to be delinquents that adolescents from middle-class neighborhoods, whereas being from a broken home as no effect on delinquency. Troubles with peers, Harris concludes, have a much deeper effect on children than do troubles at home.

Flinn's work shows just the opposite. Soon after Jane, Kathy, and Valerie's fight, he collected saliva from each of the participants. None of them had high levels of cortisol. "None," he repeats. "And this is typical of mild peer conflicts." Yet several weeks later, when Jane returned home late from a shopping errand, her saliva told a different story. This time it was her real mother, rather than Kathy, who did the scolding, and though Jane quietly went about her schoolwork afterward, her cortisol rose 60 percent above normal.

Flinn has seen the same pattern time and again. He has taken cortisol measurements from children engaged in 30 different types of activities—from "family fight" to "fight with peer"—and they consistently show that families cause more stress than peers do. Only major fights with friends elevate cortisol levels as much as family troubles do.

FLINN'S WORK GETS AT A FUNDAMENTAL truth about children, one that distinguishes them from the offspring of almost any other species. Most mammals are weaned within days or weeks of their birth. But human infants have to nurse for months, and they need a year just to learn how to walk. Their parents do more than usher them into the world; they feed, clothe, shelter, and protect them for a good portion of their lives.

"Humans have the luxury of extended families who can care for these mental larvae," Flinn says. "And because of that protection, children can afford to have a brain that is in the process of growing." At the same time, he adds, children are designed to be exquisitely attuned to their caregivers: "There is nothing more important to a child than figuring out what makes those close to them happy, and what makes them sad."

Contrary to the studies that Harris cites, Flinn has found that children who live with both biological parents clearly do best. They have lower average cortisol levels, weigh more, and grow more steadily than those living with stepparents or single parents with no support from kin. Flinn has also found that boys from households without fathers (though not girls) have cortisol levels that are *too* low in infancy and grow slower than boys with fathers at home. Once again, parents do matter; their impact is sometimes just too deep to notice.

We expect our children to be happy-go-lucky and resilient, but Flinn has found that they aren't as adaptable as we think. In Bwa Mawego, for instance, Aretha and Arnie Belle have five children, three of them still at home. But Arnie fools around, and so Aretha left him in the fall of 1990 and stayed with her sister in Martinique. During Aretha's absence, her children's cortisol levels shot up and did not come down until she came home a year later. It seems the children never adapted to living in a single-parent home.

Children with such chronically high cortisol levels can suffer permanent damage. In Romania, for instance, orphans raised under the dictatorship of Nicolae Cesusesscu were often so completely neglected—aside from perfunctory feedings and diaper changings—that they became withdrawn and temperamental, prone to rocking in place and staring blankly at visitors. Psychologist Elinor Ames, of Simon Fraser University in British Columbia, studied two groups of orphans. Those in the first group were adopted by American families by the age of 4 months; the second group spent eight months or more in an orphanage. Three years after adoption, the children in the first group had caught up to their peers in terms of size and maturity. But many of those who spent the longest time in the orphanage still suffered from depression and withdrawal.

SOME STUDIES SUGGEST that stress can make children develop subtle asymmetries in their bodies. To check for such problems, Mark Flinn and his graduate student David Leone set up in front of the local school and use calipers to measure students. After the measuring, each child gets a little money to bring home and a lollipop from Dave, the "Poppie Man."

Data gathered on 238 children over the past four field seasons have shown that children who live with a stepfather—a situation often rife with stress—weigh less than others but are surprisingly more symmetrical. There seems to be no relationship, so far, between stress and growth asymmetry in these children.

ONE SUNNY MORNING IN JANUARY, A chubby little girl named Maryann, from the apartment downstairs, toddles up to Flinn's apartment and crawls onto his sofa. Maryann has on a bright pink dress and her hair is pleated into cornrows topped with plastic bows, but she isn't feeling quite so sunny. She has been running a fever and coughing all night, her grandmother explains, as several adults jump up with a tissue to wipe the girl's runny nose.

"She's had this cold for a few days," Flinn guesses. But unlike so many illnesses he has seen these past 13 years, this one probably wasn't exacerbated by stress. Day and night, Maryann is surrounded by loving family members, he says. "It seems like she's related to everyone in town." Such extended families, in turn, allow for much more flexibility in child care. In Bwa Mawego, 36 percent of households with children changed composition at least once between 1990 and 1995—a statistic not unusual for the Caribbean; over the same period about a third of the children lived in more than one household. Fathers often spend the late summer and fall working on farms in Canada; mothers work away from the village at resorts; children go to the city to live with their grandparents. But even when children change houses, many of them are still with relatives who know all about them—and they are demonstrably healthier for it. Children with many kin connections, Flinn has found, are both

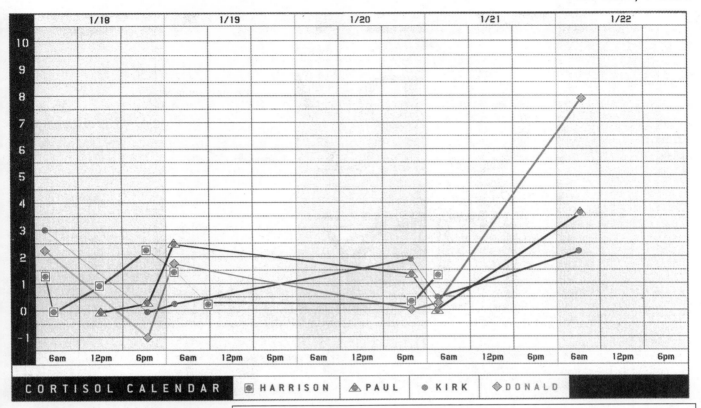

CORTISOL CALENDAR   ◉ HARRISON   △ PAUL   ◉ KIRK   ◇ DONALD

taller and heavier for their age than children with few relatives.

There may be an underlying lesson here for Dominica's more industrialized neighbors: Although nuclear families are the bedrock of Western societies, they're also prone to rifts and tremors—and children tend to fall through the cracks. In that sense, Harris may be partly right, and her differences with Flinn are partly a function of the different cultures they study. In the United States, families are an infant's first peer group, but children soon grow out of them. Without cousins, grandparents, and other relatives nearby to fill out their lives, they have to find their role models on the playground. In Bwa Mawego, by contrast, families tend to be fluid, amorphous entities, with kin networks extensive enough to guide and support children well past adolescence.

Maryann probably caught her cold from her father, a taxi driver. But with

THIS WEEK, THE CABOT FAMILY IS A LIVING experiment in the physiology of stress. Their middle child, 6-year-old Harrison, was born with one leg shorter than the other—a handicap so severe that he can't walk to school. Now, after working and saving for many years, Harrison's father, John, is taking him to Shriner's Hospital in Tampa Bay, Florida, for an operation. Afterward, Harrison must undergo four months of intense physical therapy before he and John can return home. Meanwhile, Harrison's mother, Joyce, will have to care for his three brothers, Kirk, Paul, and Donald, as well as the new baby Louise. To see how the family is coping, Mark Flinn measures the boys' cortisol several times a day before and after the departure and talks to them about how they feel. Although the brothers act as if Harrison's trip is no big deal, their cortisol levels (adjusted according to their natural daily fluctuations) tell a different story. In the chart above, the mean cortisol level for the village is zero. Anything above that indicates unusual stress. Over the nine years that he has been following the Cabots, Flinn has found them to be relatively stable, loving, and relaxed—"just a real happy family"—with a mean cortisol level of −0.29. Yet in the week before Harrison's departure their mean level rose to 1.32, and on the morning after Harrison left, 4-year-old Donald's cortisol rose nearly eight standard deviations above the mean. "That's pretty darn dramatic," Flinn says. "You might see that only once every 10,000 cases. Obviously, their brains are kind of working to see how they are going to deal with the new situation."—*M.F.S.*

everyone in her family keeping close watch, Flinn knows that she will be fine soon. Money may be scarce here on Bwa Mawego, and health care may not be up to Western standards. But when it comes to avoiding stress, a happy family is a child's greatest asset—greater even than nice friends and billion-dollar view, and a house by the sea in a small slice of paradise.

Unit 4

Unit Selections

Key Points to Consider

❖ How does an abusive relationship develop? What, if anything, can be done to prevent it? How can we help someone involved in such a relationship?

❖ If you felt your sexual relationship was troubled, how would you act? Would you discuss it with your partner? Would you hope that it would correct itself without your doing anything?

❖ How would you react if you learned that your spouse or partner had been unfaithful? Under what circumstances would you consider extrarelational sex?

❖ What is the best way to work out the competing demands of work and family? Assuming that there is an option, discuss whether or not both partners should work outside the home if there are small children in the home. What are your expectations regarding children's attitudes toward their parents' working?

❖ Discuss how the breakup of a relationship or a divorce affects the people involved.

❖ What is your responsibility to the members of your family? What is their responsibility to you? What would you give up to care for your parents? What would you expect your children to give up for you? What is the relationship among loss, grief, and care?

 **Links** ## www.dushkin.com/online/

These sites are annotated on pages 4 and 5.

Stress is life and life is stress. Sometimes stress in families gives new meaning to this statement. When a crisis occurs in families, many processes occur simultaneously as families and their members cope with the stressor and its effects. The experience of a crisis often leads to conflict and reduces the family members' ability to act as resources for each other. Indeed, a stressor can overwhelm the family system, and family members may be among the least effective people in coping with each other's responses to a crisis.

Family crisis comes in many forms; it can be drawn out or the crisis event can be clearly defined. The source of stress can be outside or inside the family, or it can be a combination of both. It can directly involve all family members or as few as one, but the effects will ripple through the family, affecting all of its members to one degree or another.

In this unit, we consider a wide variety of crises. Family violence and chaos are the initial focus. "Anatomy of a Violent Relationship" identifies patterns of abuse, two types of abusive men, and reasons why women stay in abusive relationships. The next article in this subsection specifically focuses on children. "Resilience in Development" documents characteristics of children who show amazing ability to recover and adjust, even in highly dysfunctional families.

The next subsection deals with problems in sexuality and sexual relationships. A good sex life is important to the life of a relationship, yet the underlying meaning attributed to it makes it difficult to discuss. In "Sex & Marriage," ways in which a couple can improve their sex life are addressed. Taking another view of sexuality in a committed marriage, an interview with Hara Estroff Marano, in "Shattered Vows," presents what she has learned about infidelity via her therapy practice and research.

The subsection that follows looks at the work/family connection, with interesting results. "The Politics of Fatigue: The Gender War Has Been Replaced by the Exhaustion of Trying to Do It All" addresses gender differences in the workplace and the impact on family life, as well as the overwhelming nature of the struggle to balance work and home. The view of children of their working parents is presented in "Do Working Parents Make the Grade?" The changing role of fathers in the everyday life of the family is addressed in the final article, "Balancing Work and Family."

Divorce and remarriage are the subjects of the next two subsections. In the first article in the first subsection, Peter Kramer asks the question, "Should *You* Leave?" or should you stay in a difficult relationship? Then Benedict Carey, in "Is Divorce Too Easy?" says that women are especially paying the price of easy divorce, which has led a coalition of

feminists and conservatives to want to change divorce laws in order to make breaking up more difficult to do. In the same vein, Aimee Howd in "Smart Plan to Save Marriages" describes a program that links church and community in an attempt to help more couples follow through on their marriage vows. Stresses faced by children of divorce are the focus of "The Children of Divorce." The other side of divorce—remarriage—is the focus of the next two articles. "Divorced? Don't Even Think of Remarrying Until You Read This" provides insights on what should be dealt with before one remarries, while "When Strangers Become Family" addresses issues that arise when stepfamilies are formed.

The nature of stress resulting from caring for others in the family is the subject of the final subsection. "Elder Care" presents a variety of methods by which family members can provide aid to an elderly family member. Then Tanya Fitzpatrick explains that men face unique bereavement issues and her article "Bereavement Events Among Elderly Men: The Effects of Stress and Health" details the character of these issues. "Failing to Discuss Dying Adds to Pain of Patient and Family," the final article in this subsection, presents a more personal journey through death and grief for a dying man and his daughter.

ANATOMY OF A
Violent
RELATIONSHIP

By Neil S. Jacobson, Ph.D., and John M. Gottman, Ph.D.

Each year at least 1.6 million
U.S. women are beaten by their husbands

Yet we know surprisingly little about why so many men erupt into violence, and why they feel such a need to control their women with brutal behavior.

Here, two leading marriage researchers plunge into the red-hot core of domestic abuse—observing violent couples in the heat of conflict—and surface with some startling answers.

Don was having a miserable day. There were rumors of layoffs at work, and his supervisor had been on his case for coming in late. Not only was he sick of not getting credit for doing his work well, he was sure he was about to get caught in some kind of vise he could not control. Now Don was test-driving the car he had asked his wife, Martha, to pick up from the garage. As he listened to his car's motor, he knew instantly that she had been hoodwinked. That damn rattle was still there when he drove up hills! By the time he pulled into their driveway, he was so mad that he almost hit Martha's car.

"What is it with you?" Don railed as he walked into the house. "Couldn't you tell that the damn car still wasn't running right?"

Martha, who was cooking dinner, responded calmly. "Is something wrong with the car? It sounded fine to me."

"Couldn't you tell you'd been had by the garage mechanics? Are you really that stupid?" he continued.

Martha started defending herself. "Wait a minute. I may know nothing about cars, but I resent being called 'stupid.'"

From *Psychology Today*, March/April 1998, pp. 60–65, 81, 84. Excerpted from *When Men Batter Women: New Insights into Ending Abusive Relationships*. Reprinted with the permission of Simon & Schuster. © 1998 by Neil Jacobson and John Gottman.

Don continued railing against the mechanics and against Martha for not standing up to them. He was beginning to see red, and he warned her to shut up.

But Martha didn't shut up. "If you're such a big man, why didn't you stand up to the mechanics the last time they gypped you?"

Don punched Martha in the face—hard. It was not the first punch of their marriage. But she deserved it, he told himself as he continued to hit her and yell at her. All he had wanted, he said, was a little empathy about his problems—and here she was siding with the enemy. Only a small part of him, a dim whisper in his brain, wanted to beg her forgiveness, and by the next day he would manage to squelch even that dim light of remorse.

How does a marital argument like this, one that seems to start out in near-ordinary frustration, escalate so quickly into violence? This question had come up time and again in our work as creators of couples-therapy techniques and in our two decades as social scientists studying marriage. We knew that the existing studies of the dynamics of battering didn't provide

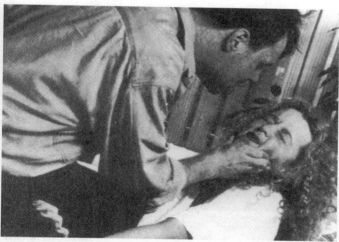

Esbin-Anderson/The Image Work

adequate answers, because they relied on after-the-fact reports by batterers and their victims, reports which are often biased and easily distorted. Particularly with battering, abundant psychological research shows that people are simply not reliable observers of their own or their intimate partner's behavior. So we decided to do something that no one had ever done before—directly observe the arguments of violent couples ourselves.

Using a simple public service announcement asking for couples experiencing marital conflict, we were able to obtain a sample of 63 battering couples, as well as a control group of couples who were equally dissatisfied with their marriage but had no history of violence. All these volunteers agreed to come into the laboratory, have electrodes hooked up to their bodies to record heart rate

and other vital signs, and be videotaped in the midst of arguments. (We also provided important safeguards, including exit interviews to ensure the woman's safety, and referrals to battered women's shelters.)

As you'll see, in the eight years of this study we made a number of myth-shattering discoveries:

- Batterers share a common profile: they are unpredictable, unable to be influenced by their wives, and impossible to prevent from battering once an argument has begun.
- Battered women are neither passive nor submissive; sometimes they are as angry as the batterers. But women almost never batter men.
- Batterers can be classified into two distinct types, men whose temper slowly simmers until it suddenly erupts into violence, and those who strike out immediately. This difference has important implications for women leaving abusive relationships.
- Emotional abuse plays a vital role in battering, undermining a woman's confidence.
- Domestic violence can decrease on its own—but it almost never stops.
- Battered women do leave at high rates, despite the increased danger they face when leaving the relationship.

Battering's Beginnings

Battering is physical aggression with a purpose: to control, intimidate, and subjugate another human being. It is always accompanied by emotional abuse, often involves injury, and virtually always causes fear in the battered woman. In our study, battering couples had at least two episodes of kicking or hitting with a fist, or at least one incident of potentially lethal violence, such as strangling.

Can women ever be batterers? In our study, we found that some battered women defend themselves, and hit or push as often as their husbands do. Some people claim that there is a huge underground movement of battered husbands. However, statistics on violent women do not take into account the impact and function of the violence. According to research conducted by Dina Vivian, Ph.D., at the State University of New York at Stonybrook, women are much more likely to be injured and in need of medical care than men, and much more likely to be killed by their husbands than the reverse. Women are the ones who are beaten up. These injuries help to sustain the fear, which is the force that provides battering with its power.

What about couples who periodically have arguments that escalate into pushing and shoving, but not beyond? We discovered large numbers of these couples, and we found that the husbands almost never become batterers.

While it is important to know about this low-level violence, we were concerned with the dynamics of severely violent couples.

Arguments under The Microscope

Through our research, we were able to reconstruct hundreds of violent arguments. Although we knew we would not directly observe violence between our subjects, we could observe their nonviolent arguments in the laboratory, ask them about these encounters, then judge their accounts of violent arguments by the accuracy of these reports.

When we put violent arguments under a microscope this way, we discovered a number of familiar themes. One of the most startling was our inability to predict when batterers would cross over into violence. While emotional abuse often preceded physical abuse, it was such a common occurrence in the relationship that it did not serve as an accurate warning sign. Further, there was no way for the battered woman to control when emotional abuse would turn into physical abuse. Martha could have shut up when Don told her to. But would this have stopped Don from hitting her? We have discovered that once an episode starts, there is nothing that the woman can do to affect its course.

Despite this inability, the women in our study did not become passive or submissive. Even when the batterers reacted to everyday requests with emotional abuse, the women typically responded calmly and assertively. We found that they wanted to inject as much normalcy into their lives as possible, and they didn't want to give up on their dream of the family life that they wanted.

However, in all the videotapes we made, never did we hear a batterer say anything like, "That's a good point," or "I never thought of that,"—comments that most married men (and women) say all the time during an argument. Instead, we observed that batterers became more aggressive when their wives asserted themselves. When Martha challenged him, we saw that Don responded violently in an attempt to maintain his dominance, no matter what the costs.

Another way that batterer's arguments diverged from those of nonviolent couples—perhaps the key difference—is that nonviolent couples have what we call "a withdrawal ritual," where at some point the escalation process stops or reverses itself. Some couples take breaks, other couples compromise, still others do both. In battering couples, the women are typically quite willing to stop at a point where they start to sense danger, but once the husbands are "activated," violence follows. Although the violence is unpredictable, we were able to identify certain warning signs. When belligerence and contempt during an argument were combined with attempts to squelch, control, or dominate a wife's behavior, that was a sign that a batterer was close to crossing the line. Don's contemptuous way of asking Martha whether she was "really that stupid," and his attempt to dominate her by telling her to shut up, demonstrate a classic prelude to battering.

Surprisingly, both in the lab and at home, battered women expressed as much belligerence and contempt as their husbands did. Like most people, battered women get angry when they are insulted and degraded. We saw much effort on the part of the women to contain their anger, but it tended to leak out anyway. Nevertheless, their initial responses—like Martha's retort to Don about not standing up to the mechanics—could hardly be considered provocations to violence.

The Slow Burn: "Pit Bulls"

Men like Don metabolize anger in a kind of slow burn: it gradually increases but never lets up. We call them "Pit Bulls" because they grow more and more aggressive until they finally attack. These men, we have found, constitute about 80 percent of batterers.

Pit Bulls have unrelenting contempt for women, and yet are extremely dependent on them. This creates a unique dynamic in their behavior. In many unhappy marriages, when one partner (usually the woman) requests change, the other one (usually the man) resists change, and eventually the woman's requests become demands, and the man's avoidance becomes withdrawal. But Pit Bulls often both demand and withdraw. We can see this in the incessant demands that Don made of Martha. Everything she did (including getting the car fixed) was wrong because nothing she did was quite enough for Don. Martha had to watch every move she made, give up her friends and family, account for all of her time, avoid Don's jealousy, and try to satisfy what he called his "simple need for a little empathy." Yet even as she walked on eggshells, she was attacked for being a "stupid bitch." Don blamed Martha for his own neediness, and punished her for it almost every day they were together.

Through this scrutiny and these constant demands, Pit Bulls establish control. Control is important to these men because they genuinely feel that they will be abandoned if they do not maintain constant vigilance over their wives. One particularly sinister form of control they use is known as "gaslighting." This technique—which gets its name from the film *Gaslight,* in which Charles Boyer convinces Ingrid Bergman she is going insane—involves a systematic denial of the wife's experience of reality. For example, when one of our subjects slapped his wife in front of a neighbor, he denied that he had done it, telling her that this kind of behavior was inconsistent with his personality, and that her accusations of abuse came from

Can Batterers JUST STOP?

"Why do women stay?" That question haunts anybody who has observed domestic violence. But a far more practical question is, How can the men be stopped? Maryland psychologist Steven Stosny, Ph.D., has developed a remarkable and effective treatment program for battering men. Even a year after treatment, an astonishing 86 percent have ended the physical abuse, and 73 percent have stopped the verbal and emotional abuse. The national dropout rate for battering programs is one out of two; Stosny's is only one out of four.

Treating batterers is something that most therapists shy away from. How did you get into it?

I became interested in spouse and child abuse at the age of two. I grew up in a violent family, where we had police and ambulances coming to the door. It took a while for me to get up the courage to get into this field, and when I started a group with severe batterers, I wanted to learn how they got that way, to learn how to prevent abuse. I was surprised when they stopped being abusive.

So how do you approach batterers?

Our program is based on the idea that most batterers can't sustain attachment, and because of this, they become flooded with feelings of guilt, shame, and abandonment, which they regulate with aggression. We teach them a five-step technique called HEALS. First, we start with the concept of *Heal*. Our clients learn that blame is powerless, but compassion is true power, and has the ability to heal. Next, you *Explain* to yourself the core hurt that anger is masking: feeling unimportant, disregarded, guilty, devalued, rejected, powerless, and unlovable. All abusive behavior is motivated by these core hurts. Then you *Apply* self-compassion. Let's say your wife calls you a brainless twit, and you feel she doesn't love you. You want to punish her for reminding you that you're unlovable. We teach men to replace this core feeling with self-compassion. "She feels unloving, but she still loves me. My instinct might be to call her a filthy slut, but she said what she said because she's hurt and feeling bad." Then you move into a feeling of *Love*, for yourself and your wife. And finally, you solve the problem by presenting your true position without blaming or attacking the other person: you say, "I care about you, but I have a problem with your calling me a brainless twit." You are healing your core hurt through love rather than anger.

So you're saying the batterer is really trying to heal his hurt core, and he can do it

with compassion instead of abuse. Still, how can someone used to physical aggression learn to be so rational?

We call it teaching Mr. Hyde to remember what Dr. Jekyll learned. These men have to learn emotional regulation and the rewards of change based on compassion. We ask them to remember an incident that made them angry, to feel the anger again, and follow the steps of HEALS 12 times a day for four weeks. It almost works like a vaccination. You feel the core hurt for five seconds at a time when you practice, and you develop an immunity to it.

Why is your dropout rate so low?

It's a 12-week program, and if they don't do their homework, they go to jail. We have surprisingly little resistance. I also say "If you don't feel much better about yourself, we'll give you your money back. You'll like yourself better when you're compassionate." I've treated over 1200 abusers in my career, and even the antisocial ones—no matter how justified they felt at the time—never felt proud of hurting someone they loved. Our group is about becoming proud.

Does this work even for the true sociopaths, the ones Jacobson and Gottman call Cobras?

These people are not afraid of the criminal justice system and they don't usually come to treatment. Most people in treatment are different. They're the dependent personalities who only hurt ones they love, and who get over-involved in the relationship. If sociopaths and people with antisocial personality disorders do come into treatment, they don't learn compassion. But they do learn to use emotional regulation techniques to keep from getting upset. Some of them use this as another form of superiority—you're going to get hysterical and I'm not—but it's better than beating up their wives in front of the children. It's a form of harm reduction.

Why does this work better than traditional treatment?

Most treatment programs focus on how men's domination causes domestic violence. We say that the real gender variable is that culture doesn't teach men to regulate their negative emotions, or sustain trust, compassion, and love. Numerous studies have shown that. We socialize girls and women to have an emotional vocabulary, and this has nothing to do with education level. We look into the eyes of little girls and reward them when they cry or express other emotions, but when a little boy expresses emotions, we call him a sissy. Boys are taught to keep vulnerable emotions sub-

merged, and don't develop an emotional vocabulary.

And if you can't tell sadness from loneliness from disappointment from rejection from being devalued, the bad feelings get overloaded easily. The strongest emotion is anger.

What about the women? Do you counsel them at all?

We put the safety of the victim first. We say, "We're sure you're not going to be abused any more, but it's very unlikely you'll have a good relationship with your abuser." We tell the women that there's more to life than not being abused. And we have a higher separation rate than the average. While 75 percent of women and children in shelters go back to their husbands, out of 379 couples to go through our program so far, 46 percent of them have left their spouses.

How do you treat substance abusers?

We conduct our treatment simultaneously with substance abuse treatment. Even though this hurts our treatment outcomes—98 percent of our recidivism is from alcohol and drugs—it's important because the nervous system bounce makes a person more irritable when coming off a drug, and I prefer they have some skills first.

Roland Maiuro, Ph.D., of the University of Washington, has been conducting a controlled study using the antidepressant Paxil to treat abusers. Maiuro found that abusers has consistently low serotonin levels, which were perhaps rendered even lower by their negative patterns of behavior. Have you seen Prozac-like drugs work with batterers?

I always tell abusers to try antidepressants. Anything that increases serotonin will reduce shame. And shame causes anger and aggression. I'll bet money that when studies like Maiuro's come out, we will see a significant reduction in violence. The problem is getting them to take it.

They'll take any illicit drug, but they won't take Prozac. But Prozac and HEALS will work best. It may even get the sociopaths.

How can we prevent domestic violence from happening in the first place?

If you treat it in the early stages you can prevent murders from happening. But you can't do this with a gender war. Community meetings against domestic violence have one or two men, and few minorities. Saying you're against domestic violence scares off people, and attracts the ones who really believe in the battle of the sexes. By demonizing the batterer, it makes him more isolated.

But if we make community organization about being for the creation of safe and secure families, they will have a much broader appeal.

her own disturbed mind. Although her face still hurt from the slap, she thought to herself that maybe she had made it all up. The neighbor, a friend of the husband's, went along and said he didn't see anything.

This technique of denying the woman's reality can be so effective that, when used in combination with methods to isolate the woman from other people, it causes battered women to doubt their own sanity. This is the ultimate form of abuse: to gain control of the victim's mind.

Lightning Strikes: "Cobras"

When Don and Martha started arguing, Don's heart rate would go up, he would sweat, and he'd exhibit other signs of emotional arousal. Most people show this response. However, we were astonished to find that as some batterers become more verbally aggressive, there is a decrease in heart rate. Like the cobra who becomes still and focused before striking its victim at over 100 miles an hour, these men calm themselves internally and focus their attention while striking swiftly at their wives with vicious verbal aggression.

When we separated these calm batterers from those who became internally aroused, we found other profound differences between the two groups. These "Cobras"—who constituted about 20 percent of our sample—were more likely to have used or threatened to use a knife or a gun on their wives, and were more severely violent than the other batterers. Only three percent of Pit Bulls had a history of extramarital violence, while 44 percent of Cobras did. And while about 33 percent of Pit Bills qualified for a diagnosis of "antisocial personality disorder"—which includes a long history of impulsive criminal behavior, childhood episodes of lying, stealing, fire setting, and cruelty to animals—fully 90 percent of the Cobras met the criteria. Finally, even though both groups abused alcohol at high rates, Cobras were more likely to be dependent on illegal drugs, such as cocaine and heroin, and were much less emotionally attached to their wives.

George was a typical Cobra. In the year prior to entering our research project, George had threatened to kill Vicky numerous times. One night several weeks before coming to see us, George came home late after he'd been out drinking and found Vicky and their two year-old daughter Christi sharing a pizza. Vicky was angry with him for missing dinner, and ignored him when he arrived. Her silence angered him, and he shouted, "You got a problem?" When she remained silent, he slammed his fist into the pizza, knocked her off the chair, dragged her across the room by her hair, held her down, and spat pizza in her face. He then beat her up, yelling, "You've ruined my life!"

The contrast between this incident and the altercation between Don and Martha over the car shows how Cobras are far more emotionally aggressive towards their wives at the start of their arguments than Pit Bulls. While Don became increasingly heated and less controlled over the course of the argument, George escalated the situation extremely rapidly, using both physical and verbal abuse in the service of control, intimidation, and subjugation. He was in Vicky's face twice as fast as she ever expected. This quick response is typical of the way Cobras control their wives—a tactic which they use because it often quiets the partner quickly and with minimal effort.

Another main difference between Cobras and Pit Bulls is that Cobras come from more chaotic family backgrounds. In our study, 78 percent of the Cobras came from violent families, compared to 51 percent of Pit Bulls. (In the population at large, 20 to 25 percent of children grow up in violent homes.) George's childhood was a classic example. He was beaten and neglected by both parents, and sexually abused by his prostitute mother's male customers. Like other Cobras, he came from a background that seriously crushed the implicit trust that every child has in his or her parents. This horrible childhood background, we believe, had somehow led the Cobras to vow to themselves that no one would ever control them again.

MEN CAN CHANGE

An astonishing 54 percent of our male volunteers showed decreases in violence during the second of two follow-up years. In fact, some men no longer met our standards for being included in our violent group. But

> **Batterers subscribe to an "honor code" that makes them unable to accept any influence—no matter how gentle—from women.**

this decrease in violence may be misleading. Once control is established over a woman through battering, perhaps it can be maintained by continued emotional abuse with intermittent battering used as a terrifying reminder of what is possible in the marriage. Cobras' violence was so severe that it may have been easier for them than for the Pit Bulls to maintain control through emotional abuse alone. Still, only seven percent of batterers in our study stopped their violence altogether in the two-year follow-up period.

We did observe several examples of husbands stopping the violence when it was unsuccessful in controlling their wives. George stopped beating Vicky as soon as she responded to his bullying with anger of her own.

WHEN WOMEN WON'T LEAVE

Three years after our two-year follow-up, we recontacted many of the battered women and their husbands. Despite the greater incidence of mental illness, drug addiction, emotional abuse, and severe violence in Cobra relationships, the typical pattern among the Cobra couples was for the wives to be committed to the marriages. While almost half of Pit Bull marriages dissolved within two years, by the five-year follow-up point, only 25 percent of women married to Cobras had left them; these women not only recognized the danger of trying to leave them, but often were quite attached to them.

Why would a woman be attached to a man as dangerous as George? Surprisingly, Vicky—like 80 percent of women married to Cobras—tested normal on our personality scales. However, she described her childhood as a "war zone" where her father would one day be absent and disengaged, and then suddenly become physically abusive toward Vicky's mother and all of the kids. She ran away from home to find a better life. And when she became pregnant by George, she tried to build her dream life. With her dashing new husband, she would finally have the home she had always wanted.

But when Vicky realized her dream of a normal, nonabusive relationship would never come to pass with George, she made the decision to leave. With Vicky and other battered women, "giving up the dream" was a pivotal step in shifting from fear to contempt and a determination to leave. Battered women need to be helped to "give up the dream" sooner, and this process should occur in conjunction with a careful safety plan and the support of an experienced helper.

Once Vicky implemented her safety plan, which included restraining orders against George and notifying his employer, the Navy, she found that George lost interest in her and went on to new pursuits. We found that Cobras will not pursue women who leave them unless it is easy and causes them little hassle to do so. But there are exceptions, and this is where help from an expert is essential.

Pit Bulls are the opposite of Cobras: easier to leave in the short run, but harder to leave in the long run. When Martha left Don and called it a trial separation, Don had little problem with it. But when she continued the separation for more than a month, he began to abuse and stalk her.

After three years of this, Martha consistently and forcefully asserted her rights. She divorced him. She hung up on him. She ended a definitive conversation with a "F___ you!" and refused to talk to him. Don might have killed her at this time. Pit Bulls have a great capacity to minimize, deny, or distort reality, and they can often justify to themselves stalking, continued abuse, and at times even murder. But Martha got lucky. Don began to leave her alone when it was clear that she would no longer be responsive to his threats. By that time, she had decided that even death was preferable to being under Don's spell.

EMERGING FROM HELL

We began this study with the goal of learning about the relationship between batterers and battered women, and we learned a great deal. We expected to focus on the men, especially when we came upon the distinction between Pit Bulls and Cobras. But during our exit interviews, we found the women in our study to be resourceful and courageous, and over time we began to realize that our work was also about the heroic struggle of battered women. These women start with a dream and truly descend into hell, and for a period of time seem stuck there. But they do not give up. They continue to struggle. Our main cause for optimism is that many of them emerge from hell and live to love again.

Resilience in Development

Emmy E. Werner

Emmy E. Werner is Professor of Human Development at the University of California, Davis. Address correspondence to Emmy E. Werner, Department of Applied Behavioral Sciences, University of California, Davis, 2321 Hart Hall, Davis, CA 95616.

During the past decade, a number of investigators from different disciplines—child development, psychology, psychiatry, and sociology—have focused on the study of children and youths who overcame great odds. These researchers have used the term resilience to describe three kinds of phenomena: good developmental outcomes despite high-risk status, sustained competence under stress, and recovery from trauma. Under each of these conditions, behavioral scientists have focused their attention on protective factors, or mechanisms that moderate (ameliorate) a person's reaction to a stressful situation or chronic adversity so that his or her adaptation is more successful than would be the case if the protective factors were not present.[1]

So far, only a relatively small number of studies have focused on children who were exposed to biological insults. More numerous in the current research literature are studies of resilient children who grew up in chronic poverty, were exposed to parental psychopathology, or experienced the breakup of their family or serious caregiving deficits. There has also been a growing body of literature on resilience in children who have endured the horrors of contemporary wars.

Despite the heterogeneity of all these studies, one can begin to discern a common core of individual dispositions and sources of support that contribute to resilience in development. These protective buffers appear to transcend ethnic, social-class, and geographic boundaries. They also appear to make a more profound impact on the life course of individuals who grow up in adversity than do specific risk factors or stressful life events.

Most studies of individual resilience and protective factors in children have been short-term, focusing on middle childhood and adolescence. An exception is the Kauai Longitudinal Study, with which I have been associated during the past three decades.[2] This study has involved a team of pediatricians, psychologists, and public-health and social workers who have monitored the impact of a variety of biological and psychosocial risk factors, stressful life events, and protective factors on the development of a multiethnic cohort of 698 children born in 1955 on the "Garden Island" in the Hawaiian chain. These individuals were followed, with relatively little attrition, from the prenatal period through birth to ages 1, 2, 10, 18, and 32.

Some 30% of the survivors in this study population were considered high-risk children because they were born in chronic poverty, had experienced perinatal stress, and lived in family environments troubled by chronic discord, divorce, or parental psychopathology. Two thirds of the children who had experienced four or more such risk factors by age 2 developed serious learning or behavior problems by age 10 or had delinquency records, mental health problems, or pregnancies by age 18. But one third of the children who had experienced four or more such risk factors developed instead into competent, confident, and caring adults.

PROTECTIVE FACTORS WITHIN THE INDIVIDUAL

Infancy and Early Childhood

Our findings with these resilient children are consistent with the results of several other longitudinal studies which have reported that young children with good coping abilities under adverse conditions have temperamental characteristics that elicit positive responses from a wide range of caregivers. The resilient boys and girls in the Kauai study were consistently characterized by their mothers as active, affectionate, cuddly, good-natured, and easy to deal with. Egeland and his associates observed similar dispositions among securely attached infants of abusing mothers in the Minnesota Mother-Child Interaction Project,[3] and Moriarty found the same qualities among infants with congenital defects at the Menninger Foundation.[4] Such infants were alert, easy to soothe, and able to elicit support from a nurturant family member. An "easy" temperament and the ability to actively recruit competent adult caregivers were also observed by Elder and his associates[5] in the resourceful children of the Great Depression.

By the time they reach preschool age, resilient children appear to have developed a coping pattern that combines autonomy with an ability to ask for help when needed. These characteristics are also predictive of resilience in later years.

Middle Childhood and Adolescence

When the resilient children in the Kauai Longitudinal Study were in elementary school, their teachers were favorably impressed by their communication and problem-solving skills. Although these children were not particularly gifted, they used whatever talents they had effectively. Usually they had a special interest or a hobby they could share with a friend, and that gave them a sense of pride. These interests and activities were not narrowly sex typed. But the boys and the girls grew into adolescents who were outgoing and autonomous, but also nurturant and emotionally sensitive.

Similar findings have been reported by Anthony, who studied the resilient offspring of mentally ill parents in St. Louis;[6] by Felsman and Vaillant, who followed successful boys from a high-crime neighborhood in Boston into adulthood;[7] and by Rutter and Quinton, who studied the lives of British girls who had been institutionalized in childhood, but managed to become well-functioning adults and caring mothers.[8]

Most studies of resilient children and youths report that intelligence and scholastic competence are positively associated with the ability to overcome great odds. It stands to reason that youngsters who are better able to appraise stressful life events correctly are also better able to figure out strategies for coping with adversity, either through their own efforts or by actively reaching out to other people for help. This finding has been replicated in studies of Asian-American,

Caucasian, and African-American children.[2,9,10]

Other salient protective factors that operated in the lives of the resilient youths on Kauai were a belief in their own effectiveness (an internal locus of control) and a positive self-concept. Such characteristics were also found by Farrington among successful and law-abiding British youngsters who grew up in high-crime neighborhoods in London,[11] and by Wallerstein and her associates among American children who coped effectively with the breakup of their parents' marriages.[12]

PROTECTIVE FACTORS WITHIN THE FAMILY

Despite the burden of chronic poverty, family discord, or parental psychopathology, a child identified as resilient usually has had the opportunity to establish a close bond with at least one competent and emotionally stable person who is attuned to his or her needs. The stress-resistant children in the Kauai Longitudinal Study, the well-functioning offspring of child abusers in the Minnesota Mother-Child Interaction Project, the resilient children of psychotic parents studied by Anthony in St. Louis, and the youngsters who coped effectively with the breakup of their parents' marriages in Wallerstein's studies of divorce all had received enough good nurturing to establish a basic sense of trust.[2,3,6,12]

Much of this nurturing came from substitute caregivers within the extended family, such as grandparents and older siblings. Resilient children seem to be especially adept at recruiting such surrogate parents. In turn, they themselves are often called upon to take care of younger siblings and to practice acts of "required helpfulness" for members of their family who are ill or incapacitated.[2]

Both the Kauai Longitudinal Study and Block and Gjerde's studies of ego-resilient children[9] found characteristic child-rearing orientations that appear to promote resiliency differentially in boys and girls. Resilient boys tend to come from households with structure and rules, where a male serves as a model of identification (father, grandfather, or older brother), and where there is some encouragement of emotional expressiveness. Resilient girls, in contrast, tend to come from households that combine an emphasis on risk taking and independence with reliable support from a female caregiver, whether mother, grandmother, or older sister. The example of a mother who is gainfully and steadily employed appears to be an especially powerful model of identification for resilient girls.[2] A number of studies of resilient children from a wide variety of socioeconomic and ethnic backgrounds have also noted that the families of these children held religious beliefs that provided stability and meaning in times of hardship and adversity.[2,6,10]

PROTECTIVE FACTORS IN THE COMMUNITY

The Kauai Longitudinal Study and a number of other prospective studies in the United States have shown that resilient youngsters tend to rely on peers and elders in the community as sources of emotional support and seek them out for counsel and comfort in times of crisis.[2,6]

Favorite teachers are often positive role models. All of the resilient high-risk children in the Kauai study could point to at least one teacher who was an important source of support. These teachers listened to the children, challenged them, and rooted for them—whether in grade school, high school, or community college. Similar findings have been reported by Wallerstein and her associates from their long-term observations of youngsters who coped effectively with their parents' divorces[12] and by Rutter and his associates from their studies of inner-city schools in London.[13]

Finally, in the Kauai study, we found that the opening of opportunities at major life transitions enabled the majority of the high-risk children who had a troubled adolescence to rebound in their 20s and early 30s. Among the most potent second chances for such youths were adult education programs in community colleges, voluntary military service, active participation in a church community, and a supportive friend or marital partner. These protective buffers were also observed by Elder in the adult lives of the children of the Great Depression,[14] by Furstenberg and his associates in the later lives of black teenage mothers,[15] and by Farrington[11] and Felsman and Vaillant[7] in the adult lives of young men who had grown up in high-crime neighborhoods in London and Boston.

PROTECTIVE FACTORS: A SUMMARY

Several clusters of protective factors have emerged as recurrent themes in the lives of children who overcome great odds. Some protective factors are characteristics of the individual: Resilient children are engaging to other people, adults and peers alike; they have good communication and problem-solving skills, including the ability to recruit substitute caregivers; they have a talent or hobby that is valued by their elders or peers; and they have faith that their own actions can make a positive difference in their lives.

Another factor that enhances resilience in development is having affectional ties that encourage trust, autonomy, and initiative. These ties are often provided by members of the extended family. There are also support systems in the community that reinforce and reward the competencies of resilient children and provide them with positive role models: caring neighbors, teachers, elder mentors, youth workers, and peers.

LINKS BETWEEN PROTECTIVE FACTORS AND SUCCESSFUL ADAPTATION IN HIGH-RISK CHILDREN AND YOUTHS

In the Kauai study, when we examined the links between protective factors within the individual and outside sources of support, we noted a certain continuity in the life course of the high-risk individuals who successfully overcame a variety of childhood adversities. Their individual dispositions led them to select or construct environments that, in turn, reinforced and sustained their active approach to life and rewarded their special competencies.

Although the sources of support available to the individuals in their childhood homes were modestly linked to the quality of the individuals' adaptation as adults, their competencies, temperament, and self-esteem had a greater impact. Many resilient high-risk youths on Kauai left the adverse conditions of their childhood homes after high school and sought environments they found more compatible. In short, they picked their own niches.

Our findings lend some empirical support to Scarr and McCartney's theory[16] about how people make their own environment. Scarr and McCartney proposed three types of effects of people's genes on their environment: passive, evocative, and active. Because parents provide both children's genes and their rearing environments, children's genes are necessarily correlated with their own environments. This is the passive type of genotype-environment effect. The evocative type refers to the fact that a person's partially heritable characteristics, such as intelligence, personality, and physical attractiveness, evoke certain responses from other people. Finally, a person's interests, talents, and personality (genetically variable traits) may lead him or her to select or create particular environments;

this is called an active genotype-environment effect. In line with this theory, there was a shift from passive to active effects as the youths and young adults in the Kauai study left stressful home environments and sought extrafamilial environments (at school, at work, in the military) that they found more compatible and stimulating. Genotype-environment effects of the evocative sort tended to persist throughout the different life stages we studied, as individuals' physical characteristics, temperament, and intelligence elicited differential responses from other people (parents, teachers, peers).

IMPLICATIONS

So far, most studies of resilience have focused on children and youths who have "pulled themselves up by their bootstraps," with informal support by kith and kin, not on recipients of intervention services. Yet there are some lessons such children can teach society about effective intervention: If we want to help vulnerable youngsters become more resilient, we need to decrease their exposure to potent risk factors and increase their competencies and self-esteem, as well as the sources of support they can draw upon.

In *Within Our Reach*, Schorr has isolated a set of common characteristics of social programs that have successfully prevented poor outcomes for children who grew up in high-risk families.[17] Such programs typically offer a broad spectrum of health, education, and family support services, cross professional boundaries, and view the child in the context of the family, and the family in the context of the community. They provide children with sustained access to competent and caring adults, both professionals and volunteers, who teach them problem-solving skills, enhance their communication skills and self-esteem, and provide positive role models for them.

There is an urgent need for more systematic evaluations of such programs to illuminate the process by which we can forge a chain of protective factors that enables vulnerable children to become competent, confident, and caring individuals, despite the odds of chronic poverty or a medical or social disability. Future research on risk and resiliency needs to acquire a cross-cultural perspective as well. We need to know more about individual dispositions and sources of support that transcend cultural boundaries and operate effectively in a variety of high-risk contexts.

Notes

1. A. S. Masten, K. M. Best, and N. Garmezy, Resilience and development: Contributions from the study of children who overcame adversity, *Development and Psychopathology, 2,* 425–444 (1991).
2. All results from this study that are discussed in this review were reported in E. E. Werner, Risk resilience, and recovery: Perspectives from the Kauai Longitudinal Study, *Development and Psychopathology, 5,* 503–515 (1993).
3. B. Egeland, D. Jacobvitz, and L. A. Stroufe, Breaking the cycle of child abuse, *Child Development, 59,* 1080–1088 (1988).
4. A Moriarty, John, a boy who acquired resilience, in *The Invulnerable Child*, E. J. Anthony and B. J. Cohler, Eds. (Guilford Press, New York, 1987).
5. G. H. Elder, K. Liker, and C. E. Cross, Parent-child behavior in the Great Depression, in *Life Span Development and Behavior*, Vol. 6, T. B. Baltes and O. G. Brim, Jr., Eds. (Academic Press, New York, 1984).
6. E. J. Anthony, Children at risk for psychosis growing up successfully, in *The Invulnerable Child*, E. J. Anthony and B. J. Cohler, Eds. (Guilford Press, New York, 1987).
7. J. K. Felsman and G. E. Vaillant, Resilient children as adults: A 40 year study in *The Invulnerable Child*, E. J. Cohler, Eds. (Guilford Press, New York, 1987).
8. M. Rutter and D. Quinton, Long term follow-up of women institutionalized in childhood: Factors promoting good functioning in adult life, *British Journal of Developmental Psychology, 18,* 225–234 (1984).
9. J. Block and P. F. Gjerde, Early antecedents of ego resiliency in late adolescence, paper presented at the annual meeting of the American Psychological Association, Washington, DC (August 1986).
10. R. M. Clark, *Family Life and School Achievement: Why Poor Black Children Succeed or Fail* (University of Chicago Press, Chicago, 1983).
11. D. P. Farrington, *Protective Factors in the Development of Juvenile Delinquency and Adult Crime* (Institute of Criminology, Cambridge University, Cambridge, England, 1993).
12. J. S. Wallerstein and S. Blakeslee, *Second Chances: Men, Women and Children a Decade After Divorce* (Ticknor and Fields, New York, 1989).
13. M. Rutter, B. Maughan, P. Mortimore, and J. Ousten, *Fifteen Thousand Hours: Secondary Schools and Their Effects on Children* (Harvard University Press, Cambridge, MA, 1979).
14. G. H. Elder, Military times and turning points in men's lives, *Developmental Psychology, 22,* 233–245 (1986).
15. F. F. Furstenberg, J. Brooks-Gunn, and S. P. Morgan, *Adolescent Mothers in Later Life* (Cambridge University Press, New York, 1987).
16. S. Scarr and K. McCartney, How people make their own environments: A theory of genotype-environment effects, *Child Development, 54,* 424–435 (1983).
17. L. Schorr, *Within Our Reach: Breaking the Cycle of Disadvantage* (Anchor Press, New York, 1988).

Recommended Reading

Haggerty, R., Garmezy, N., Rutter, M., and Sherrod, L., Eds. (1994). *Stress, Risk, and Resilience in Childhood and Adolescence* (Cambridge University Press, New York).

Luthar, S., and Zigler, E. (1991). Vulnerability and competence: A review of research on resilience in childhood. *American Journal of Orthopsychiatry, 61,* 6–22.

Werner, E. E., and Smith, R. S. (1992). *Overcoming the Odds: High Risk Children From Birth to Adulthood* (Cornell University Press, Ithaca, NY).

SEX
& Marriage

Experts say sex is vital to healthy relationships. Why is it so difficult for couples to do what's good for them?

By Patricia Chisholm

Max is recalling what sex was like before the big job, kids and mortgage. "I was a walking hormone," he says, laughing a little with his wife, Julie, in the basement of their comfortable Montreal home. The thirtysomething parents of two young children, who asked that their real names be withheld, used to fool around at least five times a week. Now, they say, they are lucky to make love that many times a month because they are either physically exhausted or mentally distracted by their demanding daytime roles—his as a boss, hers as a stay-at-home mom. Unlike many couples, though, Max and Julie haven't lost their sense of humour about what they view as a temporary decline in their physical intimacy. "It's a little sad—sex is such an enjoyable, amazing experience, " Max says. "We still really enjoy it. But now I find I'm often just too tired at night. I can get it up, but I just can't get up off the couch." Ah, sex. It's one of the few pleasures left that doesn't bloat the waistline, cause cancer or break the family budget. Researchers claim it even helps prevent wrinkles, and psychologists say it can rejuvenate the most tired relationship. According to a 1998 *Maclean's*/CBC poll, 78 per cent of married Canadians (as opposed to 61 per cent of single respondents) said they were sexually active, and 87 per cent of married Canadians said they were "satisfied" with their sex lives. Sexual monogamy has never been easy, though, and that fact has become depressingly clear to the great glut of baby boomers who grew up with the pill and unprecedented sexual freedom but now are struggling with aging bodies, sexual boredom, marital

spats and plain old exhaustion. So much for the Summer of Love.

There is no easy way out, either. The divorce rate is falling as concerns about splintered families and AIDS prompt more people to recognize that breaking up really is hard to do. Statistics Canada reported this year that the number of divorces has fallen for four years in a row, from 78,880 in 1994 to 67,408 in 1997—a 14.5-per-cent drop. Edward Laumann, a University of Chicago sociologist who studies sexual dysfunction, says people appear to be staying together longer, despite lots of problems with sex, because they are realizing that changing partners costs huge amounts of time, money and energy, with no guarantees. "They are aware that divorce is not a one-year experience," he says.

Of course, some passions cannot be revived, and some couples find it's easier to stay put and just be celibate. But in general, therapists say good sex is a hallmark of solid, long-term relationships. It's an opportunity to relax, to put everyday pressures aside and, especially, to reinforce emotional intimacy and physical closeness. More couples are turning to sex aids like toys and videos to ignite passions, while others are exploring unconventional options like long-term affairs and group sex. The permutations may be endless, but one thing is clear: sex, or the lack of it, still speaks volumes. "If you want to look at what is going on in your relationship, look at your sex life—it won't lie to you," advises Sig Taylor, a Calgary marriage counsellor. "It's a barometer, and it's usually the last thing to go. If couples get to the point

The elation people experience at the beginning of a relationship is really more akin to a drug-induced high

where there is no sexuality anymore, the relationship is pretty much dead."

Most people are reluctant to talk about an unconventional or problematic sex life, making it one of the last real taboos. But in fact, problems of one kind or another are strikingly common. One of Laumann's recent studies found that, over a one-year period, 43 per cent of women and 31 per cent of men between the ages of 18 and 59 experienced some kind of sexual impediment, including lack of desire, erectile dysfunction and pain during intercourse. "These are huge numbers," he said, "and it's probably an underestimate—people don't like to admit they have problems with sex."

No wonder people don't want to talk about their troubles—the message in the media is that only losers are sitting it out. Explicit, even kinky sex now permeates movies, magazines and the Internet. *Eyes Wide Shut*, the late Stanley Kubrick's heavily hyped film, features the unlikely scenario of a married couple descending into the depths of their own, profoundly disturbing sexual fantasies. Against that backdrop, simple sex with a partner who never changes—except to acquire a few more sags and bags every year—can start to seem, well, ordinary.

What's to be done? Experts say the vast majority of aging-related sexual ailments—erectile dysfunction, pain during intercourse and lack of lubrication—can be cured medically. But lasting solutions have to start with talk. "If couples pretend nothing is wrong, it only prolongs the problem," says Laumann. "Discussing it takes the edge off." The consequences of not talking can blight a life. "At the beginning of our marriage, things were great," says Frank, a 68-year-old retired Ontario businessman who asked for anonymity. "We had sex a couple of times a week and we were great friends." But their sex life declined sharply after they started having kids—he and his wife now have three grown children. "I felt I was inadequate," he says. "There were so many times I quietly hid my face under the sheets and cried."

He and his wife separated, but they have since struck an uneasy truce and now live together, although their sex life never resumed. Recently, he learned from a TV talk show that it is common for sexual appetites to fluctuate widely from year to year, and that the combination of life pressures and hormones is usually to blame. "I think we need to talk more about sex," he says now. "If I had known this was her body and not me, I would have done everything to fight for her."

Hormones can be responsible for the ups as well as the downs. The elation people feel early in a relationship is akin to a drug-induced high and is just about as sustainable, experts say. "The amount of adrenaline in the body is so great, you can get by with almost no sleep," says Richard Dearing, director of the Marriage Therapy Program at the University of Winnipeg. "You just don't have the energy to keep that going for more than a few months."

As passions abate, couples stand back and take a hard look at one another. Details of character and temperament kick in, and partners begin to make decisions based on compatibility. They may also notice that sex plays different roles in their respective lives. Libidos can differ wildly, partly because of natural hormonal levels—testosterone in men, androgen in women—and partly because of the approach that individuals take to sex. Dearing, like many therapists, has found that, typically, men use sex to feel good, while women need to feel good before they get into bed. The result when life gets stressful? He wants to, she doesn't.

Of course, there are no rigid categories when it comes to sex drive, and for many couples the roles are reversed. In either case, a mismatch can create big problems. Sipping a glass of white wine on a restaurant patio in Vancouver, a 38-year-old woman reflects on the recent breakup of her four-year, live-in relationship. "I realize that sex can't always be the priority," she says. "But for me, it's a way to let go of the day's hassles. You can get into it, just for the sake of pure, physical pleasure." She stayed with her partner for two years after their sex life ended, a phase that began when he was laid off. Despite her repeated efforts, it never resumed. "There was nothing I could do to reach him, and after a while I stopped trying because the rejection was too hard to take. It was horrible," she recalls. "A relationship to me is a partnership—you play as a team. When something as basic as your physical intimacy breaks down, it's impossible to think of yourself that way anymore. One of you has broken the contract."

Even when two people agree on what they want out of life, and seem to be getting it, sex can suffer. Phil Bentley, 44, and John Doleman, 37, have lived together in Toronto for more than a decade. Unlike many couples, gay or straight, their early years together were tough because they decided to put all their efforts into paying off a large mortgage. They took in boarders and each worked at two jobs. "The house was always full of people so we didn't have many opportunities to be alone," says Bentley. Now, they have more time for one another, and that has translated into better sex. "After this amount of time being together, we are more honest with each other about our sexual needs," says Doleman.

National TV sex-show host Sue Johanson bursts into laughter when the subject of sex and marriage is raised. "The two are not simpatico, " she chortles, only half in

The payoff for couples who remain intimate through a marriage's stress-plagued middle years can be extraordinary

jest. But this grandmother has listened to thousands of tales of woe, and she believes there are many ways to revive flagging sexual appetites. As a first step, she says, couples should set aside time for the occasional date. She counsels couples to play games, such as hide-and-seek—in the nude and in the dark. Sex toys can rev things up as well, she contends, although she has found that men are often threatened if a woman buys a vibrator. "They say, 'What do you need that thing for, you've got Mr. Ever Ready here.' But once men use it to stimulate their partner, they're home free—they think it's great."

In fact, there is something of a revolution under way in the area of sex aids, especially for women. Shops like Womyns' Ware in Vancouver and Good For Her in Toronto coax women inside with tasteful decor and shelves free of hard-core videos and magazines, or cheap, crudely made products. At Womyns' Ware, for instance, a sound system plays warm jazz in a light-filled room where merchandise is arranged so that those browsing for lubricants can avoid coming face-to-face with customers sampling handcuffs and leather floggers.

There is also a relatively new line of erotic videos aimed at women, called Femme. Developed by retired porn star Candida Royalle, 48, the videos feature complex story lines and shun sex scenes that degrade women. "There's a lot more out there that is couple-oriented," notes Montrealer Josey Vogels, who writes a syndicated weekly column called *My Messy Bedroom*. "Women want to explore their sexuality more, but they don't want to go to some sleazy hole in the wall—they don't want to feel creepy."

But bedroom toys cannot save a sex life that is undercut by marital conflict or fatigue. "Women are angry because they are aware that they are doing much more of the housework than men are," Johanson says. "A couple gets into bed and he has this copulatory gaze and she just looks at him and thinks, 'This is just one more person to service.'" If they want more sex, she says, men will "have to pick up more of the slack around the house—enough of this nonsense."

Leslie, a mid-40s Victoria-area mother of two young boys, can relate. With a demanding managerial job, and jammed off-hours—daily commutes to two schools, plus appointments for tutoring, soccer, sailing—Leslie says she retreats to the bedroom with one thing in mind. "By the time my head hits the pillow, I'm ready to pass out," she says. Her husband helps a lot with the kids, she says, but she is still the one who knows if it's pizza day at school or whether the dog needs a rabies shot. Too often, sex simply falls to the bottom of her "to-do" list. "Making a date with your mate is good advice, but I also know I should be doing two miles a day on the

treadmill," she says wryly. "Trying to recapture the fun you had when you were young is like trying to remember Grade 9 chemistry—you know what apparatus to use, but you're not sure which chemicals you need to get a reaction."

Experts say there are peaks and valleys in everyone's sex life. Claude Guldner, professor emeritus at the University of Guelph and one of Canada's leading sex therapists, says desire tends to follow a U-shaped pattern in most marriages: it is intense during the courtship phase, dips down with the arrival of children and—if couples are lucky—swings strongly upward again when children are older. Often, those at the bottom of the U fail to realize that they may be devoting too much energy to parenting at the expense of their marriage. "We need to educate people that 'husbanding and wifing' continues, even though you are now fathering and mothering," he says.

Some people understand that lesson without being taught. Cheryl, a 40-year-old Halifax hairdresser, and Bob, 43, who works in the offshore gas industry, have been married for 10 years. When their now-five-year-old son was born, the first three months were "challenging," recalls Cheryl, who with her husband requested anonymity. "We just realized that every time we would get intimate, our son would start crying. That was a given and we would just laugh." She says grabbing a few moments here and there is enough to keep sex alive. "Even if it's five minutes in the shower in the morning, when junior is having his catnap, it's better than nothing," she says.

Cheryl says she and her husband have ups and downs, and that things can be especially difficult when her husband arrives home after a month offshore. "I always think of my relationship as the hardest thing I will do in my life, as well as the best thing," she muses. "It's hard to keep yourself present with somebody, to keep yourself vulnerable and open. It's hard to be intimate."

Mutual neglect can do much more than lead to bad sex—it can torpedo a marriage if it spawns infidelity. Guldner, who specializes in counselling couples grappling with the fallout from cheating, says that except for chronic philanderers, affairs are rarely about sex. Usually, the cheater is avoiding another issue: they are turned off by a partner's weight gain, for instance, or they are too often left alone by a spouse obsessed with work. "Many, many people say that sex in the affair isn't nearly as good as it was with their partner," Guldner says. But if couples are willing to confront one another with their problems, they often survive an event that, in the past, was widely viewed as unforgivable. That is partly because cultural shifts have weakened old notions of sexual possessiveness. "There is less exclusivity to the sexual act now because so many people have had premarital sex," Guldner points out.

Some see a discreet affair as a viable alternative. Susan, a Toronto manager in her late 30s who requested anonymity, is deeply committed to her family, even though she has carried on a secret affair for nine years. What she gets from her lover is not better sex, she explains, but intellectual companionship and support in her professional life. Despite that, she has no intention of leaving her husband, with whom she has three school-age children. "Marriage is such a difficult, complex relationship," she says. "I would just be exchanging one set of problems for another if I left. And I think that children have the right to grow up in a home with both parents."

The payoff for couples who remain intimate through a marriage's stressful middle years can be extraordinary. Dartmouth, N.S., residents Les and Joan Halsey have treated sex as a precious, fragile wonder that is integral to the success of their 44-year marriage. "We realized early that it was very important," says Les, 65. "Once a month, we would go out for a candlelight dinner. Taking the time is so important—it's not just going to the bedroom and saying, 'OK, let's have sex now.'"

Joan, 64, recalls times when life got in the way of their physical intimacy—job changes, caring for their three children, periods of depressed libido. And she candidly admits that it was sometimes work for a couple married at 21 to keep themselves from straying. "The seven-year itch, living in suburbia, wild parties—it's only by the grace of God we didn't go that route," she says. And she has some advice for those still battling it out in the trenches. "Don't just have a home, children, work," she advises. "Do things that interested you before you were married. We always had a little bit of something just to ourselves—it keeps us healthy. And now that our family has left the nest, we have this whole new journey together." The motto for marriage, then, is "better sex than sorry."

With Ruth Atherley and Chris Wood in Vancouver, and Susan McCelland in Toronto

Shattered Vows

Hold on to your wedding ring. It's difficult, but possible, to repair the damage caused by infidelity. Increasingly, that's what couples want. But let go of assumptions. In an interview with Editor at Large Hara Estroff Marano, a leading expert challenges everything you think you know about the most explosive subject of the year. By Shirley Glass, Ph.D.

Infidelity appears to be the topic of the year. What has struck you most about the reaction to what may or may not be some kind of infidelity in high places?

Whatever horror or dismay people have about it, they're able to separate the way the President is performing in office and the way he appears to be performing in his marriage. That's especially interesting because it seems to reflect the split in his life. We don't know for sure, but he apparently is very much involved in his family life. He's not an absentee father or husband. Whatever it is that they share—and they share a lot, publicly and privately—he has a compartment in which he is attracted to young women, and it is separate from his primary relationships.

Is this compartmentalizing characteristic of people who get into affairs?

It's much more characteristic of men. Most women believe that if you love your partner, you wouldn't even be interested in an affair; therefore, if someone has an affair, it means that they don't love their partner and they do love the person they had the affair with. But my research shows there are many men who do love their partners, who enjoy good sex at home, who nevertheless never turn down an opportunity for extramarital sex. In fact, 56% of the men I sampled who had extramarital intercourse said that their marriages were happy, versus 34% of the women.

That's how I got into this.

Because?

Being a woman, I believed that if a man had an affair, it meant that he had a terrible marriage, and that he probably wasn't getting it at home—the old keep-your-husband-happy-so-he-won't-stray idea. That puts too much of the burden on the woman. I found that she could be everything wonderful, and he might still stray, if that's in his value system, his family background, or his psychodynamic structure.

I was in graduate school when I heard that a man I knew, married for over 40 years, had recently died and his wife was so bereaved because they had had the most wonderful marriage. He had been her lover, her friend, her support system. She missed him immensely. I thought that was a beautiful story. When I told my husband about it, he got a funny look that made me ask, What do you know? He proceeded to tell me that one night when he took the kids out for dinner to an out-of-the-way restaurant, that very man walked in with a young blonde woman. When he saw my husband, he walked out.

How did that influence you?

I wondered what that meant. Did he fool his wife all those years and really not love her? How is it possible to be married for over 40 years and think you have a good marriage? It occurred to me that an affair could mean something different than I believed.

Another belief that was an early casualty was the hydraulic pump theory—that you only have so much energy for something. By this belief, if your partner is getting sex outside, you would know it, because your partner wouldn't be wanting sex at home. However, some people are even more passionate at home when they are having extramarital sex. I was stunned to hear a man tell me that when he left his affair partner and came home he found himself desiring his wife more than he had in a long time, because he was so sexually aroused by his affair. That made me question the pump theory.

Many of our beliefs about the behavior of others come from how we see things for ourselves. A man who associates sneaking around with having sex will, if his wife is sneaking around, find it very hard to believe that she could be emotionally involved without being sexually involved. On the other hand, a woman usually cannot believe that her husband could be sexually involved and not be emotionally involved. We put the same meaning on it for our partner that it would have for us. I call that the error of assumed similarity.

What infidelity research have you done?

My first research study was actually based on a sex questionnaire in *Psychology Today* in the '70s. I analyzed the data, looking at the effect of extramarital sex, length of marriage, and gender difference on marital satisfaction and romanticism. I found enormous gender differences.

Men in long-term marriages who had affairs had very high marital satisfaction—and women in long-term marriages having affairs had the lowest satisfaction of all. Everybody's marital satisfaction went down the longer they were married, except the men who had affairs. But in early mar-

Reprinted with permission from *Psychology Today*, July/August 1998, pp. 34-42, 68-70. © 1998 by Sussex Publishers, Inc.

riages, men who had affairs were significantly less happy. An affair is more serious if it happens earlier in the marriage.

Explaining these gender differences was the basis of my dissertation. I theorized that men were having sexual affairs and women emotional affairs.

Are affairs about sex?

Sometimes infidelity is just about sex. That is often more true for men. In my research, 44% of men who said they had extramarital sex said they had slight or no emotional involvement; only 11% of women said that. Oral sex is certainly about sex. Some spouses are more upset if the partner had oral sex than if they had intercourse; it just seems so much more intimate.

What is the infidelity in infidelity?

The infidelity is that you took something that was supposed to be mine, which is sexual or emotional intimacy, and you gave it to somebody else. I thought that we had a special relationship, and now you have contaminated it; it doesn't feel special any more, because you shared something very precious to us with someone else.

There are gender differences. Men feel more betrayed by their wives having sex with someone else; women feel more betrayed by their husbands being emotionally involved with someone else. What really tears men apart is to visualize their partner being sexual with somebody else.

Women certainly don't want their husbands having sex with somebody else, but they may be able to deal with an impersonal one-night fling better than a long-term relationship in which their husband was sharing all kinds of loving ways with somebody else.

Why are affairs so deeply wounding?

Because you have certain assumptions about your marriage. That I chose someone, and the other person chose me; we have the same values; we have both decided to have an exclusive relationship, even though we may have some problems. We love each other—and therefore I am safe.

Voices of *Infidelity*

I was working full-time, as was my wife; I was going to school and we were caring for our son. Little time was left for each other. The night I received my acceptance to medical school, in April, she told me she was unhappy and was attracted to someone else.

We began counseling. A month later, she told me she was in love with him and was very confused. I was feeling insecure in the relationship; it was coming out as anger.

In June, the wife of the guy called and told me that Lori was having an affair with her husband. The heat in my chest began to slowly grow. Lori beeped in on the line; I told her, "I know and I'm on my way" to her office; he worked with her. Now in a full rage, I stalked through the office looking for him, but she had told him I was coming and he'd left the building. I announced that "[He] is screwing my wife!" Then I verbally vented all my anger in front of the building, where Lori was waiting before leaving to get my son from daycare.

When you find out your partner has been unfaithful, then everything you believe is totally shattered. And you have to rebuild the world. The fact that you weren't expecting it, that it wasn't part of your assumption about how a relationship operates, causes traumatic reactions.

And it is deeply traumatic.

It's terrible. The wounding results because—and I've heard this so many times—I finally thought I met somebody I could trust.

It violates that hope or expectation that you can be who you really are with another person?

Yes. Affairs really aren't about sex; they're about betrayal. Imagine you are married to somebody very patriotic and

---

then find out your partner is a Russian spy. Someone having a long-term affair is leading a double life. Then you find out all that was going on in your partner's life that you knew nothing about: gifts that were exchanged, poems and letters that were written, trips that you thought were taken for a specific reason were actually taken to meet the affair partner.

To find out about all the intrigue and deception that occurred while you were operating under a different assumption is totally shattering and disorienting. That's why people then have to get out their calendars and go back over the dates to put all the missing pieces together: "When you went to the drugstore that night and said your car broke down and didn't come home for three hours, what was really happening?"

This is necessary?

In order to heal. Because any time somebody suffers from a trauma, part of the recovery is telling the story. The tornado victim will go over and over the story—"when the storm came I was in my room . . ."—trying to understand what happened, and how it happened. "Didn't we see the black clouds? How come we didn't know?"

And so they repeat the story until it no longer creates unmanageable arousal?

Yes. In fact, sometimes people are more devastated if everything was wonderful before they found out. When a betrayed spouse who suspected something says, "I don't know if I can ever trust my partner again," it is reassuring to tell them that they can trust their own instincts the next time they have those storm warnings. But if somebody thought everything was wonderful, how would they ever know if it happened again? It's frightening.

One question people these days are asking you is, Is oral sex really infidelity?

The question they ask is, Is oral sex really adultery? And that's a different question, because adultery is a legal term. It is also a biblical term. The real issue is, Is

---

ADVICE TO *Hillary*, ALL DEARLY *betrayed*, AND *nearly* BETRAYED

• Yes, oral sex really is infidelity.

• It's a boundary problem, not a love problem.

• Some woman or other is going to give him a second chance to prove that he can be faithful. Decide if that woman can be you.

• Faithfulness is not a virtue that falls out of the heavens—it's a skill. And it can be learned. . . . [see] (www.smartmarriages.com).

• Disregard what other people say. All that matters is your ability to rebuild trust.

• Recognize your power and use it to renegotiate your relationship from the bottom up.

• Despite the hurt and anger, love can still survive.

• You may want to consider your shared history, shared goals, and shared commitment to important causes.

• Affairs are less a reflection of the partner and the marriage than of broader forces in the culture that undermine monogamy.

• You may look realistically at your partner's other qualities and decide that on balance you prefer your spouse to other potential partners.

—*The Editors, with Peggy Vaughan, author of* The Monogamy Myth.

oral sex infidelity? You don't need to ask a psychologist that—just ask any spouse: "Would you feel that it was an infidelity for your partner to engage in that type of behavior?"

Would women answer that differently from men?

It is not necessarily a function of gender. People might answer it differently for themselves than for their partners. Some people maintain a kind of technical virginity by not having intercourse. However, even kissing in a romantic, passionate way is an infidelity. People know when they cross that line from friendship to affair.

So you don't have to have intercourse to have an affair?

Absolutely. There can be an affair without any kind of touching at all. People have affairs on the Internet.

What is the *sine qua non* of an affair?

Three elements determine whether a relationship is an affair.

One is secrecy. Suppose two people meet every morning at seven o'clock for coffee before work, and they never tell their partners. Even though it might be in a public place, their partner is not going to be happy about it. It is going to feel like a betrayal, a terrible deception.

Emotional intimacy is the second element. When someone starts confiding things to another person that they are reluctant to confide to their partner, and the emotional intimacy is greater in the friendship than in the marriage, that's very threatening. One common pathway to affairs occurs when somebody starts confiding negative things about their marriage. What they're doing is signaling: "I'm vulnerable; I may even be available."

The third element is sexual chemistry. That can occur even if two people don't touch. If one says, "I'm really attracted to you," or "I had a dream about you last night, but, of course, I'm married, so we won't do anything about that," that tremendously increases the sexual tension by creating forbidden fruit in the relationship.

Another question you told me people now ask is, "Are you a liar if you lie about an affair?" How do you answer?

Lying goes with the territory. If you're not lying, you have an open marriage. There may be lies of omission or lies of commission. The lie of omission is, "I had to stop at the gym on my way home." There is the element of truth, but the omission of what was really happening: "I left after 15 minutes and spent the next 45 minutes at someone's apartment."

The lies of commission are the elaborate deceptions people create. The more deception

Lori had asked me not to tell my family we were having problems; thus, I was cut off from my major support system. I wanted to punish her by holding her up to public scrutiny. I gathered everyone from both families and proceeded to tell them the whole story.

After I cooled down, we spent a month "working" on the relationship. Then she filed for divorce. I am left with a huge amount of anger at him and at her even though it is so many months later. I've never had the opportunity to vent my anger at him and still fantasize about tracking him down and beating him senseless. After all the time and emotional investment I'd put into this relationship, they intentionally damaged it until it was unsalvageable.

I am now beginning med school, and we are sharing physical and legal custody of our son. Oh, and her love was fired from his job as a result of this indiscretion.—*BH*

⁻ᦂ⊚⋟⁻

I had an affair with my neighbor. I was friends with his wife. We spent a

and the longer it goes on, the more difficult it is to rebuild trust in the wake of an affair.

The deception makes a tremendous psychological difference to the betrayed spouse. What about to the person who constructed the deception?

Once the affair's been discovered, the involved partner could have a sense of relief, if they hate lying and don't see themselves as having that kind of moral character. They'll say, "I can't understand how I could have done a thing like this, this is not the kind of person I am."

Some people thrive on the game. For them, part of the passion and excitement of an affair is the lying and getting away with something forbidden.

There are some people who have characterological problems, and the affair may be a symptom of that. Such people lie about their accomplishments; they are fraudulent in business. When it's characterological, I don't know any way to rebuild trust; no one can ever be on sure footing with that person.

So there is always moral compromise just by being in an affair?

Which is why some people, no matter how unhappy they are in their marriage, don't have affairs. They can't make the compromise. Or they feel they have such an open relationship with the spouse that they just could not do something like that without telling their partner about it.

Do affairs ever serve a positive function—not to excuse any of the damage they do?

Affairs are often a chance for people to try out new behaviors, to dress in a different costume, to stretch and grow and assume a different role. In a long-term relationship, we often get frozen in our roles. When young couples begin at one level of success and go on to many achievements, the new person sees them as they've become, while the old person sees them as they were.

The unfortunate thing is that the way a person is different in the affair would, if incorporated into the marriage, probably make their spouse ecstatic. But they believe they're stuck; they don't know how to create opportunity for change within the marriage. A woman who was sexually inhibited in marriage—perhaps she married young and had no prior partners—may find her sexuality in an affair, but her husband would probably be thrilled to encounter that new self.

How do you handle this?

After an affair, I do not ask the question you would expect. The spouse always wants to know about "him" or "her": "What did you see in her that you didn't see in me?" Or, "What did you like about him better?" I always ask about "you": "What did you like about yourself in that other relationship?" "How were you different?" and "Of the way that you were in that other relationship, what would you like to bring back so that you can be the person you want to be in your primary relationship?" "How can we foster that part of you in this relationship?"

That's a surprise. How did you come to know that's the question to ask?

There is an attraction in the affair, and I try to understand what it is. Part of it is the romantic projection: I like the way I look when I see myself in the other person's eyes. There is positive mirroring. An affair holds up a vanity mirror, the kind with all the little bulbs around it; it gives a rosy glow to the way you see yourself. By contrast, the marriage offers a makeup mirror; it magnifies every little flaw. When someone loves you despite seeing all your flaws, that is a reality-based love.

In the stories of what happened during the affair, people seem to take on a different persona, and one of the things they liked best about being in that relationship was the person they had become. The man who wasn't sensitive or expressive is now in a relationship where he is expressing his feelings and is supportive.

Can those things be duplicated in the marriage?

That's one of the goals—not to turn the betrayed spouse into the affair partner, but to free the unfaithful spouse to express all the parts of himself he was able to experience in the affair.

I see a lot of men who are married to very competent women and having affairs with very weak women. They feel: "This person needs me." They put on their red cape and do a lot of rescuing. They feel very good about themselves. That makes me sad, because I know that even though their partner may be extremely competent, she wants to be stroked too. She wants a knight in shining armor. Perhaps she hasn't known how to ask.

Do people push partners into affairs?

No. People can create a pattern in the marriage that is not enhancing, and the partner, instead of dealing with the dissatisfaction and trying to work on the relationship, escapes it and goes someplace else.

That is the wrong way to solve the problem?

Yes. Generally when a woman is unhappy, she lets her partner know. She feels better because she's gotten it off her chest. It doesn't interfere with her love. She's trying to improve the relationship: "If I tell him what makes me unhappy, then he will know how to please me; I am giving him a gift by telling him."

Unfortunately, many men don't see it as a gift. They feel criticized and put down. Instead of thinking, "She feels lonely; I will move toward her and make her feel secure," they think, "What is wrong with her? Didn't I just do that?" They pull away. If they come in contact with somebody else who says to them, "Oh, you're wonderful," then they move toward that person. They aren't engaged enough in the marriage to work things out. The partner keeps trying and becomes more unpleasant because he's not responding.

She becomes a pursuer, and he becomes the distancer.

When she withdraws, the marriage is much further down the road to dissolution, because she's given up. Her husband, unfortunately, thinks things are so much better because she's no longer complaining. He doesn't recognize that she has detached and become emotionally available for an affair. The husband first notices it when she becomes disinterested in sex—or after she's left! Then he'll do anything to keep her. That is often too little too late.

By then she is often committed to someone on the outside?

Yes, which is why when women have affairs, it's much more often a result of long-term marital dissatisfaction.

Can you predict which couples will get involved in affairs?

Social context is a predictor. If you're in an occupational or social group where many people have affairs, and there's a sexually per-

lot of time together. (My husband works long hours and all weekend.) I started to work for my neighbor part-time and started to feel excitement build.

The affair lasted five months. We stopped many times but would find ourselves back in each other's arms. The sex was O.K.; I felt that was what I had to give him to get what I wanted—the words about how sexy I was, something I never heard from my husband.

His wife found out and told my husband last year; he left for three months. He would show up nightly after the kids were asleep, call me a whore, and scream at me. I'd be sobbing on the floor. I never wanted to end my marriage.

My husband finally started counseling with me and moved back in. The neighbors moved away three months ago.

My husband told me last week he wants a divorce. After a week of begging him to stay, I found love letters and hotel reservations from a girl in Houston. He said it's his second chance for love. I am devastated. My kids will suffer the rest of their lives for my mistakes.—*NC*

missive attitude, you're more likely. Also if you come from a family where there's a history of affairs—the most notorious are the Kennedys, where the men have a certain entitlement. Coming from one of the Mediterranean cultures, like the Greek, where the double standard is alive and well, is another predictor.

You're saying that an affair is not always about the marriage. There are often cultural or contextual pulls into affairs. This is important information for women, because women blame themselves.

And society blames women.

So affairs can happen in good marriages. Is the marriage really good?

Sometimes one person thinks the marriage is fine and the other doesn't. That may be because the more dissatisfied person hasn't communicated their dissatisfaction. Or they've communicated it and the partner has discounted it. But after an affair, people often try to justify it by rewriting unhappiness into the marital history. They say, "I never really loved you," or "You never really acted like you loved me." That is just a way to make themselves feel that they didn't do such a terrible thing.

Why do some people in unhappy marriages have affairs and others do not?

Number one is opportunity. Number two is values. Some people do not think an affair is justified for any reason. Others think it's okay if you're not getting it at home or if you "fall in love" with another person.

Surveys show that for women, the highest justification is for love; emotional intimacy is next. Sex is last on their list of justifications. It's the opposite for men; sex scores the highest.

Is infidelity in a long-standing marriage the same as in one of shorter duration?

It is potentially more threatening to the marriage when it happens earlier, and the chances of the marriage surviving are less, particularly where the woman is having an affair.

Did she choose the wrong mate?

She thinks so, especially if her affair partner is the opposite of her husband.

From your perspective, what's going on?

She's growing and changing, and she chooses somebody she sees as more similar to herself. Usually it's someone at work. Her husband may be working very hard in his profession or going to school and not paying much attention to her. She feels a little lonely, and then she gets involved. Or maybe her husband is very caring, and the relationship is so supportive and stable that it doesn't have a challenge for her.

The opportunities for affairs have changed radically in the past 20 years. Men and women are together all the time in the workplace, and workplaces are sexy places. You dress up, you're trying your best, there's energy in the air.

And you're not cleaning up vomit or the hot water heater that just flooded the basement. And it's not at the end of the day when you're exhausted. Also, you're working together on something that has excitement and meaning.

One of the major shifts is that more married women are having affairs than in the past. There are several reasons. Today's woman has usually had more experience with premarital sex, so she's not as inhibited about getting involved sexually with another man. She has more financial independence, so she's not taking as great a risk. And she is working with men on a more equal level, so the men are very attractive to her.

What do people seek in an affair partner?

Either we choose somebody very different from our partner, or we choose somebody like our partner used to be, but a younger version. A woman married to a really sweet guy who helps with the dishes, who is very nurturing and very secure, may at some point see him as boring and get interested in the high-achieving, high-energy man who may even be a bit chauvinistic. But if she's married to the man with the power and the status, then she's interested in the guy who is sensitive and touchy-feely, who may not be as ambitious.

Is this just the nature of attraction?

It has to do with the fact that people really want it all. Probably the only way to get it all is to be in more than one relationship at the same time. We have different parts of ourselves.

The other flip-flop in choice of affair partner reflects the fact that the marriage often represents a healing of our family wounds. Somebody who lacked a secure attachment figure in their family of origin chooses a mate who provides security and stability. It's healthy to seek that balancing.

But after we've mastered that, we often want to go back and find somebody like that difficult parent and make that person love us. There is a correlation between the nature of the attachment figure and the affair partner; the person is trying to master incomplete business from childhood. As a result, some people will choose an affair partner who is difficult, temperamental, or unpredictable. Under those circumstances, the unfaithful partner is often caught in a triangle.

What do you mean?

The person maintains the marriage, and can't leave it, and maintains the affair, and can't leave that either. Tension arises when either the affair partner or spouse applies pressure on them to get off the fence. The spouse provides security and a sense of family, the affair partner excitement and passion. When the involved spouse says, "I don't know which person to be with," what they really want is to keep both.

The challenge is, how do people satisfy all of their needs within the marriage?

It is a false belief that if I'm incomplete, I have to be completed by another person. You have to do it through your own life, your own work, for your own pleasure,
through individual growth. The more fulfilled you are, in terms of things that you do separately that please you, the more individuated and more whole you are—and the more intimate you can be. Then you're not expecting the other person to make you happy. You're expecting the other person to join you in your happiness.

> ## When women have affairs, it's much more often a result of long-term marital dissatisfaction.

Are more couples trying to survive affairs these days?

People are more willing to work through them. People are saying, I'm willing to work this through, but we have to solve whatever problems we have; we have to get something out of this; our marriage has to be even better than it was before.

More men are calling to come in for therapy. That's a very positive sign. The downside is, it's often too late. By the time men are alarmed, the woman is too distanced from the marriage.

What other changes do you see in affairs these days?

Cyber affairs are new. For some people the computer is very addictive. They get very caught up in it. It's hiding out, escaping. And an affair is an escape—from the
realities of everyday life. These two escapes are now paired.

The other danger on-line is that people can disguise who they are. Think of the roles you can take on if you hide behind a screen. More so than in workplace affairs, you can project anything onto the other person.

You can act out any fantasy you want. You can make this other person become anybody you want them to be. There's a loosening up, because you're not face-to-face with the person.

This attracts only a certain kind of person, doesn't it?

We don't know yet. I always get e-mail questions from people who are concerned because their partner is having an on-line relationship with somebody. Or their partner had an affair with somebody they met on-line. It's very prevalent, and it's very dangerous.

If you're talking to somebody on the computer, and you begin to talk about your sexual fantasies, and you're not talking to your partner about your sexual fantasies, which relationship now has more sexual chemistry? Which has more emotional intimacy? Then your partner walks in the room, and you switch screens. Now you've got a wall of secrecy. It has all the components of an affair. And it's easy.

Technology has impacted affairs in another way, too. Many people have discovered a partner's affair by getting the cellular phone bill, or by getting in the car and pushing redial on the car phone, or by taking their partner's beeper and seeing who's been calling. We're leaving a whole new electronic trail.

Has that changed the dynamics or the psychology of affairs in any way?

In the past, when someone was suspicious they could ask their partner: "What's going on? You seem distant lately." If the

'HOW DO I *Know* YOU WON'T *Betray* ME *Again*'

The following are signs of recovery, healing, and hope for a committed future together.

The unfaithful partner:
• recognizes and understands the individual vulnerabilities that contributed to the affair—curiosity, depression, need for excitement, and rescue fantasies are common ones—and views them as danger signals.
• shows empathy for the pain caused by the infidelity.
• assumes responsibility for the betrayal, regardless of any problems that existed in the marriage.

The betrayed partner:
• is able to recognize when his/her partner might be lying again.
• refuses to put his/her head in the sand.
• refuses to give without getting anything back.

Together you develop a united front:
• You can refer to affair-related events with calmness, perhaps humor.
• You can make united decisions concerning fallout from the affair, such as intrusive phone calls or a request for AIDS testing, and jointly manage present and future encounters with the affair partner.
• Your marriage is stronger; there's more reciprocity, more caring and communication, and better conflict management.
• You see eye to eye on the value of exclusivity and monogamy because of the pain the infidelity caused.
• You share responsibility for changing the relationship.
• You make more time for yourselves as a couple, apart from your children's needs, as a way to strengthen the friendship and erotic bond between you.—SG

partner denied anything was wrong, there wasn't a whole lot a person could do. Now there's tangible evidence people can utilize to find out if their hunches are indeed true.

There is a public conception of affairs as glamorous, but the aftermath is pretty messy. How do we square these views?

They're both true. In those captured moments, there is passion and romance. We're in Stage One of relationship formation—idealizing the partner. This Stage One can go on for years, as long as there's a forbidden aspect.

The admiration and positive mirroring can go on for a long time—until you get to a reality-based relationship. And this is why so many affairs end after the person leaves the marriage.

How many affairs survive as enduring relationships?

Only 10% of people who leave their relationship for affairs end up with the affair partner. Once you can be with the person every day and deal with all the little irritations in a relationship, you're into Stage Two—disillusionment.

How do most affairs get exposed?

Sometimes the betrayed partner will just ask, "Are you involved with somebody else?" Sometimes the affair partner, when it's a woman, does something to inform the wife—she sends a letter or even shows up on the doorstep. She asks, "Do you know where your husband's been?" Her motivation is not to be helpful but to break up the marriage. But often she's the one who then gets left out.

Sometimes people find out in horrible ways. They read about it in the newspaper, or they get a sexually transmitted disease. Or the cell phone bill arrives. Or their partner gets arrested—if there is a sexual addiction, the partner may be caught with prostitutes. Sometimes, somebody is suspicious and checks it out by going to the hotel room to see whether their partner's alone, or by hiring detectives.

Can all relationships be fixed?

No. What I look for is how the unfaithful partner shows empathy for the pain that they have caused when the betrayed spouse starts acting crazy.

In what way do they act crazy?

They're very emotional. They cry easily, their emotions flip-flop. They are hypervigilant. They want to look at the beeper. They have flashbacks. In the car, they hear a country-western song and start crying or accusing. They obsess over the details of the affair. Although these are common post-traumatic reactions to infidelity, their behavior is very erratic and upsetting to them and their partner. How

much compassion the partner has for that is one hallmark.

Another sign of salvageability lies in how much responsibility the unfaithful partner takes for the choice they made, regardless of problems that pre-existed in the marriage. (We definitely need to work on the weaknesses of the marriage, but not to justify the affair.)

If the unfaithful partner says, "You made me do it," that's not as predictive of a good outcome as when the partner says, "We should have gone to counseling to deal with the problems before this happened." Sometimes the unfaithful partner doesn't regret the affair because it was very exciting.

One of the big strains between the partners in the primary relationship is the way they perceive the affair partner.

> **People often try to justify an affair by rewriting the marital history. They'll say, 'I never really loved you.'**

How so?

A lot of the anger and the rage the betrayed spouse feels is directed toward the affair partner rather than the marital partner: "That person doesn't have any morals"; "That person's a home wrecker." To believe that of the marital partner would make it difficult to stay in the relationship.

At the same time, the person who had the affair may still be idealizing the affair partner. The unfaithful spouse perceives the affair partner as an angel, whereas the betrayed person perceives them as an evil person.

It's important at some point in the healing process for the involved person to see some flaws in the affair partner, so that they can partly see what their partner, the betrayed spouse, is telling them. It's also important for the betrayed spouse to see the affair partner not as a cardboard character but as a human being who did some caring things.

Is there anything else that helps you gauge the salvageability of a relationship after an affair?

Empathy, responsibility—and the degree of understanding of the vulnerabilities that made an affair possible.

What vulnerabilities?

There are individual vulnerabilities, such as curiosity. Somebody gets invited for lunch, and they go to the house because they're curious. They must learn that getting curious is a danger sign. Or if some damsel or guy in distress comes with a sad story, they learn to give out the name of a great therapist instead of becoming their confessor and confidante. Knowing what the vulnerabilities are helps you avoid them.

And relationship vulnerabilities?

The biggest one I see today is the child-centered marriage. I tell couples, If you really love your kids, the best gift you can give them is your own happy marriage. You can't have a happy marriage if you never spend time alone. Your children need to see you closing the bedroom door or going out together without them. That gives a sense of security greater than what they get by just by being loved.

Today's parents feel guilty because they don't have enough time with their kids. They think they're making it up to them by spending with them whatever leisure time they do have. They have *family* activities and *family* vacations. To help them rebuild the marriage, I help them become more couple-centered.

There has to be a separate layer of adult relationship?

The affair represents a man and a woman getting together in a dyad and just devoting themselves to each other. Very busy couples sometimes have to actually look at their calendars and find when they can spend time together.

Are there other vulnerabilities?

One is: getting too intimate with co-workers. One way to guard against danger is, if there's somebody you really like at work, then include them as a couple; invite that person and their partner to come over so that there isn't a separate relationship with that person. That's not a guarantee; people do have affairs with their best friend's spouse.

Can you tell whether someone is secretly continuing the affair?

A sign that the affair is continuing is when the unfaithful partner isn't doing anything caring and keeps making excuses—"I don't feel it yet," or "It would be false if I did it now." Sometimes it feels disloyal to the affair partner to be too caring.

Is it hard to get over an affair without a therapist?

It's hard to do *with* a therapist. People can get over it, but I don't know that they resolve the issues. Usually the unfaithful person wants to let it rest at "Hi hon, I'm back. Let's get on with our lives. Why do we have to keep going back over the past?" The betrayed person wants to know the story with all the gory details. They may begin to feel *they're* wrong to keep asking and may suppress their need to know because their partner doesn't want to talk about it. They may stay together, but they really don't learn anything or heal.

Can it ever be the same as it was before?

The affair creates a loss of innocence and some scar tissue. I tell couples things will never be the same. But the relationship may be stronger.

How do you rebuild trust?

Through honesty. First, I have to build safety. It comes about by stopping all contact with the affair partner and sharing your whereabouts, by being willing to answer the questions from your partner, by handing over the beeper, even by creating a fund to hire a detective to check up at random.

It also requires sharing information about encounters with the affair partner before being asked; when you come home, you say, "I saw him today, and he asked me how we're doing; I said, I really don't want to discuss it with you."

That's counterintuitive. People think that talking about it with the spouse will create an upset, and they'll have to go through the whole thing again. But it doesn't. Instead of trying to put the affair in a vault and lock it up, if they're willing to take it out and look at it, then the trust is rebuilt through that intimacy. The betrayed spouse may say, "I remember when such-and-such happened." If the unfaithful spouse can say, "Yeah, I just recalled such-and-such," and they bring up things or ask their partner, "How are you feeling? I see you're looking down today, is that because you're remembering?," trust can be rebuilt.

Eventually, the questioning and revealing assume a more normal level?

Yes, but things will often pop up. Someone or something will prompt them to remember something that was said. "What did you mean when you said that?" Or, "What were you doing when that happened?"

In the beginning, the betrayed partner wants details. Where, what, when. Did you tell them you love them? Did you give them gifts? Did they give you gifts? How often did you see them? How many times did you have sex? Did you have oral sex? Where did you have sex, was it in our house? How much money did you spend? Those kinds of factual questions need to be answered.

> ### Unless the unfaithful partner shows empathy for the pain they have caused, the marriage can't be helped.

Eventually the questions develop more complexity. How did it go on so long if you knew that it was wrong? After that first time, did you feel guilty? At that point they're in the final stages of trauma recovery, which is the search for meaning.

And they have come to a joint understanding about what the affair meant?

By combining their stories and their perceptions. A couple builds trust by rewriting their history and including the story of the affair. Some couples do a beautiful job in trying to understand the affair together, and they co-create the story of what they've been through together. When couples really are healed, they may even tease each other with private little jokes about something that they know about the affair partner or about something that happened during the affair. You can see that they finally have some comfort with it.

One of the signs that they are working in a much more united way is that their perception of the affair partner becomes more integrated—not all evil or all angel, but a human being who perhaps did manipulate but also was caring.

Some people, particularly men, are philanderers; they have repeated affairs. What's going on?

First of all, there are different kinds of philanderers. Sometimes it's easier to deal with this kind of infidelity, because there isn't the emotional involvement; sometimes it's harder, because it's such an established pattern.

One question I explore with somebody who has had lots of sexual relationships is whether it's an addiction or, in the case of men particularly, a sense of entitlement. There are some women now in positions of power who also seem to be treating sex in the same casual way and exploiting power in the same way as male philanderers. Nevertheless, in our culture, there is a sense of male privilege that condones and even encourages affairs.

How does entitlement affect matters?

If a man feels entitled, he experiences little guilt. Also, it is not necessarily a compulsive behavior; he has the ability to choose to stop it—if he changes his attitudes, if he sees what the consequences are, if he comes to believe that marriage means more than being a provider but being a loving father or caring husband. Even if he doesn't see anything wrong with philandering, if he can see the pain it causes someone he loves, he may really make the vow not only to his partner but to himself.

A sexually addicted person usually uses sex the way others use drugs: they get anxious, they say they're not going to do it, but then they're driven toward it. They get a momentary gratification followed by remorse. They decide they're not going to do it again, then they do.

There's a compulsive quality.

There is also often remorse and guilt. If they get into therapy, they may learn what addiction means in their life. Often, there's an emptiness that's linked to a need for excitement. There may be an underlying depression. They then begin to deal with the underlying source of that compulsive behavior.

What is the single most important thing you want people to know about infidelity?

BOUNDARIES. That it is possible to love somebody else, to be attracted to somebody else, even if you have a good marriage. In this collegial world where we work together, you have to conduct yourself by being aware of appropriate boundaries, by not creating opportunities, particularly at a time when you might be vulnerable.

That means that if you travel together, you never invite someone for a drink in the room; if you just had a fight with your spouse, you don't discuss it with a potential partner.

You can have a friendship, but you have to be careful who you share your deepest feelings with. Although women share their deep feelings with lots of people, particularly other women, men are usually most comfortable sharing their feelings in a love relationship. As a result, when a relationship becomes intimate and emotional, men tend to sexualize it.

There may be a history of incest or sexual abuse. Some woman may be turning the tables by using their sexuality to control men rather than be controlled by them, or they may be using sex as a way to get affection, because they don't believe that they can get it any other way. Some people may be acting out like rebellious adolescents against a spouse who is too parental.

What is happening in relationships that are parental or otherwise unequal?

Sometimes there is an over-functioning spouse and an under-functioning spouse. One partner takes on a lot of responsibility—and then resents it. The more a person puts energy into something and tries to work on it, the more committed to the relationship that person is. The other partner, who is only semi-involved in the relationship, is freer to get involved in an affair; they're not as connected to the marriage.

This is interesting because the popular notion is that the person who has the affair wasn't getting enough at home. The reality is that they weren't giving enough at home.

How do you handle that?

In rebuilding that relationship, more equity has to be created. The issue isn't what can the betrayed spouse do to make the partner happy—it's what can the unfaithful spouse do to make their partner happy. In research and in practice, my colleague Tom Wright, Ph.D., and I have observed that when you compare who does more—who is more understanding, who is more romantic, who enjoys sex more—the affair is almost always more equitable than the marriage. Usually, the person was giving more—more time, more attention, more compliments—in the affair than in the marriage. If they can invest in the marriage what they were doing in the affair, they'll feel more.

There is some research showing that people are more satisfied in equitable relationships. When relationships are not equitable, even the over-benefited partners are not as satisfied as those in equitable relationships.

You seem to be constantly reversing the conventional wisdom about affairs.

I've noticed that when younger women get involved in affairs early in the marriage and then leave, often they have not been invested in the marriage. They're working hard, climbing a ladder; the husband is the one making dinner while she's working late. He is the devastated one, because he is really committed and has given a lot. But he is peripheral in her life.

I've seen several couples who had a plan they agreed on, to build a house, or for one partner to go back to school. The person who had the responsibility for carrying out the plan was totally engrossed in it, while the other person felt so neglected that they then had an affair. The betrayed person felt terribly betrayed, because he or she thought he was working for their future. But he didn't necessarily listen to distress signs.

A relationship is like a fire. You can let it go down, but you can't let it go out. Even though you're in another part of the house, you have to go back every once in a while to stoke the coals.

> **People think a person having an affair isn't getting enough at home. The truth is, the person isn't giving enough.**

Do you ever counsel people directly to leave a relationship?

I would support a betrayed spouse ending the relationship if a period of time has gone by in which they have tried to work on the relationship but the affair continues secretly.

Leaving a bad marriage without trying to repair it first is like buying high and selling low. Better to see how good you can make it, then look at it and ask: Is this good enough?

What percentage of couples make it?

Those who stay in therapy and have stopped the affair have a real good chance. After an affair is first uncovered and the involved person vows to stop it, it usually doesn't stop right away. That would be coitus interruptus; there has to be some kind of closure. There will be secret meetings to say good bye or to make sure that you can really let go. But that should happen in the first few weeks or months.

Are some occupations or settings particularly conducive to affairs?

I don't know any place where the risk is low. When I was doing research for my dissertation, I went to the Baltimore-Washington airport and to an office park and gave out questionnaires. I'd go up to the men, quite imposing in their pinstripe suits and starched collars, and ask if they'd complete an anonymous research questionnaire on marriage.

I was stunned when the forms came back; so many of the men who had looked so conservative had engaged in extramarital sex. It is now known that, while we suspect the liberals, conservative men are actually more likely to be having extramarital affairs—because they split sex and affection. There are the nice girls you marry and the wild girls you have sex with.

The double standard is alive and well.

Men who score high on traits of authoritarianism are more likely to separate sex and affection than men who are low in authoritarianism. Military officers fall into this category.

People in high-drama professions—among doctors, those in the ER, trauma surgeons, cardiologists—engage in a certain amount of living on the edge that is associated with affairs. Certainly, being in the entertainment business is a risk; there's a lot of glamor, and people are away from home a lot. Often you're in a make-believe world with another person.

To hear that a person can be happily married and having an affair is surprising.

I often get asked, "How can women stay with men who have repeated affairs?" Many people believe the Clintons have some kind of an arrangement.

I don't know anything about their marriage, but I do know that it's more comfortable for people to believe they have an arrangement. When something bad happens to others, we distance ourselves from it, try to find an explanation that couldn't possibly apply to us.

You use the metaphor of walls and windows in talking about affairs.

There is almost always a wall of secrecy around the affair; the primary partner does not know what's happening on the other side of that wall. In the affair, there is often a window into the marriage, like a one-way mirror.

To reconstruct the marriage, you have to reverse the walls and windows—put up a wall with the affair partner and put up a window inside the marriage. Answering a spouse's questions about what happened in the affair is a way to reverse the process. It's a matter of who's on the inside and who's on the outside. Sometimes people will open windows but not put up walls. Sometimes they put up walls but don't open the windows. Unless you do both, you cannot rebuild safety and trust in the marriage.

The Politics of Fatigue

The gender war has been replaced by the exhaustion of trying to do it all

By Richard Morin and Megan Rosenfeld
Washington Post Staff Writers

Men and women have declared a cease-fire in the war that raged between the sexes through much of the last half of this century. In its place, they face common new enemies—the stress, lack of time and financial pressure of modern life.

A new national survey has found that after nearly a generation of sharing the workplace and renegotiating domestic duties, most men and women agree that increased gender equity has enriched both sexes. But both also believe that the strains of this relatively new world have made building successful marriages, raising children and leading satisfying lives ever more difficult.

The problem that now unites them, as warehouse operations manager James Lindow, 35, of Green Bay, Wis., puts it, is "the lack of time you spend with your life."

Large majorities of more than 4,000 men and women questioned in a series of surveys last fall placed high importance on having a successful marriage and family. At the same time, equally large majorities of working men and women said they felt bad about leaving their children in the care of others, and wished they could devote more time to their families and themselves.

Surprisingly, although men and women agreed they should have equal work opportunities, and men said they approved of women working outside the home, large majorities of both said it would be better if women could instead stay home and just take care of the house and children.

Majorities of men and women believe there still are more advantages to being a man rather than a woman, and that most men don't understand the problems women face. And the survey shows that in some areas, the reality of daily existence for two-career families still has not caught up with changed attitudes.

Most men in the polls said they were happy to share child care and domestic chores with wives who work outside the home. Yet household duties remain sharply divided along gender lines. Working mothers still do twice as much housework as their husbands, and more than half of all women questioned expressed at least some dissatisfaction with the amount of help their husbands provide around the house.

"I think men are beginning to get it, at least some are, some of the time," says survey respondent Traci Hughes-Velez, 34, of Brooklyn, N.Y., director of compensation for a major corporation. "But there are times they don't. My husband just doesn't seem to get it when I tell him that I feel I'm always on duty. When we're at home, I'm the one who always has an eye out for our son, making sure he's eating on time, things like that."

The survey shows that real differences in perspective and perception remain between the sexes. Men are more likely to support increases in defense spending; women more favorably disposed toward health care for uninsured children. Women are more likely than men to be religious and to value close friendships; men are more likely than women to want successful careers and wealth, and more likely to value an "active sex life."

But rather than emphasizing their differences and blaming many of life's problems on each other, men and women share a sense of conflict and confusion about how to make it all work under today's pressures. To a large extent, the politics of resentment have become the politics of fatigue.

The Washington Post is examining how men and women are managing in this transformed world based on a series of five nationwide surveys sponsored by The Washington Post in collaboration with researchers from Harvard University and the Henry J. Kaiser Family Foundation.

The people surveyed came from all walks of life and all parts of the country. They included people like B. J. Sande, a 32-year-old mechanical engineer from Chattaroy, Wash., and Phyllis Wilkes, a 68-year-old San Franciscan retired from waitressing in a restaurant called Clown Alley. A sewing machine operator, a preschool teacher, a woman on welfare, a man looking for a job—they all spoke with conviction about how their lives are mostly better but definitely harder.

This story describes some of the consequences of the gender revolution, as revealed in survey data, in conversations with men and women, and in interviews with social scientists.

❖

IN JUST THE PAST THREE DECADES, MOST AMERICANS agree that changing gender roles have dramatically altered their lives at work and at home.

Government statistics confirm what they see every day: The world of work is increasingly a man's and a woman's world. Between 1970 and 1995, the percentage of women ages 25 to 54 who worked outside the home climbed from 50 percent to 76 percent, sociologists Suzanne Bianchi and Daphne Spain reported in their recent book "Balancing Act."

Changes in Gender Roles

Men and women agree that the changes in gender roles in recent years have been both good and bad, and nostalgia for the lifestyle of the 1950s lingers, according to a new series of national surveys by The Washington Post/Henry J. Kaiser Family Foundation/ Harvard University.

Q: **How much change do you think there has been in recent years in the relationship between men and women in their roles in families, the workplace and society?**

	Men	Women
A great deal	36%	33%
Quite a lot	**40**	**43**
Only some	20	21
None at all	4	3

Q: **Do you think these changes have been mainly good for the country, mainly bad, or have they been both good and bad?**

	Men	Women
Mainly good	23%	13%
Mainly bad	14	12
Both good and bad	**62**	**72**
No difference	1	1

Q: **Considering everything, do you think it would be better or worse for the country if men and women went back to the traditional roles they had in the 1950s, or don't you think it would make a difference?**

	Men	Women
Better	35%	**42%**
Worse	35	33
No difference	29	21

Changed Roles Make Things Harder

For each of the following aspects of life, please tell me whether you think this change [in the relationship between men and women in their roles in families, the workplace and society] has made things easier or harder for people in this country, or whether it hasn't made much difference:

	Men	Women
For parents to raise children		
Easier	12%	14%
Harder	**80**	**80**
Not much difference	6	5
For marriages to be successful		
Easier	12%	15%
Harder	**70**	**72**
Not much difference	13	11
For families to earn enough money to live comfortably		
Easier	31%	22%
Harder	**60**	**69**
Not much difference	7	8
For men to lead satisfying lives		
Easier	22%	30%
Harder	**53**	**44**
Not much difference	22	21
For women to lead satisfying lives		
Easier	42%	34%
Harder	**44**	**50**
Not much difference	10	14

Other numbers tell a richer story. The percentage of lawyers and judges who are women doubled to 29 percent between 1983 and 1996, while the percentage of female physicians increased from 16 to 26 percent. Today, nearly a third of all professional athletes are women—almost double the proportion in 1983.

Women currently make up nearly half of all entry- and mid-level managers in American corporations, up from 17 percent in 1972. But the executive suite remains disproportionately male: A 1995 survey of Fortune 500 corporations found that only 1 in 10 corporate officers and fewer than 3 percent of all chief executive officers are women.

In higher education, gender equity is a reality. Slightly more than half of all bachelor's degrees were awarded to women last year, and the percentage of doctoral degrees granted to white women has increased from 25 percent in 1977 to 44 percent in 1993. Among African Americans, women receive more of the doctorates.

At home, men do more around the house than their fathers ever did. But the burden still falls on women: On average, working mothers do about 20 hours of housework a week, down from 30 hours two decades ago, while their husbands are doing 10 hours a week, up from five hours, Bianchi said in the book. And it's still women who say they're responsible for the way the house looks, according to the Post-Kaiser-Harvard polls.

The survey of couples with children found that women still do most of the food shopping, laundry, cooking, cleaning, arranging for child care and babysitters, and taking children to appointments or after-school activities—even when both parents work full time. Men tend to mow the lawn, shovel the snow and take out the trash, the survey found.

○

IN IMPORTANT WAYS, THE SURVEY SUGGESTS THAT WE have yet to find new patterns of living that recognize the real workloads of two-career couples with children, and some resentment, nostalgia and fatigue are reflected in the survey results.

"I work, my husband works, I come home and I work. I clean the house and I do my laundry," says Susan Gehrke, 44, a tenant assistant for the elderly in La Crosse, Wis. "Someone comes over and the house is a mess, they don't look at the man and think, 'What a slob,' they look at her and say, 'What a slob.' "

Says Lindow, 35, the Green Bay warehouse operations manager, whose wife also works full time: "Your kids are going to the day care, or wherever they are taken care of by somebody else. By the time you get done with your job, you've got to rush home and make supper, do whatever, and then you have to run your kids somewhere else. You don't get enough time to spend with your wife anymore, either, because you are both working. You're lucky if you get to see your wife one or two hours a day. What kind of quality time is that?"

Age, more than sex, shapes attitudes toward the changing roles of men and women, the survey suggests. Younger men and women were far more likely than their elders to say the change in gender roles has made their lives better.

"These changes have made a lot of people's lives better and it's made some people's lives worse," says the 32-year-old Sande, who is single. He adds: "Any time there is a change like there has been in my generation, there is always going to be some growing pains. But as a whole I think it's moving toward the direction of making things easier, better."

Powerful social and economic forces nourish and sustain the trends that create these tensions. Two out of three men and women surveyed agreed that it takes two incomes to get by these days; about half the respondents—men and women—said they work mostly because they must.

○

ONE OUT OF EVERY FIVE WORKING WOMEN SAID she would cheerfully quit her job if only she could afford to— but so did 1 in 5 men surveyed. Today, even mid-career crises are gender-neutral.

"I did stay home with my daughter the first couple years, but financially you just can't make it on one salary anymore," says Kelly Lynn Cruz, 22, of Henderson, Md., who is between jobs and has one child and another on the way. "It's hard on my family, anyway. I don't get to spend as much time with my child. The housework isn't always done, which makes me feel like I'm not always doing my job."

Why is the housework her work? "It just is," she says with a laugh, adding that "he helps. But it's mainly my job. I take care of the inside, he takes care of the outside."

Perhaps not even the '50s housewife worked this hard at home: "I've had grandmothers tell me their daughters work far harder and spend more time with their children than they did" in the 1950s, says Sharon Hays, a sociologist at the University of Virginia who studies family structure.

Many Americans say that mounting pressures to be it all and to have it all put many relationships on the rocks. In the survey, 7 in 10 said there's too much pressure on both men and women today to realize the American ideal: marriage, family and a successful career. Many survey respondents in subsequent interviews said they put the pressure on themselves. Not surprisingly, those who felt this tension most acutely also were more likely to say it's harder to make marriages and families work.

"There's too much pressure on everyone, period, whether they're men or women," says Karen Mapp, a 42-year-old PhD candidate and researcher in Boston.

In response to these pressures, 4 in 10 of those surveyed said, it would be better to return to the gender roles of the 1950s, a dimly remembered world of television's Ozzie and Harriet and their blithe suburban existence.

"I definitely think it would be good to go back," says Rose Pierre-Louis, 40, a social worker in Brooklyn, N.Y., who was among those interviewed in the poll. "Kids aren't being raised, they're just growing up. Nobody's getting married anymore. There's no respect between men and women, [or from] children for their parents."

○

BUT JUST AS MANY AMERICANS SAY THEY AREN'T eager to go back—particularly young people, who do not bear the burden of their parents' nostalgia.

"I've never been under the impression that I couldn't do something because I was a woman," says Jennifer Wedberg, 25, a graphics designer who lives in Lisle, Ill. "It would be a shame if things went back to the way they were in the '50s. . . . It's easier to grow up knowing that some day you're just going to get married and be a mom or a wife, and now it's more complex, you have to figure out what you want to do with your life. . . . But I think more choices is always a good thing."

Young women like Wedberg have many of the same conflicts—over whether to stay home or take an outside job after having children—that their mothers might have had. But they also believe they are entitled to be full participants in areas of life their mothers had to fight to enter, and they assume their personal identity includes a job or a career.

Similarly, young men generally accept that their lives at work and in the home have changed, and with these transformations have come new duties, responsibilities and rewards. "I'd just as soon stay home with the kids," says Lindow, who adds that it doesn't bother him that his wife has a better job than he does.

"I think a lot of the problems we hear of now are because we have raised our standards," says Christopher M. Moeller, 22, a radio reporter in Des Moines. "We're more involved in each other's lives. . . . We value equality, we value everybody wanting to have self-esteem, to get everything they want, and I don't see where imposing a limit on more than half of our population accomplishes that."

Washington Post assistant director of polling Claudia Deane and staff researcher Robert Thomason contributed to this report.

Book Excerpt: In the debates over quality time and how to balance work and family, kids are rarely heard. A new 'Ask the Children' study reveals how kids rate their moms and dads—and what children really want. BY ELLEN GALINSKY

Do Working Parents Make The Grade?

WHENEVER I MENTION THAT I AM STUDYing how kids see their working parents, the response is electric. People are fascinated. Parents want to know what I have found, but inevitably they are nervous, too. Sometimes they say, "I wonder what other people's children would say. I'm not sure that I'm ready to hear what mine have to say!"

Why has a comprehensive, in-depth study of this question never been conducted? Because we have been afraid to ask, afraid to know. But now I feel the time is right. The answers of children are illuminating, not frightening. They help us see that our assumptions about children's ideas are often at odds with reality. Ultimately, this information will help us be better parents—and better employees, too. In fact, adding children's voices to our national conversation about work and family life will change the way we think about them forever.

Many of the debates we've been having about work and family miss the mark. For example, we have been locked in a longstanding argument about whether it is "good or bad" for children if their mothers work. Numerous observational studies have found that having a working mother doesn't harm children, yet the debate still rages. Another way to assess this issue is to see whether children of

mothers who are not employed and children of working mothers differ in the way they feel they are being parented. In our "Ask the Children" study, we had a representative group of more than 1,000 children in grades three through 12 to evaluate their parents in 12 areas strongly linked to children's healthy development, school readiness and school success. In their responses—rendered in actual letter grades—having a mother who worked was never once predictive of how children assess their mothers' parenting skills. We also found that while the amount of time children and parents spend together is very important, most children don't want more time with their parents. Instead, they give their mothers and fathers higher grades if the time they do spend together is not rushed but focused and rich in shared activities.

It may seem surprising that children whose mothers are at home caring for them full time fail to see them as more supportive. But a mother who is employed can be there for her child or not, just as mothers who are not employed can be. Indeed, children of nonworking fathers see their dads less positively when it comes to making them feel important and loved and to participating in important events in the children's lives. Fathers who work part time are less likely to be seen as encouraging their children's learning. Perhaps fathers who work less than

Family Values

56% of parents think their kids want more time together; only 10% of kids want more time with Mom, 15.5% with Dad. Most kids, however, feel they have enough time.
62.5% of parents say they like their work a lot. Only 41% of children say Dad enjoys his job, and 42% says the same about Mom.
44.5% of kids say time with Mom is rushed, 37% say so with Dad. Only 33% of parents think time with their kids is rushed.
23% of kids want their parents to earn more; 14% of parents think kids want this.

From *Newsweek*, August 30, 1999, pp. 52-56. Excerpted from *Ask the Children* by Ellen Galinsky (Morrow, 1999). © 1999 by Ellen Galinsky. Reprinted by permission of William Morrow and Company, Inc.

Grading
Dad

He instills good values, but doesn't always know what 'really' goes on

SUBJECT	A	B	C	D	F
Raising me with good values	69%	18%	8%	4%	2%
Appreciating me for who I am	58	21	11	8	2
Encouraging me to enjoy learning	57.5	24	12	4	2
Making me feel important and loved	57	22	13	6	2
Being able to go to important events	55	22	13	5	5.5
Being there for me when I am sick	51.5	20	16	8	4
Spending time talking with me	43	24	19	10	4
Establishing traditions with me	41	26	15	11	7
Being involved in school life	38	24	19	12	7
Being someone to go to when upset	38	22	15	12	13
Controlling his temper	31	27	20	10	12
Knowing what goes on with me	31	30	17	12.5	10

NOTE: GRADES GIVEN BY CHILDREN IN SEVENTH THROUGH 12TH GRADES

full time or who are unemployed are feeling financial and role strain, which could affect how they interact with their children.

That children can appreciate the efforts of working parents is clear. Said one 12-year-old son of working parents: "If parents wish to provide some of the better things in life, both parents need to work and share the home and children responsibilities." A 15-year-old girl whose father works full time and whose mother does not said: "Your children may not like you working now, but it will pay off later on."

The problem isn't that mothers (and fathers) work: it is how we work and how work affects our parenting. For example, we asked the children in this study, "If you were granted one wish to change the way that your mother's or your father's work affects your life, what would that wish be?" We also asked more than 600 parents to guess what their child's response would be. Taken together, 56 percent of parents assume that their children would wish for more time together and less parental time at work. And 50 percent of parents with children up to 18 years old say they feel that they have too little time with their child—fathers (56 percent) even more so than mothers (44 percent).

But only 10 percent of children wish that their mothers would spend more time with them, and 15.5 percent say the same thing about their fathers. And surprisingly, children with

employed mothers and those with mothers at home do not differ on whether they feel they have too little time with Mom.

What the largest proportion of children (23 percent) say that they want is for their mothers and their fathers to make more money. I suspect that money is seen as a stress-reducer, given children's other answers. The total number of children who wish that their parents would be less stressed or less tired by work is even larger: 34 percent make this wish for their mothers and 27.5 percent for their fathers. Sympathy for working parents comes through loud and clear: "I would like to thank the parents of America for working so hard to earn money," says one 15-year-old girl. "I know that a working parent goes through so much for their children."

The study also reveals what children learn from their parents about the world of work. Only about two in five children think their parents like their work a lot, compared with 62.5 percent of parents who say they do. That's probably because many of us have said to our kids, "I have to go to work." Or "I wish I didn't have to leave." We seem to talk around children rather than with them about our jobs. And our reluctance to talk to our children about our work has meant that young people are getting haphazard rather than intentional information, sometimes blaming themselves for distress we pick up on the job, and not fully appreciating the potential of their own future careers.

As a result, many children play detective to figure out what is going on in our jobs that upsets or elates us. They study our moods at the end of the workday. One of our young subjects says you can tell if your parents are in a bad mood "because you get a short and simple answer. If they had a bad day, they won't talk. Or they will just go off by themselves."

What makes a good parent? Through our interviews with parents and children, eight critical parenting skills emerged. We then asked the children in our national survey to grade their own mothers and dads on those criteria. They are:

1. Making the child feel important and loved
2. Responding to the child's cues and clues
3. Accepting the child for who he or she is, but expecting success
4. Promoting strong values
5. Using constructive discipline
6. Providing routines and rituals to make life predictable and create positive neural patterns in developing brains
7. Being involved in the child's education
8. Being there for the child

Which of these skills earned parents the highest—and lowest—grades? Among children in the seventh through the 12th grades, mothers are given the highest grades for being there when the child is sick (81 percent gave their mothers an A) and for raising their children with good values (75 percent). They receive the lowest grades for controlling their tempers

Time spent in shared activities wins parents high marks— but not if it feels hurried or rushed

when their children make them angry (only 29 percent gave their mothers an A) and for knowing what is really going on in their children's lives (35 percent). The age of the child makes a difference. Younger children consistently rate their parents more favorably than older ones, which no doubt reflects the way teenagers separate emotionally from their parents.

Money also matters. In analysis after analysis, the children's perception of their families' economic health is strongly linked to how they rate their moms' and dads' parenting skills. Although the public often views the problems of children as primarily moral in nature, our analyses show that families that do not have to worry about putting bread on the table may have more to give to their children emotionally. They also may be able to raise their children in more positive, cohesive communities.

These findings illustrate why it is so important to ask the children rather than to rely on our own assumptions. The issue of time with children has typically been framed in the public debate as a mothers' issue. But when we ask the children, we see that fathers need to be front and center in this discussion, as well.

Children in the seventh through the 12th grades judge their fathers less favorably than their mothers in some important respects, such as making their child feel important and loved and being someone whom the child can go to if upset. Teenagers are more likely than their younger counterparts to want more time with their fathers. Thirty-nine percent of children 13 through 18 years old feel they have too little time with their fathers, compared with 29 percent of children 8 through 12 years old.

We found that the quantity of time with mothers and fathers does matter a great deal. Children who spend more time with their mothers and fathers on workdays and nonworkdays see their parents more positively, feel that their parents are more successful at managing work and family responsibilities, and see their parents as putting their families first. "I think that if the parents spend more time with their children, they will become better people in life," says a 12-year-old boy whose father works part time while his mom stays home.

But to move beyond simply cataloging the number of hours children and parents spend together, we looked at what parents and children do while they are together, such as eating a meal, playing a game or sport or exercising, doing homework (together) and watching TV. For all these activities, the same pattern holds: the more frequently parents and children engaged in them together, the more positive the assessment parents got from their children.

But spending time together isn't enough. Many children said their interactions with parents feel rushed and hurried, and they gave their mothers and fathers lower marks as a result. More than two in five (44.5 percent) children feel that their time with their mother is rushed, while 37 percent feel their time with their father is rushed. Some mentioned mornings as

Grading Mom

She's there during illness, but sometimes loses her temper

SUBJECT	A	B	C	D	F
Being there for me when I am sick	81%	11%	5%	2%	1%
Raising me with good values	75	15	6	3	2
Making me feel important and loved	64	20	10	5	1
Being able to go to important events	64	20	10	3	3.5
Appreciating me for who I am	64	18	8	6	5
Encouraging me to enjoy learning	59	23	11.5	3	3
Being involved in school life	46	25	14	10	6
Being someone to go to when upset	46	22	14	8	9
Spending time talking with me	43	33	14	6	4
Establishing traditions with me	38	29	17	10	6
Knowing what goes on with me	35	31	15	10	9
Controlling her temper	29	27.5	20.5	12	11

particularly hectic times for their families. One 12-year-old girl said of her mother: "She's rushing and telling me to rush . . . And my backpack weighs a ton, so if she walks me to school, it's like running down the street. I'm like, 'wait up . . .'"

Predictably, children are more likely to see their parents positively if their time together is calmer. For example: of children 8 through 18 years of age who rate their time with their mothers as very calm, 86 percent give their mothers an A for making them feel important and loved, compared with 63 percent of those who rate their time with their mothers as very rushed. And 80 percent of children who feel their time with their fathers is very calm give them an A for "appreciating me for who I am," compared with only 50.5 percent of those who rate their time with their fathers as very rushed.

The flip side of feeling rushed and distracted with children is concentration and focus. In one-on-one interviews, we asked parents to describe moments when they felt particularly successful at home. Over and over, we heard the word "focus." The mother of a 12-year-old says: "It's the time you spend with your children [when] you are really focused on them that's good; not a distracted time."

Of children in the seventh through 12th grades, 62 percent say that mothers find it "very easy" and 52 percent say that fathers find it very easy to focus on them when they are to-

Kids who think their families are financially secure feel more positive about Mom and Dad

gether. And children are very attuned to the times when their parents are truly focused on them: "They're not just saying normal things like 'uh huh . . . uh hmmm.' They seem to be very intent on what I'm saying, they're not just looking away," said a 10-year-old boy. Some children even have "tests" of whether their parent is focusing on them. For example, one 13-year-old boy throws nonsense statements — like "a goldfish on the grass"—into the middle of a sentence to check out whether his parents are really listening to him.

Every analysis we conducted revealed that when children feel that their mothers and fathers can focus on them, they are much more likely to feel that their parents manage their work and family responsibilities more successfully and put their families before their work. And they give their parents much higher marks for all of the parenting skills we examined.

So, is it quantity time or quality time? Clearly, the words we're using to describe time within the family are wrong. To change the debate, we need new words. Since "focus" is the word that parents use to describe the quality of time they treasure most, I suggest we use it. And since parents and children highly value the quantity of time they spend being together, whether sharing a meal or just being around each other in a nonrushed way, we need a phrase for that, too. Children need focused times and hang-around times.

I hope that, as a result of this book, the conversations around work and family will change. When parents and children talk together about these issues, reasonable changes can be made. Children will tell us how some things could be better. Yes, they will still try to push our guilt buttons. Yes, they will still read our moods and plead their case for what they want because kids will be kids. But we are the adults, and we set the tone for our relationships with our children.

I repeat the wisdom of a 12-year-old child: "Listen. Listen to what your kids say, because you know, sometimes it's very important. And sometimes a kid can have a great idea and it could even affect you." So let's ask the children.

Balancing
Work and
Family

by Joseph H. Pleck

Fathers who live with their families are spending more time with their children. At the same time, more fathers are not living with their families

Stories in the media often portray contemporary men balancing an active family role with the breadwinning responsibilities of a career. At the same time, commonly held wisdom suggests that yesterday's men—even those from just a few decades ago—often failed at that juggling act, serving primarily as full-time workers and participating in few, if any, family activities. These images of present and past men, however, might arise more from folklore than fact. By studying exactly what activities American men do now, and have done in the past, social scientists find an interrelated web of trends that are changing men's roles.

In 1956 Swedish sociologist Alva Myrdal and British historian Viola Klein published *Women's Two Roles: Home and Work.* Their title introduced what became the leading understanding of the change in adult women's lives in industrial societies over the first half of the 20th century. In addition to their traditional child-rearing and homemaking role within the family, women were increasingly engaging in a second role: paid employment outside the family. In the decades subsequent to *Women's Two Roles*, Myrdal and other sociologists have tentatively suggested that in the long run, women could not succeed at both roles unless men also took on more family responsibilities. Our society is still just beginning to recognize that men, too, face the challenge of dual roles.

Are Men Doing More in the Family?

Since the mid-1970s other social scientists and I have systematically studied the changing ways in which contemporary American men combine and prioritize their work and family responsibilities. In attempting to analyze these changes, many people—especially students, journalists and scholars—often ask: Are men doing more in the family now than they did in the past? That question can be examined on many levels. For example, beyond simply knowing how much time men spend with their families, one might examine what men do during their family time and what it means to them. This changing role for men also leads to larger social implications.

Reprinted with permission from *Scientific American Presents—Men: The Scientific Truth About Their Work, Play, Health, and Passions,* Vol. 10, Issue 2, Summer 1999, pp. 38-43. © 1999 by Scientific American, Inc. All rights reserved.

Although men still perform less child care than women, good evidence indicates that the participation of men in family activities is increasing.

Today's American men spend less of their lives working than their predecessors did. In comparison to men of the early 20th century, they now enter the labor force later and retire earlier. In addition, the average number of hours that men work each week also decreased substantially during the first half of this century, but there is some controversy about whether such decreases have continued. Even more interest—and controversy—surrounds a related question: Do today's men spend more time taking care of children and doing housework?

One long-term comparison came from the so-called Middletown project, in which sociologists Robert and Helen Merrill Lynd studied Muncie, Inc., in the 1920s. In 1924 about 10 percent of Muncie's working-class wives reported that their husbands spent no time with their children, and 68 percent said that their husbands spent more than an hour a day. In 1978 Theodore Caplow of the University of Virginia and Bruce A. Chadwick of Brigham Young University repeated most of the Lynds' interview procedures with a similar sample in Muncie. In their study, only 2 percent of

working-class wives reported that their husbands spent no time with their children, and 77 percent reported that their husbands spent more than an hour a day. In both studies, the figures were similar for what the Lynds called "business-class" families, in which the husbands held white-collar jobs.

Many more comparisons can be made with data collected since 1965. Some of the most important of these studies have used so-called time diaries. Home economists developed this technique in the 1920s, but it fell into disuse until its reinvention in the 1960s. With this method, respondents report—in their own words—what they were doing at each moment of the previous day, starting at 12 A.M. The respondents list each activity, when that activity stopped, what they did next, when that stopped, what they did after that and so on, until reaching the following midnight. They might also be asked other questions about each activity, such as whether a television was on or who was with them. Responses are then coded into specific categories, such as baby care and indoor playing, which can be combined into broader categories, such as child care.

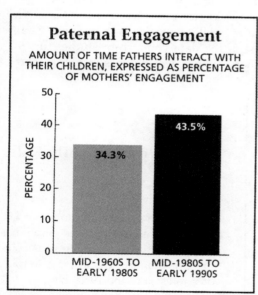

Paternal Engagement

AMOUNT OF TIME FATHERS INTERACT WITH THEIR CHILDREN, EXPRESSED AS PERCENTAGE OF MOTHERS' ENGAGEMENT

34.3% — MID-1960S TO EARLY 1980S

43.5% — MID-1980S TO EARLY 1990S

LAURIE GRACE

PATERNAL ENGAGEMENT is the category of activities in which fathers interact with their children. Examples include playing with children (right), reading to them and helping with their homework. Paternal engagement is increasing, but mothers still spend more than twice as much time interacting with their children (above).

BERND AUERS

In the studies that do not use time diaries, fathers are often asked to simply estimate how much time they spend with their children each day. To make sense of the more recent data collected with time diaries as well as with other methods for estimating time-use patterns, Michael Lamb of the National Institute of Child Health and Human Development, James Levine of the Families and Work Institute and I proposed two categories: paternal engagement and paternal availability. Paternal engagement consists of direct interaction with a child, which is described by the father in language indicating that he thought of the activity as taking care of the child. Paternal availability adds to this the amount of time the father and child are in the same vicinity but engaging in different activities.

Lamb, Levine and I discovered that different time-diary studies often interpret the same behavior differently. For example, "talking with children" might be considered part of child care in some studies but not in others. To identify trends across studies, we converted the data about fathers' time with children in each study from an absolute amount, such as 76 minutes a day, to a percentage of the mothers' interactions, such as 32 percent. Consequently, results of the different studies could be converted to a common standard of measurement—fathers' time as a proportion of mothers.

Using this approach to review 11 national or local studies that collected data between the mid-1960s and the early 1980s, Lamb, Levine and I found that fathers' engagement was on average about one third of mothers' and their availability was about half of mothers'. When I recently examined 13 similar studies that reported data collected between the mid-1980s and the early 1990s, fathers' engagement had risen to 43.5 percent of mothers', and paternal availability had risen to 65.6 percent. In addition, many studies have shown that when fathers are more involved with their children because they want to be, the fathers' involve-

BERND AUERS

PATERNAL AVAILABILITY is a measurement of the amount of time fathers spend in the vicinity of their children, either interacting with them or not. The category covers activities such as working on the computer while the children play video games (above). In recent years, paternal availability has risen to nearly two thirds of maternal availability (bottom).

ment benefits the children's cognitive and social development.

Although men still perform less child care than women, good evidence indicates that the participation of men in family activities is increasing. Nevertheless, most of the data come from studies of married fathers, which overlook a substantial part of the adult male population.

More Diverse Family Roles

Even though some data show that U.S. men's involvement with the family has risen, other indicators suggest the contrary. For example, the increase in divorce rates since the 1950s has weakened many men's family ties. Most divorced fathers' contact with their children drops off rapidly after divorce. Almost half of all divorced fathers have not seen their children in the past year, and high proportions of them do not

Paternal Availability

AMOUNT OF TIME FATHERS ARE NEAR THEIR CHILDREN, EITHER INTERACTING OR NOT, EXPRESSED AS PERCENTAGE OF MOTHERS' AVAILABILITY

MID-1960S TO EARLY 1980S: 51.8%
MID-1980S TO EARLY 1990S: 65.6%

LAURIE GRACE

pay child support. (More than 80 percent of court-ordered child-support money is never actually paid.) What is more, the recent increase in the proportion of men who never marry also indicates decreasing family involvement. Most unmarried fathers—teen and adult—refuse to accept any responsibility for their children.

These phenomena, however, are more complex than they first appear. For example, although the increase in divorce during the 1960s and 1970s appeared dramatic compared with the unusually stable divorce rate during the 1950s, rates of divorce have actually been relatively stable at about 50 percent for nearly two decades. In addition, divorced fathers' loss of interest in their children is not the only possible source of the rapid decrease in contact. For instance, many divorced mothers do not want continuing contact between their ex-spouses and their children.

In their 1991 book *New Families, No Families?*, Frances K. Goldscheider of Brown University and Linda J. Waite of the University of Chicago perceptively argue that American family life is not changing in two contradictory directions. In two-parent families, fathers' involvement with children and overall gender equality are increasing; however, two-parent families have become a smaller proportion of all families. Families headed by single mothers are becoming more common, and thus, more children overall do not have a resident father.

Goldscheider and Waite's analysis helps to make sense of the perhaps surprising finding that ethnicity and socioeconomic status show little if any consistent association with the amount of child care performed by married fathers. These variables primarily influence fathers' behavior by determining whether fathers get and remain married, not by affecting how fathers act when they are married.

How might these demographic and behavioral trends play out in the future? The downside trend—more children in single-parent families—has leveled off, because the divorce rate has been stable for nearly two decades and the out-of-wedlock birth rate has also leveled off in recent years. The upside trend—greater father involvement in married two-parent families—appears to be continuing. This produces a positive overall trend toward greater paternal involvement. Nevertheless, the disparity between the experiences of children growing up in married two-parent families and those of children in single-parent families will continue to grow.

This discussion usually contrasts two groups—resident, married fathers versus nonresident, never-married or divorced fathers—but my research suggests that there is a surprisingly large and unrecognized third group: resident, unmarried fathers. Jeffrey L. Stueve of the University of Illinois and I analyzed a nationally representative sample of fathers between the ages of 22 and 26 who live with their children. Nearly 60 percent were the children's biological father, residing with and married to the children's biological mother, but more than 40 percent were not. Resident, unmarried fathers have several subtypes: cohabiting biological fathers (13 percent of the total number of resident fathers), cohabiting stepfathers (8 percent) and fathers raising biological and unrelated children alone (6 percent). Married stepfathers have been studied more than any of these subgroups but are less frequent (5 percent). Fathers in "blended" families—in which they are living with children *and* stepchildren—make up 8 percent of the total. Men were defined as "cohabiting" if they were living with a female partner at the time of the study; there was no minimum length of time for the relationship. This wide variety of family types suggests that researchers need to broaden their studies to include all kinds of fathers.

For a long time, social scientists assumed that men's and women's experiences must be opposite in all respects. For example, past researchers often thought that if family is more central than work for women's identities, work must be more central than family for men's identities. Nevertheless, research has never borne out this expectation. My research in the 1970s, using self-report questionnaires, showed that family is far more psychologically central to men than work, just as is true for women. Other recent studies concur.

Someone might say that men merely report the socially desirable response. To sidestep that potential criticism, one could compare how strongly men's overall psychological well-being is linked to their satisfaction with either family life or work life. Using two mid-1970s surveys, I found the men's levels of family satisfaction explained twice as much variance in their psychological well-being as their levels of work satisfaction did—just like women. Rosalind C. Barnett of Brandeis University replicated my findings with more recent samples.

Of course, more subtle differences might exist between the family identities of men and women. In studies of so-called emotional transmission from work to family, for example, Reed W. Larson of the University of Illinois showed that a father's mood at the end of a workday influences a mother's mood when they're together at home far more than her prior mood affects him. In fact, a father's mood at work more strongly influences a mother's mood at home than her own mood at work affects her mood at home. Larson's findings suggest an important difference in the place of work and family in fathers' and mothers' personalities: fathers carry their workplace emotions home with them, but mothers keep their family experience insulated from workplace pressures.

Other research, however, suggests unexpected similarities. For example, Ellen Hock and Wilma Lutz of Ohio State University found that fathers and mothers experienced similar levels of anxiety over separation from their children during the first two years of parenthood. Research today is just beginning to flesh out a full understanding of the differences and similarities in men's and women's family identities.

Actions and Expectations

Less evidence exists about how the character of men's behavior in the family has changed. What is available continues to find gross differences between fathers' and mothers' behavior with children. With infants, mothers' behavior is more smoothing and predictable, and fathers' is more stimulating and unpredictable. With older children, mothers provide more caregiving, and fathers engage in more play.

Some conservatives suggest that a new social pressure encourages fathers to "act like mother." For instance, David Blankenhorn of the Institute for American Values says that a new cultural "script" pushes dad toward androgyny under the label of "Mr. Mom." I see little evidence, though, of this alleged new ideal. Other researchers and I recognize the importance of fathers' providing children with financial support and developmental guidance as well as supporting the mother in her relationship with the children. Moreover, we have not claimed that greater paternal involvement necessarily has positive effects, and we have not recommended that fathers should act like mothers. Indeed, several of my colleagues and I contend that fathers' play with children might have more positive consequences for their children's development than fathers' caretaking time, because play interaction is more socially and cognitively stimulating. In any event, no recent evidence finds fathers actually acting more like mothers in terms of their specific activities or behavioral style, so conservatives need not be so concerned.

I also question whether the current cultural script about fathering really has shifted in favor of greater involvement with children. Within the general belief that it is desirable for fathers to be more involved lurks a hidden qualification: not if it negatively impacts their jobs. For example, a recent survey of large companies showed that fathers are usually entitled to parental leave on the same basis as mothers—but when company employees were asked how many days a father should be entitled to take, 90 percent said none.

Social Implications

Although men's changing work-family balance affects their children, their spouses and the men themselves, we must also consider broader effects: the consequences of these changes on social institutions. The two different directions in which men's work-family patterns have changed—an increase in paternal involvement among married men and a simultaneous increase in divorce and fatherhood outside marriage—must be considered separately.

Men's decreasing tendency to be married fathers forces more children to face significant risks in their development. In recent years, our society has developed better strategies to increase the number of child-support court orders directed at absent fathers and to encourage their compliance with the orders. Nevertheless, even with the highest feasible child-support payments and maximum paternal compliance, many children in these families will live in poverty, and most of them will need some form of public assistance.

Robert E. Emery of the University of Virginia found that court data over the past two decades indicate a large rise in the proportion of fathers who share legal custody but only a small increase in the proportion sharing physical custody—in other words, actually living with their children. Emery's studies, however, point to a possible intervention effort: divorce mediation, in which the couple negotiates a settlement instead of fighting it out in court. Emery found that divorce mediation leads to more contact between fathers and children 12 years after divorce than the standard divorce process does.

Other intervention efforts can effectively promote parental responsibility among teenage fathers and reduce the incidence of out-of-wedlock births, especially among

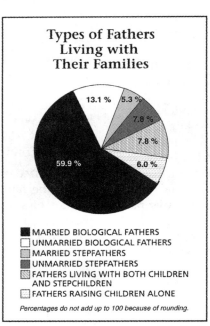

Types of Fathers Living with Their Families

13.1 % 5.3 %
7.8 %
7.8 %
59.9 % 6.0 %

■ MARRIED BIOLOGICAL FATHERS
□ UNMARRIED BIOLOGICAL FATHERS
▨ MARRIED STEPFATHERS
▧ UNMARRIED STEPFATHERS
▨ FATHERS LIVING WITH BOTH CHILDREN AND STEPCHILDREN
▧ FATHERS RAISING CHILDREN ALONE

Percentages do not add up to 100 because of rounding.

LAURIE GRACE

UNCONVENTIONAL FATHERS make up about 40 percent of all fathers who live with their children. Studies show that cohabiting fathers and stepfathers are particularly common, at 13.1 and 7.8 percent, respectively.

teenage women. Unfortunately, our government's recent approach—eliminating increases in benefits to mothers who have additional children while on welfare—is not one of them. This approach has not resulted in lower rates of out-of-wedlock births in the states that have passed such laws. Recently attention has turned to possible ways of reducing the incidence of divorce by making it more difficult to obtain or by creating a class of marriage in which divorce is not permitted. These latter efforts are, at best, controversial in their feasibility and desirability.

Married fathers' increasing involvement with their children also has social ramifications for the workplace. In a 1977 national survey that I co-directed for the U.S. Department of Labor, I developed the first measures of the extent to which employed married men and women experience conflict between their work and family roles. In that survey, and in much of the research conducted subsequently by other investigators, the married mothers and fathers reported similar levels of conflict. Other studies show that parenthood is associated with increased absences or lateness at work to a similar degree for men and women and that work-family disruptions, such as a breakdown in child-care arrangements, affect men's well-being at least as much as women's.

Impetus for Change

Men's conflicts between their work and family responsibilities create pressure to change the workplace, which adds to the impetus for change already created by the rising numbers of employed mothers. Over the past two decades, for examples, enough men fought for parental leave on the same basis as women—generally unpaid—to generate a well-established body of case and administrative law affirming this right. In fact, fathers initiate a significant proportion of the grievances regarding denial of parental leave filed with the U.S. Department of Labor under the 1993 Family and Medical Leave Act. In January 1999 one father—Kevin Knussman, a helicopter paramedic with the Maryland State Police—received a $375,000 jury award for denial of leave. Knussman's award was the largest ever granted to a father in a parental leave case.

Although men's changing work-family patterns are triggering demands for more flexible workplace poli-

cies, the changes are sure to be contested. In fact, considerable resistance to greater workplace flexibility exists today, despite the social attitudes favoring more involvement of fathers in family life. The resistance stems from the hidden qualification mentioned earlier: the belief that fathers' family involvement should not affect their job performance in any way.

As a result, the shifting pattern of work-family commitments for men will most likely mirror the pattern experienced by women. Policy changes in the workplace have been important, but we should remember that employed mothers have nonetheless needed to work out accommodations between their work and family lives largely on an individual basis, relatively invisible from public view. And the widespread resistance to paternity leave suggests that companies are even less sympathetic to their male employees' work-family problems. So it is likely that the accommodations that most employed fathers create to balance their work and family responsibilities will, to an even greater degree, be largely private and thereby socially unrecognized and unsupported.

The Author

JOSEPH H. PLECK has studied the changing roles of men and women for more than 25 years. He earned a Ph.D. in clinical psychology from Harvard University in 1973 and is now professor of human development and family studies at the University of Illinois. In 1997 he received the Distinguished Contribution to Family Psychology Award from the American Psychological Association. He serves on the editorial boards of *Sex Roles: A Journal of Research*, the *Journal of Gender, Cultural Diversity and Health*, and *Men and Masculinities*; he is also an associated editor of the *Journal of Men's Studies*.

Further Reading

BETWEEN FATHER AND CHILD: HOW TO BECOME THE KIND OF FATHER YOU WANT TO BE. Ronald Levant and John Kelly. Penguin Books, 1991.

FATHERHOOD: CONTEMPORARY THEORY, RESEARCH, AND SOCIAL POLICY. Edited by William Marsiglio. Sage Publications (Thousand Oaks, Calif.), 1995.

THE ROLE OF THE FATHER IN CHILD DEVELOPMENT. Third edition. Edited by Michael E. Lamb. John Wiley & Sons, 1997.

WORKING FATHERS: NEW STRATEGIES FOR BALANCING WORK AND FAMILY. James A. Levine and Todd L. Pittinsky. Harvest Books, 1998.

Should *You* Leave?

HERE THE AUTHOR OF **LISTENING** TO **PROZAC** TURNS HIS EAR TO **PEOPLE** ON THE THRESHOLD OF LEAVING A **ROMANTIC** RELATIONSHIP. BUT GIVING **ADVICE** TO SUCH FOLK, HE FINDS, ISN'T AS STRAIGHT-FORWARD AS YOU **MIGHT** THINK.

BY PETER D. KRAMER, M.D.

"How do you expect mankind to be happy in pairs when it is so miserable separately?"
—Peter De Vries

YOU ARE IN A DIFFICULT RELATIONSHIP, ONE THAT FEELS painful to stick with or to leave. You imagine there is something particular a psychiatrist can offer—perhaps the fresh perspective of a neutral observer. You want to know how your relationship looks from the outside. Is your partner impossible, or do you bring out the worst in others? Are you too tolerant, or too demanding? If you could decide which view to accept, you would know just how to behave. You have had it with the slow, self-directed process of psychotherapy; you want a frank and immediate response, an expert opinion.

I am sympathetic toward your wish for immediacy and plain talk. But often people who ask for advice in such matters are really looking for someone to blow up at when the rules indicate they should leave, but they dearly want to stay. Or perhaps you want permission. Sometimes a child can skate only when a parent is on the ice right beside; the parent becomes the child's nerve or guts, even the stiffness in the child's ankles. You may need what the child skater needs: additional self. If this is what you require of me, you will tell me what you already know you should do, and I will confirm your conclusions. But if you have a good supply of self, then the choice you are confronting must be a difficult one, or else you would have already made a decision.

I take it that you are in love, or have been, or think you might be in time. Love, not operatic passion: Those who are swept off their feet rarely ask questions. And since you go to the trouble to seek an expert opinion, you must value the investment of emotion and the crea-tive effort you have put into your relationship. Intimacy matters to you, shared experiences, time together. And you imagine that people should and can exercise control in affairs of the heart.

To this picture I might add that you already know the conventional wisdom. Television, romance novels, late-night radio call-in shows, and self-help books all provide exposure to the tenets of psychotherapy. Characters advise one another continually: Walk away from abuse. Don't bet on actively reforming an alcoholic. Communicate. Compromise on practical matters. Hold fast to your sense of self. Take emotional crises to be opportunities for growth. Expect and accept imperfection. No one is a stranger to these commonplaces.

But you hope to be an exception. You feel different enough to ask whether the conventional bromides illuminate your special predicament. Perhaps you fear that you are inept at judging partners, so that when it is time for others to leave, you should stay, because you will do no better next time. Or you are more vulnerable than others, less able to bear transitions. You have been telling yourself as much, and you hope that a neutral observer will agree.

IRIS'S STORY

HERE IS HOW I IMAGINE WE COME TO MEET. THE BELL RINGS, and you are at my office door. "Iris," I say, not concealing my surprise. My daughter used to play on the same soccer team as your nephew, and I remember admiring your spirit while your marriage and publishing career were unraveling. You assure me that you are not here for psychotherapy. You want help with a predicament.

You have not done well with men, you say. Your large-boned and angular stature, and what they call your fierceness, scares them off. Those few who are attracted to tough women don't give support when you need it,

Reprinted with permission from *Psychology Today*, September/October 1997, pp. 38-45, 72, 74. © 1997 by Sussex Publishers, Inc.

HOW CAN YOU **STAY** *WITH A* **MAN** *WHO SEES* **YOU** *THIS* **WAY?** *AND YET YOU ARE* **TEMPTED** *TO.*

hate any sign of vulnerability—or are outright sadists. Randall seemed the sole exception. He is a man with enough confidence to enjoy forthright women and enough awareness of his own wounds to allow for frailty.

Randall courted you vigorously, tried to sweep you off your feet. He has given you the happiest two years of your life. He is sweetly handsome, separated, en route to divorce. Having grown up in a difficult family in a neighborhood that chews up its children, he now works with wayward youth. Best of all, unlike your ex-husband, who publicly humiliated you with a younger woman, Randall loves you alone.

At least that's what you thought until two weeks ago, when you went to download your e-mail. You received an extraordinary bundle of messages, all forwarded from bunny@univ.edu. You knew who this Bunny was: a touchy-feely social worker who runs a clinic Randall consults to. She had sent you the modern equivalent of the stack of letters, tied in a ribbon, deposited on the wife's dressing table. Although there was no evidence in the e-mail that Randall had slept with Bunny, he had revealed a few of your intimate secrets—enough to make you physically sick. And in his postings, Randall kept referring to you as Prickly Pear—barbed on the outside, tender within—the same term he had once used for an ex-girlfriend. You suddenly understood his m.o.: commit to one woman, then denigrate her to another.

When you felt able to stand, you left work, stopped for a moment at a florist, and drove to Randall's condo. Once there you shoved your purchase, a small cactus, into the open lips of the disk drive on his PC. For good measure, you erased his hard drive and threw his modem in the oven and set it to self-clean. You packed your clothes and bathroom

paraphernalia. Then you pulled a jar of gravy from the fridge. You spread the contents onto Randall's favorite rug and left his dog Shatzi to do her worst.

As you drove home, you were overcome with the awareness that you love Randall as you have never loved another person. And indeed, since then Randall has done all of the right things. He's broken off contact with Bunny, plied you with flowers, called the lawyer and directed that his divorce be set in motion, resumed treatment with his therapist and invited you in for joint sessions. But you realize that you are in one of the classic bad arrangements between lovers. Ran-

HEADS I STAY, TAILS I LEAVE . . .

For most of human history, the question of whether to leave a long-term relationship was almost irrelevant. Marriage was seen as an unbreakable contract, and the economic perils of a solo existence made abandoning one's partner difficult, particularly for women. Throw in legal and religious restrictions against divorce and leaving simply wasn't an option. As late as 1930 famed psychiatrist Karl Menninger refused to advise women to leave their husbands—even in cases of repeated philandering or abuse.

Today, most of the social and practical impediments to leaving have fallen, but the decision to do so remains psychologically daunting. "There's no litmus test you can give a partner that determines whether you should leave, or whether this person is good partner material," notes family therapist Diane Sollee, M.S.W. So figuring out whether to leave remains a complex and intensely personal calculation incorporating issues ranging from the philosophical—How happy am I?—to the profoundly practical: Can I find somebody better?

The upshot: Nobody can give you a definitive formula for when to try to salvage a relationship and when to move on. But here are some issues to keep in mind:

THAT'S MY STORY AND I'M STICKING TO IT

When pondering whether to leave, most people retrace the history of their relationship, taking a mental inventory of the good times and the bad. But there's a hidden pitfall in this technique, notes University of Minnesota psychologist William J. Doherty, Ph.D., author of *Soul Searching: Why Psychotherapy Must Promote Moral Responsibility*. The problem: Our memories tend to be biased by how we're feeling at the moment. So when people are feeling pessimistic about their relationship, says Doherty, they "unconsciously put a negative spin on everything—how they met, why they got married." And they're more likely to overlook happier times.

Let's say you and your spouse eloped right after high school. If you're feeling hopeless about the relationship at the moment, you're especially likely to describe the elopement as the act of two impulsive, foolish kids. "But two years earlier, when you were feeling better about the relationship, you would have told the story in a whole different way," says Doherty. Instead of viewing your teenage marriage as impulsive, you might have fondly remembered it as an exceedingly romantic act by two people passionately in love.

This memory bias colors the relationship history you present to friends, family, counselors, and other confidants. So these individuals may wind up advising you to pull the plug on a relationship that isn't as bad as you've portrayed. (The same bias, of course, gives you an unrealistically rosy view of your relationship during good times.) And even if you don't consult others, your own ruminations on whether to leave will be similarly slanted. None of this means that your relationship history is irrelevant to the decision to leave—only that the evidence may not be as clear-cut as you initially think.

dall is behaving like a naughty boy who buries himself in the skirts of the mother he has injured and sobs apologies. Looking back, you see that even your tornado-like attack on his apartment was only an enactment of his basic fantasy: woman as avenger. How can you stay with a man who sees you this way?

And yet you are tempted to. That there is something flawed about Randall makes him seem more accessible, less puzzling. Now that his flaws are laid out, you feel peculiarly well-matched with him. After the fall, he seems more truly yours. You feel alive when you are with Randall. You still trust and admire him. Besides, you want to sustain this complex, intimate liaison you have done so much to nurture. Are you mad? Do these things ever work?

To say the obvious—that you must leave a man who has been dishonest, contemptuous, and incapable of commitment—doesn't seem to suffice. I know too little about you to answer the question you are asking, which is not whether most people should leave in these circumstances (they should) but whether you and Randall form an exception. I am taken with the odd detail that you feel more comfortable with Randall after the fall; to you, it is a relief to know that for all his kindness he is as crazy as you. I like your argument that even after the betrayal, there remains in your ledger a balance of trust in Randall's column. And since you are indicating that you have every intention of letting the relationship proceed, I feel unmotivated to throw myself in your path. You're making a bad bet, but I have seen worse bets succeed.

"To go ahead with the relationship will require all of your skills," I say. Business skills, people management skills, negotiation skills, every skill you possess. But you can risk continuing the relationship if you make that risk an occasion for your own maturation, for attaining something you can bring with you if the relationship fails, as it likely will. If you can be single-minded about what you need, and if you can let him be who he is—in that delicate combination of self-assertion and caring and disengagement, there will be hope that you will grow and that he will then grow to meet you.

HOW MOTIVATED IS YOUR PARTNER?

"Assessing whether you should leave may require assessing whether you have tried to stay," notes psychiatrist Peter Kramer, M.D., What he means is that relationships take work, and that couples often abandon relationships that would be successful with a little more effort. Indeed, adds Sollee, it's ironic that couples who are expecting a baby "will take months of classes to get ready for that one hour in which the mother pushes out the baby, but they don't take the time to [get counseling] on how to keep the marriage alive."

Given that every relationship requires effort, the fact that a relationship is somewhat rocky is not in itself a sign that a couple should split. What's more important, says Peter Frankl, M.D., a psychiatrist at New York University School of Medicine, is how motivated the partners are to give each other a chance to work out viable solutions to their particular problems. This motivation, says Frankl, is the best predictor of whether a troubled relationship will succeed. "I've turned around some marriages that were on the brink of divorce," he says. But if your partner isn't motivated to put some work into the relationship, the odds of success fall—and leaving may make more sense.

ADVICE DEPENDS ON THE ADVISOR

Visit three different doctors for your sore throat and you're likely to get similar diagnoses and treatments. Ask three different therapists whether you should leave your ailing relationship, however, and the advice you get may differ dramatically. The reason: a therapist's speciality—marriage counseling, individual therapy, groups—is linked to his or her feelings about commitment.

Marriage and family therapists are, by nature, inclined to keep people together. "I would never advise a couple to divorce," says Atlanta psychiatrist Frank Pittman, M.D., who feels that telling people to end a marriage is akin to advising a parent to put a child up for adoption. "You don't do it, especially when there are kids involved." (Pittman *did* feel comfortable, however, advising a pair of newlyweds to break up when he learned that the wife had cheated on her husband during the honeymoon.)

On the other hand, individual therapists, whose training in treating troubled relationships may range from extensive experience to a single seminar in graduate school, are more likely to see a relationship as something that should be sacrificed if it interferes with a client's happiness. "I read a case study of a woman who stayed with the same analyst through five marriages," says Sollee. "And that analyst helped end all five marriages." Minnesota's Bill Doherty calls such cases "therapist-assisted marital suicide," noting that by repeatedly asking their clients whether they are happy, "the therapist is basically saying, 'Why do you stay?'"

Because therapists typically maintain a neutral stance with regard to what a client does—the better to appear objective—these philosophical differences on the importance of saving relationships may not be immediately apparent. But they're always present, warns Doherty. The lesson for those who seek counsel from therapists: Keep in mind that the advice you get may be more of a reflection of your therapist's personal values than a scientifically valid assessment of the "correct" thing to do.—P.D.

WHY STAY?

AS A THERAPIST, I LEAN IN THE DIRECTION of reconciliation. I lean that way in part because of my experience that simple interventions sometimes suffice to hold together couples who seem on the verge of separation, and that those repaired relationships proceed ordinarily well. Moreover, second marriages do not seem gloriously better than first marriages, or if they do, it is

I **LIKE** *YOUR* **ARGUMENT** *THAT EVEN* **AFTER** *THE* **BETRAYAL** *THERE REMAINS A BALANCE OF* **TRUST.**

often because the second marriage benefits from efforts or compromises that might as readily have been applied to the first.

People tend to choose partners who operate at an emotional level similar to their own. To stay with a flawed relationship thus may entail tacit acknowledgment of your own limitations. And coming to grips with your limitations, and those of your relationships, is an important form of personal development. If you are loyal and slow to say goodbye, I might say leave, because leaving would represent facing your fears. But if your tendency is to cut and run, I lean towards staying and altering perspective. If you leave, will you find greater satisfaction elsewhere? Most relationships, after all, are practice. That's why, in a culture that allows dating, people have more relationships than they have marriages. Not only because they're finding the right person, but because they're learning how to do it.

SANDY AND MARK

PERHAPS YOU HAVE LITTLE IN COMMON WITH IRIS. YOUR STORY is simpler, quieter. As you enter my office, I am aware of a critical sensibility. You approve, I think, of the framed photographs of the walls, though you squint at one and judge it prosaic.

In your soft voice, you say that you have known almost from the start that there were problems in your marriage. Now that you have the chance, you are determined to get a little help about whether to stay on.

You and Mark married just after high school and then moved from your hometown. It has always been Mark-and-Sandy: People run the words together, like warm and sunny or, lately, cool and cloudy. You shared fine taste, an appreciation of the arts and of the art in daily life. Having seen enough fighting and drinking in your own families as you grew up, you promised implicitly to protect each other from any more indignities.

Then you panicked when Mark leaned on you in his childish way. He resented the stress of competition on the job and the pressures associated with being a bread-winner, and would come home feeling unappreciated. In childhood, you had the responsibility for the care of your brothers, and you never felt you could do right by them. You lacked confidence that you could make another person feel better. So merely to think of Mark heading home worn out and hungry for affection made your day seem black. When he walked through the door and saw you

already drained, he would shrink away. You felt his withdrawal as another sign of your inability to give or elicit nurturance. You became hopeless and more needy than Mark could bear. I hope you will not feel diminished when I say yours has been a marriage between melancholics.

But you maintained the marriage in its early years by carrying on affairs with married men. To you, an adoring man is solace from the isolation Mark imposes. Although you felt dirty, in your bluest states you were buoyed by these dalliances. You felt that you had no choice, that life is too bleak without at least the pretense of admiration. As a result of these affairs, you were more emotionally available for Mark, and your support allowed Mark to do better at the office. And what surprised you through the course of these events is how much tenderness you continued to feel for Mark. He tries hard in a world he is not made for, and sometimes he succeeds.

Over the past couple of years, your odd jobs—making up gift packages in pharmacies and florist shops, designing window displays for boutiques—have turned into a career. Your work in a fabric shop led to requests that you consult on interior design. A former lover has begun small-scale commercial production of your decorated mirrors, boxes, and picture frames. This good luck has allowed you to feel secure month in, month out. There are no more lovers, though with your patron the door is open, especially now that his own marriage is headed for divorce.

For a while Mark seemed to disapprove of your commercial success, as if you had gone over to the enemy, the movers and shakers, in a way that were disloyal to your joint view of the world. Now Mark has told you he has a platonic girlfriend. He needed you to know of his near-peccadillo, because for him it throws the marriage into question. You know he does not really want a lover. He is asking for reassurance that you, despite your success, still want him. Lately, however, you have found yourself thinking that here is an opportune moment for you to leave.

I recognize this crisis—change in a member of a depressive couple. Marriages between emotionally sensitive people can be models of the best human beings are capable of. But the result can also be a stifling sort of peas-in-a-pod marriage such as yours, one made overtly stable by an implicit promise never to change, never to move toward the wider world. Although the stalemate

IF YOU ARE **LOYAL,** *I MIGHT SAY* **LEAVE,** *BECAUSE LEAVING* **REPRESENTS** *FACING YOUR* **FEARS.**

is often broken when a patient is "transformed" by medication, career success such as yours can have this function too. Now you are over your depression, and the question is whether you should stay.

This is a moment for remarriage or separation. Since you care so deeply for Mark and admire so many of his qualities, and since you have come so far with him, you may choose to let the marriage play itself out further. You could suggest to Mark that he seek treatment for depression, although what seems to be at issue is personality style rather than illness. If you stay put, you may next find Mark turning angry, which I would consider progress. Or you may find instead that he will move forward to join you, and you will be able to judge, after these many years together, whether a period of real marriage is possible.

Are you thinking of divorce and marriage to your patron entrepreneur? How could you not be? This is a frequent response to recovery from prolonged depression—entry into a highly "normal" marriage, one focused on pleasure rather than ideals, on the future rather than the past. This solution has its dangers. The patron may be someone who enjoys and demands dependency in a wife, while you take pride in your hard-earned autonomy, your quiet toughness and firm balance. And yet I have seen such relationships work. Perhaps your entrepreneur will treasure you and challenge you and rejoice with you in the bounty of life, and you will hold on to what is precious in your sadness without having sadness possess you.

The only apt advice is to say that you will need to fiddle with this problem as you have with others, quietly, from around the edges, at your own pace. You will need to be an artisan, here as elsewhere, and to rely on your unerring sense of the fitting. You seem someone who would prefer to find just the right time for leaving and to craft your exit in a way that pleases you—if you are to leave at all.

MATTER OF TRUST

HOW DOES A PERSON WHOSE FAITH IN HIS OR HER PARTNER HAS been breached decide whether to stay? Hungarian psychiatrist Ivan Boszormenyi-Nagy refers to what he calls "residual trust." Loss of trustworthiness, he observes, is rarely absolute. Each relationship contains an invisible slate or ledger of give and take, what I might call a "trust fund." Partners deposit trustworthy acts, earn merited entitlement, and owe due obligations. Strong balance sheets make stable marriages. But if one partner continually overdraws the account, the other will feel justified in retaliating or leaving—though other factors, such as good sex, excessive guilt, or power arrangements, might complicate the decision.

An additional complication is that people are poor bookkeepers. They attribute credits and debts to the wrong accounts. In Nagy's view, ethical relations are intergenerational. A child is due reliable care by his parents and is owed restitution if he doesn't get it, but once he reaches adulthood there is no one appropriate from whom to seek it. So the deprived child will enter adulthood with a destructive sense of entitlement. In marriage, this creates further injustice, since it is not the spouse who created the imbalance in the books. Perhaps you demand excessive loyalty because you have been treated disloyally elsewhere, just as your wife demands support that she has been denied elsewhere. If you treat the other unjustly, however, the relationship will be further depleted of resources of trust.

NORA

What made you ask for a consultation is something that will sound trivial. Philip gave you a public tongue-lashing at a recent party, and the hostess took you aside. Nora, she said, if you will not stay here with me tonight and tell Philip goodbye, you must at least promise that you will see someone else.

You want me to understand how decent Philip can be. Often you wonder what's wrong with you that you cannot bring that Philip back. What you loved was his self-assurance, his calm in the face of turmoil. Back then, you were attractive, and—you wonder whether I can believe this—accustomed to avid responses from men. In Philip, you met a man who made you want to earn his

> "The only distinctive thing I know about ending enslavement in a relationship is that sometimes you get a gift—an act by your partner that crystalizes what you should do."

admiration. You gladly merged your consulting business into his, and moved from a business relationship to courtship.

When you discovered you were pregnant by Philip, you were secretly thrilled. You had believed you were infertile, because in years of unprotected sex with an old boyfriend, you had never conceived. But Philip turned icy cold—how could you do this to him? He would marry you, but on the condition that you abort the pregnancy. You aborted, which was more horrible for you than Philip could know, or that you would let him know, since you wanted to enter the marriage as the sort of woman he demanded, a happy one. What was funny was that you loved him all the more, loved his little boy squeamishness about intimacy.

After the marriage you started falling apart, failing him in small but important ways. At the office, you might fail to pass on a phone message, or in the middle of a meeting make a comment that infuriated him. He began to demand—with every reason—that you stay in the office and do grunt work.

When Philip was finally ready to have children, you failed to give him any. There has been unspoken resentment about that, you suspect. And now you sometimes wonder if he is turning his attention elsewhere. You came across a document that seems to show he co-owns a condominium with a woman. He yells at you so much over little things, you can't image what would happen if you asked him about the condo.

What put you up to asking for advice was a word in Philip's diatribe at the party—he called you a dried-up prune. You know what he meant: infertile. That one epithet seemed to step over the line. You realized, in a confused moment, that some of what has kept you in the marriage is loyalty to your lost pregnancy—your lost unborn child. After what you sacrificed, the marriage *has* to work. You feel foolish asking whether you should leave a man you love and who has put up with so much from you.

If I thought I could get away with it, if you were not too skittish, I would advise you to leave. But I am afraid that if I give you advice in full measure you will bolt. My first goal is not to lose you; my second is to make you less isolated within your fearful perspective. The only rhetoric at my service is the look on my face when you say "prune." Not horror or astonishment, just your expression plus a little extra. I want to underline what you have said.

Sometimes I think of enslavement in relationships as a hypnotic phenomenon: The enslavers induce a substitution of their will for the subject's. They are vampires, gaining strength as their victim wastes away; the commanding and decisive executive by day flourishes on the blood of the wife he drains by night. Lesser degrees of possession are the root of many ordinary relationship troubles. The demanding impose expectations, while the loyal are exploited for their loyalty.

After 20-odd years in the field, the only distinctive thing I know about ending enslavement is that sometimes you get a gift—an act by your partner that crystalizes what you should do—and if you receive such a gift you had better recognize and accept it. Usually I hear about these gifts in retrospect. A woman who is now doing well tells me about an incredible act of overstepping by her former possessor: He knocked up a single mother with four kids and wanted to move them in. Or the act may seem indistinguishable from the person's habitual behavior, as with Philip's shockingly unreasonable diatribe at the party.

I take your response to the gift Philip offers as an important part of our transaction because it is your own. If you have filled your life with authoritative others who tell you what to do, I will not want to validate that behavior. In highlighting this gift, I hope to instead validate what remains of your perspective. I offer the self-help bromide "listen to your own voice," with this difference: I point to one of your voices and say this one, and not the others. The voice that says: No human being should be asked to give what that man demands nor accept what he imposes.

MY MISGIVINGS ABOUT GIVING ADVICE

Despite the psych jockeys on the radio, despite the widespread acceptance under managed care of therapies that entail little more than the quick proffering of an opinion, despite my own enduring curiosity about advice, I find the prospect of advising slightly illicit. I am suspicious of books of advice: When I read a self-help precept, I think that the opposite advice might be equally apt, for someone. The advice that I have valued in my own life has never turned on fixed maxims or canned metaphors. More crucially, lists of precepts don't work like targeted advice because lists contain inherently constraining messages. They seem to say that complex matters are knowable, that a given process leads to

> *"I am suspicious of advice books: When I read a self-help precept, I think that the opposite advice might be equally apt. The advice I have valued has never turned on fixed maxims."*

foreseeable results. It implies a thin and predictable world, whereas the sort of advice that has mattered to me bespeaks a quite tentative optimism, the optimism of the quest of whose outcome is finally unknowable.

Thus, even after an extended interview, as we have had, you might remain unknown to me in important ways. This, then, is the advisor's dilemma: Like a partner in a troubled relationship, an advisor faces an other who is at once transparent and opaque. I will offer a perspective, you will add it to those you already entertain, and you will stay, or leave, or remain in limbo.

is divorce too easy?

By Benedict Carey

We have stopped taking marriage seriously, say the experts and women are paying the price. That's why a surprising coalition of conservatives and feminists want to make breaking up harder to do.

HE MUST HAVE BEEN RELIEVED to get out of the house and into the open. He'd tried to be casual, waiting until breakfast was over, when the kids were preparing for school, waiting until his wife, almost ready for work herself, came to the door to see him off. What was it he had said? "We're getting a divorce. Give me a call later." The basics, anyway. Then he was gone.

"It was an announcement, not a conversation," Susan Blumstein, now remarried, says of the day her first husband left, in 1990. "We talked that day, and then that same week we went to see his brother the lawyer, who had already prepared papers. It was a done deal."

Susan had assumed all along that their marriage was the done deal–an assumption, she now concedes, that may have blinded her to her husband's discontent. After 18 years of partnership, after raising two children to adolescence, after all the diapers and dishes and damp dental floss, one does indulge a few simple faiths. "You don't just *think* of yourself as a married person," she says, "you *are* a married person. It's part of what you are, everything you do." But the family's life together vaporized in less time than it takes to put out the recycling bins, and there was nothing she could do about it.

She had no idea what might be next, no notion of what slights the world reserves for a divorced, middle-aged mother of two. She had to break the news to everyone: her friends, her coworkers, her boss. She lost her place in her social group. Many mornings she woke up afraid, profoundly unsure of who she was. "I have heard divorce described as a kind of death," Blumstein says. "That sounds right to me."

She kept the Birmingham, Alabama, house and got custody of their two children, a girl, then age 17, and a boy, 11. She dropped several rungs on the economic ladder. (Divorce on average leaves ex-wives 20 to 30 percent poorer than ex-husbands, mainly because child support doesn't cover all of a child's living expenses.) Once comfortable, the family was suddenly strapped. And she had scant expectation of starting a new relationship; divorced mothers who retain custody don't get bachelor pads and long nights out in the bargain.

It would have come as no surprise to Susan to hear that, compared to married people, divorced individuals are three times as prone to depression, twice as likely to drink heavily, and three times more liable to commit suicide. She might have been too overwhelmed to care that they're also at higher risk of developing cancer or heart disease. "We have been studying this subject for a long time now," says Linda Waite, a University of Chicago sociologist whose book, *The Case for Marriage,* is due out next year. "Being married changes people's behavior in ways that make them better off."

Susan did gain one thing from her divorce: a set of previously undreamed-of anxieties about her children's future. The kids were suddenly subdued, spending more time at friends' houses. "They just didn't want to be here," she says. But they were old enough, fortunately, to understand what was happening; kids under the age of ten don't fare as well. Sociologists have found that children who grow up in split families are twice as likely to eventually divorce, twice as likely to drop out of school earlier, and much slower to support themselves.

Americans sometimes toast their own divorces, but few would celebrate their country's distinction as the world's divorce leader. Between 40 and 50 percent of first-

"I have heard divorce described as a kind of death," says Susan Blumstein. "That sounds right to me."

time marriages break up in the United States. Perhaps a third of divorces end poisonous unions to the benefit of everyone involved, say researchers. In the other two-thirds, the vital security of family life is evident only after it has been irrevocably lost. Women in particular pay the price, financially and emotionally.

For decades now, legislators, religious leaders, and social reformers have debated how to lower the divorce rate. It is a very tall order. No policy can re-create the society of the 1950s that supported traditional households. No one is going to abolish the economic sovereignty and independence women have earned in the past few decades, which has given them the freedom to leave an unbearable marriage. And no advertising campaign can convince a nation of divorced people to seriously stigmatize divorce.

But legislators can change laws, and they are beginning to do just that. In August 1997 the state of Louisiana started allowing people to choose a marriage option more binding than the standard no-fault contracts that have governed marriage and divorce in most states since the 1970s. Called covenant marriage, the new statute is a favorite among religious conservatives. What's surprising is that some feminists and many progressives have allowed themselves to be counted among the faithful–especially those who, like Waite, have studied the consequences of divorce for women.

Diane Sollee is founder and director of the Coalition for Marriage, Family, and Couples Education, a group of professional counselors, researchers, educators, and policy-makers. "No-fault laws were originally meant to give people an easy way out of a bad marriage," she says, "but we've been using the statutes to make a quick exit from any marriage."

Covenant marriage is sometimes called "I do, and I really mean it" marriage. It differs from the conventional contract in two important ways. First, it requires that couples receive professional marital counseling—before

the wedding and, if it comes to it, prior to filing for divorce. Second, the law prohibits a mutually agreed-upon, nofault split until husband and wife have lived apart for two years. Currently, in most states, the waiting period for a divorce can range from six to 18 months and can be waived altogether. The only way to dissolve a covenant marriage in less than two years is by going to court and proving that your spouse committed adultery, a felony, or physical or sexual abuse, or has moved out for a year and won't return.

The agreement gives leverage to spouses who want to preserve their marriage, says the statute's composer, Katherine Spaht, a law professor at Louisiana State University in Baton Rouge. "What we have now amounts to legalized abandonment," she says. "This law says, 'You leave me, I set the terms.'"

Spaht's zeal derives from what she has witnessed among Louisiana's modern professional class of lawyers, doctors, and academics. "I was seeing friends of mine, women in their forties and fifties, being left behind when their husbands decided they were tired of them. A man I know, a surgeon, just left his wife of 23 years for a younger woman. He was just up and gone. I believe that is simply not right. It shouldn't be that easy," she says. "Many of these women chose to raise their children. Even if they kept working, they made significant sacrifices to put their families first. What's a woman supposed to think when half of all marriages fail and here's a man proposing to her, asking her to give up a career? It's crazy.'

In 1996 Spaht met a state representative named Tony Perkins who shared her view. Together they drew up the covenant bill, which passed by a vote of 99 to 1. "We had liberal Democrats with us from very early on," says Perkins, a Republican. "Here was a bill that commits people to at least try to make their marriages work, and it's voluntary. It was hard to vote against."

NOT LONG AGO, voting against marriage counseling would have been easy. New York State had laws on the books in the 1960s and early 1970s that required couples to get therapy, yet the effect on the divorce rate was negligible. If anything rates increased, helping to expose marriage counseling for what it then was: a profession as starved for answers and direction as its clients.

"The professional stance of the American Association for Marriage and Family Therapy was neutrality," says Sollee, a past associate director. "That meant we were neither pro-marriage nor pro-divorce. We thought we should be working for what was best for each spouse. Often the so-called marriage therapist would be advising couples to divorce."

Nine years ago when Susan met Chris Blumstein, the man who would become her second husband, one of the things they talked about, besides the surreal suddenness of being abandoned (Chris had been, too), was the absence of effective counseling. Susan doubts it would have saved her first marriage, but she still feels cheated that they couldn't at least have given it a chance.

Chris and his first wife *did* seek advice—in vain. "We went to a professional counselor who said, 'Come back with a list of what you want most out of marriage.' Well, I came back with a list of 26 things, and she just had one: 'I want him to spend more time with the kids.' She was right. But our problems went deeper than that, and we refused to deal with them. So did our counselor. What kind of counseling is that?"

It's the traditional kind, Sollee says, and it's on the way out, thanks to groundbreaking marriage research done in the 1980s. Psychologists interested in relationship dynamics began using videotape to observe how couples spar over the small, I-thought-you-were-going-to-pack-that nuisances that often escalate into scalding arguments. The scientists also started using blood pressure monitors, stress hormone tests, and urinalysis to provide a record of physiological stress during these spats.

"The new technology allowed you to see what was going on inside," says Sollee, "even if you had stoic New Englanders there holding everything in."

These experiments demonstrated something astonishing: Couples who stayed to-

> Our laws tell a story, and for 30 years now they've been telling us that committed marriage isn't important.

gether fought as frequently, and over precisely the same things, as did couples who split up. "Experiment after experiment showed this, until we couldn't avoid it," says Sollee. "We *all* have irreconcilable differences. Every couple has them. Those who have successful marriages simply have learned ways of talking about their problems. They may never solve them. But they know how to talk about them."

The importance of this discovery to the field of marriage counseling cannot be overstated. Most marriage advisers are neutral no

longer. Barring extreme circumstances, they don't put personal needs before the relationship. Most have abandoned the traditional emphasis on solving each spouse's individual problems in favor of what Sollee calls marriage education–a relationship course, in effect, that teaches skills and strategies for disarming emotional grenades.

The model is called PREP, for Prevention and Relationship Enhancement Program, developed in 1980 by clinical psychologist Howard Markman. Markman's methods are straightforward. For example, he coaches couples to discuss problems in what he calls speaker-listener technique, in which one person gripes, then the listener paraphrases the complaint, and vice versa.

In practice, this technique is not all that unnatural; it simply provides a framework for the sort of empathetic conversations most couples have had. Other tactics include taking time-outs when tempers flare, and spending an hour weekly to discuss your relationship.

In an ongoing Denver-area study, Markman found that 8 percent of couples who took his course broke up, separated, or divorced within five years. But that number rose to 16 percent of the couples in the control group. A similar trial in Germany reported that only 4 percent of a PREP group divorced after three years, compared to 24 percent of those who got no counseling. On every measure of marital stability–number of fights, amount of affection, level of trust–the

Making Divorce Work

My husband and I divorced when our son Patrick was four and our daughter Morgan was six. Patrick cried and asked for cookies, then couldn't eat them. "I told you not to do this," said Morgan.

"I know, baby," I said, tears sliding down my face. This was my first taste of that curious callousness of a mother. I would have died for them, but I would not, for their sake, go on living with a good man I no longer loved.

Jim was 21 years my senior–he had been my college English professor–and we had begun to grow apart. He once snapped off a radio I was listening to, saying he had only a finite number of hours left on earth, and did not want to spend any of them listening to rock music. I snapped it back on.

One day while sitting at a red light, I realized I was no longer in love, and hadn't been for some time. It seemed to me then reason enough to leave. It still

does. But I went home and cried, desperately afraid of what I was about to do–to him, to the kids, to myself, condemning us all to the bitterness and the pain of divorce.

Shortly after I made my decision, a comment from an acquaintance took me by surprise. "I think it's terrible when people give up like that," she said. "I can't respect that at all." Her parents had been married for 45 years, she said, through some very hard times. She respected that kind of commitment. Anything short of it was giving up.

I respected it, too; it seemed to me an immense achievement. But what my husband and I were doing also struck me as immense. We were attempting to divorce without destroying the family.

"You should know joint custody works in only 10 percent of cases," said the first lawyer I spoke to. I found another lawyer.

Jim kept the kids Sunday through Wednesday night, and they were mine the

rest of the week. By the time the divorce papers came thumping through the mail slot, several years after we had separated, Jim and I were neighbors. I had moved into the flat below his so we could raise the kids together more easily. It took civility, effort, and luck, but we made it work.

Would my kids have been happier had we stayed together? Of course. But they're doing fine. Over the years, we've developed an odd kind of extended family. The other night we had our usual Sunday dinner together: My husband of seven years, Bill, grilled steaks, Jim brought down fresh strawberries, Morgan had a tofu burger, and Patrick, now 19 and 6 foot 3, ate an entire T-bone before heading out to his summer restaurant job. Afterward, as I was getting ready to go to the movies, I heard Morgan tell a friend on the phone, "All of my parents are going out. Want to come over?"
—ADAIR LARA

couples who had taken the course were better off.

"I don't give people wedding presents anymore," says Sollee. "I give a weekend of marriage education. It's far more valuable than a table setting or a salad bowl."

The covenant statute doesn't specify any particular type of counseling; lawmakers decided against that. It is the binding promise to do *something,* however, that sells covenant marriage to people who otherwise wouldn't buy it.

Bob Downing, a Louisiana District Court judge, and his wife, Pamela, decided last year to renew their vows under the covenant license. "It was his idea," says Pamela, "and I asked myself, Why? I mean, my first vows were my vows, and this wasn't going to make them any more sacred. But I eventually decided that the counseling was a good safety valve, and I like the agreement up front to do it. If you can't agree to that, what kind of commitment do you have?"

NOT MUCH OF ONE, most married people would agree. But behind the commonsense appeal of the law, some see a dark trend: covenant marriage as a step back to the more acrimonious days of fault-based divorce. Back in the sixties, divorce laws were relaxed in the United States because they were out of step with people's behavior. Throughout this century, Americans who wanted out have found a way to make it happen—by heading off to Reno, by leaving the country, most of all by fabricating evidence of infidelity or abuse. No-fault laws made the system a more honest one.

They've also made the process more humane. "The most offensive thing to me is the suggestion that somehow no-fault divorces are easy," says Terry O'Neill, a law professor at Tulane University in New Orleans and past president of the Louisiana chapter of the National Organization for Women. "Just think of the divorced people you know. They all got divorces for reasons that were very important, very real for them. This covenant law is really all about punishment. It punishes people for wanting to get out of a marriage, even a bad marriage. As if it weren't already difficult enough to go through a divorce."

Linda Waite doesn't deny the real pain of no-fault divorce; she's been through one herself. She's nonetheless concerned by a telling statistic: Thirty years ago, just 40 percent of Americans believed ending a troubled marriage could benefit a husband or a wife. These days, 80 percent share that belief, according to the General Social Survey, a government poll of social attitudes. "This amounts to a very large and very real change in attitudes toward committed marriage," she says.

Most Americans still want to be married; surveys are clear about that. The romantic ideal is intact. It is the reality of marriage, the thing itself, that has lost its place in the public imagination. All the mundane give-and-take that is part of a normal relationship can disappoint sentimental couples, Waite says. And the ease of walking out makes the union that much more fragile.

"When people are in more binding contracts they tend to invest more in the kids, and become more emotionally dependent on each other in the best ways," Waite says. "They put their well-being in a partnership, in a trust. They become part of a larger network of people, including spouses' parents, siblings, and friends. All of this helps enormously."

Katherine Spaht puts it more simply. "I believe our laws tell a story," she says. "And for 30 years now they've been telling us that committed marriage isn't that important."

Spaht's legislation tells an imperfect story, to be sure; experience suggests that many of these Louisiana covenants will blow up for perfectly valid reasons. But the law does provide for a different narrative than the one we've been hearing for decades. It challenges couples to honor their promises and marriage counselors to do their job, and has prompted lawmakers around the country to think seriously about the benefits of marriage preparation and rehabilitation. Deeper than that, the law says that there is more to marriage than romantic love.

ON VALENTINE'S DAY LAST YEAR, dozens of churches in Louisiana held collective ceremonies in which married parishioners renewed their vows. In Baker, near Baton Rouge, the Bethany World Prayer Center had 500 couples in attendance. Another 100 convened in the venerable First Presbyterian Church downtown. "I think we were all surprised at how emotional the ceremonies were," says Russ Stevenson, senior pastor at First Presbyterian. "One fellow came up to me and said, 'Reverend that was more beautiful than the first time.'"

The ceremonies had the feel of a mass public demonstration–a March for Marriage, so to speak–and the sensation persists in the humid delta air around the city. Says Pamela Downing: "Our own kids have so many friends whose parents are divorced that I felt this was a way to let them know we are in this for keeps."

She and husband Bob joined the Valentine's Day ceremonies, affirming 18 years of marriage. Katherine and Paul Spaht (28 years) also participated, along with Russ and Sherrill Stevenson (38 years). And at the Baton Rouge Christian Center Church, after seven years together, stood Susan and Chris Blumstein, ready to make the long walk down the aisle for the last time.

Benedict Carey is a contributing editor.

Smart Plan to Save Marriages

By Aimee Howd

Gloomy divorce rates are the norm in the United States, but a program linking church and community could help more couples follow through with their wedding vows.

Pragmatic, booming America has become a cold place for romance. Today's staggering divorce statistics suggest six in 10 marriages in the United States will fail, most within the first few years.

The rate of cohabitation is up 700 percent since 1970, as a divorce-shy generation looks unsuccessfully for the way back to the stability their grandparents enjoyed but their parents left behind. More than half of all marriages in the United States are preceded by cohabitation, as couples "try to get to know each other first." Yet those who live together before marriage increase their odds of divorce by 50 percent. In fact, fewer people than ever bother to marry today and three-fifths of America's children will grow up in single-parent homes. The price of disintegrating family ties may be seen in social ills ranging from increased alcoholism to doubled school dropout rates for single-parent families to higher mortality rates for divorced men and women.

"All of this in a nation where 74 percent of marriages still occur in church," pondered syndicated *New York Times* ethics and religion columnist Mike McManus. The gloomier the figures for the institutions of marriage and family, the more desperately McManus looked for answers. In 1995, he wrote a book, *Marriage Savers: Helping Your Friends and Family Avoid Divorce,* proposing a private-sector program to tap church and community resources to strengthen existing marriages and provide "marriage insurance" for engaged couples. His ideas are catching on.

"The core reform is a simple idea," says McManus. "In every congregation there are couples with solid, vibrant marriages who could be of help to other couples but have never been asked, trained or inspired to do so." After all, according to George Gallup, 69 percent of Americans are members of a church or synagogue, and 43 percent attend services each week. If people lived the faith they professed, reasoned McManus, the United States no longer would host one of the world's highest divorce rates. Churches should encourage rigorous premarital counseling, teaching the skills necessary for a healthy marriage instead of just serving as "blessing machines." Marriage Savers engages the churches and the community, says Harriet McManus, who cochairs the small nonprofit with her husband, rendering it more effective than pro-marriage legislation. "A law can only work at the margins in helping people love each other," she says. "Churches can help couples bond."

And its broad community appeal makes Marriage Savers more than just another well-meaning church program. In February 1999, 20 local clergy made Culpeper, Va., the 100th community to hammer out a marriage preparation and enrichment document—dubbed by McManus a "community marriage policy." He explains: "Specifically, congregations across denominational lines are agreeing to require couples to undergo a rigorous four months of marriage preparation that includes taking a premarital inventory, meeting with a mentoring couple and attending classes on 'the Biblical foundations of

marriages, management of finances, conflict resolution and the influence of intergenerational family history and dynamics,' as the Culpeper clergy put it. It communicates the conviction by pastors that what God has joined together the church should hold together."

Less than 10 months had passed between the day Chris, 32, and Sarah, 25, met in their work at a local hospital and the November day they said "I do." Their church held a hush as bridesmaids in dark green gathered at the altar of Christ Lutheran Church, crimson flowers in hand. Pachelbel's Canon was played and 150 heads turned to follow Sarah's progression down the aisle toward a new life as the wife of Chris Arnold.

While many churches invest far more in helping an engaged couple prepare for the day of the wedding than for a lifetime union, Christ Lutheran's director of pastoral care and family life, the Rev. Jeffrey Meyers, had led 40 other suburban Kansas City, Kan., clergy in signing a Community Marriage Covenant and was committed to doing whatever he could to strengthen the marriages of couples who came to him.

"He told us there would be some guidelines: They request that couples promise not to live together and that they commit to chastity. And he said we would be matched up with a mentor couple," says Sarah. She and Chris admit that they hesitated a bit before discussing intimate matters with a mentor couple they never had met. But the Weisses had been trained in administering a premarital inventory called PREPARE, which gave both couples a starting point for discussion. Although the inventory showed that Chris and Sarah matched fairly closely on most issues, "there were some areas where we had been wearing rose-colored glasses," Sarah says.

Both strength and growth areas were probed. After watching marriages around them founder, they welcomed the help and motivation to work through their expectations and their plans for their family. Most importantly, says Sarah, the mentors "made us responsible to God."

Already convinced by McManus' book that building strong couples is the first step toward stronger families and communities, Meyers in 1996 had accepted McManus' challenge to pool his resources with others in his community. He began calling other pastors. By May 1997, the community agreement was signed among the city's clergy. Inquiries about their policy keep coming in from surrounding communities. At the grass-roots level, "Mike's movement is starting to take on a life of its own," Meyers says.

Citing a Harvard University Press study which claims that 70 percent of divorces occur needlessly, Meyers says a church's commitment to responsible marriage creates the opportunity to reach 40 percent of those who walk away from a marriage for no good reason. "It challenges them to stick with it for their own well-being, the well-being of their community, their church and their children."

Marriage Savers literature says divorces have plummeted 35 percent in Kansas City and its suburbs in the two years since the Community Marriage Policy was implemented. (Across the river, in Kansas City, Mo., there was no Community Marriage Policy and divorces increased during the same period.) In Modesto, Calif., the divorce rate also fell 35 percent over a decade, following the implementation of a Community Marriage Policy; in only one year there was a 7 percent decrease in Eau Claire, Wis., and a 14 percent decrease in Chattanooga, Tenn. In 18 cities with a marriage policy, Marriage

'Any effort to link people in marriage is praiseworthy. Marriage is not this magic thing that just happens. Couples need a level of competence going into it.'

Savers reports, there are decreasing divorce rates at 10 times the national average.

Demographer Robert Rector of the Heritage Foundation in Washington says the data are difficult to contradict. "The burden of proof lies with anyone else who would try to figure out what [else would be] going on here. There is a fire behind the smoke. This is the most optimistic and effective program that we have in the United States today."

Meyers is careful. "Who knows? Let's look at it 10 years from now and see if we can sustain those rates."

But Larry Bumpass of the University of Wisconsin's Center for Democracy tells **Insight** it is too early for family-values advocates to feel secure. He believes data from his heavily cited National Survey of Families and Households suggest that any stabilization or decrease in divorce may be attributed to increasing rates of cohabitation among the undecided. "I would be very skeptical—based on what I know—of their ability to evaluate how divorce had changed in these communities," he says of the figures cited by Marriage Savers.

But if all the statisticians in the world were laid end to end, it is pos-

sible they still wouldn't reach a conclusion. Regardless of whether the hopeful statistics pan out, say those who have seen this program in action, Marriage Savers makes sense. In February the McManuses spoke to the Wisconsin Assembly at the invitation of House Speaker Scott Jansen. On Jan. 15, Florida's newly elected governor, Jeb Bush, signed onto Tallahassee's new Community Marriage Policy along with 64 clergy, saying he hoped it would be a "model for the rest of the state."

Glenn Stanton, director of the conservative Palmetto Family Council and author of *Why Marriage Matters,* puts it this way: "Although more research is needed to document results, any effort to link people in marriage and link them well is praiseworthy. Marriage is not this magic thing that just happens. It is work. Couples need a level of competence going into it."

Stanton says that competence is most effectively taught not by marriage authorities, but at the community level. "If the couple next door has been married 40 years, they are obviously doing something right." As for the future, he is optimistic: "Generation X is the first generation of Americans coming of age under their parents' divorces. This has affected them deeply and significantly. They are not necessarily traditionalists or conservatives, but they do know what they want—family stability."

For the Arnolds, unlike many of their generation, the transition from single to married life has been relatively easy with few surprises, thanks to a continued relationship with their mentor couple. "Our vows weren't the traditional ones," says Sarah. "We added, 'Depending upon God for strength and wisdom, we pledge ourselves to the establishment of a Christian home. Together we will constantly seek God's will and honor Christ in our marriage.' It kind of wrapped up all the planning we had done. We wanted to say with all of those witnesses there that this was how our marriage was going to be."

The Children of Divorce

by Glenn T. Stanton

Nineteen seventy-four was the first year that more marriages in America were ended by divorce than by death.

This made it a watershed year, for at that point the majority of family change became something we chose to do to ourselves rather than something that happened to us.

Today, approximately 45 percent of children born to married parents are likely to see their parents divorce before they reach the age of 18.

Prior to the late 1960s, it was generally believed that a child's need for family security was greater than a parent's need for marital happiness. It was thought, therefore, that significant effort should be invested in keeping rocky marriages together "for the sake of the children."

But then a psychological revolution emerged that focused on the well-being of the individual rather than the larger social fabric. This spawned a new and influential profession of family therapists and child-welfare advocates who believed that a child's greatest need was not stability but parents happy in their relationships. This would be guaranteed, the therapists said, if parents could move freely out of bad relationships into "better," more fulfilling ones. Only then could children have the loving, nurturing parents their fragile development required.

This thinking is seen in psychologist Fritz Perls' mantra of individualism, which became the tacit wedding vow of many couples marrying in the early '70s:

I do my thing, and you do your thing.
I am not in this world to live up to your expectations
And you are not in this world to live up to mine.
You are you and I am I,
And if by chance we find each other, it's beautiful.
If not, it can't be helped.

Therefore, divorce shifted from constituting a social ill to virtually being a personal good, a liberating and enriching event for parent and child. The country plunged into a new age of family formation, exhibiting near-absolute confidence that family health and child welfare would blossom.

In the intervening quarter century, social scientists have observed, collected data, and reported on the outcome of this experiment with the American family. What have the researchers found?

WALLERSTEIN'S PIONEERING WORK

One of the first scholars to undertake a long-term study of divorce's impact on children was Judith Wallerstein, a psychologist who founded the Center for the Family in Transition in Corte Madera, California. When she started her work in 1971 at the University of California at Berkeley, little was known about how people coped with the death of marriage, and she wanted to conduct a serious and thorough analysis.

The conventional wisdom at the time was that divorce was a brief crisis that soon resolved itself, leaving life better for all concerned. But very little serious work had been done in this area.

Based on this early understanding of divorce, Wallerstein sought enough grant money to observe 60 just-divorced families over a period of 12 to 18 months. She assumed the families would resolve their problems and move on with their lives. She wanted to learn the processes by which families coped with and overcame divorce.

But what she found stunned her. At the one-year mark, most of her subject families had not resolved their problems.

"Their wounds were wide open," she explained. "An unexpected number of children were on a downward course. Their symptoms were worse than before. Their behavior at school was worse. Our findings

COREL

■ *Permanent pain:* Research shows that, no matter how old the child, the impact of the parents' divorce increases rather than subsides over time.

were absolutely contradictory to our expectations."

Realizing she needed a longer observation period with her subject families, Wallerstein presented another grant proposal to extend her follow-up to five years. Those results are presented in her first book, *Surviving the Breakup: How Children and Parents Cope with Divorce,* in which she explains that while some of their children were doing better at the five-year mark, "we were deeply concerned about a large number of youngsters–well over a third of the group–who were significantly worse off than before."

Many of these children were clinically depressed, were doing poorly in school, and had difficulty with peer relationships. Some early disturbances, such as sleep, education, and behavior problems, had become persistent. Wallerstein also found that the divorce was not welcome news to the children.

"Many of the children, despite the unhappiness of their parents," she wrote, "were relatively happy and considered their situation neither better nor worse than that of other families around them.... The lightning that struck them was the divorce, and they had not even been aware of the existence of a storm."

A BROODING, BUILDING SADNESS

Wallerstein extended her observation of these families for five more years, and these findings are found in her highly acclaimed book *Second Chances.* The children's experiences she relates are, for the most part, very sad.

But data from her 25-year follow-up, which she presented this summer at a professional meeting, reveal the greatest cause for alarm.

As adults, these children speak with great sadness of their "lost" childhood, which vanished at the news of their parents' divorce, and their constant fear of total abandonment. The pain stemming from their parents' breakup increased rather than subsided over time.

"Unlike the adult experiment," Wallerstein explains,

the child's suffering does not reach its peak at the breakup and then level off. On the contrary. Divorce is a cumulative experience for the child. Its impact increases over time.... The effect of the parents' divorce is played and replayed throughout the first three decades of the children's lives.

Specifically, half the children in this group developed severe drug and alcohol problems in their early teens. Only two of the families made a serious effort to interrupt these substance-abuse problems.

165

Divorce's Ripple Effect

Some 45 percent of children born to married parents today are likely to see their parents divorce before they reach the age of 18. A 25-year study of the children of divorced families found that divorces often caused children:

◆ to become clinically depressed,

◆ to do poorly in school,

◆ to struggle with peer relationships.

This and other scientific studies showed that children of divorce exhibited:

◆ a surge in alcohol and drug problems,

◆ more negative self-concepts,

◆ greater conflict with parents,

◆ a lower standard of living,

◆ a greater risk of being a single parent,

◆ poorer physical health.

Although all of their parents had college educations and professional careers, the great majority of the children were unable to attain the same level of success their parents had. Most of the adult children expressed anxiety about romantic relationships and the prospect of marriage. They bitterly regretted the fact they had not grown up embraced by a healthy marital relationship.

One of the study subjects said, "Sometimes I think I was raised on a desert island. Love with sexual intimacy is a strange idea to me." Another lamented her predicament as follows: "I don't ever want to get divorced. So, I can't marry."

WALLERSTEIN'S CRITICS

Wallerstein's research is not without its critics. Two of the most notable are Frank Furstenberg of the University of Pennsylvania and Andrew Cherlin of Johns Hopkins University.

In their book, *Divided Families: What Happens When Parents Part,* they claim it is "highly likely" that Wallerstein's data exaggerate the prevalence of long-term problems of divorce. This exaggeration, they explain, is attributable to methodological problems in her sample selection. Her study population was relatively small, they note, and the families came to Wallerstein voluntarily for short-term therapy, indicating there were preexisting problems.

Defending herself, Wallerstein says the children were prescreened and accepted into the study only if they proved to be "developmentally on target" (normal) prior to the divorce.

But Furstenberg and Cherlin note that Wallerstein had no control group of children from intact families. They charge that this makes it impossible to attribute the children's problems solely to divorce with any scientific certainty. While the two critics do not disagree that divorce

can have deleterious effects on children, they question Wallerstein's findings on the severity of those effects.

Wallerstein responds that she never claimed her work was broadly representational but rather was a unique, long-term observation of how one group of adults and children fared in the shadow of divorce. Rather than collecting impersonal, quantitative data on the families, she pursued a qualitative and subjective approach, sitting down and talking with them, drawing from their personal stories and experiences.

Most important, her conclusions have largely been vindicated by a significant and growing scientific literature.

THE LARGER BODY OF DATA

E. Mavis Hetherington, a psychologist from the University of Virginia, is another early pioneer in the study of divorce and its impact on adults and children. She conducted a six-year follow-up in the early 1970s on 180 families, comparing divorced *and* intact families.

Like Wallerstein, Hetherington found that young children of divorce grossly distorted fears of total abandonment, reasoning that if one parent could just leave, so could the other. They were also unrealistically optimistic about their parents reconciling and bringing the family back together.

Hetherington discovered that divorced parents monitor the activities and whereabouts of their children less than do parents who are together. Divorced parents, she found, "know less about where their children are, who they are with, and what they are doing than do mothers in two-parent households."

In fact, boys from divorced homes reported being involved in more antisocial behavior without their parents' knowledge than children in any other type of family group. Girls from broken homes are more likely to become involved in sexual activity and at a younger age than children from intact homes.

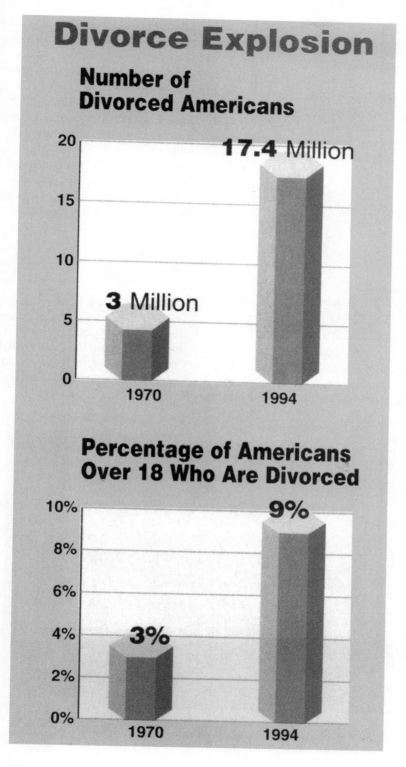

Divorce Explosion

Number of Divorced Americans

17.4 Million

3 Million

1970   1994

Percentage of Americans Over 18 Who Are Divorced

9%

3%

1970   1994

Another leader in this field of research is Nicholas Zill. Working with data from the National Survey of Children, he discovered that the tide of divorce not only negatively affects the children of broken families but even youngsters in intact families. He found that more than half of all elementary-school children, based on the knowledge that friends' parents have split, become afraid for the future of their family when their parents argue.

Regarding the health of parent-child relationships after divorce, Zill found that 55 percent of children in intact families reported positive relationships with both parents, compared with only 26 percent in situations of divorce.

Conversely, in intact families, only 18 percent of children reported having negative relationships with both parents, while 30 percent of kids from broken homes reported the same.

Zill, like Wallerstein, found the "effects of marital discord and family disruption were visible for 12 to 22 years later in poor relationships with parents, and [there is] an increased likelihood of dropping out of high school and receiving psychological help."

'METAANALYSES' OF PUBLISHED STUDIES

Paul Amato, a sociologist from the University of Nebraska, has done some interesting studies on how divorce affects children. Rather than observing children and analyzing their experiences as Wallerstein and Hetherington did, or looking at nationally representative statistics as Zill did, Amato examined the substantial body of published data on how divorce touches children.

In this process, called *metaanalysis,* a researcher examines a whole body of data, considering all its disagreements and inconsistencies, and attempts to come to an informed, balanced conclusion.

One of Amato's metaanalyses, looking at how divorce affects young children, draws from 92 published studies and a collective sample of more than 13,000 children. Another piece of research, involving 37 separate studies and a collective population sample of over 80,000 children, examined how divorce affects children as they enter their adult years. He required that each of the studies examined in both analyses contain a sample of children living in both broken and intact homes.

Amato found that, compared with kids in intact families, young children of divorce had lower aca-

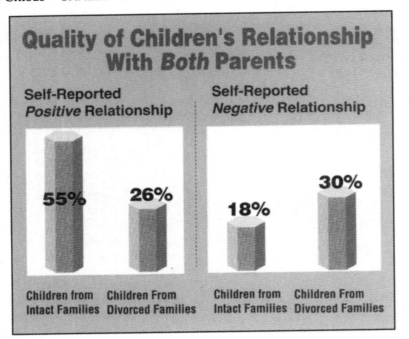

Quality of Children's Relationship With *Both* Parents

Self-Reported *Positive* Relationship

- Children from Intact Families: 55%
- Children From Divorced Families: 26%

Self-Reported *Negative* Relationship

- Children from Intact Families: 18%
- Children From Divorced Families: 30%

demic achievement, more behavioral problems, poorer psychological adjustments, more negative self-concepts, greater social difficulties, and more problematic relationships with both mothers and fathers.

This led him to conclude that "the view that children of divorce adapt readily and reveal no lasting negative consequences is simply not supported by the cumulative data in this area."

Amato's examination of how divorce affects children in their adult years confirms Wallerstein's findings: The pain does not subside but in many areas becomes more intense.

Amato found that, compared with adults from intact homes, people who grew up in broken homes had lower job status, poorer psychological well-being, a lower standard of living, less marital satisfaction, a heightened risk of divorce, a greater risk of being a single parent, and poorer physical health.

Based on his research, Amato concludes that "the long-term consequences of parental divorce for adult attainment and quality of life may prove to be more serious than the short-term emotional and social problems in children that are more frequently studied."

In general, then, although all the facts may not yet be in, the picture that is emerging of the new "divorce culture" from the available research is one of troubling grimness, the effects of which may hit America with waves of social and economic problems for generations to come.

Glenn T. Stanton is director of public policy research at Focus on the Family in Colorado Springs, Colorado. He is also the author of **Why Marriage Matters: Reasons to Believe in Marriage in Postmodern Society** *(Piñon Press, 1997).*

COREL

■ *Drag on education:* Divorce has been shown to impair children's performance in the classroom and to promote dropping out. Here youngsters wait for a school bus.

DIVORCED?

Don't Even Think of Remarrying

Until You Read This

Divorce rates prove that conventional wisdom is wrong: The dirty little secret is that when it comes to relationships, experience doesn't count. Experts take a close look at why we don't learn from our mistakes and how we can start—right now.

By Hara Estroff Marano

Americans are an optimistic lot. Perhaps nowhere is our optimism more apparent than in our approach to marriage.

One of every two marriages can be expected to end in tears. Still, 90% of Americans marry. Surveys consistently show that marriage holds an honored place on our wish list, something we believe is necessary of attaining life happiness—or its slightly wiser sibling, fulfillment.

If our optimism steers us into marriage, it goes into overdrive with remarriage. Despite the disappointment and the pain and the disruption of divorce, most of us opt to get back on the horse. An astonishing 75% of the broken-hearted get married all over again. And if you count among the remarried those who merge lives and households without legal ratification, the de facto remarriage rate is even higher.

Yet a whopping 60% of remarriages fail. And they do so even more quickly; after an average of 10 years, 37% of remarriages have dissolved versus 30% of first marriages.

If divorce and remarriage rates prove one thing, it is that conventional wisdom is wrong: When it comes to remarriage, experience doesn't count. A prior marriage actually *decreases* the odds of a second marriage working. Ditto if you count as a first marriage its beta version, living together; three decades of a persistently high divorce rate have encouraged couples to test the waters by living together before marrying. But this actually dims the likelihood of marital success.

"It's so counterintuitive," says Diane Sollee, M.S.W., a family therapist and director of the Coalition for Marriage, Family and Couples Education, based in Washington, D.C. "It seems obvious that people would be older and wiser. Or learn from the mistake of a failed first marriage and do better next time around. But that's like saying if you lose a football game you'll win the next one. You will—but only if you learn some new plays before you go back onto the field."

Remarriage may look a lot like any other marriage—two people, plenty of hope, lots of love and sex, and a desire to construct some form of joint life. It even smells like an ordinary marriage—the kitchen is busy once again. But it has its own subversive features, mostly invisible to the naked eye, that make it more tenuous. It's not impossible to make remarriage work, but it takes a concerted effort.

Reprinted with permission from *Psychology Today*, March/April 2000, pp. 56–62. © 2000 by Sussex Publishers, Inc.

Why Experience Doesn't Count

No, when it comes to relationships, people don't automatically learn from experience. There seems to be something special about relationships that prevents them from recognizing their failures. A close look at marriage suggests several reasons why.

Love deludes us. The rush of romance dupes us into believing our own partnership uniquely defies the laws of gravity. "We feel that this new, salient, intense relationship fills the firmament for us," observes William J. Doherty, Ph.D., director of the Marriage and Family Therapy Program at the University of Minnesota and author of *The Intentional Family* (Avon, 1999). "You really think 'problems are for regular people and our relationship certainly isn't regular,'" Doherty adds. "Partners bring to remarriage the stupidity of the first engagement and the baggage of the first marriage."

Marriage deflects us. Marriage, in fact, contains a structural psychological loophole: Being a two-party event from the get-go, it affords us the (morally slippery) convenience of thinking that any problems reside in our partner. We simply chose the wrong person last time. Or despite our shining presence and best efforts, the other person developed some critical character flaw or craziness. Either way, we focus—wrongly, it turns out—on the characteristics of our partner rather than on the dynamics of the relationship, by definition involving both people.

"Till our last dying breath we still think, "Someday I'll meet a mensch and it will be perfect; he will fit with all my wonderfulness in such a way that it will all work," says Diane Sollee. "We indulge the illusion that, with the right partner, conflict will be minimal."

Jeffry Larson, Ph.D., psychology professor at Brigham Young University, confirms, "partners don't reflect on their own role. They say 'I'm not going to make the same mistakes again.' But they do make the same mistakes unless they get insight into what caused the divorce and their role in the marriage failure." Larson is quick to admit that our culture generally provides us with no road map for assessing ourselves or our relationships. And some people are just too narcissistic to admit they had any role in the relationship's failure. They will never understand what went wrong. And that makes them lousy bets as new partners.

What's more, we are deeply social creatures, and even distant rumblings of a threat to our most intimate social bond are intolerable. When problems develop, marriages become so painful that we can't bear to look at our own part in them.

Conflict confuses us. Our ability to learn about relationships shuts down precisely when marriage begins to get tough—and they all get tough. Conflict is an inevitable part of relationships. But many people have no idea how to resolve the conflict; they see it instead as a sign that there's something wrong with the relation-

ship—and their partner. With low expectations about their own ability to resolve conflict, explains psychologist Clifford Notarius, Ph.D., professor of psychology at Catholic University in Washington, D.C., people go into alarm mode. This distorts the couple's communication even further and prevents any learning from taking place. "When a husband hears 'let's talk about money,' he knows what's coming," says Notarius. "He doesn't think anything different can happen. He shuts down."

Conflict rigidifies us. Arguments engage the Twin Terminators of relationship life: blame and defensiveness. These big and bad provocateurs destroy everything in their path, pushing partners further apart and keeping them focused on each other.

Invariably, marriage experts insist, whether in the first marriage or the fourth, couples tend to trip over the same mistakes. No. 1 on the list of errors is unrealistic expectations. A decline in intensity is normal and to be expected, says Notarius. In its own way, it should be welcomed. It's not a signal to bail out. "You will be disappointed—but that opens the potential for a relationship to evolve into something wonderful, a developmental journey of adult growth. Only in supportive relationships can we deal with our personal demons and life disappointments. We get the reassurance of having a partner who will be there no matter what, someone who can sit through our personal struggle for the hundredth time and support us. The promise of long-term relationships is the sharing of the secret self."

Absent this awareness, partners tend to start down the road to divorce as soon as the intensity wanes. Happiness, observes Pat Love, Ph.D., a marital therapist based in Austin, Texas, is the ratio between what you expect and what you get. "You have to suffer the clash of fantasy with reality in some relationships," adds Notarius. "Either you do it in the first relationship or you have 10 first relationships."

How To Remarry

Why is remarriage so difficult? The short answer is because it follows divorce. People who divorce are in a highly vulnerable state. They know what it's like to have a steady dose of love, that life's burdens are better when shared. But, say Love, "They go out, so they're hungry. And when you're hungry, you'll eat anything." The longing for comfort, for deep intimacy, impels the divorced to rush back into a married state. Says Love: "People tend to want to go back into the woodwork of marriage."

Yet prospective remarriage partners need to build a relationship slowly, experts agree. "They need to know each other individually and jointly," says Robert F. Stahmann, Ph.D., professor of family sciences and head of the Marriage Preparation Research Project at Brigham

Young University. "This means time for bonding as a couple because the relationship will be under stress from each partner's various links to the past," none more tangible than children and stepchildren.

Couples also need enough time to allow for the cognitive and emotional reorganization that must take place. Says Love, "You've got to replace the image in your head of what a man or a woman is like based on your ex. It happens piece by piece, as with a jigsaw puzzle, not like a computer with the flick of a switch."

When choosing a mate the second time around, people typically look for traits and tendencies exactly opposite those of their first partner. A woman whose first husband was serious and determined will tend to look for someone more fun. "Unfortunately," observes Howard K. Markman, Ph.D., "to the extent that they are making conscious choices, they are looking at the wrong factors." At the University of Denver, where he is professor of psychology, Markman and his colleagues are videotaping couples in a second marriage who were also studied in a first marriage.

"The motivation to do it differently is there," says the researcher, "and that is good. But they don't know exactly what to do differently. They're not making changes in how they conflict, which is predictive of relationship quality."

Further, he notes, both parties need to use the second marriage to become better partners themselves. "They both need to nourish the relationship on a daily basis . . . and refrain from things [such as hurling insults at one another] that threaten the marriage in the face of disappointments."

Learn to Love Complexity. There is even more opportunity for conflict and disappointment in remarriages because the challenges are greater. "There are always at least four people in bed," says Love. "Him, her, his ex and her ex. Not to mention the kids." The influence of exes is far from over with remarriage. Exes live on in memories, in daydreams, and often in reality, arriving to pick up and deliver the kids, exerting parental needs and desires that have to be accommodated, especially at holiday and vacation times. The ex's family—the children's grandparents, aunts, uncles and cousins—remains in the picture, too. "When you remarry," says Brigham Young's Larson, "you marry a person—and that person's ex-spouse." It just comes with the territory.

Defuse Anger, Vent Grief. Nothing keeps exes, and the past itself, more firmly entrenched in the minds of one-time spouses than anger. But we can minimize anger by finding ways to minimize the impact of ghosts from the past.

Unless people grieve the loss of the prior relationship and the end of the marriage, they are at risk of staying overtly attached to it. "When they don't grieve, often they remain angry," Larson says. "Exploring the feelings of sadness, and understanding the ways in which the first marriage was good, is a way of unhooking from it."

Many are the sources of loss that require acknowledgment:

The loss of an attachment figure. "It has nothing to do with how you were treated," says Love. "You lost someone you once cared about."

Loss of intact family. We all harbor the idea of a perfect family, and it's one in which emotions and biology are drawn along the same tight meridians.

A sense of failure. "A powerful element contributing to vulnerability in a second marriage," observed Love, "is a sense of shame or embarrassment stemming from relationships failure," denial of any role in the marital breakdown notwithstanding.

"There is pain and fear from the fact that former relationships did not go well," adds Hawkins, "which inhibit commitment to the new relationship and distort communication between partners."

A sense of grief. Grief is bound to be especially great for those who were dumped by their first spouse. "You can't grieve and try to get used to a new relationship at the same time," says Jeff Larson, who recommends waiting at least one or two years after a divorce before remarrying.

Digging Up the Past

Stahmann emphasizes that for remarriage to be successful, couples need to look at their previous relationships and understand their history. How did they get into the first marriage? What were their expectations, hopes and dreams? Through the soul-searching, people learn to trust again.

"It is essential that they do this together," Stahmann says. "It helps each of them break from the past relationship and sets a precedent for the foundation of the new one."

Pat Love stresses that this joint exploration must include a look at the partners' own role in the failure of the past relationship. "You have to list what you didn't like in your partner and own your own part in it. If you don't understand your part, then you are bound to do it again."

"When you do something that reminds me of my old partner," Love explains, "I project all the sins of that partner onto you. If you don't want sex one night, then you are 'withholding,' just like the ex." The fact is, Love insists, "the things you didn't like in your old partner actually live on in you."

But such joint exploration doesn't always take place. Couples are often afraid that a partner who brings up the past will get stuck there. Or that a discussion will reignite old flames, when in fact, it helps extinguish them. "Couples often enter remarriage with their eyes closed more than the first marriage," reports Hawkins. "It's as if they are afraid the marriage won't happen if they confront the issues."

Once a couple has opened up and explored their past, they need to bring the kids in on the discussion. "Kids don't have the same understanding of how and why the prior relationship ended." Explains Stahmann. "Yet they need it." On the agenda for discussion: how the adults got together, why the past failed, how contact with the biological parents will be maintained, and all the couple's dreams and hopes for the future. Most experts would reserve this conversation for after the wedding.

Clearing Customs. In any marriage, each partner to some degree represents a different culture with different traditions and rituals and symbols. The two distinct sets of highly structured traditions are not simply deeply emotionally resonant; they carry the force of commandment. The subtlest departure from them can make anyone feel like an outsider in his own home. One or both partners is bound to feel bad, even unloved, when their current family does a celebration "the wrong way."

The problems is, culture clash is built in to marriage, says Frank Pittman III, M.D., an Atlanta-based family therapist whose most recent book is *Grow Up! How Taking Responsibility Can Make You a Happy Adult* (Golden Books, 1998).

That, however, is where the fun begins. "The conflict causes electricity and the need to discuss things and compare perspectives, and thus come to know one another and oneself. That is the source of a marriage's energy," he says.

It's wise for couples heading into remarriage to explicitly discuss and agree on which ritual styles with prevail when. Even the everyday ones: Will dessert be served with dinner? Are evening snacks allowed? Then there are the big celebrations sprinkled throughout the calendar, culturally designated as holidays but more likely hurdles of stress in remarriage households.

Negotiating External Forces. As if there aren't enough internal hurdles, remarriage can be undermined by outside forces, too. "People who lived independently before remarriage often have jobs, friend networks and hobbies that are anti-relational," says Stahmann. "These are spheres in which they have come to invest a lot of themselves as a regular source of gratification." He counts among them learned workaholism. "Such individual-gratifying activities can be hard to give up. Couples need time to work out these patterns."

Coping with Kids. Nothing challenges a remarriage more than the presence of children from a prior marriage, and 65% of remarriage households contain kids. Their failure rate is highest in the first two years, before these multiplex families have even sorted themselves out.

"All you need is one active conspirator," says Minnesota's Doherty. "It's not uncommon for an ex to play on the ambivalence or outright hostility that kids have for a remarriage, especially at the beginning. An ex can have you talking about him every day."

Take one of his clients for example: Bob, who is remarried, gets a visit from his two children. After the weekend, the kids mention to their mother that the house felt cold. She calls her ex-husband, furious. When he agrees to turn up the thermostat, the new spouse feels powerless in her own home and angry at her husband because she thinks he is not standing up for himself, or her.

With kids present, partners in a remarriage do not get time to develop as a couple before becoming parents. Their bond is immediately under assault by the children. Family experts agree that this is yet another reason for couples heading into remarriage to prolong the period of courtship despite the incentives to merge households.

Even noncustody can pose problems. "Custody is a legal solution," says Stahmann. "It implies nothing about the emotional reality of family. A parent who shares custody or one who has only visitation rights is already experiencing some degree of loss regarding the children."

And the children themselves are in a state of postdivorce mourning over the loss of an intact family and full-time connection to a parent. No matter which parent a child is with, someone is missing all the time. "This leads to upset, depression and resentment at the new marriage," says Emily Visher, Ph.D., a psychologist in California and co-founder of the Stepfamily Association of America. The resentment is typically compounded by the fact that the children do not have the same perspective as the adults on how and why their parents' marriage broke up.

Financial obligations add more stress. Many a stepfather thinks: "I don't what to be putting my money into your kids' college education when I didn't put it to mine."

"There is an existential, moral dimension to remarriage families that is not talked about," says Minnesota's Doherty. "The partners will always be in different emotional and relational positions to the children. One is till death do us part. The other is till divorce do us part. The stepparent harbors a deep wish that the children did not exist, the very same children the parent could not live without."

People need to develop "a deep empathic understanding of the different emotional worlds parent and stepparent occupy." To be a stepparent, Doherty adds, "is to never be fully at home in your own house in relation to the children, while the original parent feels protective and defensive of the children. Neither 'gets' it until each describes what the emotional world is for him or her." Each partner is always an outsider to the experience of the other.

The role of the nonbiological parent is crucial—but fuzzy. "Twenty plus years into the divorce revolution and remarriage is an incomplete institution," observes Andrew Cherlin, Ph.D., professor of sociology at Johns Hopkins University. "It's not clear what rules a stepparent should follow." In successful families, the stepparent is somewhere between a friend and a parent, what he calls "the kindly uncle role." Using first names can help enhance that relationship.

But most importantly, "the more a couple can agree on expected roles, the more satisfied they will be," says Carlos Costelo, a Ph.D. candidate focusing on the dynamics of remarriage at the University of Kansas.

The key to remarriage, says Stahmann, is for couples to be less selfish that they used to be. "They have to realize there is a history there. They can't indulge jealousy by cutting off contact with kids. They can't cut off history." Selfishness, he insists, is the biggest reason for failure of remarriages.

"We all have a lot to learn from them," notes Doherty. "Remarriage families hold the secrets to all marriage. Remarriage with stepchildren illuminates the divergent needs and loyalties that are always present but often invisible in original families."

It Takes a Village

With so much vulnerability, and the well-being of so many people at stake, prospective partners in a remarriage need a little help from others. "The impression of family and friends on whether this remarriage will work is important," says Stahmann.

Pat Love, herself in a remarriage, couldn't be more emphatic. "You've got to do it by consensus. It takes a village. You've got to listen to friends. You're in an altered state by way of infatuation. The failure factor is there, making you fragile."

In face, Stahmann contends, the opinion of family members and friends is predictive of remarriage success. "Friends and family know who you are. They knew you married, and they can see how you are in the context of the new relationship." The trick is to listen to them.

Hara Estroff Marano is PT's editor-at-large and author of Why Doesn't Anybody Like Me? *(William Morrow, 1999).*

READ MORE ABOUT IT

Stepfamilies: Love, Parenting and Marriage In the First Decade, James H. Bray, Ph.D., and John Kelly (Broadway Books, 1998)

How To Win As A Stepfamily, Emily B. Visher, Ph.D., and John S. Visher, M.D. (Brunner/Mazel, 1991)

When Strangers Become Family

The art of being a stepparent, learned not easily but well

By Wray Herbert

Tori La Londe hosts a large Thanksgiving gathering every year at her home, but she's never sure who will show up. It could include any combination of her four biological children from two marriages, her stepson, the two foster kids she raised, or the several strays the others bring home. Although La Londe has little contact with her two former husbands, she has a close, enduring relationship with Jud, the stepson she helped raise. She also has a strong friendship with Jud's mother (when the two get together one will quip, "How's our husband?"). Once, when she ran into Jud's grandmother—his mother's mother—they embraced warmly, and Jud's grandmother cheerily introduced Tori to her friends: "This is my ex-son-in-law's wife."

Ex-wife now, which means the U.S. Census Bureau doesn't count Tori La Londe's family as a stepfamily. Social scientists label it a broken stepfamily, but calling her a "step" mother presiding over a "broken" home belies the warmth and wholeness she sees in her recombinant family. Like many Americans, she considers the collection of children and in-laws she has inherited in her marriages as family, plain and simple. The ties may not be biological, but they are strong nonetheless.

In fact, La Londe's extended family and other stepfamilies of various configurations are becoming standard issue: The government estimates that stepfamilies will outnumber traditional nuclear families by the year 2007. But a more inclusive estimate of anyone in any kind of step relationship brings the number of people who are "steps" to about 60 percent of the population. Which means that sitting down this week to the final Thanksgiving dinner of the 20th century will be more than 5.5 million American stepfamilies.

Their stories have become familiar in the two decades since *Kramer vs. Kramer:* the uneasy navigation of strangers suddenly confronting each other at the breakfast table, over the holidays, on the way to the bathroom in the middle of the night. In interviews with *U.S. News,* they spoke of awkward intimacies, jealous anxieties—and the strange alliances that make stepparenting an experiment in heartbreak and joy. Many of them are prospering, instinctively coming up with strategies that social scientists and family experts have just begun to understand.

Name game. The challenges begin on the level of language: What do members of new stepfamilies call themselves? Consider Kris Allen, 18, of Boulder Creek, Calif. His mother is Kim Allen, Allen being the name she took from her ex-husband, Kris's father. But Kris's father only became an Allen when he himself became part of a stepfamily in his youth; his given name was Hoops, and Kris is thinking of taking Hoops as his name. Just to make it interesting, Kris's stepfather, Jerry Kaiser, was originally Jerry Cohen. His widowed mother changed his name to Kaiser when she remarried, when Jerry was 10.

As complicated as it is to deconstruct the Allen-Hoops-Kaiser-Cohen family tree, in practice they act like any old American family. Both parents are fully involved in family decision making and discipline, as they have been since Jerry and Kim got together eight years ago. Kris is a well-adjusted kid, no more directionless or cynical than the other 18-year-olds attending nearby Cabrillo College. Social scientists haven't studied this family, but if they did they would point to a couple of things that Kim and Jerry have done that most successful stepfamilies do. First, they talk openly and daily, anticipating and defusing many potential land mines. Jerry and Kim are both counselors, and the communication skills that they teach to corporate managers are the same ones they bring to parenting. They also developed their relationship very slowly at first. Jerry and Kris actually became friends before Jerry and Kim started dating—Kris attended a work-site day-care center where they worked—so he was excited when his mother told him that Jerry would be moving into their house. The 10-year-old had only one question: "Where's he going to sleep?"

The Kaiser-Allen family is typical of what psychologist James Bray calls "neo-traditional" stepfamilies, the most successful stepfamilies he identified in his nine-year study for the National Institutes of Health. Their most striking characteristic is that they take a realistic—and flexible—approach to building a family out of strangers. They know they're not a 1950s-vintage nuclear family and don't try to be; but they are also the type of stepfamily that after a few years most closely resembles the traditional nuclear family, in intimacy and unconditional support of one another.

But successful stepfamilies come in many different shapes. Brenda and Jeff Micka of Joseph, Ore., have staked out a bold position, perhaps at odds with what the experts counsel, but which works for them. All four of their boys—three from his first marriage and one from hers—call them Mom and Dad. They also call their other biological parents Mom and Dad—an arrangement that the kids seem comfortable with. But the Mickas are well aware that they have an unusual setup. For one thing, Jeff's ex lives eight hours away in Eugene, so every other weekend the three boys have to travel 16 hours round trip to visit their mother. Still, they've been able to turn this awkward arrangement into an acceptable routine. For Michael and Simone Humphrey of Overland Park, Kan., the sacrifice has been even greater: They recently moved their new family to Kansas from Dallas, following Michael's son and daughter and their mother—his ex-wife—who had relocated in 1996. Says Simone: "We were flying Jennifer and Matthew to Dallas and back once a month. It was just too much, and too little time with them."

Every successful stepfamily has stories about compromises and adjustments it has had to make. In the case of Drew Myers and Anne Marie O'Connell-Myers of Westport, Conn., a major issue was religion. Anne Marie and her daughter, Jackie, are practicing Catholics; Drew and his four kids—Brad, Carter, Garrett, and Libby—were not churchgoers when Drew and Anne Marie got together. Anne Marie had no interest in converting her new family, but she did think as a matter of shared values that it was important for all of them to attend church. So Drew and his children began attending the Congregational Church, where they now go on the first Sunday of each month. It was an adjustment at first for the formerly unchurched Myers kids, but now they sometimes choose to join Anne Marie and Jackie at their services, too.

Lifestyle change is inevitable when a new stepfamily is formed, and it can be especially difficult for only children. In the Micka family, for instance, Brenda's son, Cody, inherited three younger brothers overnight. "Cody had some difficulty at first," says Brenda Micka, "going from having me to himself to sharing a mother with three younger brothers." But the three younger boys' adoration of their new "older brother" brought Cody around. For 10-year-old Jackie O'Connell, the adjustment had more to do with family finances. An only child who had lived with her single mom since birth, she had never really wanted for anything; when she joined the Myers clan, she inherited four siblings and a stepdad who was used to running a disciplined family budget. "We had to negotiate family finances," says Drew. "I was budgeting for four, and Jackie had been used to getting what she wanted."

Baby makes three. The arrival of new half-siblings can also be disruptive, although it doesn't have to be; indeed, it can be tonic if the parents involve the older children in the excitement of the pregnancy early on. That's certainly how 12-year-old Madeleine Schlefer of Brooklyn, N.Y., sees it. She and her 9-year-old sister, Gwen, live primarily with their mother, but her dad and stepmom live close by in the same Park Slope neighborhood. That proximity makes it easy for the two older sisters to stop by after school and check in on their baby sister, Juliet, who was born 10 months ago. Meg Schlefer, the girls' stepmom, credits their mother with helping to make Madeleine and Gwen's comings and goings uncontentious.

RELIGION, FAMILY FINANCES, DIET, DISCIPLINE— these are all issues that stepfamilies around the country are struggling with every day. And most of them are doing it gracefully. Even so, there is a sizable minority of stepfamilies in America that are not doing well at all. A variety of studies have demonstrated that stepkids do more poorly on a variety of measures than do kids who live in traditional, two-parent families—even adjusting for income level. They are more apt to repeat a grade in school, have disciplinary problems, and drop out of school altogether. In fact, these studies collectively indicate that stepchildren do about as well as kids who live with a single parent, which is to say much worse than kids in traditional nuclear families.

And that's not the worst of it. According to extensive research by Martin Daly and Margo Wilson of McMaster University in Ontario, stepchildren are more likely to be abused, both physically and sexually, and even more likely to be killed by a parent—100 times as likely—compared with kids being raised by two biological parents. Another line of research indicates that they are less likely to be provided for. For example, American children living with a stepparent are less likely to go to college and to receive family financial support if they do. New research also shows that biological mothers around the world spend more of family income on food—particularly milk, fruit, and vegetables—and less on tobacco and alcohol, compared with mothers raising nonbiological children. The list goes on.

Unsolved mysteries. Just why these families fare so poorly as a group is a matter of dispute. It's widely accepted that kids in single-parent families have troubles at least in part because the parent—usually the mother—has money problems following divorce. Facing financial difficulties, she is more apt to be absent—actually or emotionally. But remarriage doesn't seem to ameliorate the children's problems. And while few doubt that the dislocating effects of the initial divorce contribute to the situation, many experts believe that these experiences cannot fully account for the problems.

Experts offer several ideas about what might be going on. For example, unsuccessful stepfamilies often overromanticize the new family. What psychologist Bray calls "romantic" stepfamilies picture themselves as the idealized nuclear family, and they do whatever they can to fit into that mold—usually with unhappy results. The main problem, Bray says, is that in their impatience to be seen as traditional, these families push things that should evolve slowly. In most families, for example, family members spend a fair amount of time apart, more and more so as the kids become teenagers. Romantic stepfamilies, on the other hand, spend a lot of time in forced camaraderie, and teens are especially quick to detect the falseness. The decidedly unromantic Kris Allen wasn't even comfortable being photographed for this article taking a walk with his parents. A friend asked him, "So, Kris, you mean that photographer dude tried to make you act normal doing

EVIL STEPMOTHERS

The uses and abuses of Cinderella

Who's the fairest of them all? asks Snow White's stepmother before plotting to kill her young, raven-haired competition. Hansel and Gretel head to the forest knowing their father's new wife would like to see them dead. Cinderella is relatively lucky: Her stepmother relegates her to the chimney corner, but at least she doesn't threaten her life. Similar tales starring evil stepmothers can be found in cultures around the world, leading social scientists to wonder if this archetype might be rooted in fact.

Indeed, scientists who study modern stepfamilies generally agree that families with a full-time stepmother do worse than families with a stepfather. It may be that stepmothering is simply harder, because the children's bond with the biological mother is often very powerful. As University of Nebraska–Lincoln sociologist Lynn White notes, a man can be a decent stepfather simply by being a provider and a nice guy, but a stepmother is often called upon to establish "gut-level empathy and attachment"—traits that are difficult, if not impossible, to fabricate. It's also possible, White adds, that the children have a poorer relationship with their father to begin with, a frailty that may weaken the basic foundation of the new family. Whatever the reason, stepmothers and stepchildren are the "big losers" in these reconfigured families.

Evil stepfathers? But such stepfamilies are actually quite rare. In fact, most stepfamilies are formed when a biological mother remarries. So why isn't literature filled with evil stepfathers instead? According to Martin Daly and Margo Wilson, authors of *The Truth About Cinderella,* stepfathers don't come off all that well either; they're often lustful as well as cruel. But there aren't as many of them, and Daly and Wilson speculate that stepmothers weren't always so vanishingly rare. In earlier times, when the mortality rate for women during childbirth was much higher, a lot of widowers ended up replacing their first wife with another. According to historian Stephanie Coontz, these stepfamilies were often plagued by feuds, divorces, and even murders—not infrequently because of competition over inheritance. In societies like those of medieval Europe, she says, where primogeniture ruled inheritance, "it makes sense for people to be obsessed with wicked stepmothers who might try to substitute their own (often older) children for the oldest biological child of the dad."

Daly and Wilson offer one additonal theory. If a story is to persist through the ages, they contend, it must serve some social purpose, not only for the audience but for the storytellers as well. The audience for stories like *Cinderella* and *Snow-White* was most likely children; the storytellers, however, were their mothers. It's not hard to imagine why mothers might prefer tales whose subtext runs: "Remember, my dears, that the worst thing imaginable would be for me to disappear and for your father to replace me with another woman."—W.H.

in navigating the tricky territory of step-relationships. When she's trying to get her stepdaughters to attend to chores, for example, she'll say: "Your wart-covered, foul-smelling, evil stepmother asks you, 'Please clean your room.'"

Biological nuclear families form gradually, allowing a couple time to negotiate rules, responsibilities, and traditions before children come along. But in stepfamilies these processes unfold helter-skelter. From the point of view of the child, it can seem that one life has been torn away and replaced with another—and all without the child's vote. Jerry Kaiser, for example, was 10 when his widowed mother remarried. Seemingly overnight, he inherited two older siblings and had to share a room with one of them in a strange house. Perhaps most disconcerting, he lost his name and the name of the father he grieved for. He was Jerry Cohen one day, Jerry Kaiser the next. He was never clear on what he was supposed to call his stepfather—nobody ever told him—so he simply avoided addressing him at all. "I got very good," Kaiser recalls, "at positioning myself in the room so I didn't have to call him Norm *or* Dad."

If stepfamiles shouldn't pretend they're traditional intact families, how should they act? Nobody really knows, including stepparents. In one recent research project, adults were asked to rank various roles according to their importance as sources of their sense of self. Not surprisingly, "parent" topped the list, but "stepparent" ranked extremely low, below such identities as neighbor, in-law, or churchgoer. Because of the low regard accorded stepparenting, it's not surprising that many stepparents are tempted to put more of their time and energy into other roles, making their presence in the new family shadowy at best. But this can set in motion a vicious circle: When a stepparent lacks a clear mandate as the authority figure within the family, he or she may err on the side of disciplining too much—or too little, withdrawing from that traditional parental role completely. The result may be that the stepchildren receive less attention, monitoring, and supervision than children in nuclear families.

Being somewhat disengaged as a stepparent isn't always bad, however. The third type of stepfamily to emerge from Bray's study is what he calls "matriarchal" stepfamilies, and as the name suggests, the mother plays the dominant

stuff with your parents that you'd never do?" Kris: "Yeah. Like I'd ever be walking on the beach with my parents!" In extreme cases, stepfamilies actually pretend they are nuclear families, hiding their step-status from schools, for example. And the bottom line is that they break up at a higher rate than other stepfamilies.

The problem, experts say, is that stepfamilies are not nuclear families—even if they wish they were—and trying to squeeze into that mold can backfire. According to historian Stephanie Coontz, author of *The Way We Really Are: Coming to Terms With America's Changing Families,* stepfamilies are not a new phenomenon in American life, but the dynamics have changed in important ways. Before divorce rates exploded in the 1970s, stepfamilies were usually formed after the death of a parent, and those stepfamilies could in effect create a second nuclear family. But modern stepfamilies are mostly the product of divorce (or out-of-wedlock births), and it's nearly impossible for these families to fit the traditional mold. Most have to deal with ex-spouses—the "ghost at the dinner table," in one expert's phrasing—and often with the exes' new families as well. These interactions can be complex under the most congenial circumstances, and more often than not the circumstances are not congenial. Meg Schlefer has found that humor goes a long way parenting role in these families. Matriarchal stepfamilies often come into existence when a single mom finally remarries; since she has been carrying the full parenting load, perhaps for several years, she often simply continues to do so. These stepfamilies usually do best when the new stepfather takes a somewhat marginal role; this is especially true if the stepchildren are teenagers, who are just beginning the psychological process of distancing themselves from parental authority. Indeed, matriarchal stepfamilies are more likely to experience problems when circumstances force the new father into a disciplinary role with which he is unfamiliar or uncomfortable.

WHEN PAUL AND GALE HALPERN DECIDED TO end their marriage, Paul expected he would at least have some kind of continuing relationship with their 1-year-old daughter, Laurie. Although he was not the girl's biological father, he felt that he had been a committed "psychological parent": He had coached Gale through the birth and cut the umbilical cord; his name was on the birth certificate, evidence of the couple's intention to raise the child together. And he had been a stay-at-home dad since Laurie's birth. Indeed, she had even called him "Daddy."

No relationship. But when Paul Halpern petitioned for visitation rights, the California courts denied his request in what has become an often-cited legal landmark. Because he was a stepparent during the marriage, the dissolution of that union made him nothing more than a "nonparent" in the eyes of the court. The judge dismissed Paul and his claims with this terse comment: "He absolutely has no relationship to the child bloodwise or otherwise, and I can't accept I should burden all of the parties in this matter, including Mr. Halpern, with conflicts, struggles, and disruptions for years to come because of Mr. Halpern's present emotional state in connection with the child."

The Halpern case took place nearly two decades ago, but it has remained a symbol in the legal profession of the gross disregard and lack of protective laws that beset stepparents and stepfamilies. Sadly, the shaky status of stepparents is just as much a fact of life today as it was in the Halperns' time. Indeed, it is now under fresh assault: Conservative critics have recently embraced the sweeping biological indictment of stepfamilies proposed by evolutionary psychologists, who contend that parents have evolved over eons to care only about the welfare of their genetic offspring. The critics are using the scientific theory as ammunition to lobby for stronger "pro-family" social policies. If stepfamilies are so unnatural from a genetic point of view that they imperil children's welfare, the argument goes, then anything that can be done to prevent divorce and preserve traditional families ought to be. This includes a number of ideas proffered by the nascent "marriage movement"—from pro-marriage tax policies to the so-called covenant marriages that are intended to make divorce (and thus remarriage) more difficult.

Biological determinists represent a minority viewpoint in family-policy debates. Other social critics contend that if there is a genetic predisposition that favors biological children over stepchildren, it's just that—a predisposition—and predisposition is not destiny. Creating social policies that keep unhappy families trapped in the same house, these critics argue, would be wrongheaded and far more risky psychologically than life in a stepfamily. What's needed, these critics argue, is not more stigmatizing of stepfamilies, but rather policies that strengthen stepfamilies and reduce any risks that might exist.

Changes in their legal status are one possibility. Like domestic partners, stepparents currently have almost no legal standing in most states, which means that even when they assume responsibility for their stepchildren—supporting them emotionally and financially, for example—they have no corresponding rights. If the marriage ends, the stepparent has no legal standing to ask for custody or visitation. Similarly, stepchildren rarely have rights—to life insurance benefits, for example—or, if the marriage ends, to continued support or inheritance. Existing family law has been challenged in various ways in different localities, but the resulting legal rulings have been inconsistent. In a case now pending before the Supreme Court, a child's grandparents are suing for visitation rights, but some legal experts believe that a ruling for the grandparents could be interpreted as an affirmation of stepparents' rights as well.

Many family experts are now arguing for legislation that explicitly spells out both the rights and responsibilities of stepparents, perhaps modeled on England's Children Act of 1989. That law gives stepparents who have been married to a child's parent for at least two years the right to petition the court for a "residence order," which conveys many of the same rights and responsibilities as the biological parents'. Children in these stepfamilies in effect have legal relationships with three adults: both biological parents and the stepparent. The theory is that giving the stepparent enhanced status will legitimate his or her role, both in the family and in society, and that the very process of asking for rights and responsibilities will bolster the stepparent-stepchild bond. (The law only went into effect in 1991, so its effects are not yet known.)

Cultural connection. Ultimately, the changes that will strengthen stepfamilies will likely come from shifts in cultural prejudices. Such change is slow, but there are signs that some preliminary movement along this line is beginning to take place. For instance, Roger Coleman, a clergyman in Kansas City, Mo., performs marriage ceremonies specifically designed to include children when a parent remarries. In years of officiating second marriages, he says, he became acutely aware of the confusion and insecurities of the children, and the ceremony—which includes a special medallion worn by the child—aims to celebrate the "new family" and move the church beyond mere condemnation of divorce. This year, Coleman says, over 10,000 families across the country will use the medallion in their remarriage ceremony.

Similar changes are occurring in public schools around the country. One of the difficulties for stepfamilies is that schools and other public institutions have typically not recognized the stepparent as a legitimate parent; school registration forms, field trip permission slips, health emergency information—none of these required or acknowledged the stepparent. The message, whether intended or not, has been that only biological parents count. It's a message that the stepparent and stepchild internalize, undermining what's often an already difficult relationship, and one which the larger community takes as another sign of the stepfamily's illegitimacy in American society. Through the efforts of the Stepfamily Association of America and other advocates, schools around the country have begun changing their policies to acknowledge the increasingly important role of stepparents.

Change is also evident in a marketplace eager to exploit this wide social trend. In a particularly American sign of the times, the Hallmark greeting card company, that longtime arbiter of normalcy, is about to launch a line of cards devoted entirely to nontraditional families. The cards never use the word "step," but most of the "Ties That Bind" line is clearly aimed at people who have come together by remarriage rather than biology—or, as one card puts it, "Thrown together without being asked, no chance of escape." Some are straightforward ("There are so many different types and ways to be a family today"), while others are more elliptical ("It's like looking at a puzzle where the pieces aren't where they used to be"). But all are aimed at the vast and growing market of people who don't identify with the old definitions of family, and who—like the Mickas and Kaisers and Allens and Schlefers—are finding ways to make

MAKING STEPFAMILIES WORK

Taking it step by step

*S*ome lessons experts have distilled from research on successful stepfamilies:

•**Don't go nuclear.**
Parents often cling to the dream of being a nuclear family, but it's a mistake to push it too fast. The most successful stepfamilies are realistic about the challenges they face—dealing with exspouses, negotiating rules and traditions—and communicate openly about them.

•**Work on the relationship.** Stepchildren need attention, but the family won't last if the parents' relationship doesn't. Anyway, it's not normal for families to be together all the time.

•**Don't rush it.** It usually takes up to two years for the stepfamily to emerge from an initial period of conflict. It can be difficult for everyone if a stepparent tries to take on the role of full parent too quickly. Kids generally want their own parents to be responsible for them.

•**Define roles.** The stepparent and stepchild need to figure out what feels right. Some form close bonds over time, but in many cases both the parent and child are better off if the stepparent acts more like a kindly aunt or uncle.

—*W.H.*

their new families work. Who knows— soon there may even be a card Tori La Londe can send to her ex-husband's ex-mother-in-law.

ELDER CARE: MAKING THE RIGHT CHOICE

Nursing homes used to be the only stop for seniors who need help. Now there are options

By JOHN GREENWALD

MARJORIE BRYAN'S HUSBAND DIED 14 years ago. That was when she lived in Mississippi, and for some time afterward she went on living on her own. Now she's 82. A few years ago, she started having trouble with her balance and taking falls. Bryan has a grown son in Georgia, but moving in with him didn't seem like the answer. It's one thing to have a roof over your head. It's another to have a life. "I didn't want to live with my children," she says. "I think it would bore me to death. I don't drive anymore. If I'd stayed there, I'd be sort of a prisoner during the day."

So Bryan went looking at the alternatives. It turned out there were more than she had imagined. A couple of decades ago, seniors like her who were basically healthy but needed some assistance had limited choices. Among them, they could move in with their grown children, if they had any and were willing to risk the squabbling and sulking. Or they could be bundled off to a nursing home that was like a hospital, only less inviting. All that began to change in the early 1980s with the growth of a new range of living arrangements for older people who want to live as people, not patients, without the physical confinement and spiritual dead air of many nursing homes.

Eventually Bryan came upon the Gardens of Towne Lake in Woodstock, Ga., a landscaped complex where about two dozen sen-

iors live in their own apartments and have round-the-clock staff members to help with daily tasks such as dressing and bathing.

There are regular social events. There's a beauty shop. "I love living here," she says. "I got out that first day to learn names."

AGING IN AMERICA

The number of American seniors is growing. They're independent now, but it won't last forever

76
Currently the average life expectancy for Americans

43
Percentage of today's seniors who will use a nursing home in their lifetime

25
Percentage of elderly housing residents in assisted-living facilities now

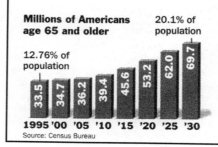

Millions of Americans age 65 and older

12.76% of population

20.1% of population

33.5 — 1995
34.7 — '00
36.2 — '05
39.4 — '10
45.6 — '15
53.2 — '20
62.0 — '25
69.7 — '30

Source: Census Bureau

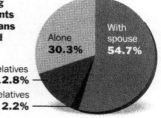

1999 living arrangements for Americans age 65 and older

With spouse **54.7%**
Alone **30.3%**
With other relatives **12.8%**
With nonrelatives **2.2%**

From *Time*, August 30, 1999, pp. 52–56. © 1999 by Time, Inc. Magazine Company. Reprinted by permission.

THE OPTIONS	HOME CARE	CONGREGATE HOUSING	ASSISTED LIVING	CONTINUING-CARE FACILITIES	NURSING HOMES
WHAT IS IT?	■ Services ranging from shopping and transportation to physical therapy brought to the home	■ A private home within a residential compound, providing shared activities and services	■ Residential units offering private rooms, meals, 24-hr. supervision and other assistance	■ A variety of housing options and a continuum of services all in one location	■ Residential medical care for the aged who need continual attention
WHOM IS IT FOR?	■ Seniors who are able to continue living at home but need some help	■ Seniors in good health who want both independence and companionship	■ Seniors who may need help with bathing, dressing, medication, etc.	■ Seniors who want to provide for health needs as they age without having to relocate	■ Seniors with deteriorating mental or physical abilities or great difficulty with daily activities
WHAT DOES IT COST?	■ Some services are free; a home health-care visit can be $80	■ Often $1,200 to $2,00 a month, yet can cost much more	■ Averages $2,000 a month, but can be far more for high needs	■ $1,500 to $5,000 a month. Most require an entry fee	■ Average close to $50,000 a year
WHAT DOES IT OFFER?	■ Independence at home, but can be costly depending on level of care needed	■ The advantages of home, plus services like 24-hr. security and laundry	■ A greater level of care while maintaining some independence	■ Guaranteed care as a resident ages—at a relatively high price	■ About the only option for those who need constant care

The late 20th century has done for the retirement years what it did for TV channels and fancy coffee. It multiplied the choices but also the consumer bewilderment. For seniors who want to stay in their homes as long as they can, there is home care for the masses—agencies everywhere that provide nurses and aides who either come by your place on a regular basis or live in. Traditional nursing homes are still widely used, though they are evolving away from long-term care and toward rehabilitative facilities, for short-term stays following hospitalization. The most popular new options are assisted-living facilities. There are an estimated 20,000 to 30,000 such places in the U.S., according to industry figures. Assisted-living complexes are home to one-fourth of the 2.2 million Americans who live in housing for seniors, according to the American Seniors Housing Association. Some are free-standing facilities. Some are part of continuing-care retirement communities, which offer increasing levels of help and medical supervision as residents move through the years.

"The assisted-living movement has really changed the way people age," says Karen Wayne, president of the Assisted Living Federation of America (ALFA), an industry trade group. "We've proved that people don't want to be in institutional settings." The facility provides each resident with a room or suite; meals, usually in a common dining room; and round-the-clock members who help with the no-big-deal chores of the day that can still defeat the mostly capable elderly—bathing, dressing, taking medication. Assisted living gives the elderly some measure of independence, a chance to socialize and needed privacy. Privacy for all sorts of

things—sex has hardly disappeared from these seniors' lives. A survey released this month by the American Association of Retired Persons revealed that a quarter of those 75 or older say they have sex at least once a week.

The widening flood of Americans into later life—Tina Turner turns 60 this year!—guarantees that elder care will be a 21st century growth industry. The market, which was $86 billion in 1996, is expected to reach $490 billion by 2030. That potential is attracting such big developers as the Hyatt Corp. and Marriott International hotel operators. The 3,300 units of senior housing that Hyatt operates in 16 communities around the country are worth an estimated $500 million.

The old people that assisted living caters to are usually able to get out of bed and walk around. But their average age, estimated by ALFA, is 83, so they can also be frail. Almost half have Alzheimer's or some degree of cognitive impairment. (Alzheimer's patients tend to have their own, more closely supervised area.) John Knox Village, in Pompano Beach, Fla., is a not-for-profit continuing-care operation on a landscaped campus with meandering walks and duck ponds. In an arrangement typical of such places, the elderly buy a residence—studio apartments are $48,500; two-bedroom "villas" are $142,500—and a continuing-care contract that sets a monthly maintenance fee covering all services. While they may begin life there in a mostly independent mode, taking an apartment with meals, they can later move to assisted-care rooms or even the on-campus nursing home for about the same monthly maintenance fee, usually a fraction of what a regular nursing home demands.

Carl Kielmann, 73, is a retired banker and the second generation of his family to

live at John Knox in the Health Center. He and his wife Lillian moved there in 1985, joining his mother, who was also a resident. His mother's contract with Knox allowed her to spend her last six years in the village medical center without eating up her savings. "In a lot of ways," says Kielmann, "this type of place is your ultimate insurance policy."

Other assisted-care facilities can be a single building. Sunrise Assisted Living in Glen Cove, N.Y., is a 57,000-sq.-ft. soft yellow mansion with white gingerbread trimmings. The 83 seniors who live there each pay between $2,850 and $4,800 a month. On a recent day the buttery smell of fresh popcorn wafted through the vestibule. One the door of its suites, framed "memory boxes" display mementos of the lives of the people who live behind those doors—family photos, military dog tags and other souvenirs of long lives. In the special section for residents with Alzheimer's, one area is stocked with old tool kits, weeding gowns and a crib with several dolls, haunting but therapeutic props meant to engage the minds of people who have returned in fantasy to younger days when they worked and raised families. "We want to create pleasant days for these folks," says Jennifer Rehm, who runs the busy activity room. "This is not usually a neat place by the end of the day."

Keeping the elderly connected to the larger world is a big part of the idea behind assisted living. At the Munné Center in Miami, where family gatherings are featured, residents look forward to seeing their neighbors' grandchildren as eagerly as they do their own. Cecilia Struzzieri, 95, recently moved into Munné after living with her daughter. "I was getting feeble, and she wanted her freedom," Struzzieri says with a

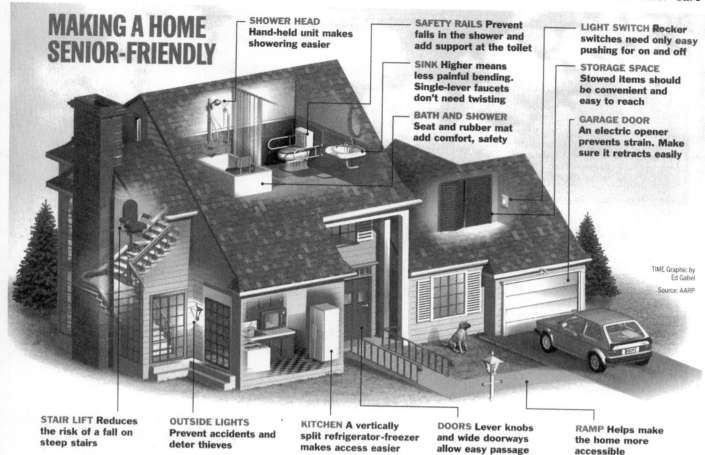

MAKING A HOME SENIOR-FRIENDLY

SHOWER HEAD Hand-held unit makes showering easier

SAFETY RAILS Prevent falls in the shower and add support at the toilet

SINK Higher means less painful bending. Single-lever faucets don't need twisting

BATH AND SHOWER Seat and rubber mat add comfort, safety

LIGHT SWITCH Rocker switches need only easy pushing for on and off

STORAGE SPACE Stowed items should be convenient and easy to reach

GARAGE DOOR An electric opener prevents strain. Make sure it retracts easily

TIME Graphic by Ed Gabel
Source: AARP

STAIR LIFT Reduces the risk of a fall on steep stairs

OUTSIDE LIGHTS Prevent accidents and deter thieves

KITCHEN A vertically split refrigerator-freezer makes access easier

DOORS Lever knobs and wide doorways allow easy passage

RAMP Helps make the home more accessible

sigh. "Here I get all the attention I need." Miami developer Raul Munné, who built the place, is a Cuban immigrant. "Where I grew up," he jokes, "the elderly sat on the porch and fought with the neighborhood kids. It gave them incentive to get out of bed in the morning." But in the U.S., he says, "old folks are told, 'Don't open your door and go out at night. You might get mugged.' So, many of them have no one to talk to all day. They can only sit and watch television."

Later life lived this way doesn't come cheap. The Del Webb company, which made its name building luxury spas and retirement communities in the Sun Belt, last year opened a Sun City retirement community in Huntley, near frost-belted Chicago, an acknowledgement that seniors increasingly prefer to locate near longtime friends and family and not move to far-off sunny climes. Prices range from $130,00 for a single-level fourplex to $750,000 for customized estate homes that include home theaters, Jacuzzis and wine cellars, where eminent Bordeaux can age along with its owners.

The typical assisted-living unit rents for about $2,000 a month, meals and basic services included. And prices can go much higher. Furthermore, assisted-living communities are not medical facilities, so their costs are not covered by Medicare or Medicaid, though 32 states do permit the limited use

of Medicaid funds for assisted living. No wonder, then, that the average assisted-care resident has an income of $26,000 annually, while the typical retiree has $20,700.

The boomtown growth of the assisted-living industry has left it a bit rough around the edges. While nursing homes are federally regulated, assisted-living communities are overseen by the states and thus subject to widely varying standards. A federal study in four states (California, Florida, Ohio and Oregon) found "unclear or potentially misleading" language in sales brochures for about one-third of the 60 assisted-living homes surveyed. The most common problem

USEFUL WEBSITES

www.senioralternatives.com ■
A virtual tour of selected retirement communities around the country

www.edlerweb.com ■
Lots of links to specific subjects, including a useful housing guide

www.aarp.org ■
Includes detailed tips on modifying a home to accommodate seniors

www.ec-online.net ■
Comprehensive information about Alzheimer's disease

was a failure to disclose the circumstances under which a resident can be expelled. One Florida home promised that seniors would not have to move if their health deteriorated, but the fine-print contract said physical or mental decline could be grounds for discharge.

Congress has begun poking into the problem, partly by way of its work to update the 1965 Older Americans Act, which provides penalties for scams on the elderly. "New services that meet the needs of our growing senior population are necessary and exciting," says Louisiana Senator John Breaux, ranking Democrat on the Senate Special Committee on Aging. "But the facilities are market driven and are susceptible to a bottom-line mentality that can lead to consumer fraud and abuse."

Of course, they are. Late-century American life is a social experiment in which we hope that market institutions can be fashioned to meet the most personal requirements. And sometimes they can be. New living arrangements for the elderly are still evolving. If that evolution isn't finished in time for all out parents to take advantage of, for many of us there will be a second chance—when it's our turn. —*Reported by Aixa M. Pascual/New York, Greg Aunapu/Miami, Leslie Everton Brice/Atlanta, Anne Moffett/Washington and Kermit Pattison/St. Paul*

Bereavement events among elderly men: The effects of stress and health

Tanya R. Fitzpatrick

Abstract:

Fitzpatrick reviews the literature on bereavement events as they relate to elderly men who have experienced the loss of a spouse, adult child, parent, sibling or friends.

Previous bereavement studies have focused on the loss of a spouse and have been limited to surviving women. Studies of the effect of the death of a friend or of male survivors remain sparse. This article reviews the literature on bereavement events as they relate to elderly men who have experienced the loss of a spouse, adult child, parent, sibling, or friends. Several psychoanalytic, cognitive and sociobiological theories are examined along with stress and health-related factors that are said to influence grief and mourning. The review of the literature indicates that health is particularly affected by stressful life events such as the loss of a spouse, child, parent, sibling, or friend, and that elderly men are at a disadvantage as evidenced by higher rates of psychological and physical disorders. The necessity to extend research beyond present theories and to consider specific social supports as they buffer the impact of stress on the health of bereaved elderly men is discussed.

Given the likelihood of experiencing losses associated with the death of significant loved ones as people age, it is important for health care professionals to consider the impact of bereavement as it relates to the physical and mental health of elderly men. Many studies have indicated that the loss of a spouse is the most stressful life event experienced for aging persons and is directly related to a decline in physical and mental health (Duran, Turner, & Lund, 1989; Gallagher, Breckenridge, Thompson, & Peterson, 1983; Gass, 1989; Hershberger & Walsh, 1990; Lund, 1989; Stroebe & Stroebe, 1983; Zandt, Mou, & Abbott, 1989), yet most investigators have studied elderly widows (Gallagher et al., 1983). Although some investigators have addressed the relationship between bereavement and aging men, few have considered grief reactions aside from the loss of their wives, such as those associated with the death of other intimate relationships (i.e., children, siblings, parents, and friends). In the few studies that have taken into account specific bereavement events among older adults—that is, parents (De Vries, Della Lana, & Falck, 1994; Moss, Lesher, & Moss, 1986–1987), siblings (Hays, Gold, & Pieper, 1995), and friends (Roberto & Stanis, 1994)—scant attention has been directed toward aging men. However, studies on familiar bereavement events have found that the death of a parent, a child, or a sibling is equally as stressful for men as the death of a spouse, and can greatly influence future emotional and physical health (De Vries et al., 1994; Hays et al., 1995; Moss & Moss, 1983, 1984-1985; Perkins & Harris, 1990). The purpose of this review is to examine specific bereavement events as they relate to elderly men and to focus attention on the meaning of these losses through relevant theoretical perspectives and other bereavement-related factors including gender, mortality, stress, health, and social support.

From the *Journal of Applied Gerontology*, June 1998, pp. 204-228. © 1998 by Sage Publications, Inc. Reprinted by permission.

The limitations of extant empirical research make this study unique in that it will add to the general bereavement literature among aging men and also contribute to the integration of scant knowledge concerning elderly men who have lost other significant loved ones in addition to their spouse. This review has implications for practitioners and community interventions in addressing the bereavement needs of this ignored population. Implications are discussed for the use of social supports when coping with stressful bereavement events as they influence health and mortality among elderly men.

Although not extensive, relevant literature on grief and bereavement events is presented to assist in understanding the bereavement process among aging men who have experienced the death of spouse, child, parent, sibling, or friend. In addition, several factors thought to be associated with specific bereavement events, including mortality, gender, stress, health, and social support, are considered along with pertinent theoretical perspectives as a conceptual framework to examine the relationship between bereavement, stress, and health.

Bereavement and Health Bereavement is usually followed by a normal but painful adjustment to the loss. The period of grief and mourning may be lengthy, although it is difficult to generalize, as the duration of this process may vary depending on the individual. The bereavement process may become complicated as symptoms of depression frequently overlap with normal reactions to bereavement such as sleep disturbance, crying, weight loss, concentration difficulties, and anger or aggression. Factors associated with normal bereavement in the elderly are the preexistence of life stressors that may coincide with the bereavement experience, such as low socioeconomic status, poor physical health, and the unavailability of a confidant. Kalish (1987) attempts to provide a description of the physiological and psychological process of grief and bereavement. Bereavement reactions can be expressed physically (physical health), cognitively, affectively, and behaviorally. Physical health expressions may include a hollow feeling in the stomach, tightness in the chest and throat, dry mouth, sensitivity to noise, shortness of breath, muscular weakness, or lack of energy. Cognitive expressions may include disbelief, confusion, preoccupation with thoughts of the deceased, and an attempt to put the event into perspective and find meaning and understanding. Affective expressions are recognized as depression, sorrow, sadness, guilt, anger, relief, and denial. Behavioral reactions may be the result of physical, affective, or cognitive changes and may present as a slowing down of movements or "longer reaction times" (Kalish, 1987, p. 35). Osterweis (1985) describes physical problems of the bereaved as typically ranging from sleeping and eating difficulties to respiratory symptoms and pains that may even resemble those of the deceased prior to their death. Psychological or emotional reactions associated with bereavement may include sadness, rapid emotional changes, disruption in so-

cial relationships, anger, guilt, and remorse. In addition, there is the potential for the bereaved individual to develop health problems precipitated by an increase in self-destructive behavior, such as smoking, drinking, or overeating. Individuals may also experience an increased risk for an exacerbation of present health problems, which can lead to sudden death or suicide. Nevertheless, Wortman and Silver's (1989) research indicates that considerable variability exists in the individual's response to loss and coping and that individuals may not grieve in the standard way. Professionals may tend to minimize or maximize the requirements of the mourning process and may assume that the individual is experiencing either more or less distress following the loss than is actually present.

Earlier studies have presented conflicting findings as to the vulnerability of the elderly toward health problems resulting from stressful life events such as bereavement (Aldwin, 1990; Murrell, Himmelfarb, & Phifer, 1988; O'Brien, 1987; Rogers & Reich, 1988). When life events such as the death of a family member or a friend are placed on the individual in such a way as to create a low self-image or poor self-concept, stress results. Additionally, role changes (as a result of the death of a loved one) are said to represent a link between a major life event and stress. Stress is created directly by the individual's need to compensate or readjust to the disruption in their lives, and also indirectly through the increase or "exacerbation of role strains" (Pearlin, Lieberman, Meneghan, & Mullan, 1981, p. 343). Stress can manifest itself in many forms in the human system; it may be manifest in "endocrine, immunological, metabolic, or cardiovascular system, particular diseases" (Pearlin et al., 1981, p. 341) and has been associated with symptoms such as pain, depression, strain, fatigue, restlessness, panic, shortness of breath, headache, and tension (Cohen & Wills, 1985; Parkes, 1972; Pearlin et al., 1981).

Bereavement Events

Bereavement refers to the status of persons following the loss of someone they love. Depending on the type of loss, the older adult may experience the loss in the status of a bereaved child, as a bereaved spouse, sibling, or parent, or even as a bereaved grandparent or great-grandparent.

Death of a spouse. As many researchers have indicated, the death of a spouse can be considered one of the most stressful life events (Moss & Moss, 1984-1985). Moss and Moss note that there are over 8 million widows and widowers in the United States. Their findings emphasize the strength of the bond with the deceased spouse, which tends to persist long after the initial year or two following the bereavement event. The death of a spouse may coincide with physiological changes associated with aging and as a result lead to increased stress and a decline in physical or mental health. For a 1-year period after the death of a spouse, a physical health or a mental health problem will affect at least 25% of surviving spouses (Balkwell, 1981; Tudiver, Hilditch, Permaul, & McKendree, 1992).

Widows and widowers live in a high-risk environment, as a sense of hopelessness and helplessness may produce further stress and subsequent health problems or illness (Hayslip & Leon, 1992). The death of a spouse for men may involve the loss of a sexual partner and companion, changes in decision making regarding household tasks and finances, relocation, and changes in social roles and lifestyles. Additionally, the supportive nature of the spousal relationship is lost as reminders or cues are absent for important daily activities. For the widower, changes in routine household chores can have adverse effects on health, especially if chronic health problems exist, such as heart disease, diabetes, or hypertension, which may require special diets and medications that his spouse previously prepared (Kalish, 1987; Osterweis, 1985). Furthermore, the loss of an occupational role and status for the retired widower may complicate the adjustment process (Berardo, 1970). Meaningful relationships with friends and coworkers may be disrupted and may contribute to an increased sense of social isolation and loneliness, which has been associated with high rates of suicide, mental disorders, and mortality. Psychological stress has been recognized as a major factor contributing to earlier deaths among widowers due to associated biochemical changes (Balkwell, 1981; Parkes, 1972).

Death of an adult child. The death of an adult child usually has a devastating and lasting impact on the physical and emotional health of aging parents (Aldwin, 1990; Arbuckle & De Vries, 1995; Goodman, Rubinstein, Alexander, & Luborsky, 1991; Osterweis, 1985; Rogers & Reich, 1988). Besides the mental and physical implications of the loss resulting from a major disruption in life expectations associated with an untimely death, the adult child's death may leave an older parent without a caretaker if illness or disability develops. Hayslip and Leon (1992) cite statistics from Moss, Lesher, and Moss (1986–1987) that indicate that approximately 10% of adults over the age of 60 experience the loss of an adult child. This figure is expected to rise with an increase in the elderly population, although presently, support from others may be less available due to the rare occurrence of this loss.

Additionally, surviving elderly parents may be forced to assume caretaking or financial responsibilities for the remaining grandchildren. Furthermore, less support or assistance is available for health or instrumental needs of grandparents who lose their children (Hayslip & Leon, 1992). This may produce an increase in stress-related illnesses as a result of the additional caregiving demands. DeVries et al. (1994) further state that elderly parents may experience a loss of continuity in their lives or a loss of integration and interpretation of their successes and failures. In addition, there is a loss of a sense of closeness or intimacy resulting from the death of a friend, helpmate, or companion (Goodman et al., 1991). Although Goodman and colleagues primarily focus their research on the meaning of death for elderly women and the influence of culture, they present a comprehensive review of pertinent theories addressing the experience of this monumental loss for elderly parents. They report that most generalized models in the grief literature fail to address and explain the impact of this unique loss for elderly parents, as there are barriers at each of the normal grief resolution stages that may interfere with adjustment and adaptation due to their secondary role or removal from the day-to-day role of parenting. Goodman et al. (1991) explain that Erik Erikson's theory of generativity as a developmental stage of old age can be viewed as a reciprocal relationship from significant other loved ones involving caring and receiving care. The relationship between grandparents, children, and grandchildren is a process called "grand-generativity" (p. S323), in which children and grandchildren are the primary source of generativity for aging parents. However, a crisis may occur if the developmental sequence is severed when elderly parents outlive their own children or grandchildren.

Parkes (1972) notes that the death of a child appears to produce greater emotional devastation for mothers than for fathers. Osterweis (1985) discusses the aspect of extreme guilt and anger that bereaved parents may experience due to the inherent need to prevent or actually save their child from the untimely death. Yet, these studies have not completely addressed gender differences or the impact of bereavement among aging men following the death of their adult child.

Death of a parent. Research on the effect of the death of a parent for an aging male remains extremely limited. In one of the few studies available, Kalish (1987) attempts to explore the experience faced by the "older adult as a bereaved child" (p. 35). Assumptions as to the nature of the situation reveal that most parents of older adults are in their mid-80s or mid-90s and suffering from various forms of chronic illnesses. Because parental deaths are perhaps anticipated, future expectations and roles for the remaining family members may be diminished resulting in a less destructive impact from the death.

Parkes (1972) reports that the death of a parent did not produce an increase in health-related illnesses. However, it is not to be assumed that the death of a parent is less painful than other important losses. Residual feelings of guilt, anger, and hostility over unresolved issues may surface (Perkins & Harris, 1990). Moss and Moss (1983) report that a parent's death can be a severe blow to physical and mental health and stability. Similar to the work by Hays et al. (1995) on the loss of siblings in later life, the death of a parent places the individual in the position of the "omega generation," the oldest living generation or the next in line for a decline in health or impending death (p. 17). These findings suggest that the bereavement outcome for an aging son following the death of a parent would represent a stressful life event and would also be influenced by prior health status and the quality of the earlier relationship.

Death of a sibling. Few empirical studies have explored the death of a sibling and the relevance of such loss to elderly men (Perkins & Harris, 1990). Past studies have primarily focused on the death of siblings in childhood and the special meaning of the sibling relationship, yet have failed to examine bereavement reactions among later-life families. As with the loss of a spouse, familial ties and relationships have extended for many years. Regardless of the level of past and present involvement, "The loss of a sibling remains a powerful reminder of one's own mortality" (Brubaker, 1985; Hays et al., 1995; Osterweis, 1985, p. 11). Furthermore, the process of grieving may be considerably heightened for surviving siblings who have experienced the loss of a younger sibling (Brubaker, 1985). Regardless of the level of emotional closeness or the degree of participation shared in daily activities prior to a sibling's death, feelings of vulnerability to inheritable diseases and impending mortality are increased (Osterweis, 1985). Additionally, shared family responsibilities may require readjustment. Due to the nature of possible long-standing sibling conflicts or geographical separation, the grieving process may become even more difficult or complicated. Another relevant study found that elderly bereaved brothers reported more activities of daily living (ADL) deficits than elderly men who had lost friends (Hays et al., 1995). In fact, this group reported worse self-reported health than any other bereaved group, including widowers.

Death of a friend. The death of a friend has been given the least attention. Of the few studies available, researchers have indicated that the experience of bereavement is similar to that associated with the loss of significant family members (De Vries, Lehman, & Arbuckle, 1995; Roberto & Stanis, 1994; Sklar & Hartley, 1990). Similar themes are present, such as a decreased coping ability; anger; guilt; anniversary syndrome; visions of the deceased; and economic, legal and health consequences. Roberto and Stanis (1994) studied elderly women who had lost friends within the past 12 years and found that the suffering for these women extended for many years and was not forgotten easily. Sklar and Hartley (1990) suggest that "survivor-friends" carry a double burden, as society does not recognize their grief, thus representing a hidden population of bereaved people. Doka's (1989) research on disenfranchised grief supports this view, and pays particular attention to the "friend as griever" experience (p. 77). He defines disenfranchised grief as "the grief that people experience when they incur a loss that is not or cannot be openly acknowledged, publicly mourned, or socially supported" (p. 4). Compared to the death of family members, Murrell's et al. (1988) findings revealed that the death of a friend was a powerful predictor and placed the individual at

an even greater risk for developing health problems. Other environmental influences such as the loss of home, job, or business may also compound health outcomes. Similar to the loss of one's parents or a sibling in later life, the death of a friend is also a powerful reminder of one's own mortality, which generates fear and a sense of relief "that it was not my turn" (Deck & Folta, 1989). Elderly people are said to experience extremely close and intimate relationships with friends, which can serve as a substitute for unavailable family or as a safety valve for the pressures of family obligations and responsibilities.

Balkwell's (1981) review of the literature on widowhood and friendship concludes that the level of interaction with friends was not lower for widowed men than women. Furthermore, widowed people of both sexes interacted more with friends than with married people, suggesting that the death of friends for widowed men would also represent a traumatic experience and would greatly affect the numbers of available social supports. Although Roberto and Stanis (1994) focus mainly on the reactions of older women to the death of close friends, their study addressed differences in the quality of interactions with friends among elderly men and women. Men tend to engage in friendships that coincide with their involvement in various activities and may underreport feelings of grief, whereas women who share activities with their friends tend to maintain supportive and intimate exchanges.

In comparison to other researchers, De Vries and colleagues (1995) have found that bereaved friends reported better health, greater positive affect, and more future preparation in contrast to the nonbereaved group of controls. These unexpected differences may be explained through individual personality or affiliate traits. Furthermore, "The mental and physical health benefits of social activity, particularly in later life: that is, individuals embedded in a social network tend to fare better than those without satisfactory access to such social relationships" (p. 11). For example, those who have more friends may experience repeated losses, and although suffering is not diminished, there are more remaining friends available for support and a sense of resilience may result. The nature and quality of friendship relationships may also differ from family relationships. De Vries et al. (1995) further state that in contrast to the ritualized, structured, and socially defined family relationships, friendships are subjectively defined "with criteria that vary from individual to individual" (p. 11). Therefore, the responses to the loss of a friend may be related more to the social organization of individuals than to psychological or stressful reactions to death. The frequency of lost friendships that elderly men experience is similarly described by Kemeny et al. (1994) in the repeated bereavement situations among the HIV and gay community of men who have lost several close friends or lovers (p. 15).

Although some of the questions have been answered, previous studies have not adequately addressed bereavement events among aging men. It also appears that most studies on familial and friendship deaths may have only accounted for the first few months or the first year following the event, yet potential health complications may arise over a longer period of time (Perkins & Harris, 1990).

Factors Associated With Bereavement Among Elderly Men

Mortality and gender. A number of gerontologists have attempted to determine if the effects of bereavement and stress are greater for men than for women (Gallagher, Thompson, & Peterson, 1982; Stroebe & Stroebe, 1983). Widowers have higher mortality and suicide rates than widows (Stroebe & Stroebe, 1983), and appear to experience higher levels of psychological distress than women (Umberson, Wortman, & Kessler, 1992). One study found that bereaved elderly men and women share more similarities than differences regarding selected social and psychosocial bereavement outcomes (Lund, Caserta, & Dimond, 1986). Yet, the process of bereavement is not always experienced in a similar manner for men and women (Wortman & Silver, 1989), despite the evidence suggesting that adaptation follows a similar course during the first 2 years after the loss of a spouse. Other studies show an increase in the death rate among widowers over the age of 54 of almost 40% during the first 6 months of bereavement (Gass, 1989; Parkes, 1972; Stroebe & Stroebe, 1983). In a study focusing on factors that affect mortality after widowhood, no differences in mortality rates were found between women who were married and those who were widowed, based on person-years at risk, but significantly higher mortality rates were observed for widowed men than for those who were married (Helsing, Szklo, & Comstock, 1981). According to one report, widowed men, regardless of age, are more susceptible to early death than their married counterparts (Osterweis, 1985). Furthermore, the effects of stress and poor self-care contribute to the high mortality rate among newly bereaved widowers (Gass, 1989).

Stroebe and Stroebe (1983) conclude from their review on conjugal bereavement reactions and health risks that men suffer more than women. They attempt to analyze gender differences across marital status based on stress theory, role theory, and the buffering hypothesis. Stress theory assumes that stressful life events will have harmful effects on both the physical and mental health of the individual, especially if a predisposition to illness is already present. As Murrell et al. (1988) explain, a major loss can produce a stressful situation that will increase one's vulnerability to disease or illness. Stress has been linked in a multitude of studies to various detrimental effects on the immune system, cardiovascular system, mortality and morbidity rates, suicide, and various emotional disorders (Ferraro, Mutran, & Barresi, 1984; Parkes, 1972; Rogers & Reich, 1988; Stroebe & Stroebe,

1983; Thompson, Breckenridge, Gallagher, & Peterson, 1984). It is therefore assumed that elderly people, especially men, will experience considerable stress during the grieving and mourning process. Stroebe and Stroebe (1983) further explain gender differences and bereavement outcome in terms of a biological predisposition to specific health problems or diseases to which men and women are differentially susceptible. The evidence supports the notion that there is an interaction among biological, social, and psychological factors. It appears that elderly men, especially in the first 6 months, are more vulnerable than women and younger age groups to the adverse affects of bereavement due to the positive relationship among age, declining health, and functional ability (Bowling & Windsor, 1995). Furthermore, "Life events that appear to be harmful for the health of older men tend to be those involving disruption of social networks, i.e. bereavement and relocation" (Aldwin, 1990, p. 56). Murrell et al. (1988) support this view and state that the death of family members or the loss of a home are the most undesirable or stressful events for the aging individual, along with health problems involving the self, family, or friends. The death of siblings, grandchildren, and close friends also have a strong effect on health similar to bereavement experiences associated with the death of a spouse, parent, or child (Murrell et al., 1988).

Rogers and Reich (1988) discuss the association between bereaved elderly men and physiological vulnerabilities to heart disease, coronary artery disease, and the effects of stress and depression on the immune system. Aldwin (1990) studied the relationship between egocentric stress (losses affecting the self) and nonegocentric stress (concern for others) on health status among aging male veterans and found that events causing a disruption in relationships such as losses related to bereavement or relocation were the most harmful and stressful events affecting their health. Murrell and colleagues (1988) explain that vulnerability to disease associated with the stress of bereavement is due to the "desolation effect" (the attachment bonding is severed in bereavement) creating changes in the endocrine, cardiovascular and nervous system (p. 92). Yet, their findings reveal that past and present health status is likewise a predictor of future health along with losses or stress associated with bereavement. The nature of the bereavement process may reflect a multidimensional experience and specific cognitive, behavioral, and emotional coping strategies may coexist with significant grief and emotional distress (Gallagher, Lovett, Hanley-Dunn, & Thompson, 1989). These authors also report that aging male widowers whose wives have suffered from a long-term chronic illness experience both elevated mortality and an increase in physical and emotional health symptoms. Hayslip and Leon (1992) also explain that pathological grief reactions among men may take on many forms of behavior and can be accompanied by additional life stressors and losses (e.g., retirement, relocation, and illness).

The death of a spouse or a child is clearly documented as the most stressful life event affecting health status (Rogers & Reich, 1988). For widowers, Parkes (1972) reports an increase in the mortality rate during the first 6 to 12 months following the death of a spouse, primarily from coronary heart disease, but the rate of death declines after the first year. Rogers and Reich (1988) discuss studies that report an excess in mortality following the first year after the loss of a spouse among widowers and also a higher death rate from infectious diseases, accidents, and suicide than among widows. However, some studies indicate that health differences between widows and widowers are minimal; the only difference reported is reflected in the widow's perception of poorer health (Thompson et al., 1984). These authors suggest that widowers may develop health problems over a longer period of time and may also tend to underestimate or underreport health difficulties immediately after the loss of their wives. One study found that newly bereaved widowers perceived their health as poor or worse in the year following a wife's death and also reported less activity because of health problems (Vinick, 1983a).

Stress, social support, and gender. Married people tend to have less strain than single people of either sex. The death of a spouse eliminates the supportive characteristics of the marriage relationship in which roles were validated and assistance was shared among various tasks (Stroebe & Stroebe, 1983). However, widows may have less to lose in terms of roles than widowers due to the general idea that women carry the greater burden in the marriage role as housewife, mother, employed worker, or a volunteer outside the home. The tasks and responsibilities associated with these roles for widows are usually continued after the death of a spouse. On the other hand, men have a greater tendency to remarry than women and are less prone to experience extreme role shifts. Nevertheless, elderly widowed men are especially vulnerable to loneliness, illness, and suicide (Vinick, 1983b), which may be associated with the nature of their support system.

The type and quality of support the bereaved person receives will have an effect on the bereavement outcome and adjustment. Women seem to fare better on measures of health than do men, as the nature of the support they receive is different. It is less socially acceptable for men to express feelings of grief and loneliness. Men tend to be more isolated outside their work environment and depend on their wives for social activities. Finally, because widows outnumber widowers, there are fewer widowers available for socialization purposes. In this regard, attempts have been made to develop and analyze the relationship between a stressful life event such as bereavement and social support as they relate to the promotion and maintenance of health (Aldwin, 1990; Ferraro et al., 1984; Murrell et al., 1988; Perkins & Harris, 1990; Rogers & Reich, 1988; Stroebe & Stroebe, 1983; Thompson et al., 1984). Research has focused on the re-

lationship between social support and social stressors (Krause, 1986, 1987, 1990; Wheaton, 1985), which ultimately affect the individual's psychological and physical well-being.

The stress-buffering hypothesis. Social support, in general, and specifically in the form of various leisure or formal community supports (Howe-Murphy & Charboneau, 1987; Tudiver et al.,1992; Weiner, Brok, & Snadowsky, 1987), has been positively associated with psychological well-being and physical health, and in some cases serves as a buffer against stress among the elderly (Fitzpatrick, 1993, 1995; Krause, 1986). The buffering hypothesis implies that support buffers or protects the individual from stressful life situations and makes the stressful experience less detrimental (Cohen & Wills, 1985; Krause & Tran, 1989; Thoits, 1982; Wheaton, 1985). Tudiver et al. (1992) examined the efficacy of a mutual-help group intervention for new widowers and a control group focusing on the grief process, nutrition, new relationships, exercise, and lifestyle issues. Their findings revealed a significant improvement for all subjects over time on health, psychological, and social measures, although no differences were found between the two groups during the initial 8 months. The maintenance of physical health may therefore depend on the maintenance of social supports for bereaved elderly individuals, and especially for bereaved men (Stroebe & Stroebe, 1983; Tudiver et al., 1992).

Theoretical Perspectives

Although Cleiren (1993) focuses his attention primarily on theories of adaptation after bereavement, he presents a comprehensive review of psychodynamic, cognitive, and sociobiological theories in an attempt to understand certain aspects of the bereavement process. A brief review of these theories will assist in explaining their relevance to the purpose of this article. Freud's (1917) psychoanalytic theory on mourning and melancholia focuses on the intrapsychic aspects of bereavement with regard to the concept of the libido, which is attached or cathected to a lost loved object or person. This aspect of grief work is associated with a "de-attachment" or a "decathecting" from the lost object. This can be an extremely difficult task for the ego. Melancholia (abnormal or depressive illness), according to Freud, results when the loss remains unconscious and the defense mechanism of repression acts to inhibit these unconscious feelings from one's awareness or consciousness. Lindemann's (1944) theory focuses on acute grief and bereavement reactions. His theory, however, does not include aspects of anticipatory grief reactions or stress reduction after the loss (Cleiren, 1993). The main premise of the early theories on grief lies in the assumption that identification with the lost loved one or object is viewed in a compensatory manner for the actual death or loss. Neither Freud's nor Lindemann's theories account for gender or specific bereavement experiences. However, their ideas provide a reasonable explanation and understanding of the unconscious attachment mechanism and the persistent tendency for the grieving individual to experience ongoing stress as a result of the intense work during the mourning and bereavement experience.

Bowlby (1969), Parkes (1972), and Marris (1978–79) offer a perspective that combines psychoanalytic thinking and cognitively oriented theories. Bowlby (1969) postulated that "attachment behavior" is a survival mechanism for joining human beings to each other, originating in childhood with the initial mother-child interaction. Grief and loss (bereavement) is essentially "separation anxiety," in which an unwanted separation from the deceased occurs, resulting in anxiety, protesting, and searching behavior (Cleiren, 1993, p. 16). The relationship with the deceased is never completely severed. This model does not clearly make the connection between childhood reactions to loss and adult responses to bereavement events. Furthermore, immunobiological and/or other stress-related factors may influence reactions to loss, depending on the individual and the circumstances. Parkes (1972) discusses an earlier study (Parkes, 1970), focusing his attention on cognitive restructuring to explain the bereavement process. He employs three models: medical, cognitive, and cathartic. He attempts to explain the process of grief through medical classifications, yet includes instinctual responses to separation. He believes that the recovery period (cognitive restructuring) following a bereavement event for an individual must include the experience of pain, distress, and impaired functioning before recovery can be attained. Marris (1978–1979) moves beyond attachment and instinctual behavior and proposes a cognitive theory of grief. His theory focuses on approach and avoidance tendencies in the bereaved as an attempt to restore predictability in their environment.

Littlefield and Rushton (1986) introduce a sociobiological perspective that endeavors to address the aspect of kinship relationships in the grief process by making predictions about gender and age differences among family members. They propose that kinship groups should be ranked in order of bereavement difficulties—that is, older parents and spouses would experience the most difficulties; parents and spouses would follow; then siblings and children—however, older adult siblings sustain a greater loss than adult children. This theory offers considerable merit from the perspective of different bereavement events elderly men experience. A major criticism is the indirect method used for assessing the intensity of the grief reactions, in that parents were requested to provide retrospectively subjective ratings of other family members (Cleiren, 1993).

Cognitive stress theorists attempt to examine and explain the bereavement process from an information-processing viewpoint: "Central to these models is that they accentuate the combination and interaction of physical and psychological arousal, which is based on the perception of events, and which in turn influences perception" (Cleiren, 1993, p. 26). Stress is created when the demands of the situation outweigh the individual's coping resources. This is usually based on the individual's perception and interpretation of past experiences and on primary and secondary appraisal and assessment of the bereavement situation (Lazarus, 1966).

In summary, although these theories provide a basis for understanding certain aspects of the bereavement process and bereavement events, there are limitations that should also be considered. Psychoanalytic theorists such as Freud (1917) and Lindemann (1944) explain personal and individual reactions to grief as originating from the early infant-mother relationship, yet have not provided an explanation for stress-related aspects of specific bereavement events in the elderly. Of the theoretical perspectives that attempt to bridge the gap between the psychoanalytic and the cognitively oriented theories (Bowlby, 1969; Marris, 1978–1979; Parkes, 1970), Bowlby's theory of attachment, as Hays et al. (1985) describe it, suggests that siblings, similar to the mother-infant bond, also form close and early emotional bonds. Attachment theory also posits that the death of a significant other produces separation anxiety, thus leading to anger, frustration, and fear of abandonment. Because sibling relationships are inclined to become closer over the years, the death of a sibling for an older adult can produce extreme feelings of anger and loss. Unfortunately, these studies make it impossible to determine how this would apply to an elderly man or if elderly men would become more or less distressed at this type of loss than would elderly women. Yet, behaviorally oriented theories of grief do have relevance for this article as they present a more clinically oriented and intervention approach and include pathological reactions and deviations in the grief process (Ramsay, 1977). Ramsay's theory of grief includes the role of reinforcement, the environment, and situational factors such as social support. This theory ties in with the model of social support and stress reduction Wheaton (1985) proposes. From a sociobiological perspective, Littlefield and Rushton (1986) address the role of kinship relationships, specifically indicating that men experience a lessor degree of grief intensity and difficulties than women. These findings are in contrast to the findings from the stress and health literature concerning bereaved elderly people that implies that elderly men have a greater vulnerability to stress and illness following the death of their spouse than do their female counterparts. Of the few available studies on the impact of grief among different family members, Littlefield and Rushton's research has made a beginning contribution toward addressing this unique issue by considering the rank order of difficulty by the kinship groups following a bereavement event and by including a comparison between men and women. Cleiren (1993) further suggests that the present trend in the theoretical approach to bereavement is to encompass a broad and global psychological stress theory. This perspective may be more in line with specific loss events (i.e., spouse, child, parent, sibling, friends, or other family members) and could be linked with an increase in stress and physical health problems experienced by elderly bereaved men. Although stress-reduction and buffering perspectives address the clinical and more practical aspects of the health and bereavement process, they do not take into account individual differences and other personality factors or the early developmental bonding that occurs between an individual and his or her significant loved object. This theoretical review suggests that further research be conducted to include a broader personality and stress-reduction approach in the study of bereavement events among elderly men.

Discussion

The purpose of this article was to review the literature on bereavement events among elderly men, drawing attention to the meaning of these losses through empirical research and theoretical perspectives. It is appropriate to summarize the three central themes of the review. The summary is divided into two parts. The first presents a summary table of the themes, together with a listing of associated theories and recommendations for practice and research (Table 1). Next is a discussion and review of the three themes—bereavement and health, bereavement events (death of spouse, parent, child, sibling, friend), and gender differences—integrating recommendations for theory, practice, and research.

Bereavement and health. The literature reviewed in this article indicates that bereavement represents a stressful life event and elderly men are at a particular health disadvantage as evidenced by findings reporting high rates of psychological and physical disorders, mortality risk, and suicide. In general, the review of literature on bereavement and health has implications for theories on human development and the processes associated with bereavement. A broad theoretical perspective that contains aspects of psychoanalytic theory, cognitive theory, and sociobiological models—including concepts of attachment, cognition, the role of kinship relationships, and the stress-reduction process—should be further examined as a conceptual framework for the study of older male survivors.

Theories of stress have focused on the negative and detrimental aspect of bereavement and its impact on physical health and psychological well-being. Krause's (1986) major findings reveal that specific types of social supports (informational support, tangible help, and emotional support) buffer the impact of specific types of stressful major life events such as bereavement. O'Brien's (1987) findings demonstrate the relationship between social support and negative life events (bereavement), in

which the presence of an individual's support system can reduce the negative effects of stress during the experience of bereavement. Research endeavors should focus on a comprehensive search for factors associated with the impact of the environment, the bereavement process, and health among aging men. This will contribute to a knowledge base that will assist in the development of social policy and health programs directed toward relieving stress related to bereavement and maintaining maximum physical and mental health.

This review has practical importance for gerontologists and health care practitioners who provide services to noninstitutionalized elderly men and for those serving elderly men in Veterans Administration medical centers, acute care hospitals, or long-term care facilities. Hayslip and Leon (1992) have fittingly described specific suggestions for helping all grieving persons experiencing various losses in relation to the loss of a spouse, parent, and a child. For example, clinicians should be more readily available to understand that the grieving person may need to repeatedly recall his or her story. It is necessary to adopt a patient and nonjudgmental attitude toward both positive and negative feelings, to express caring directly, and to focus on the here-and-now thoughts and feelings of the griever. By making eye contact and even touching persons on the shoulder, one can offer a sense of security and support, suggesting that one is not "uncomfortable" with their pain (p. 195).

The literature suggests that for those elderly men who have experienced the loss of a loved one, social supports may in fact serve as a buffer against the harmful impact of bereavement and thus reflect on physical and mental health. It is important for clinicians to continue to foster supportive relationships throughout the life span, and especially for elderly men, as the nature of their relationships is often subjected to increasing loss of friends and loved family members. Social activities such as sponsoring support groups for bereaved men may provide an atmosphere to express grief openly, to receive beneficial feedback, and to promote and develop the elderly male's continued participation in an active lifestyle, thus preventing further health problems, isolation, or other maladaptive and self-destructive behavior.

Bereavement events. Beyond the death of a spouse, the death of an adult child, parent, sibling, or friend are also representative of stressful life events affecting the health of elderly men. Future bereavement research among elderly men should account for Bowlby's (1969) theory of attachment and include other bereavement events (parent, child, friend) aside from siblings (Hays et al., 1995). Additionally, future studies might consider Rando's (1986) developmental perspective, which describes parental grief as influenced by factors such as the untimeliness of the death, the nature and quality of the lost relationship, the role of the deceased, the characteristics of the death, and the available support system. These variables should also be considered to assist in

Table 1. Themes, Theories, and Recommendations for Future Practice and Research

Theme	Theory	Practice Recommendations	Research Directions
Bereavement and health	Psychoanalytic: Mourning Melancholia Cognitive theory Stress theory Attachment theory	Use social supports as buffers	Investigate factors associated with bereavement and health status
		Adopt a nonjudgmental approach Improve the availability of clinicians	Explore the role of health programs in relieving stress Investigate the impact of environment on stress and health
Bereavement events[a]	Psychoanalytic Sociobiological	Broaden definitions of loss Help families grieve together Engage in grief work tailored to individual needs	Investigate parental grief factors: role, untimeliness Study the developmental stages of bereavement: patterns specific to loss of different family members Investigate relationships between peer loss and disenfranchised grief
Gender differences	Sociogiological Stress theory	Encourage letting go of gender stereotypes Reinforce specific activities and peer friendships Sponsor support groups for elderly men	Investigate different gender responses after loss of child, and male grief Conduct studies to address gender friendships and social support factors

a. Bereavement events may include the death of a spouse, parent, child, sibling, or friend.

clarifying the relationship between bereavement events, stress, and health issues among elderly men. Furthermore, the conceptualization of family developmental stages that DeVries and colleagues (1994) present could also be applied to the various bereavement events elderly men experience. For example, the death of a sibling is perceived differently than the death of a parent, spouse, child, or friend and may be associated with patterns and concerns specific to the developmental age and stage.

Additionally, Hays et al. (1995) describe Wright's (1994) recent work on evolutionary psychology, which focuses on the interaction between environmental factors and social supports on stress and health. Further exploration of this view would prove beneficial in our understanding of different bereavement reactions and losses in

later life. Because studies have shown that certain bereavement events produce a stressful and harmful impact on health, theories of stress, social support, and the stress-buffering hypothesis should also be examined further as a theoretical framework to determine if specific types of social supports (qualitative and quantitative) can buffer the harmful impact of specific bereavement events on health status among elderly men.

By broadening the definitions of loss, gerontologists and practitioners should identify the varying needs resulting from different types of bereavement events and engage in grief work tailored to specific supports that directly address these needs. Hayslip and Leon (1992) state that the pain following the death of a spouse may never completely subside. Widows and widowers may require individual attention and extended support for a ng time. There is a need to investigate parental grief reactions and to assist family members to grieve together, thus allowing for the expression of feelings in preparation for a spouse's or other family member's death. This can be particularly beneficial if the loss is anticipated. The death of older parents, siblings, and friends has received comparable, and in some cases higher, stress ratings than the death of a spouse due to the untimeliness of the event. Although all types of bereavement events are stressful, the death of a friend or peer should receive greater attention due to the hidden (disenfranchised grief) and double burden for greater health risks among survivor-friends. Roberto and Stanis (1994) focus primarily on the meaning of the death of a friend for elderly women, yet they reinforce the significance of "shared activities and intimacies" within friendships due to the harmful impact of loneliness (p. 25).

The findings of Hays et al. (1995) indicate that bereaved siblings demonstrate a health disadvantage regarding their perceived health status but do not experience emotional fluctuations or lack of social supports similar to bereaved spouses. These findings suggest that future research would be improved by examining the quality and types of social support factors that might affect stress, health, and mortality among elderly male grievers who have lost a friend, parent, or child and comparing the differences across the various groups. A recent study by DeVries et al. (1995) on the meaning of the death of a friend in later life suggests that future work is needed to address the actual meaning and nature of interpersonal ties among elderly men over the life course. The nature of male friendships, therefore, needs further exploration in a more comprehensive manner to include other factors that can ultimately be used to aid in the prevention of both psychological and physical health deterioration. As with other stress-related events for elderly men, it is important to encourage new and ongoing peer relationships to ward off the detrimental aspects of loneliness and social isolation.

Gender differences. Research findings addressing gender differences, bereavement, and health among elderly people clearly indicate that (a) widowers have a higher mortality rate and higher levels of psychological distress following the death of their spouse than do widows; (b) the social and psychosocial process of bereavement and the nature and quality of elderly male and female friendships are experienced differently for elderly men and women; (c) the effects of stress and poor self-care is more evident among elderly male survivors than their female counterparts; and (d) men have a biological predisposition to specific and different health problems and diseases, especially in the first 6 months following the loss of their spouse.

Although the work of Freud (1917) and Lindemann (1944) focuses on the process of grief and mourning and reactions to bereavement, it has not accounted for gender differences or specific bereavement events, especially

among the elderly. Similarly, Bowlby (1969) and other theorists (Horowitz, Wilner, & Alveraz, 1979; Marris, 1978–1979) who have combined psychoanalytic and cognitively oriented perspectives have addressed bereavement responses from a more universal or global perspective. However, Parkes (1972), in his research on medical and cognitive restructuring, addresses the relationship between gender and health outcomes among widows and widowers. He attributes the increase in the death rate among widowers to heart disease in the first 6 months of bereavement. Littlefield and Rushton's (1986) sociobiological perspective may offer a reasonable explanation regarding gender differences and the aspect of kinship relationships in the grief process in that men may demonstrate a lesser degree of grief intensity than women.

Their research suggests that predictions about gender and age may be attributed to the fact that (a) men are expected to react in a similar manner as women who tend to express their feelings of grief more openly than men and (b) expectations that certain bereavement events should receive more recognition than others—that is, the death of a spouse—are more important or stressful than the death of a sibling or a friend. Older men may sustain even greater emotional losses (perhaps unrecognized) than do their female counterparts due to the hidden nature of their bereavement responses and the bereavement event (Wortman & Silver, 1989). This further implies that professionals should recognize the difference in grief reactions between men and women and consider the nature and importance of the relationship of the survivor to the deceased. Genevay's (1997) recent findings stress the importance of eliminating gender and ageist stereotypes among professionals and of tailoring grief work to the unique and individual needs of men and women. In particular, future research should investigate gender responses focusing on elderly male grievers and fathers following the death of an adult child or a friend. This population is often forgotten, yet this group of survivors may experience feelings of intense grief similar to those of surviving spouses (Doka, 1989; Hamilton, 1978). Studies should also be conducted addressing gender friendships and social support factors that prove helpful following the loss of a friend or peer by examining the effects of bereavement support groups for elderly men.

The bereaved should be encouraged to maintain social involvement with their family, friends, and the community, together with the possibility of making new friendships, which may serve to reduce stress and positively affect well-being and health among elderly men. Hayslip and Leon (1992) further emphasize the intense loneliness experience of most grievers, and the necessity for workers to remain available through the long process of mourning, together with encouraging grievers to maintain necessary daily activities and social contacts. Social interaction and, specifically, direct face-to-face per-

sonal contact has been reported to be extremely beneficial for grievers. Community programs should, therefore,
be directed to this group of elderly men who have been
neglected in the past due to their inability to use fully
the available resources as a result of unrecognized or disenfranchised grief (Doka, 1989); personal inhibitions; isolation factors; or lack of family, formal community
assistance, or knowledge. Interventions should be designed to continue to reinforce elderly men's ability to
remain involved in ongoing activities and to create new
relationships and friendships. Health care workers
should continue to educate staff members and the families of elderly male clients on the need for social activities, stressing that despite health problems and physical
limitations, it is even more crucial to encourage participation in activities and groups in order to discourage
depression, loneliness, isolation, suicide, or other harmful social or physical health problems associated with the
process of grief for men. Public policy should assume
that various community or group programs are a valuable option for family caregivers and for elderly men
who experience the death of family members or friends.
Although some community interventions have been directed toward widows and bereavement groups, few
have addressed the effects of bereavement among widowers or elderly men in general.

In conclusion, this review suggests the need to examine intervening and social support variables that might
serve to provide specific benefits to bereaved elderly
men. For example, future research should address the
buffering effects of different types of social supports on
bereavement and health, such as participation in religious activities and the qualitative and quantitative aspects of confidant support. Given the different cultures
and religious affiliations in the United States, a cross-cultural examination including types of bereavement events
and reactions should be considered. Hopefully, the findings and suggestions from this review will provide the
basis for future empirical research in the area of social
and community supports and health status among bereaved elderly men who have experienced different
types of losses.

AUTHOR'S NOTE: This article was supported by a National Institute on Aging Multidisciplinary Training Grant #5 T32 AG00220.
The author wishes to thank Elizabeth Markson from Boston University Gerontology Center, and Ray Bosse Avron Spiro III, and Nancy
Kressin from the Normative Aging Study, Veterans Administration
Medical Research Center, Bedford, MA for their comments on an earlier version of this article. Correspondence concerning this article
should be addressed to Tanya R. Fitzpatrick, Assistant Professor,
Saint Joseph college, Institute in Gerontology, West Hartford, CT
06117, and the Normative Aging Study, Veterans Administration
Medical Research Center, Bedford, MA 01730.

References

Aldwin, C. M. (1990). The elders life stress inventory: Egocentric and
nonegocentric stress. In M. A. P. Stevens, J. H. Crowther, S. E. Hob-
foll, & D. L. Tennenbaum(Eds.), Stress and coping in later life fam-
lies (pp. 49–69). New York: Hemisphere.

Arbuckle, N. W., & de Vries, B. (1995). The long-term effects of lat
life spousal and parental bereavement on personal functioning. Th
Gerontologist, 35, 637–647.

Balkwell, C. (1981). Transition to widowhood: A review of the literatu
Family Relations, January, 117–127.

Berardo, F. M. (1970, January). Survivorship and social isolation: Th
case of the aged widower. The Family Coordinator, 11–25.

Bowlby, J. (1969). Attachment and loss, Vol. 1. London: Hogarth.

Bowling, A. & Windsor, J. (1995). Death after widow(er)hood: An anal
sis of mortality rates up to 13 years after bereavement. Omega, 3
35–49.

Brubaker, T. (1985). Later life families. Beverly Hills, CA: Sage.

Cleiren, M. (1993). Bereavement and adaptation. Washington: Hem
sphere.

Cohen, S., & Wills, T. A. (1985). Stress, social support and the bufferin
hypothesis. Psychological Bulletin, 98, 310–357.

Deck, E. S., & Folta, J. R. (1989). The friend-griever. In J. K. Dota (Ed.
Disenfranchised grief. Recognizing hidden sorrow (pp. 77–89). Ne
York/Toronto: Lexington Books.

De Vries, B., Della Lana, R, & Falck, V. T. (1994). Parental bereavemen
over the life course: A theoretical intersection and empirical review
Omega, 29, 47–69.

De Vries, B., Lehman, A. J., & Arbuckle, N. W. (1995, November). Re
actions to the death of a close friend in later life. Paper presente
at the annual meeting of the Gerontological Society of America, An
nual Meeting, Los Angeles, CA.

Doka, K. J. (1989). Disenfranchised grief. Recognizing hidden sorrow
New York/Toronto: Lexington Books.

Duran, A., Turner, C. W., & Lund, D. (1989). Social support, perceive
stress, and depression following the death of a spouse in later life
In D. A. Lund (Ed.), Older bereaved spouses (pp. 69–77). New York
Hemisphere.

Ferraro, K. E., Mutran, E., & Barresi, C. M. (1984). Widowhood, health
and friendship in later life. Journal of Health and Social Behavior
25, 245–259.

Fitzpatrick, T. R. (1993, November). Gender, recreational services and
well-being among the frail elderly. Paper presented at the annua
meeting of the Gerontological Society of America, New Orleans
LA.

Fitzpatrick, T. R. (1995). Stress and well-being among the elderly: The
effect of recreational services. Journal of Applied Social Sciences, 19
95–105.

Freud, S. (1917). Mourning and melancholia. Merck, Sharpe, & Dohme,
1972.

Gallagher, D. E., Breckenridge, J. N., Thompson, L. W., & Peterson. J.
A. (1983). Effects of bereavement on indicators of mental health in
elderly widows. Journal of Gerontology, 38, 565–571.

Gallagher, D. E., Lovett, S., Hanley-Dunn, P., & Thompson, L. W. (1989).
Use of select coping strategies during later life bereavement. In D.
A. Lund (Ed.), Older bereaved spouses. (pp. 111–120). New York:
Hemisphere.

Gallagher, D. E., Thompson, L. W., & Peterson, J. A. (1982). Psychosocial
factors affecting adaptation to bereavement in the elderly. International Journal of Aging and Human Development, 14, 79–95.

Gass, K. A. (1989). Health of older widowers: Role of appraisal, coping,
resources, and type of spouse's death. In D. A. Lund (Ed.), Older
bereaved spouses. (pp. 95–108). New York: Hemisphere.

Genevay, B. (1997). Men, women and unmasking grief. In Aging Today,
Focus, pp. 9, 13.

Goodman, M., Rubinstein, R. L., Alexander, B. B., & Luborsky, M.
(1991). Cultural differences among elderly women in coping with
the death of an adult child. Journal of Gerontology, 46, S321–S329.

Hamilton, J. (1978). Grandparents as grievers. In O. J. Z. Sabler (Ed.),
The child in death (pp. 219–225). St. Louis, MO: C. V. Mosby.

Hays, J. C., Gold, D. T., & Pieper, C. F. (1995, November). Sibling bereavement in late life. Paper presented at the annual meeting of the
Gerontological Society of America, Los Angeles, CA.

Hayslip, B., & Leon, J. (1992). Grief and bereavement. In Hospice Care
(pp. 180–197). Newbury Park, CA: Sage.

Helsing, K. J., Szklo, M., & Comstock, G. W. (1981). Factors associated
with mortality after widowhood. American Journal of Public
Health, 71, 802–809.

Hershberger, P. J., & Walsh, W. B. (1990). Multiple role involvement and the adjustment to conjugal bereavement: An exploratory study. Omega, 21, 91–102.

Horowitz, M., Wilner, N., & Alvarez, W. (1979). A measure of subjective stress. Psychosomatic Medicine, 41, 209–218.

Howe-Murphy, R., & Charboneau, B. G. (1987). Therapeutic recreation intervention. Englewood Cliffs, NJ: Prentice Hall.

Kalish, R. (1987). Older people and grief. Generations, Spring, 33–38.

Kemeny, M. E., Weiner, H., Taylor, S. E., Schneider, S., Visscher, B., & Fahey, J. L. (1994). Repeated bereavement, depressed mood, and immune parameters in HIV seropositive and seronegative gay men. Health Psychology, 13, 14–24.

Krause, N. (1986). Social support, stress and well-being among older adults. Journal of Gerontology, 41, 512–519.

Krause, N. (1987). Chronic strain, locus of control, and distress in older adults. Psychology and Aging, 2, 375–382.

Krause, N. (1990). Perceived health problems, formal and informal support and life satisfaction among older adults. Journal of Gerontology, 45, S193–S205.

Krause, N., & Tran, T. V. (1989). Stress and religious involvement among older blacks. Journal of Gerontology, 44, S4–S13.

Lazarus, R. S. (1966). Psychological stress and the coping process. New York: McGraw-Hill.

Lindemann, E. (1944). Symptomatology and management of acute grief. American Journal of Psychiatry, 101, 141–148.

Littlefield, C. H., & Rushton, J. P. (1986). When a child dies: The sociobiology of bereavement. Journal of Personality and Social Psychology, 51, 797–802.

Lund, D. A. (1989). Older bereaved spouses. New York: Hemisphere.

Lund, D. A., Caserta, M. S., & Dimond, M. F. (1996). Gender differences through two years of bereavement among the elderly. The Gerontologist, 26, 314–320.

Marris, P. (1978–1979). Conservatism, innovation and old age. International Journal of Aging and Human Development, 9, 127–135.

Moss, M. S., Lesher, E. L., & Moss, S. Z. (1986–1987). Impact of the death of an adult child on elderly parents: Some observations. Omega, 17, 209–218.

Moss, M. S., & Moss, S. Z. (1983). The impact of parental death on middle aged children. Omega, 14, 65–75.

Moss, M. S., & Moss, S. Z. (1984–1985). Some aspects of elderly widow(er)'s persistent tie with the deceased spouse. Omega, 15, 195–206.

Murrell, S. A., Himmelfarb, S., & Phifer, J. E. (1988). Effects of bereavement/loss and pre-event status on subsequent physical health in older adults. International Journal of Aging and Human Development, 27, 89–107.

O'Brien, R. A. (1987, November). Role of social support in bereavement outcomes. Paper presented at the annual scientific meeting of the Gerontological Society of America, Washington, DC.

Osterweis, M. (1985). Bereavement and the elderly. Aging, 348, 8–13, 41.

Parkes, C. M. (1970). The psychosomatic effects of bereavement. In O. W. Hill (Ed.), Modern trends in psychosomatic medicine. London: Butterworth.

Parkes, C. M. (1972). Bereavement: Studies of grief in the adult life. New York: International Universities Press.

Pearlin, L. I., Lieberman, M. A., Meneghan, E. G. & Mullan, J. T. (1981). The stress process. Journal of Health and Social Behavior, 22, 337–356.

Perkins, H. W., & Harris, L. B. (1990). Familial bereavement and health in adult life course perspective. Journal of Marriage and the Family, 52, 233–241.

Ramsay, R. W. (1977). Behavioral approaches to bereavement. Behavioral Research and Therapy, 15, 131–135.

Rando, T. A. (1986). Loss and anticipatory grief. Lexington MA: Lexington Books.

Roberto, K. A. & Stanis, P. I. (1994). Reactions of older women to the death of their close friends. Omega, 29, 17–27.

Rogers, M. P., & Reich, P. (1988). On the health consequences of bereavement. The New England Journal of Medicine, 319, 510–512.

Sklar, E, & Hartley, S. E (1990). Close friends as survivors: Bereavement patterns in a "hidden" population. Omega, 21, 103–112.

Stroebe, M. S., & Stroebe, W. (1983). Who suffers more? Sex differences in health risks of the widowed. Psychological Bulletin, 93, 279–301.

Thoits, P. A. (1982). Conceptual, methodological, and theoretical problems in studying social support as a buffer against life stress. Journal of Health and Social Behavior, 23, 145–159.

Thompson, L. W., Breckenridge, Gallagher, D., & Peterson, J. (1984). Effects of bereavement on self-perceptions of physical health in elderly widows and widowers. Journal of Gerontology, 39, 309–314.

Tudiver, E. Hilditch, J., Permaul, J. A., & McKendree, D. J. (1992). Does mutual help facilitate newly bereaved widowers? Evaluation & The Health Professions, 15, 147–162.

Umberson, D., Wortman, C. B., & Kessler, R. C. (1992). Widowhood and depression: Explaining long-term gender differences in vulnerability. Journal of Health and Social Behavior, 33, 10–24.

Vinick, B. H. (1983a). Three years after bereavement: Life styles of elderly widowers. Interdisciplinary Topics in Gerontology, 17, 50–57.

Vinick, B. H. (1983b). Loneliness among elderly widowers. Paper presented at the annual meeting of the Gerontological Society of America, San Francisco, CA.

Weiner, M. B., Brok, A. J., & Snadowsky, A. M. (1987). Working with the aged (2nd ed.). Norwalk, CT: Appleton-Century-Crofts.

Wheaton, B. (1985). Models for the stress-buffering function of coping resources. Journal of Health and Social Behavior, 26, 352–364.

Wortman, C. B., & Silver, R. C. (1989). The myths of coping with loss. Journal of Consulting and Clinical Psychology, 57, 349–357.

Wright, R. (1994). The moral animal: Evolutionary psychology and everyday life. New York: Pantheon.

Zandt, S. V., Mou, R., & Abbott, D. (1989). Mental and physical health of rural bereaved and nonbereaved elders: A longitudinal study. In D. A. Lund (Ed.), Older bereaved spouses (pp. 25–34). New York: Hemisphere.

Article accepted December 30, 1997.

Tanya R. Fitzpatrick, D.S.W, R. N., received her doctorate in social work from Boston College Graduate School of Social Work in 1992 and has been teaching in the field of gerontology since graduation. Additionally, she was employed as a project director on a research grant at Boston University School of Public Health. She recently completed a 2-year postdoctoral traineeship at Boston University Gerontology Center and conducted her research at The Normative Aging Study, VA Medical Research Center, Bedford, MA. She is also an assistant professor in gerontology at St. Joseph College in West Hartford, CT, and continues her research at the VA. Her research interests include ethnic and minority issues and aging, bereavement and health among elderly men, and most recently, religion, retirement, and health issues. She is in the process of coediting a book on therapeutic interventions for ethnic elders and has contributed a chapter on the Russian elderly. She has presented this material at several national gerontology conferences. Her recent publications include "Age, gender and health among African Americans" (with T. V. Tran) in Social Work in Health Care (1996), and "Acculturation, health, stress, and psychological distress among the Hispanic elderly" (with T. V. Tran) in the Journal of Cross-Cultural Gerontology (1996).

Failing to Discuss Dying Adds to Pain of Patient and Family

TALKING AROUND DEATH

ESTHER B. FEIN

Joan Siff and her father, Martin Isaacs, were as close, she thought, as parent and child could be. She had always enjoyed the facility of his mind and the generosity of his heart. Though he never went to college, they would have lengthy talks about classical literature and class division in American society. His passion was poetry, and in 1991, Mrs. Siff's sons, Andrew and Michael, published a volume of their grandfather's verse as a family legacy.

But for all the time they spent talking about his life, Mrs. Siff and her father never once talked about his death. When he was young and healthy, working as a social worker for New York City, it never occurred to Mrs. Siff to raise the subject.

As he aged, Mr. Isaacs had no real physical problems until he reached his late 80's, when he suffered a series of strokes that compromised his memory, his balance and eventually his thinking. Yet even then, as the situation grew more urgent, father and daughter never talked about death.

Mrs. Siff and Mr. Isaacs are not unusual. For all the vociferous political debates about how best to allow people to die with dignity, few people discuss with their doctors or their families what kind of treatment they want when they are dying.

Talking in advance about death is clearly no salve for the pain of losing a mother, a child or a friend. But when people avoid the subject, many health care experts say, dying often becomes even more traumatic to patients and those caring for them, compounding the loss that even the most careful planning can never erase.

People die after undergoing lengthy and frequently painful treatments that they never told anyone they did not want. Families are forced to make critical decisions for loved ones who are no longer mentally competent and who never voiced their wishes. And doctors—many of whom do not initiate discussions about care at the end of life even with terminally ill patients—treat the dying not knowing whether their patients would consider their care too aggressive or not aggressive enough.

For Mrs. Siff, the fact that Mr. Isaacs never spoke to her or to his own doctor about the kind of care he wanted at the end of life meant that three times during her father's hospitalization, as he lay in a coma unable to communicate, she was alone in making wrenching decisions about how aggressively doctors should treat him, decisions that she says still haunt her more than a year after his death.

Mr. Isaacs was among 20 people who died at Beth Israel Medical Center in Manhattan during the first 11 days of November 1995, a period chosen at random to consider the overwhelming decisions that patients, health care workers and families confront in an era of medical advances that have enabled bodies to function long after brains have ceased to.

Administrators at Beth Israel, which lies at First Avenue and 16th Street in Stuyvesant Town, agreed to contact the families and doctors of people who had died at the hospital during this period and to provide their charts to the New York Times on the condition that each name be used only with the family's consent.

Twenty deaths in 11 days is about average for Beth Israel. And as in any other 11 days, some people died slowly, others quickly, some in great pain, others more comfortably. Some came from nursing homes. One was a 5-year-old. Some were surrounded by family and private doctors. Others relied on emergency room physicians. A few had thought about death and planned what sort of care they wanted. Most had not.

In addition to the 20 who died in the hospital, 14 people died during that time in Beth Israel's hospice program, most of them at home. Although nearly 400,000 Americans will die this year in such programs, which allow them to die at home with a minimum of intrusive care, most of the 2.3 million people who die each year in this country still die in hospitals, many unprepared for the decisions that they and their families will face.

In the last decade, public debate about death and dying has intensified. The Supreme Court is reviewing two Federal court rulings that have opened the way for doctors to help mentally competent terminally ill patients who choose to end their lives—rulings that are opposed by a broad range of people who fear that the right to die will become the obligation to die.

Medical schools are revamping their curriculums to teach young doctors how to advise dying patients and their families. (Now, only 5 of 126 medical schools in the nation have a separate, required course about dealing with death.) And hospitals and insurers are creating complicated formulas to determine when to use costly life-prolonging treatments.

A growing number of people are choosing friends or relatives to act as proxies should they become unable to make decisions for themselves, and more hospitals have ethics committees to help medical

personnel, patients and families sort through the harrowing emotions and choices that dying presents.

But examining the records of the 20 people who died at Beth Israel Medical Center—a pioneer in confronting medical and ethical issues surrounding death—and speaking with surviving relatives, doctors, nurses, social workers and hospital administrators, show that to many people, death remains a subject never broached in private, a taboo.

"If people don't express what they want, or someone doesn't do it for them, it's a matter of pure luck if they get what they want," said Dr. Robert G. Newman, president and chief executive at Beth Israel and an ardent supporter of patients' rights. "There's a spectrum of horror to blessing in the death process. To leave it to luck is foolhardy at best, dangerous at worst."

The Daughter
Not Ready to Speak for Her Father

Joan Siff said she thought little about death until Oct. 23, 1995, when an ambulance brought her 91-year-old father, Martin Isaacs, to the Beth Israel Medical Center emergency room. He was disoriented, feverish and suffering from bedsores. Senility had robbed him of his ability to speak for himself, and his wife, Mrs. Siff's stepmother, was too emotionally fragile to make decisions for him. Mrs. Siff assumed the role of her father's advocate.

After several difficult days, Mr. Isaacs' bedsores began healing. A social worker was putting together a plan to sent him home.

But then, at 6:30 P.M. on Nov. 1, a nurse on routine rounds found that Mr. Isaacs had stopped breathing. His blood pressure had plummeted so low, she could not get a reading. He was deathly pale.

Doctors raced to his room and performed cardiopulmonary resuscitation. They revived his heart, but Mr. Isaacs fell into a coma. Unable

to breathe on his own, he had a stiff tube inserted down his throat and into his lungs, and he was attached to a ventilator. Instead of going home, he was transferred to the intensive care unit.

The next day, Dr. Yoav Borsuk, a second-year resident in internal medicine, and Dr. Paul Mayo, co-director of the medical intensive care unit, sat down with Mrs. Siff and her stepmother to discuss Mr. Isaacs' condition. His brain was functioning only minimally. There was scant chance he would breathe again without the ventilator. Although he had stopped writing poetry years earlier, he would now no longer even appreciate hearing its rhythms.

"Dr. Mayo was so kind," said Mrs. Siff, a teacher of adult education. "The first thing he said was: 'Tell me about Mr. Isaacs. I only see him now, like this, but tell me what he was like when he was young and healthy.' "

Nonetheless, Mrs. Siff said her meeting with Dr. Mayo and Dr. Borsuk was devastating. For the first time, she realized that her father was dying, and she was forced to make what she said was the most difficult decision of her life. Dr. Borsuk, the resident, noted in the chart that Mrs. Siff and her stepmother "expressed their wishes that no aggressive medical treatment or intervention be taken because 'he suffered so much so far.' "

Dr. Mayo's note in the chart, however, indicated that the family was still struggling with what such an approach meant, considering that Mr. Isaacs was attached to a respirator that could keep his hopeless body technically alive for a long time. "The family does not request active disconnect," Dr. Mayo wrote, "but rather a peaceful completely noninterventional approach leading to peaceful death."

To give the family time to absorb the reality of Mr. Isaacs' condition, Dr. Mayo said he waited a day before discussing with them whether they wanted to place in his chart a "do not resuscitate," or D.N.R., order, instructing doctors not to revive him should he suffer the kind of attack he had four days earlier.

Mrs. Siff agonized over the decision.

"I am in general a believer in not keeping people alive if in general they are more dead, but I had a hard time signing something saying that they shouldn't save my father," she said. "If he had told me, if we had talked, it would be different. Maybe he would want those few extra weeks or days no matter what. It's possible.

"I don't think he would, but without ever having spoken directly about it, I'm just guessing."

The Personal Physician
'I'm Still Lazy' in Preparing Patients

Mrs. Siff was not alone in her ignorance about her father's wishes. Mr. Isaacs also never talked about death with his regular doctor, Alan R. Raymond, even as he began to slide from health to infirmity.

Dr. Raymond, 42, said that he never learned about preparing patients for death either in medical school training or on the wards. "It's just not ingrained as part of our history and practice," he said.

Beth Israel has been at the forefront of demystifying the dying process by encouraging patients to name health proxies, which empower someone else to make decisions about health care when a patient no longer can, and urging doctors to have frank conversations with their patients about issues involving the end of life.

It was one of the first hospitals in the state to create an ethics committee to explore these difficult matters. It is one of the few medical centers in the nation that distributes proxy forms and information about choices for the dying to patients who make routine visits to its outpatient offices. And Beth Israel requires residents training there to demonstrate three times their ability to talk with

patients and their families about death.

But even here the reality of how patients and doctors talk about death intrudes daily on decisions about care.

As Dr. Raymond saw Mr. Isaacs began to falter, he never suggested to his patient that he name a health proxy, nor did he talk to him about how aggressively he wanted doctors to prolong his life. Dr. Raymond said he "very rarely" discussed proxies and death with any of his patients—including those in frail health—even though he had, in the past, "been nicely chastised by the ethics committee" because such omission had complicated the care of patients.

In fact, on the day he was interviewed, four of Dr. Raymond's terminally ill patients were in the hospital. Only one, who had severe heart disease, had a proxy. The other three, two with advanced lung cancer and one with pancreatic cancer, had none.

The ethics committee has no power to force private doctors who practice at Beth Israel to raise these issues with their patients, but can only try to educate and persuade them.

"As a practicing physician you'd think I'd have learned," he said. "But I'm still lazy on the subject."

In Mr. Isaacs' case, Dr. Raymond acknowledged that he "absolutely should have" talked to him about proxies and "end of life" care options, but did not. "Even if I couldn't talk with him," Dr. Raymond conceded, "I should have with his wife or daughter."

The Staff
Mixing Directness and Compassion

On Nov. 5, after getting the full support of her family, Mrs. Siff signed the request asking doctors not to revive her father if his heart stopped.

Days passed with no improvement in Mr. Isaacs' condition. He

developed bacterial pneumonia. Dr. Patricia Villamena, an attending physician in pulmonary and critical care medicine, gently suggested to Mrs. Siff that she consider disconnecting her father from the machine that inflated his lungs 10 times a minute, a hissing and whooshing sound accenting each artificial breath.

Mrs. Siff was stunned. Agreeing to the "do not resuscitate" order, not knowing her father's wishes, had been tortuous. This decision seemed unbearable. "The question of whether he lived or died was on my head," she said.

Though it is often a brutal process, it is critical to be direct, even blunt, with families, Dr. Villamena said. Too often, she said, doctors resort to medical jargon or euphemisms, either because they want to preserve a kind of superiority over patients and families or out of sheer discomfort. But that only intimidates and confuses families.

"When it's true, you need to use absolute terms, like 'There's no hope,'" Dr. Villamena said. "That allows families and patients to make appropriate decisions with the least amount of guilt and grief."

As she visited her father and stared for hours at his withered body, tethered to a web of tubes, Mrs. Siff said she became lost trying to fathom what he would want and what she had a right to do. Although a few months earlier, on the advice of an estate lawyer, she had had her father sign a document naming her as his health proxy, Mrs. Siff doubted his capacity to understand what he was signing and why. Even at that point, the two did not talk about "end of life" care and death.

Driven by indecision, Mrs. Siff turned to Navah Harlow, who started as Beth Israel's first patient advocate in 1979 and is now director of its 14-person department of medical ethics. With Mrs. Harlow's help, Mrs. Siff scoured her memory for conversations with her father, searching for a hint of what he might have wanted.

When Mrs. Siff's mother was dying of rheumatoid arthritis, her father fretted about the tormenting cream of testing and probing that would never change the fact that the woman he so adored, a woman just 8 years old, would soon die. She also remembered a discussion about the landmark case of Karen Ann Quinlan, whose parents successfully argued to the New Jersey Supreme Court that they had the right to disconnect their brain-dead daughter from a respirator.

"I remembered he had said, 'It's sad, but it's not a life,' " Mrs. Siff recalled.

Speaking to Mrs. Harlow, Dr. Mayo and Dr. Villamena, Mrs. Siff said she felt comforted by the hospital staff's compassion. But as she struggled deciding what to do, blind to her father's wishes, she said she grew increasingly distressed at what she called the "lack of sensitivity" her father's longtime doctor showed to his dying patient and at what she saw as the doctor's failure to prepare Mr. Isaacs and his family for complicated decisions they would face near his death.

"It's like he saw Dad as a patient, not as a person," she said, "like he was his symptoms, not a whole human being."

The Decision
Suddenly, Room Grows Quiet

On Nov. 8, Mrs. Siff finally asked that her father be disconnected from the ventilator. In a letter to Dr. Villamena, she wrote that although her father had left no written directions for his death, "he would clearly be opposed to any extraordinary means of life support" and "would wish to carry on in a natural way without mechanical intervention."

Dr. Raymond, as his primary care doctor, concurred. The medical center's ethics committee was brought in. As its rules require, Dr. Mark Rosen, chairman of the ethics committee, and chief of the pulmonology department, evaluated Mr. Isaacs on the morning of Nov. 10 to verify his medical status. He agreed that given the patient's irreversible condition, mechanical ventilation should be withdrawn.

Beth Israel allows families of patients with no proxies or written directions great leeway in showing proof of what a patient would have wanted. Many other hospitals, concerned over possible lawsuits or sanctions by regulatory agencies, demand either written documentation of a patient's wishes or a conversation witnessed by more than one person.

Dr. Newman said that Beth Israel's policy was based on the premise that as long as each decision was made with the best interest of the patient paramount, nobody would challenge its practice. Nobody ever has.

On Nov. 10, two hours after the ethics committee gave its approval and 18 days after Mr. Isaacs was admitted to the hospital, Dr. Deborah Ushkow withdrew the tube that ran from the ventilator down Mr. Isaac's throat to his lungs and shut the machine off.

The room went suddenly quiet. Mr. Isaacs' pulse was a steady 82 beats per minute. His blood pressure was a weak 90/40. He was taking 16 labored breaths a minute on his own. An hour and a half later, at 2:15 P.M., he was pronounced dead.

A year later, Mrs. Siff still revisits her decision. She asks herself whether in some way she betrayed her father: did she allow him to die in a way he might not have wanted? She is haunted by ambiguity.

"It's a good thing for healthy people not to be obsessed by death, but you have to be prepared," she said.

And yet, with all that she has experienced, Joan Siff has not chosen a health proxy for herself; nor has she written out her wishes for when her own end nears.

Unit 5

Unit Selections

Key Points to Consider

❖ After having charted your family's health history, what type of future do you see for yourself? What changes do you see yourself making in your life? How would you go about gathering the information you need to make these decisions?

❖ What decision have you made about long-term commitments—marriage or some other relationship? How about children? Do you see divorce as a viable option, even before marriage? Do you expect to live "happily ever after"?

❖ In what ways have secrets been integral to your family life? In what ways have you been hurt by family secrets? How have you benefitted?

❖ What is the state of rituals in your family? What rituals might you build in your family? Why?

 **Links** **www.dushkin.com/online/**

These sites are annotated on pages 4 and 5.

What is the future of the family? Does the family even have a future? These questions and others like them are being asked. Many people fear for the future of the family. As previous units of this volume have shown, the family is a continually evolving institution that will continue to change throughout time. Still, certain elements of family appear to be constant. The family is and will remain a powerful influence in the lives of its members. This is because we all begin life in some type of family, and this early exposure carries a great deal of weight in forming our social selves—who we are and how we relate to others. From our families, we take our basic genetic makeup, while we also learn and are reinforced in health behaviors. In families, we are given our first exposure to values and it is through families that we most actively influence others. Our sense of commitment and obligation begins within the family as well as our sense of what we can expect of others.

Much writing about families has been less than hopeful and has focused on ways of avoiding or correcting errors. The five articles in this unit take a positive view of family and how it influences its members. The emphasis is on health rather than dysfunction.

Increasing evidence of genetic factors in physical as well as mental health serves to promote the need for awareness of our family's health history. "To See Your Future Look Into Your Past" considers how charting your relatives' medical history can save your life. Steven Finch provides a useful technique for mapping out your family's health history so that you can anticipate, plan, and possibly change your health behaviors. One way to gather this information is through interviews, and "Getting the Word" explains just how this can be done. "What's Ahead for Families: Five Major Forces of Change," identifies five societal trends that Joseph Coates believes will have an impact on the future direction of families. Then, "The Power of Secrets" is related to family dynamics and shows the ability of secrets to shape how we relate to others. Concluding this volume, "Rituals for Our Times," by family therapists Evan Imber-Black and Janine Roberts, describes the ways in which rites and ceremonies are used to strengthen families. Through examples, readers see how they might use ritual in their own families.

Families, Now and Into the Future

TO SEE YOUR
FUTURE
look into your past

Tracing your family health history may be the most
important step you ever take toward long life

BY STEVEN FINCH

AS A CHILD Kathi Marangos always found her birthday cake a bit hard to swallow. Each sugary bite reminded her of a mother who gave her up for adoption and of a family she didn't know. But she recalls her 18th birthday as especially bittersweet.

"That's when my mother found me," she says. "She hired a private detective so she could give me information about my family."

Marangos felt at once transformed—into the proud daughter of a ski lodge manager and a Harvard graduate. But at the same instant she felt the chill from her family's dark side: its frightening predisposition for depression, heart disease, and colon cancer.

Today, at 35, Marangos, with her doctor's help, keeps an eye out for any sign of cancer while she makes sure her family sticks to a low-fat diet. "I'm so glad to know my medical history," she says, "to know I can use it to protect myself and my kids from our genetic shortcomings."

If only more Americans would see the light, says Michael Crouch, director of the Baylor Family Practice Residency Program in Houston and a leading expert on inherited risks. Tracing your roots to learn your family's health history may be the single most important thing you ever do to bolster your well-being.

Why? Because any disease that runs in your family puts *you* at risk. And regardless of whether the risks stem from your genetic code or from habits nurtured in your childhood, many family-

linked ills can be kept at bay if you know the right steps to take.

If a woman and her husband both have insulin-dependent diabetes, for example, any child of their runs a one-in-ten chance of getting the disease herself. But she greatly lowers her risk if she eats well, exercises regularly, and maintains a healthy weight. For problem such as alcoholism, the genetic connection is less certain. Children of alcoholics are between two and four times more likely to become alcoholics than other people.

> "People who see illness patterns in their families tend to note the red flags in their own lives; then they seek help."

"People who recognize patterns of alcoholism in their families tend to note the red flags in their own lives and are more likely to seek help or avoid a problem in the first place," says Crouch. What's more, doctors alerted by family histories

can aggressively look for and treat specific health problems.

"Take breast cancer," says Steven Esrick, a family physician who helps direct Kaiser-Permanente's preventive care programs in the northeastern United States. "It's reasonable for most women to start having mammograms at age 50, but I'd want a woman with a family history to start at 40." And many physicians who'd normally recommend counseling for depressed patients, says Esrick, are quicker to consider antidepressant drugs if the family history includes suicide attempts.

"I know one woman who lost her mother and one sister to ovarian cancer at a young age," says Esrick. Because this cancer tends to be fatal and is difficult to detect early, even with frequent screening, the patient chose to have her ovaries removed. Not the decision for everyone, to be sure. "But because this woman knew her risks," says Esrick, "she was better able to weigh the options and to make the right decision *for her.*"

People in this country are hardly strangers to unearthing family history. Nearly half say they've at least dabbled in genealogy, and tens of millions have compiled some kind of family tree.

Still, Crouch and Esrick are amazed by how few people know even the barest details of their relatives' medical histories. Only now, thanks to health maintenance organizations and other managed care groups, is this trend starting to change. Under Esrick, for example, Kai

Preventable Perils: Are You at Risk?

ONCE YOU FIND OUT which health problems various family members have had, your doctor can help you figure out how that affects your risk—or refer you to a genetic counselor if necessary. Many inherited conditions, alcoholism or obesity for example, are passed on by a mix of inborn tendencies and family habits, such as cocktail hour every night or a love of fried foods. But here's one rule of thumb: The more close relatives who suffered one of the conditions listed below—and the younger they were at the time—the likelier you are to have inherited a predisposition to the illness. Here's how to size up your risk—and improve your odds.

HEART DISEASE

If your father or grandfather had a heart attack or bypass surgery before age 55 or your mother or grandmother before 65, your risk rises significantly, especially if you're African American. *If it runs in your family:* Swear off smoking, and have your cholesterol tested. If it's over 240, you need to have your blood analyzed for LDL, or "bad" cholesterol. An LDL level over 160 will likely prompt your doctor to prescribe cholesterol-lowering drugs and to advise you to exercise and cut back on fatty foods.

HIGH BLOOD PRESSURE

A family history of high blood pressure increases your risk of developing the condition, which in turn boosts your odds of having a stroke sixfold. *If it runs in your family:* Have your pressure checked regularly, watch your weight, exercise, and eat a diet low in fat and high in calcium, potassium, and magnesium. Your doctor may advise you to cut down on salt or to take calcium supplements or blood pressure drugs.

DIABETES

If you have one parent with type I (insulin-dependent) diabetes, you typically have a 4 to 6 percent chance of getting it yourself. If one parent has type II (non-insulin-dependent), your risk is 7 to 14 percent. African Americans, Mexican-Americans, and Pima Indians are at highest risk. *If it runs in your family:* Exercise regularly, lose weight if you're obese, and eat a low-fat, high-fiber diet.

BREAST CANCER

Many women assume they have a genetic predisposition to breast cancer if a family member developed the disease. But only 5 to 10 percent of all breast cancers are inherited. Scientists have pinpointed a mutated gene, BRCA1, linked to both breast and ovarian cancer, and 1 percent of Jewish women carry it. *If it runs in your family:* You may want to start yearly mammograms at 40 instead of 50. If many members of your family developed the disease at a young age, you might ask your doctor about being tested for the mutated form of BRCA1.

COLON CANCER

Ten to 15 percent of all colon cancers are inherited; family genes lead to about 20,000 new cases each year. *If it runs in your family:* Ask your doctor whether you should get a sigmoidoscopy. Regular, low doses of aspirin may offer protection, as does a low-fat, high-fiber diet.

ALCOHOLISM

Thirteen to 25 percent of children of alcoholics are likely to become alcoholics. *If it runs in your family:* You need to be especially vigilant about your drinking habits; dependence develops over time. If you've ever found it hard to keep your drinking under control, or anyone close to you thinks your drinking is a problem, you may want to seek treatment.

DEPRESSION

Some types of depression run in families and occur generation after generation. Not everyone with a vulnerable genetic makeup will develop depression, but stress is believed to trigger its onset. *If it runs in your family:* Your doctor is more likely to suggest early intervention with antidepressants if you become depressed and your family history includes suicide attempts or major depressions requiring hospitalization.—*S.F.*

women whose mothers had breast cancer prior to menopause run a much higher risk themselves. "It's hardly worrisome if several relatives died in their eighties due to heart disease," says Crouch. "But it's a different kettle of fish if they died at 35 or even 55."

Crouch constructs a health history for every patient but tells people not to worry just because a couple of relatives

> "It's not just that family trees prompt more people to come in for tests. The right people are getting the right tests."

have suffered from heart disease or struggled with addiction. "My guess is that there's a genetic component to almost every disease," he says. "But few of them are caused entirely by genetics." In other words, having a diabetic grandfather raises your risk—it doesn't necessarily doom you to the disease.

Neither does a clean record mean you can quit taking good care of yourself, says Bruce Bagley, public health chairman of the American Academy of Family Physicians. "Just because you don't have a history of hypertension or heart disease doesn't mean a doctor won't still urge you to have your blood pressure checked, to eat healthily, and to exercise." But when doctors can tie in family history, he says, blanket health warnings are made personal.

"Sure, no one should smoke," Bagley says. "But if somebody looks at their family history and sees low cholesterol coupled with a two-pack-a-day cigarette habit, they may come to realize it was really Dad's smoking that caused his heart attack. That's a pretty strong impetus for a person to quit."

This type of nudge can be crucial for people with silent conditions like high blood pressure and elevated cholesterol, says Esrick. Why change your habits if the disorder doesn't make you feel bad? "What feels bad," he points out, "is what happened to your parents."

No wonder Esrick often finds that his patients aren't ready to discuss their family's medical past until they're about the same age as a mother or brother was when she or he became ill or died.

er recently began an ambitious effort to ather family health information from all 14,000 of its patients in New York, Connecticut, and Massachusetts.

"What you're really looking for is patterns," says Crouch. Most crucial, he explains, are cases of cancer, high blood pressure, heart disease, diabetes, depression, and alcoholism—all common, life-threatening hereditary diseases that you can do something about.

"Another important pattern," Crouch says, "is the age at which your relatives developed a disease." For example,

Family Facts: Where to Find Them

FEW AMERICANS KNOW even the highlights of their family's health history, but no group knows less than the 5 million people who were adopted. Confidentiality has been the watchword for adoption agencies since the 1930s. Today only Hawaii and Kansas allow open records. That means someone adopted in any other state has no right to his or her health history—although judges have sometimes ordered records to be opened in emergencies. Of course, you don't have to be adopted to be blind to some bogeyman in your bloodline. The following agencies can help you track down your relatives, research your heritage, and, after you've compiled a health history, gauge your risks or those facing your children.

IF YOU'RE BUILDING A FAMILY TREE

NATIONAL GENEALOGICAL SOCIETY Offers two publications ($6 each) that explain ways to track down family health records. 4527 17th St. N., Arlington, VA 22207.

FAMILY HISTORY LIBRARY OF THE CHURCH OF JESUS CHRIST OF LATTER-DAY SAINTS Houses the world's largest collection of genealogical records (church members are only a fraction of the database), with 2 million rolls of microfilm and 300,000 bound volumes containing 2 billion names. The staff can answer brief questions and refer you to sources. You can also check the databases at more than 1,800 Family Search Centers in the United States and Canada; call for the nearest location. 35 Northwest Temple, Salt Lake City, UT 84150; 801/240–2331.

NATIONAL SOCIETY OF GENETIC COUNSELORS Gives referrals to professionals who flag hereditary illnesses and determine your risks as well as the chances of passing an illness on to a child. Once you've compiled your family health history, send the society a written request. 233 Canterbury Dr., Wallingford, PA 19086.

IF YOU'RE SEEKING YOUR PARENTS

NATIONAL ADOPTION INFORMATION CLEARINGHOUSE Sends important facts on state adoption laws and on searching for birth relatives, including a list of mutual consent registries as well as other organizations and support groups. 5640 Nicholson Ln., Suite 300, Rockville, MD 20852; 301/231–6512.

INTERNATIONAL SOUNDEX REUNION REGISTRY Matches data on adopted children with data on biological parents who have given up a child for adoption (a free service). Call for a registration form. The registry will contact you if the computer turns up a match. P.O. Box 2312, Carson City, NV 89702; 702/882–7755.

AMERICAN ADOPTION CONGRESS Has local support groups across the country for adoptees, birth parents, and adoptive parents. Each group offers psychological as well as search guidance. 1000 Connecticut Ave. NW, Suite 9, Washington, DC 20036; 202/483–3399.

CONCERNED UNITED BIRTHPARENTS Provides support and some search help through a monthly newsletter and 14 local branches around the country. First-year membership is $50. 2000 Walker St., Des Moines, IA 50317; 800/822–2777.

ADOPTEE LIBERTY MOVEMENT ASSOCIATION Holds search workshops at 62 chapters worldwide. Also provides a registry for people adopted from foreign countries who are seeking their biological relatives. P.O. Box 727, Radio City Station, New York, NY 10101; 212/581–1568. —S.F.

relatives, both living and dead. Focus first on older family members, since they're more likely to have suffered whatever ailments run in your bloodline. After tracking down information on your parents, grandparents, aunts, uncles, and siblings, you can compile the data for your spouse and children. If you're ambitious, you can even fill in facts on cousins, nieces, and nephews.

> "Some may be afraid of finding an illness in their bloodline. But knowledge is a good thing, even when the news is bad."

Placing a few phone calls is all it takes for some people. Others send out questionnaires or plan a big reunion so family members can swap medical details. Of course, close-knit families have a distinct edge over those separated by geography or personal disputes. But even deep gaps can be bridged. One method is to send any estranged relatives a note describing how a comprehensive health tree will benefit the whole family.

Locating relatives is the easy part, says Crouch. Often tougher, he says, is convincing them to open up about their maladies—and provide details. Health topics are highly sensitive; some are taboo to older people. Remember that not long ago it was the norm in this country to keep mum on miscarriages, mental illnesses, and even cancer.

Ethnicity, too, remains a delicate topic, albeit an important one. "For example, we worry about hypertension in blacks because they suffer more damage from the disease earlier in life. But in the South especially," Crouch says, "if a mother was Creole it's often not talked about because some people don't want to know what the racial background really is."

If one relative is tight lipped, see if your chatty aunt might be more forthcoming. But in the end, says Crouch, don't sweat a few unknown details about an unreachable uncle or long lost grandparent. Your goal is simply to gather as much information as you can. For all your close relatives, try to find out:

"I had one patient who finally came in because he's 47 and his father had a heart attack at 50," says Esrick. "Now he's taken up walking two days a week, he's reduced his weight, and because he lost someone he cared about, he's agreed to take cholesterol-lowering medication."

Esrick's gospel is steadily sinking in. "A lot more people here are being counseled and screened," he says. "And it's not just that more people are getting mammograms and Pap smears and cholesterol tests. It's that the *right* people are being given the *right* tests."

Getting yourself to that stage doesn't have to be difficult, Esrick says, but it does take a little time. An ideal health tree includes details on all your close

- full name and dates of birth, marriages, divorce, and remarriage.
- ethnic background.
- height and weight.
- average amount that he or she drank or smoked.
- any health problems, from recurring headaches and frequent colds to allergies and even limps. Pay special attention to heart attacks, strokes, cancers, diabetes, high blood pressure, high cholesterol, miscarriages, and major surgeries. List the age at which an event occurred or a condition was diagnosed.
- any depression or substance abuse and all suicide attempts.
- date and cause of death. Tease out as much information as you can. If a grandmother died of stroke, was it caused by a blood clot or by bleeding in the brain? Did she also have high blood pressure? If she died of cancer, what kind?

Organize your tree so that you and your physician can easily compare the health histories of two or more family members. The more close relatives you see who developed a hereditary illness and the younger they were at the time they got sick, the more significant your own risk. Some illness patterns—all your aunts had osteoporosis—will be obvious. But your doctor might notice threats that you miss and possibly refer you for tests or even suggest that you see a genetic counselor, who can help gauge your risk of, say, kidney disease or multiple sclerosis.

"Some people will always be worried about finding an incurable disease in their bloodline—though I'm of the school of thinking that knowledge is a good thing even if the news is bad," says Crouch.

Not everyone agrees. Both patients and doctors worry that insurance companies might use this information to deny coverage to high-risk individuals, such as women who carry the gene mutation that raises the odds of breast cancer. Still, 11 states already have laws on the books banning this type of discrimination.

And though there's no advantage to finding out that a relative had an incurable illness such as Alzheimer's or Lou Gehrig's disease, the day will come when doctors can actually repair defective genes. Until then, Crouch says, there's a lot we can do about the big things people die from—heart disease, hypertension, cancer—especially if a family tree leads to an early diagnosis.

"In the balance of things," Crouch says, "learning more about your family history is about as close as you can get to controlling your destiny."

Steven Finch is a writer and research editor for Hippocrates *magazine.*

GETTING
the Word

Oral-history interviewing can enrich your family history and unlock your relatives' memories—if you go easy on the who, where *and* when *and focus instead on* why, how *and* what.

By Sharon DeBartolo Carmack

When I started to research my family history, I dutifully interviewed my grandmother, asking her questions like when and where she was born, the names of her parents, when and where they were born, the names and birth dates of her siblings, the names of her grandparents and when and where they were born and died. Then, as all the genealogy how-to books advised, I verified everything she told me in one record or another.

I hated doing oral history interviews. My grandmother hated being interviewed.

It was a long, long time before I tried again. By then, Grandma was gone, so I interviewed her cousin Isabel. I followed the same procedure, asking about names, dates and places. Finally Isabel had enough of

> "I learned to unlock my relatives' memories and to tap the family history that's not in the record books—people's thoughts, feelings and motivations."

my pestering for facts: "Please don't ask me any more questions," she said. "I've told you everything I know." She stopped answering my letters, and when I called she pretended I had the wrong number.

So much for quizzing relatives for genealogical data. Besides, why bother asking questions I could find the answers to in a record somewhere? What was the point?

Then I met a social historian who taught me a better way of doing oral history interviewing—the oral historian's way. Instead of asking *who, where* and *when,* I should have been asking *why, how* and *what.* I learned to unlock my relatives' memories and to tap the family history that's not in the record books—people's thoughts, feelings and motivations. Trust me, the census record enumerating Great-uncle Mortimer's family will still be around long after we're all dead and gone. But the sense of what life was like in the past, the memories that make a person unique, will go to the grave with that person—unless you ask the right questions.

The right questions to ask in an oral history interview go beyond "just the facts, ma'am":

- What were some of your grandfather's positive qualities?
- What about negative qualities?
- How did your grandparents meet?
- What kind of work did your grandfather do?

- What's your fondest memory of your grandfather?
- What do you think he would have wanted to be remembered for? Why?
- As you think of your grandfather, how do you remember him looking?
- How old was he then?
- What did you call him?
- What did his wife and friends call him?
- Tell me a story about your grandfather that shows what kind of a man he was.

Notice that none of these questions can be answered with a simple "yes" or "no." These questions require the person to think about the answers and will give you information that's more interesting than dry names and dates.

From who to why

When I interviewed my grandmother and poor Isabel, I was laboring under another misconception: that the right time to interview your relatives is when you're just beginning to research your family history. Actually, you should talk to relatives at least twice: once when you first begin, then again after you have gathered quite a bit of research.

The first interview should be short. Your goal is to gather the facts–names, approximate dates, places, and stories about the origins of the family–so you can begin researching in records. But don't belabor this interview, and let your relative know your limited goal. You'll be back again for more after you've done some research and found some records.

Focus the second interview on augmenting information in the records and getting historical content based on that person's life. Anything Great-aunt Esmeralda tells you about ancestors beyond her lifetime is just hearsay anyway. Concentrate on getting stories based on her own lifetime and what she remembers about the oldest people in her life.

You should prepare for this interview by thinking of questions you'll ask on events, emotions and what you found in the records, asking why did this happen, how did you feel about it, and what was it like? My favorite book for helping me to prepare questions is William Fletcher's *Recording Your Family History* (Ten Speed Press, out of print). He subdivides questions into these categories:

- family history
- childhood
- youth
- middle age
- old age
- narrator as parent
- grandchildren
- historical events

- general questions, unusual life experiences and personal philosophy and values
- questions for interviewing Jewish, black and Hispanic relatives

I use the questions Fletcher provides as a starting point, then tailor the questions to the individual I'm interviewing based on my prior or research knowledge. I write these questions out in advance, but I'm prepared to deviate if the person gives me details about a topic I hadn't considered. For example, a general question might be "Where did your father go to college?" Since I knew my subject's father went to Princeton, instead I asked her, "Did you father ever tell you stories about his Princeton years?" Even though I knew what her father did for a living, I still asked, "What kind of work did your father do?" to get her interpretation.

Getting them to talk

Before I actually begin interviews, I explain to my subjects that not all the material will be used in the family history I write and that they'll have a chance to see and approve what I write before it's published or distributed to other family members. You can't own another person's memories. Get written permission to use the material if you plan to publish or distribute parts of the interview.

I also try to put my interview "victims" at ease by telling them that they don't have to answer all the questions I ask. If it's too personal, just tell me. And if they later regret telling me something, they can contact me and I won't include it. This happened after an interview I did with a lady who commissioned me to write her family history. During the interview, she told me how she and her daughter didn't get along. Afterward, she had second thoughts about seeing that in print, so I left it out. Remember, you're a family historian, not someone out to write an exposé.

You can also put your subject at ease by beginning with a fun, easy question. If I know the person is also interested in genealogy, I ask how he became curious about his ancestry. Typically, fellow genealogy buffs make enthusiastic interview subjects. If I have a reluctant interviewee, however, who can't imagine why I'd want to interview him, I might begin by asking what he does for a living or about one of his hobbies or the family pet.

My aunt was one of those reluctant interviewees. She dreaded coming for a visit because she knew I wanted to interview her. By the second day, however, she informed her daughter who had come along, "You'll have to find something to do to entertain yourself. Sharon and I are going to do more interviewing because this is important, and we have to

Videocameras:
Recording Words and Pictures

If you're recording an oral history interview with a videocamera, here are some secrets for success.

■ Use a tripod for the videocamera and make sure it's placed in the least distracting spot you can find.

■ If your videocamera has a light that flashes when it's recording, place a piece of black electrical tape over it. This light can be distracting to your subject and is a constant reminder that the camera is rolling.

■ Pick a room that's brightly lit, or use lots of lights to ensure the best quality picture. But don't have the subject sit in front of a window, which will cause everything in front of it to photograph too dark. Do a "screen test" with the subject to make sure the lighting and sound are acceptable.

■ Have visual materials ready (photographs, artifacts, historical documents) so you can get these items on the video when the narrator begins talking about them.

■ Punch the tab on the tape as soon as you take it out of the camera, so it can't be accidentally recorded over with next week's "E.R."

■ Make a copy of the tape and store in a cool, dry place.

---

get this done." Usually, once the reluctant subject sees that I'm not asking for facts—especially about people long dead and buried—but instead for stories about her life and her memories of her parents and grandparents, the "victim" relaxes and thoroughly enjoys the attention.

An interview shouldn't last longer than an hour or two at a stretch. It's tiring for you and the person being interviewed. If you're with the relative only for a day or so, take frequent breaks during the interview, since an intensive interview like this can total six to eight hours. You may want to break up the interview with a visit to the cemetery or a walk around the old neighborhood to get more stories.

Try to interview only one person at a time, alone. People tend to talk over one another and finish each other's sentences—especially couples who've been married a lifetime—making it hard for you to keep up. If you're taping the interview, it's more difficult to transcribe or take notes from the tape with several people talking.

Ask a question, then wait and really listen to the response. Resist the urge to interrupt, to clarify a point or ask another question. Make a note and come back to it. Don't correct your subject. Even though you may have a contrary document, let your relative tell you the way he or she remembers the event and make a note of the discrepancy. Show interest in what your subject is saying by nodding, using appropriate facial expressions or occasionally saying "uh-huh."

Taping and notetaking

If the interviewee doesn't mind, it's always a good idea to tape the interview, but you should also take notes. Don't rely solely on the tape recorder. I've had recorders malfunction and lost portions of an interview because I wasn't taking notes. Recently I purchased a new tape recorder and was happily interviewing; then it dawned on me that we'd been going longer than the half hour for that side of the tape. The machine had come to the end of the tape, but it didn't click off. My subject and I had to reconstruct about 20 minutes of the interview. If I'd been taking notes, that wouldn't have been necessary.

Make a double-space printout of the questions you're planning to ask, then jot down answers and notes next to the questions. You'll want to verify spellings of names, places or unusual or archaic words, but do this at the end of the interview or at the end of a story—don't interrupt the speaker's flow.

Include in your notes a description of where you're conducting the interview. Detail what your subject is wearing, how she looks, whether she smiles over one question and frowns at another, how she fidgets. All these traits show personality, and unless you're videotaping, you won't get these recorded.

Audio taping, rather than videotaping, is the least intrusive to the interview. While videotaping (see box "Videocameras: Recording Words and Pictures") can capture a person's look, facial expressions and personality, some people are more intimidated by a camera than a tape recorder and behave unnaturally.

Always begin each tape with your name, the name of the person being interviewed, how you're related, the date of the interview, whether this is tape number 1 or 21, and where the interview is taking place. Also record this information on the tape or cassette case.

Getting personal

Some of the best questions to ask are personal—questions that may be slightly embarrassing or make the subject laugh or cry. These are the questions no one has had the nerve to ask, the answers to which you won't find recorded anywhere, except maybe in a diary. Obviously, you don't want to start the interview with a question like, "So tell me what you and your husband used for birth control in the 1940s." Or, "Tell me about the automobile accident your son died in last year." Interviewing requires sensitivity and a sixth sense of what you can ask and when.

Often I'll phrase potentially embarrassing questions so they sound general, not personal: "Were many teenage girls in your day having premarital sex?" You may be shocked by the bluntness of the answer, though. One elderly lady responded to this question with, "Oh, sure, my boyfriend and I did it." Another lady told me much more about her sex life than I really wanted to know—but only after I turned off the tape recorder.

And move over, Barbara Walters—I can make the person I'm interviewing cry, too, though that's never my intention. You just never know what question may trigger an emotional response. In one interview, the question that triggered the tears was, "Tell me how you heard World War II had begun." The tears took us both by surprise, but I just let her cry and waited while she composed herself. Uncomfortable? You bet. Hard to wait out the tears? Incredibly. Now I know how my therapist feels.

Photographs and memories

An oral history interview is the perfect time to bring along old photographs or ask your subject if he or she has any. Ask your interviewee to tell you about the people in the photograph and where and when it was taken. If your subject is also in the photo, ask if she remembers the events that led to the photograph being taken. Was it a special occasion? Did some people not want to be in the photograph? If so, who else was there? Who suggested the pose? What was the conversation before and after the photograph? Yes, these are tough questions, and it will be the rare person who can remember all these details. But it's always worth asking.

Also ask about family artifacts. My grandmother's cousin, Isabel, has the tea set my great-grandmother brought with her from Italy in 1910. I wanted to know whether it had been a wedding present or held some other special meaning and how often the set

---

interviewing toolkit

PACKING FOR AN INTERVIEW

Before making a trip to visit and interview family members, stock a tote bag with these oral history essentials:

■ Cassette tape recorder (microphone if not built in)

■ Power cord

■ Extension cord

■ Cassette tapes and labels

■ Extra batteries

■ Note pad and pens

■ List of questions or a book on oral history interviewing that has simple questions

■ An address book to note names and addresses of relatives the person you are interviewing may give you

■ Your research notebook with pedigree charts and family group sheets (you can download these from www.familytreemagazine.com/forms/download.html)

■ A watch to make sure you're not overstaying your welcome

■ Photocopies of any documents you've gathered to show the relative or photographs you need to identify

■ Magnifying glass in case the relative needs it to view the photocopies

■ Camera to photograph any documents or photographs you relative won't let you take out of the house to copy (you may also consider bringing a laptop computer and handheld scanner)

Label each tape and its storage case with identifying information:

■ The person being interviewed

■ The date

■ The place

After the interview, immediately punch out the tab, making it impossible for someone to accidentally erase the tape or record over it.

---

was used—on special occasions or every day. Perhaps there are interesting stories surrounding an item in your family.

Bring out photocopies of the documents you've been gathering and show them to your relatives. Isabel had never seen her name on the passenger arrival list when she came to this country. She got teary-eyed when I showed it to her, and even more excited when I gave her her own copy.

Using oral history

So what do you do with your interview materials after you leave your relative's house? First, you'll either need to transcribe your tapes or, if you didn't take notes during the interview, you should make notes from the tapes. Keeping the interview only on tape limits its usefulness to you and your descendants. Technology changes too fast, and the shelf life of an audio- or videotape is only about 10 years before it begins to deteriorate. The printed word is still the most widely used—and reliable—form of preserving history.

on the bookshelf

READING ABOUT ORAL HISTORY

■ *Family Tales, Family Wisdom: How to Gather the Stories of a Lifetime and Share Them With Your Family* by Robert U. Akeret (Henry Holt, out of print)

■ *Transcribing and Editing Oral History* by Willa Baum (Altamira Press, $15.95)

■ "Searching at Home and Talking With Relatives," in *The Genealogy Sourcebook* by Sharon DeBartolo Carmack (Lowell House, $16)

■ *Oral History: From Tape to Type* by Cullom Davis, Kathryn Back and Kay MacLean (American Library Association, $46)

■ *Record and Remember: Tracing your Roots through Oral History* by Ellen Epstein and Jane Lewit Lanham (Scarborough House, $10.95)

■ *Recording Your Family History: A Guide to Preserving Oral History Using Audio and Video Tape* by William Fletcher (Ten Speed Press, out of print)

■ *Nearby History: Exploring the Past Around You* by David E. Kyvig and Myron A. Marty (Altamira Press, $24.95)

■ *Video Family History* by Duane and Pat Strum (Ancestry, out of print)

■ *How to tape Instant Oral Biographies* by Bill Zimmerman (Betterway Books, $12.99, in bookstores or order direct from www.familytreemagazine.com/store)

Most out-of-print books can be obtained through bookselling Web sites such as www.amazon.com, www.bn.com or www.borders.com.

Transcribing entire tapes is incredibly time-consuming. To transcribe, edit and proof the transcript against the tape and make a final copy, plan to spend about 22-25 hours for every hour of an interview. I've never transcribed an oral history tape; instead, I take notes from the tape and pull particularly interesting quotes.

Once you have your notes or a transcript, you can combine information from the interview with the records you have researched and the general, relevant historical context to write a narrative account as part of the family history. Here's an example using oral history, a death certificate and historical information on tuberculosis:

Mary remembers visiting her cousin Ralph who had tuberculosis. "We used to visit him in the sanatorium. It was like a hospital, and because we were too young and it was a contagious disease, we weren't allowed to go up and see him. But he used to wave to us from the window as we played on the grounds." Tuberculosis was the leading cause of death in the 19th century and into the 20th century, when Ralph died from the disease in 1946. Not until 1882 was the tubercle bacillus identified, and doctors realized that the disease was infectious. Confining tuberculin patients in sanatoriums became popular in the late 1890s.[1]

Using footnotes or endnotes, make sure your readers and descendants know where all the information came from. For example:

[1]*Oral history interview with Mary Bart, October 31, 1997, Simla, Colo.; death certificate, Register of Deaths, Harrison, N.Y.; Sheila M. Rothman,* Living in the Shadow of Death: Tuberculosis and the Social Experience of Illness in American History *(Baltimore: Johns Hopkins University Press, 1994),2, 43, 6, 179.*

No source you consult while doing your genealogy is 100 percent accurate. Any record, from a birth certificate to even a tombstone, can be wrong. Oral history is no more or less reliable. Yes, memories are prone to lapses, distortions and mistakes. But it depends on the type of information you're seeking: If you're asking Great-uncle Mortimer the dates when all 12 of his brothers and sisters were born, or when they all got married, then you're also asking for trouble. If you're asking him to recount memories of the first car he owned—how did it smell? What did it feel like to get behind the wheel? What color and make was it? where did you first drive it to?—then you're on pretty safe ground.

You'll also find that talking to Great-uncle Mortimer about his memories can be personally rewarding—both for you and for your interview subject. Despite my rocky start as an oral history interviewer, I've come to really enjoy it. I now think of myself more as an oral history therapist, because it's so therapeutic for people to have my full attention for the length of the interview and to reflect on their lives and the lives of their parents and grandparents. One person I interviewed said I asked tough questions—"tough" because I made him think about his relationships, attitudes and feelings. Even though we both walked away from the interview feeling mentally drained, we felt good and knew we'd captured something that would have been lost otherwise.

As you prepare for an oral history interview, think of this African proverb: "When an old person dies, a whole library disappears." Don't let these libraries of memories disappear. With oral history interviewing, you can ensure that the why, how and what of your family's past will be remembered forever.

SHARON DEBARTOLO CARMACK is a Certified Genealogist who specializes in writing family history narrative. She is the author of *Organizing Your Family History Search* (Betterway), *A Genealogist's Guide to Discovering Your Female Ancestors* (Betterway) and *The Genealogy Sourcebook* (Lowell House).

What's Ahead for Families: Five Major Forces of Change

A research firm identifies key societal trends that are dramatically altering the future prospects for families in America and elsewhere.

BY JOSEPH F. COATES

No adequate theory in the social sciences explains how values change, so it is very difficult to anticipate changing social values. On the other hand, the social sciences are outstanding in reporting and exploring historic patterns of social change and in reporting contemporary social values through surveys, opinion polls, and observational research.

Identifying long-term shifts in values is complicated by the great deal of attention given to fads—that is, transient enthusiasms. A good example is "family values," a topic of great interest in recent political seasons. Both the family and values are undergoing shifts, and the challenge for futurists and other observers of social change is to identify the long-term trends and implications in both of these important areas. Social values are slowly evolving trends.

To help you understand the myriad of evolving patterns in families, this article describes several major trends and forecasts in families and values and suggests what they may imply for the future.

TREND 1

Stresses on Family Functions

The family in the United States is in transition. While the forces at play are clear and numerous, the outcomes over the next decades remain uncertain.

Anthropologists agree that the family is a central, positive institution in every society. It performs two functions: the nurturing and **socialization** of children and the regulation of the expression of **sexuality**. In European and North American society, the family serves another basic function: **companionship**. Also important are the **economic** functions of families, such as providing care for the elderly and sick and social support for unemployed members.

All of these family functions are being stressed by structural changes in society. Among the patterns that have long-term implications are:

• Increased life-spans mean that adults live well past the period in which nurturing and socialization of children is central to their lives. In many cases, longevity leads to the death of one spouse substantially before the other, creating a companionship crisis.

• Sexual behavior is increasingly being separated from its procreative function, thanks to reproductive technologies such as artificial insemination and *in vitro* fertilization, as well as contraceptives.

• New patterns of work and leisure mean that people are developing interests and activities that are different from other members of their family. In many cases, this

leads to conflicting interests and expectations rather than convergence and mutual support. As a result, the companionship function of families comes under increasing stress.

• Television and magazines create images of lifestyles, which may influence people's expectations of each other and the roles of families.

• The anonymity of metropolitan life eliminates many of the social and community pressures on families. There are no watchful and all-knowing eyes in the big city that compare with those in smaller and more cohesive communities, where "What will the neighbors think?" is a critical socializing factor.

These forces will not wipe out the family or the commitment to family, but they will continue to reshape it.

Implications of Stress on Family Functions:

• **Substitutes for family functions will develop.** As family members seek other sources of companionship, and nurturing children becomes less important in matured families, institutions will have a challenge and opportunity to meet human needs. Already, people are finding companionship and even forming committed relationships on the Internet. Schools, businesses, and governments are all under more demand for meeting human services once provided in families, such as

From *The Futurist,* September/October 1996, pp. 27–25. © 1996 by The World Future Society, Bethesda, MD. http://www.wfs.org/wfs. Reprinted by permission.

About the Report

This article expands on research prepared for "Social and Value Trends," the third in a series of reports by Coates & Jarratt, Inc., on critical trends shaping American business in the next 30 years.

The reports were collected under the general project title, American Business in the New Millennium: Trends Shaping American Business, 1993–2010, which was prepared for and sponsored by 15 U.S. organizations: Air Products and Chemicals, Battelle Pacific Northwest Laboratory, CH2M Hill, Discover Card Services, Dow Chemical Company, E.I. DuPont de Nemours & Company, Eastman Chemical Company, Motorola, Niagara Mohawk Power Corporation, NYNEX Corporation, Ohio Edison, Sony Corporation of America, South western Bell Corporation, Goodyear Tire & Rubber, and U.S. West.

Other reports in the series covered trends in U.S. and world demography, politics, the global economy, science and technology, environment and resources, information technology, health and safety, transportation and habitats, and more.

For more information on the reports, contact: Coates & Jarratt, Inc., 3738 Kanawha Street, N.W., Washington, D.C. 20015. Telephone 202/966–9307; fax 202/966–8349.

health and medical care, child care, retirement care, unemployment compensation, etc.

• **Interest groups will proliferate.** Support groups have burgeoned in recent years to help people with special health or emotional problems. Similarly, special-interest groups such as book-discussion salons, travel and adventure societies, or gourmet dinner circles could see a renaissance as individuals seek others with similar interests outside their own families.

• **"Recreational sex" may become more acceptable** as the connection between sexual activity and child-bearing diminishes. Greater access to information on health and "safe sex" will allow people—including the very young and the very old—to engage in sexual activity more safely, both physically and emotionally.

TREND 2

Economics Drives Family Changes

The greatest changes in families have to do less with the family structure and more with economics. The change richest in implications is the rise of the two-income household. The United States has a way to go. Sweden and Denmark are the standards for mothers participating in the labor force. Sixty-five percent of U.S. mothers with children under age 18 are in the work force, compared with 86% in Denmark and 89% in Sweden. For children under 3, the figures are 53% in the United States, 84% in Denmark, and 86% in Sweden. Among the significant patterns emerging are:

• By 2000, women will make up just under half of the work force.

• Women are older when they marry and have their first child, deferring family formation until after they finish their education and get their first job. In 1988, the median age of mothers of firstborn children was 26, the oldest at any time in U.S. history.

• Although the average income of the family household has stayed relatively flat over the last 15 years, the growth of the two-income household is allowing couples to make a higher average income.

Implications of Changes in Family And Economics

• **Two incomes, two decision makers.** Both breadwinning members of two-income households will have broader opportunities to start a new career or business initiative. Any change of job or relocation offer will thus affect two incomes rather than just one, making life/career planning doubly complicated.

• **Women disappear from the community.** Women's greater commitment to work means a long-term change in their commitment to home and the community. Like male breadwinners of the past, women may be rarely seen in stores, in their neighborhood, at home, and so on. In the shopping mall of the future, for instance, the only daytime customers may be the very old, the very young with their mothers or minders, and after-school teenagers.

• **A masculinization of the home** will spread to the community. Telecommuting allows one or both breadwinners of the dual-income household to work at home. Many

---

Enduring Family Values

(Percentage of adults saying these values are important)

Respecting your parents	70%
Providing emotional support for your family	69%
Respecting people for who they are	68%
Being responsible for your actions	68%
Communicating your feelings to your family	65%
Respecting your children	65%
Having a happy marriage	64%
Having faith in God	59%
Respecting authority	57%
Living up to your potential	54%
Being married to the same person for life	54%
Leaving the world in a better shape	51%

Source: *American Demographics* (June 1992), from the Massachusetts Mutual American Family Values Study, 1989.

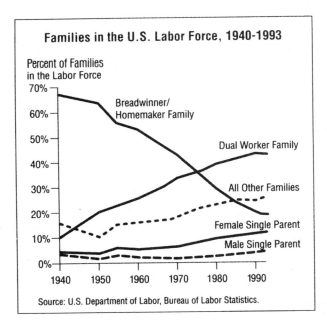

Families in the U.S. Labor Force, 1940-1993

Percent of Families in the Labor Force

Breadwinner/Homemaker Family

Dual Worker Family

All Other Families

Female Single Parent

Male Single Parent

Source: U.S. Department of Labor, Bureau of Labor Statistics.

men are choosing this option in order to be more available for domestic responsibilities such as cooking, cleaning, and chauffeuring children to various activities. Men may also increasingly become involved in volunteer activities, especially those that directly benefit their own families, such as neighborhood crime-watch groups and the PTA.

• **An economy of convenience will emerge.** A working lifestyle for most families will also continue to shape their preferences in eating, at home, for entertainment, and in shopping. Many families will be willing to pay a premium for convenience in all goods and services they purchase.

TREND 3

Divorce Continues

Divorce may be viewed as a way to correct social mistakes and incompatibility. In the 1940s, for example, there was a surge of marriage in the early 1940s as young Americans went off to war, and at the end of the war there was a surge of divorces in 1945–1947, apparently correcting impetuous mistakes. There was an even greater surge in postwar marriages.

Divorce is seen by many as the death knell of family values. On the other hand, a high divorce rate could be seen as a positive social indicator. It represents an unequivocal rejection of a bad marriage. For the first time anywhere in a mass society, the United States has had the income, the wealth and prosperity, and the broad knowledge base to allow people previously trapped in lifelong misery to reject that state and search for a better marriage. The evidence is clear, since the majority of divorced people either remarry or would remarry were the opportunity available.

Among the patterns emerging in divorce are:

• Divorce rates fell below 10 per 1,000 married women between 1953 and 1964, then surged to a high of almost 23 per 1,000 married women in 1978. Divorces have continued at about 20 to 21 per 1,000 for the last decade.

• Commitment to marriage continues, as demonstrated in the fact that the majority of divorced people remarry. One-third of all marriages in 1988 were remarriages for one or both partners. The average time until remarriage is about two and a half years.

• The shorter lifespans of many families has led to serial marriages. Almost surely there will continue to be people who have three, four, or five spouses, without any intervening widowhood. In the long term, it is much more likely

that society will settle down into a pattern of later marriage, earlier sexual engagement, and much more careful and effective selection of life mates.

• **Marriages and families will be businesses.** Families may increasingly be treated as business units, which form legal partnerships and plan and evolve their own lifecycles as an integrated activity. Families may even incorporate to obtain tax and other benefits. Divorces will be handled as simple business or partnership dissolution. [*Ed. note: The rise of "families as businesses" was predicted by Lifestyles Editor David Pearce Snyder in his article, "The Corporate Family: A Look at a Proposed Social Invention," THE FUTURIST, December 1976.*]

• **Teenage sex—but not pregnancy—will increase.** Teenagers will observe and emulate their parents' distinct separation of sexuality and commitment.

• **Companies will share and care.** Businesses will offer their employees training in household economics and management, as well as family and divorce counseling. These courses could also be marketed as a service to the community.

• **Opportunities for marketing to new families will emerge.** Many of

U.S. Divorce Rate, 1940-1992

Rate per 1,000 married women, aged 15 and over

Source: National Center for Health Statistics.

Divorce petition. Author Coates anticipates a movement to improve matchmaking in order to strengthen marriages and families.

the families in the top income segments will include remarriages and second and third families, in which the parents will have a strong incentive to tie together the new relationships. Aiming at this concern could offer opportunities. For example, a new blended family may want financial planning and related services to reallocate its resources. Club memberships for the new family, new homes, etc., all could be important among this group.

• **A "pro-family" movement will take new directions.** One of the most important underlying causes of divorce is that no institution in the United States—school, church, Boy Scouts, or other—teaches and trains people about what it is like to be married, to live in a two-income household, or to share and be involved in a new division of domestic labor. The search for a good marriage is not supported by the right tools to aid that search. Over the next decade, society will focus more on creating more-effective families. A new "pro-family" movement will encourage better and more effective matchmaking, as well as better teaching and training on marriage lifestyles and on economic and household management.

TREND 4

Nontraditional Families Proliferate

A variety of nontraditional family forms are evolving in the United States, shaped by economic and so-cial changes. For example, higher expectations for education mean young people spend more years in the educational system and marry later. The greater tolerance of divorce and remarriage affects how often people dissolve and re-form families. Many people enter long-term cohabiting relationships before marriage. And many single-parent families are being formed among low- and middle-income communities, as a result of divorce, widowhood, or out-of-wedlock childbearing.

The emerging patterns include:

• More couples are cohabiting. In 1988, one-third of all women aged 15–44 had been living in a cohabiting relationship at some point.

• The number of "boomerang" families is increasing. Young people—post-high school or post-college children who would otherwise be on their own—are returning home to live with Mom and Dad. To a large extent, this is a money-saving move more commonly practiced by men than by women.

• Blended families are becoming the norm. Blended families result from divorced parents who remarry, either linking stepfamilies together or linking the children of one partner to the subsequent children of both. It is estimated that, for nearly 16% of children living with two parents in 1990, one of those parents is a stepparent.

• Technology is creating new families. These may involve adopted children matched for similar genetic inheritance, children from surrogate parents, and eventually children from cloned embryos.

• Gay families are surfacing as a result of the new openness in society. Aside from the social approval so valuable to many in the gay community, acknowledgment offers substantial economic benefits in corporate or business health and recreation benefits packages. Time will make family resources available to members of nontraditional families.

• Group living, with or without sexual intimacy, is likely to remain a transitional life stage for an increasing number of people, often as an alternative to living alone.

• Single-parent families are increasingly common across all socioeconomic groups. The unmarried woman who bears a child is one of these family styles. It is unclear what the consequences are for middle- and professional-class mothers and children in these voluntary single-parent households. Evidence is strong

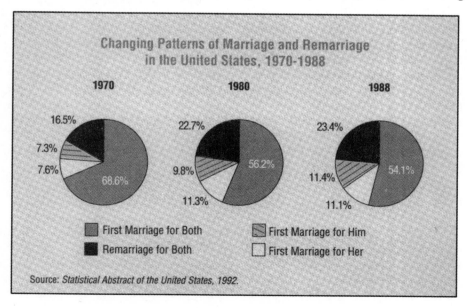

Changing Patterns of Marriage and Remarriage in the United States, 1970-1988

1970
- 16.5%
- 7.3%
- 7.6%
- 68.6%

1980
- 22.7%
- 9.8%
- 11.3%
- 56.2%

1988
- 23.4%
- 11.4%
- 11.1%
- 54.1%

■ First Marriage for Both   ▨ First Marriage for Him
■ Remarriage for Both   □ First Marriage for Her

Source: *Statistical Abstract of the United States, 1992.*

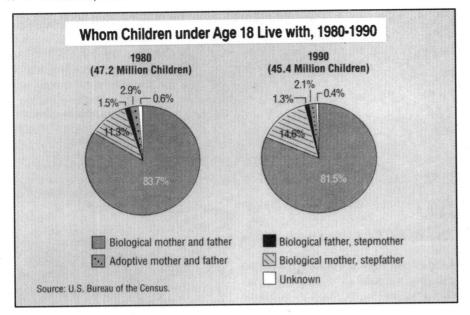

Whom Children under Age 18 Live with, 1980-1990

1980
(47.2 Million Children)

2.9%   ┌0.6%
1.5%┐ │
11.3%
83.7%

1990
(45.4 Million Children)

2.1%   ┌0.4%
1.3%┐ │
14.6%
81.5%

■ Biological mother and father
▨ Adoptive mother and father

■ Biological father, stepmother
▨ Biological mother, stepfather
□ Unknown

Source: U.S. Bureau of the Census.

that teenage childbearing, particularly by unmarried mothers, is socially destructive of the future well-being of both the mother and the child. Some single-parent families are single by divorce or separation.

Implications of the Proliferation of Nontraditional Families

• **Rearranged families will rearrange the workplace.** The work force will continue to be profoundly affected by new family structures. The proliferation of family arrangements will create new pressures on employers to be flexible and responsive in relation to working hours.

• **Businesses will make attitude adjustments.** Employers will be hard-pressed to justify accepting one type of family arrangement among their employees and not another. One company decided to offer benefits to gay couples because they could *not* get married and deny them to male-female couples living together because they *could*. Workers did not accept this justification.

• **"Nonfamily" families will gain in status.** Many groups of people consider themselves families, even though they do not fit traditional definitions (e.g., gay couples, unmarried couples with or without children, foster parents, long-term housemates, etc.). This has implica-

tions for business and nonbusiness issues, for example in marketing, housing codes and covenants, loans, billing, leasing, and so on.

• **Family-oriented organizations will reinvent themselves.** For example, Parent-Teacher Associations may broaden into Family-Teacher or Community-Teacher Associations. Schools may provide more counseling for students in nontraditional families.

• **Flexible architecture will be mandatory.** Housing will become more flexible, with walls that can be easily taken down and rearranged to form new rooms depending on the needs of new family members.

TREND 5

An Aging Society Will Redefine Families

The traditional family in past decades was the nuclear family: a working father, a homemaker mother, and children. As the children aged and left home, the traditional family was two adults with no children living at home; then one or the other died, leaving an elderly single person alone.

Aging creates a crisis in traditional families' lifecyles. The patterns to watch now include:

• Death rates of men are relatively high compared with women. Men

also tend to marry women younger than themselves. As a result, at age 75 and older, 66% of men but only 24% of women are living with a spouse. At age 65, for every 100 men there are 150 women. At age 85, for every 100 men there are 260 women.

• The savings rate among working adults is now just 4.1% of personal income, compared with 7.9% in 1980; this low rate bodes ill for Americans' economic status in retirement.

• Voting rates among seniors are traditionally higher than for younger people (60.7% of those 65 years and older voted in 1994, compared with 16.5% for 18- to 20-year olds and 22.3% for 25- to 34-year olds). It is likely that the baby boomers' influence on public policy will gain strength as they approach retirement years.

Implications of Age and Family

• **The end of retirement?** A combination of several factors may lead to the end of retirement: the emotional need of seniors to feel useful when their families no longer demand their daily attention, the financial needs of seniors who didn't save enough during their working years, the improved mental and physical health of older people, and the need in businesses for skilled, experienced workers.

• **Economic priorities shift away from children.** There is already concern among the elderly about balancing their economic assets against commitments to their children. Personal savings during their working years for their kids' college education may have left them ill-prepared for retirement.

• **Parents will "boomerang" back to their kids.** Just as adult children of the 1980s and 1990s moved back into their parents' home for economic security, elderly parents in the twenty-first century may increasingly move into the homes of their grown children. "Granny flats" and mother-in-law apartments will be common additions to houses.

• **No retirement from sex.** The sexual experimentation characteristic of baby boomers' youth may be brought to their old age. New drugs and therapies, such as penile implants, will help.

• **Elders will have roommates** or form other shared-living arrangements. A substantial increase in cohabitation offers the benefits of companionship without compromising the individual's financial survival or reducing the children's inheritance. We may see some college campuses convert into retirement communities, with dorm-style living.

The Effects of Population Changes on Values

Changes in values in the United States will depend to some extent on demographic change. Social institutions will continue to be stressed when population groups such as the aging baby boomers pass through society.

The baby boomers' children, the echo generation, now number more than 80 million people; they will be an even larger generation and a bigger social force than the baby boom was. They may be expected to stress and reshape education, justice, and work in turn, beginning now and accelerating through 2005, when they reach 20 and are ready to go to work.

Through the 1990s, the young echo boomers will increase school enrollment, then college enrollment. As they reach their late teens and move into their violence-prone years, the United States could experience an increase in violent crimes after the turn of the century. At around the same time there may be some risk of social unrest either in universities or in cities, as the echo boom goes through its years of youthful idealism and discontent.

The aging of the baby boom in the 1990s and 2000s may push the dominant values of U.S. society to be more conservative, more security conscious, and more mature and less driven by youthful expectations. In 2010, the first of the baby boomers turn 65. If the conservatism of their elders becomes repressive, the echo boomers could have more to rebel against.

As the U.S. population grows, if the economy affords only shrinking opportunities, this may promote more conservative views. At the same time, there may be an emerging social activism around worker rights, employment stability, and related issues.

Effects of Shifting Family Patterns

As a flexible institution, the family will continue to accommodate itself to the economy and the values of the Information Age. In many societies, this means an ongoing shift to dual-income partnerships.

It has also meant a shift in what work is available for the family to earn its income—away from agriculture and manufacturing and to information and services. This shift has brought millions of women into the work force because the work now requires education rather than raw physical might—mind, not muscle.

In many societies, men are finding it more difficult to find work unless they, too, can shift to information-based work. It is possible that women will become the higher wage earners in millions of families. It is also possible that as a result child care and family responsibilities will be more equally distributed between men and women.

People will continue to want to be part of families, but for some the economic necessity to do so will be less. For example, young people will need to spend more time in acquiring their education, and they will form their families later. Women with substantial careers will have less economic need to remarry after divorce.

Education, prosperity, and a decline in regard for authority will continue to secularize U.S. society, but concern for the family and community will tend to promote ties with religion. The church will continue to be a source of support for those who feel in some way disadvantaged by current values and attitudes. The other attractions of religion are its rituals, its shared experiences, its mysteries, and its social events. These will continue to bring in and keep people in religious groups, unless urban society develops some alternatives.

Conclusion: Belief in the Family Remains High

Anticipations of family life have not diminished to a significant degree in the last decades. In general, Americans are committed to the family as the core of a successful life. It is particularly gratifying to see this view widely maintained by young people. The percentage of college freshmen saying that raising a family is "essential" or "very important" has been fairly constant in the past quarter century: 67.5% in 1970 and 69.5% in 1990.

Adults' commitment to the family has become somewhat tempered by the higher likelihood of divorce. But most people still agree that being happily married and having a happy family is an important goal.

About the Author
Joseph F. Coates is president of Coates & Jarratt, Inc., 3738 Kanawha Street, N. W., Washington, D.C. 20015. Telephone 202/966–9307; fax 202/ 966–8349.

This article is based on the "Social and Value Trends" section of a major report by Coates & Jarratt for its clients, *American Business in the New Millennium: Trends Shaping American Business, 1993–2010.* The author acknowledges the assistance of Christine Keen of the Domani Group and the team support of Jennifer Jarratt, John Mahaffie, Andy Hines, Andrew Braunberg, Sean Ryan, and Nina Papadopoulos of Coates & Jarratt, Inc.

The POWER of Secrets

They divide people. They deter new relationships. And they freeze the development of individuals.

There's no question that family secrets are destructive. But it matters mightily when and how you reveal them. Resist the temptation to handle them at transition times such as weddings, graduations, and new beginnings.

BY EVAN IMBER-BLACK

As a family therapist, I'm a professional secret-keeper. I'm often the very first person with whom someone risks telling a long-held secret. Several decades of guiding people struggling with secrets have taught me that they have an awesome if paradoxical power to unite people—and to divide them.

From government conspiracies to couples having affairs, secrets permeate every level of society. Secrets have existed throughout time, but the nature of secrets has recently changed in our society. Today's families face special dilemmas about secrecy, privacy, silence, and openness.

We live in a culture whose messages about secrecy are truly confounding. If cultural norms once made shameful secrets out of too many events in human life, we are now struggling with the reverse: the assumption that telling secrets—no matter how, when, or to whom—is morally superior to keeping them and that it is automatically healing. My own experience, however, has shown me that telling secrets in the wrong way or at the wrong time can be remarkably painful—and destructive.

The questions we need to concern ourselves with are: When should I keep a secret? How do I tell a secret without hurting anyone? How do I know the time is right? I've learned the answers as I've witnessed—sometimes with terror, more often with joy, and always with deep

respect—families making the courageous journey from secrecy to openness.

Secrets are kept or opened for many complex motives, from self-serving abuses of power to altruistic protection of others. Understanding the best ways and situations in which to reveal a family secret can help you decide when and how to do so.

HOW SECRETS SABOTAGE

Although we encounter secrets in every area of life, they are perhaps most destructive when kept in the home. Families are support systems; our identity and ability to form close relationships with others depend upon the trust and communication we feel with loved ones. If family members keep secrets from each other—or from the outside world—the emotional fallout can last a lifetime.

There are four main ways that family secrets shape and scar us:

• they can divide family members, permanently estranging them;

From *Psychology Today,* July/August 1998, pp. 50-53, 62. Excerpted from *The Secret Life of Families,* by Evan Imber-Black.

- they can discourage individuals from sharing information with anyone outside the family, inhibiting formation of intimate relationships;
- they can freeze development at crucial points in life, preventing the growth of self and identity;
- they can lead to painful miscommunication within a family, causing unnecessary guilt and doubt.

A person who seeks to undo the damage caused by family secrets must accept that revealing a secret is not a betrayal but a necessity. Luckily, as you'll see, it's never too late to do so.

SHATTERING THE TRIANGLE

Not all secrets are destructive. Many are essential to establishing bonds between two people. When siblings keep secrets from their parents, for example, they attain a sense of independence and a feeling of closeness. But the creation of any secret between two people in a family actually forms a triangle: it always excludes—and therefore involves—another.

When family members suspect that important information is being withheld from them, they may pursue the content of the secret in ways that violate privacy. A mother reads her daughter's diary. A husband rifles through his wife's purse. Relationships corrode with suspicion. Conversely, family members may respond to a secret with silence and distance, which affect areas of life that have nothing to do with the secret.

Either way, the secret wedges a boulder between those who know it and those who don't. To remove this obstacle, families must break the triangle formation.

Molly Bradley first called me during what should have been a joyous time. She had recently given birth. Her happiness, however, was bittersweet. Molly felt a deep need to surround herself with family but hadn't spoken to her brother, Calvin, in six years. The reason, I discovered, reached back 30 years to a secret made by Molly's mother.

When Molly, Calvin, and their youngest sister, Annie, were teenagers, their grandmother committed suicide. Molly and Annie were told she died from a heart attack. Only Calvin, the eldest, knew the truth. His mother made him promise not to tell. His sisters sensed a mystery, but if they asked about their grandmother, their mother switched topics.

Making secrets soon became the family's modus vivendi. Their aunt committed suicide two years after their grandmother's death. Calvin fathered a child out of wedlock. Each secret was kept from Molly and Annie, amplifying the family pattern of secrecy. Calvin grew distant from his sisters, their relationship weakened by mistrust. Eventually, Molly guessed the truth of her grandmother's death but, in her family's style, told only Annie.

All families have some secrets from the outside world. Yours, no doubt, has jokes and stories told only within.

Secrets between Calvin and his mother were matched by those between Molly and Annie, tightening family alliances.

From the outside, the family looked like two close pairs—Calvin and his mother, Molly and Annie. But the pairs were actually triangles; Calvin and his mother distanced themselves from the girls with their secret, forming one triangle, while Molly and Annie, keeping their own secrets from the rest of the family, formed another.

'DON'T TELL ANYONE OUR BUSINESS'

Molly convinced her two siblings to enter therapy, but each felt that overcoming feelings of alienation was impossible. When I asked Annie if she'd ever considered confiding in Calvin as a child, she told me the thought had never occurred to her. If family members cannot even imagine a different way of interacting, then secrets have truly taken hold of their lives.

In order to bridge the distance between the Bradley children, I asked them to relive their memories of how it felt to keep—and be kept out of—secrets. Molly, Annie, and Calvin each acknowledged that their needs to connect with each other had gone painfully unmet. Calvin explained tearfully that being forced to keep information from his sisters left him unable to relate to them, causing him to withdraw into himself. Molly revealed that watching her infant son each day made her miss Calvin—and the relationship they'd never had—more and more.

The siblings finally began to share long-held secrets, realizing that they were bound and supported by their desire for closeness. After the fourth session of therapy, they went to dinner together for the first time in years. "This was so different from any other family event," Annie reported. "Things felt genuine for the first time."

As a lifetime of confessions and hopes emerged into the open, the triangle of secrecy was replaced by one-to-one relationships. When everyone in a family knows a secret, triangles cannot create barriers between members.

All families have some secrets from the outside world. Yours, no doubt, has shared jokes and stories told only within the family circle. You also have a zone of privacy that demarcates inside from outside, building your family's sense of identity. But if a dangerous secret—one concerning

> **Being the family member who opens internal secrets is difficult. It may seem like an act of betrayal.**

an individual in immediate physical or emotional jeopardy—is held within your house, the boundaries between family and the rest of the world become rigid and impenetrable. Friends and relatives are not invited in, and family members' forays out are limited. "Don't tell anyone our business" becomes the family motto.

BREAKING FAMILY RULES

Some families create inviolable rules to keep information hidden, making it impossible for members to ask for assistance or to use needed resources in the outside world. Even problems that do not touch on the secret may go unresolved if resolution requires outside help.

When Sara Tompkins, 37, first came to see me, she spoke with great hesitation. "If my family knew I was speaking to you, they'd be very angry," she confided. She told me about growing up in a family that completely revolved around her mother's addiction to tranquilizers. "My father is a physician. To this day, he writes her prescriptions. No one was supposed to know. The worst part was, we were supposed to act like we didn't know. Our family invented 'don't ask, don't tell' long before the government ever thought of it."

Even though Sara hadn't lived with her family for 15 years, this was the first time she had ever broken the family rule against speaking about the secret. When Sara left home for college, she was surrounded with new and exciting faces, each seeking lifelong friends and stimulating late-night discussions. But Sara found herself unable to open up, ultimately finding few friends and fewer lovers. She found it difficult to reveal anything personal about herself to anyone, and even suspected others of withholding from her.

Secrets were how she had learned to process and handle incoming information. Sara finally sought therapy when she realized that she had never been able to sustain a romantic relationship past the second date.

When a family's secret is an ongoing condition—such as drug addiction, physical abuse, an illness—then both family relationships and interactions with the outside

world are profoundly affected. In families like Sara's, members must organize their everyday lives around the needs of the secret while performing the breathtaking feat of pretending not to notice anything is out of the ordinary. Conversation is superficial, since what is truly important cannot be discussed. Members become paralyzed, unable to develop relationships with others or to deepen the relationships within the family. Since individual well-being takes a backseat to group fidelity, being the family member who challenges internal secrets is difficult. Taking the risk of opening a long-held secret to friends and loved ones may seem like an act of betrayal. The anticipated catastrophe of exclusion from the family stops many people—often long after leaving home.

But breaking the rules of family secrecy is necessary to ensure the achievement of freedom and honesty crucial to making and sustaining authentic relationships. One of the best ways to ease into revealing long-hidden information is to tell an objective listener, like a therapist.

ROOM FOR REHEARSAL

Only rarely do my clients want their first and final telling to be with me. Making secrets with a professional helper is a double-edged sword. A client's relationship with a therapist, minister, priest, or rabbi can be an excellent arena to dissolve shame, find acceptance and empathy, and seek new resources for support and strength.

At the same time, sharing secrets only with professionals may negatively affect marriage and other relationships. Important issues may be discussed more in therapy, for example, than at home. Instead of being a dress rehearsal for life, therapy becomes the show. Most often, I find that people want a receptive and empathetic context in which to unpack a secret initially, room to explore the consequences of telling others, then the help to do it well.

Imagine if your sister made a secret with you on the eve of your wedding and told you that you must not tell your husband. Or you are dragged into a secret about your parents just when you are taking tentative steps into the outside world. If a secret is made at a key point in development, the natural unfolding of self and relationships may be frozen. The shifting of boundaries that ordinarily would occur is suspended, creating a developmental deep freeze.

FROZEN FAMILIES

Every family experiences developmental stages. These are most evident when someone enters the family by marriage or other committed relationship, birth, or adoption, and when someone exits the family by leaving home or through separation, divorce,

Families must open secrets only during a normal time in everyday life, or else resolution can't occur.

or death. Such entrances and exits require that a family reinvent itself in order to accommodate new roles. The stages of development are not discrete events but rather processes that take place over time. When that process goes well, complex adjustments occur in every corner of the family. When a secret is made in the midst of this process, adjustment screeches to a halt.

Samuel Wheeler tried to leave home when he was 19, but his discovery of a central family secret pulled him back and short-circuited his young adulthood. When Sam came to see me, he was 34 and still struggling with the aftermath. Aimless, jobless, and depressed, Sam wondered why he had never really found his focus. As we explored his past, I realized that Sam's life had frozen when his attempts to assert independence were squelched his first year of college.

Early in his first semester, Sam invited his mother to visit. "I was more than surprised when she arrived with a close friend of the family, Duncan," said Sam. Each morning for three days, Mrs. Wheeler left Sam's apartment at five A.M. and returned to have breakfast at eight o'clock. When Sam finally asked what was going on, his mother admitted that she and Duncan were having an affair. She also revealed that his younger sister had actually been fathered by Duncan.

"My mother had kept this secret for years," Sam mused. "Why did she have to put it in my face at that moment?" The ill-timed revelation kept Sam from proceeding with his new life and developing his own identity. While very bright, Sam did poorly his first year in college, dropped out, and went back home. He had subconsciously returned to play watchdog for the family's relationships. His sister was only 15, and he was worried that she would discover the secret. He remained home until she left for college.

RESPECTING TRANSITION TIMES

Giving voice to the developmental deep freeze, Sam said, "Knowing these things about my mother's life has kept me from changing my relationship with her and my dad in ways I would like. I wanted to get closer to my dad, but this secret is like a rock between us."

Pulling Sam into a secret just as he and his family were moving apart also kept him from asserting independence. While there is no such thing as the perfect moment to open a secret, there are better occasions than a life-cycle ritual, such as a wedding or graduation. Because family relationships are already shifting, rituals may seem a perfect time to open a secret. The excitement of a major life change, however, will prevent resolution of the secret. Either the importance of the secret will be lost in the event, or the secret will diminish the importance of the ritual.

For family members to have the strength to handle a life-altering secret, it should be told during a normal time in everyday life. Otherwise, development linked to a life passage will stop in its tracks.

When secrets are as much a part of families as birthdays, it may seem impossible to extricate them from the daily routine. But I know it can be done. Each time I meet with a new client, I'm moved by the courage people bring to this endeavor, by the human desire to heal and to connect.

Rituals
FOR OUR TIMES

**Evan Imber-Black
and Janine Roberts**

Evan Imber-Black is the director of the Family and Group Studies program of the Department of Psychiatry at Albert Einstein College of Medicine. Janine Roberts is the director of the Family Therapy program of the School of Education at the University of Massachusetts.

How today's families are developing innovative rites and ceremonies to ease difficult transitions, heal relationships, and celebrate life.

E VERY FOURTH OF JULY, PAUL and Linda Hoffman pack their three children and their dog into the station wagon and drive 250 miles to Paul's sister's home, where all of the Hoffmans gather. The event is fairly unpleasant. The women spend the day cooking, which Linda resents, while the men watch sports, an activity Paul doesn't care for. The young cousins spend most of the day fighting with one another. In the evening, Grandpa Hoffman sets off fireworks, but no one really pays attention. On the fifth of July, Paul and Linda drive home, wearily vowing that this is the last year they will spend their holiday this way.

The following June, however, when Paul and Linda dare mention that they are thinking about doing something different for Independence Day, Paul's sister calls and tells them how upset their parents will be if the couple and their children don't come this year. Alternate plans fall by the wayside, and on the Fourth of July into the car they go.

Does this story sound at all familiar to you? Because of experiences like the Hoffmans', in which celebrations are static and meaningless, many of us have minimized the practice of rituals in our lives. One woman we know who grew up in a family whose rituals were particularly confining put it this way: "I don't want any rituals in my life. Rituals are like being in prison!"

Yet in these times of rapid and dramatic change in the family—with more children being raised by single parents, more mothers working outside the home, fewer extended families living in close proximity—rituals can provide us with a crucial sense of personal identity as well as family connection. Despite the changing status of the family, membership within a family group is still the primary way that most people identify themselves. Rituals that both borrow from the past and are reshaped by relationship needs of the present highlight for us continuity as well as change. A family in which ritual is minimized may have little sense of itself through time. Everything simply blends into everything else.

As family therapists who have been working with and teaching the use of rituals since the late '70s, we have encountered an increasing number of people who are longing to revitalize the rituals in their lives. They just don't know how. Rituals surround us and offer opportunities to make meaning from the familiar and the mysterious at the same time. Built around common symbols and symbolic actions such as birthday cakes and blowing out candles, or exchanging rings and wedding vows, many parts of rituals are well known to us.

A ritual can be as simple as the one that sixty-two-year-old Eveline Miller practices when she needs to sort things through. She goes to her grandmother's rocking chair, sits, and rocks. When she was a child and needed comfort, this was where she used to go to lay her head upon her grandmother's lap. Her grandmother would stroke her hair and say, "This too will pass." Now, as Eveline rocks and thinks, she repeats those words to help calm herself and provide perspective.

Rituals also can be more elaborate and creative, such as one that Jed and his wife, Isabel, a couple in their early twenties, designed for Jed's brother. Several months after Jed married Isabel, his mother died suddenly, leaving Jed's nineteen-year-old brother, Brian, orphaned. Brian came to live with Jed and Isabel. The young couple thus found themselves not only newlyweds but also new "parents." One day Brian told them, "You know, I feel like I don't have a security blanket. My friends at school, other people in my classes—most of them have at least one parent still alive. Their parents can help them if they're having trouble in school, or if they need a place to stay, or can't find a job. And I don't have that security blanket because both of my parents are dead."

What Brian had said seemed so important to him that Jed and Isabel talked about it between themselves and eventually came up with an idea: They would make Brian a quilt—a security blanket. Jed's sister had an old nurse's uniform of their mother's that they could use for material. An older brother had a Marine camouflage shirt of their father's. They found some other old fabric among their mother's things. Then, as they began to cut the material into squares, they realized that they would need help sewing them together into a quilt. Jed thought of his maternal grandmother, who had sewn a number of quilts for other family members.

The siblings and the grandmother began gathering in secret to sew the quilt and share memories of Brian's parents and their earlier life. And when the family gathered to celebrate the grandmother's eightieth birthday, Brian was given the quilt—a blanket that symbolized both the ability of Jed and Isabel to "parent" in creative ways and the new network of contact that had been built between the siblings and their grandmother. Together,

these family members had proved to be Brian's "security blanket."

The symbols and symbolic actions of rituals embrace meaning that cannot always be easily expressed in words. Eveline Miller's rocking chair, for example, was much more than a place to sit; it evoked safety, reassurance, and the memory of her grandmother. Brian's quilt was not just a cover; it represented the interconnected people in his life—from the past and the present—whom he could carry with him into the future. The textures, smells, and sounds of ritual symbols—an heirloom rocking chair, a family-made quilt—can be powerful activators of sensory memory. Family members may recall scenes and stories of previous times when similar rituals were enacted or some of the same people were together. Rituals connect us with our past, define our present life, and show us a path to our future.

FAMILY RITUALS TAKE A VARIETY OF forms. There are daily practices, such as the reading of a child's bedtime story or the sharing of a mealtime. There are holiday traditions, some celebrated with the community at large (seasonal events such as the solstice, religious events such as Passover, national events such as the Fourth of July) and others exclusive to a particular family (birthdays, anniversaries, reunions). Then there are life-cycle rituals, which mark the major transitions of life.

All human beings throughout the world and throughout time are born, and all die. All of us experience emerging sexuality. And most create sustained adult relationships to form new family units and new generations. Such changes are enormously complicated, involving both beginnings and endings; holding and expressing both pain and joy. They may shape and give voice to profoundly conflicting beliefs about our personal existence and our relationships. It's little wonder that every culture in the world has created rituals to celebrate and guide our way through these life-cycle passages.

The truly magical quality of rituals is embedded in their capacity not only to announce a change but to actually create the change. Given that volumes have been written advising people how to change, and that people spend countless hours in therapy, often agonizing over their inability to make needed changes, it is easy to see why rituals exist in all cultures, to ease our passage from one stage of life to another. Using familiar symbols, actions, and words, rituals make

> **A family in which ritual is minimized may have little sense of itself through time.**

change manageable and safe. Simply knowing which rituals lie ahead during a day, a year, or a lifetime stills our anxiety. Change is *enacted* through rituals and not simply talked about—couples don't change from being single to being married by talking about marriage, but rather by participating in a wedding ceremony. Teens don't graduate from high school when a teacher says "you're finished now"; they attend proms, picnics, and the graduation ceremony itself.

As families have changed, life-cycle events have changed too, and there are many crucial transitions for which there are no familiar and accepted rituals in our culture. Changes that often go unmarked include divorce, the end of a nonmarried relationship, adoption, forming a committed homosexual relationship, leaving home, pregnancy loss, and menopause. Since life-cycle rituals enable us to begin to rework our sense of self and our relationships as required by life's changes, the lack of such rituals can make change more difficult.

Rituals tend to put us in touch with the profound circle of life and death, so it is not surprising that healing moments emerge spontaneously during these celebrations. If you keep that in mind when changes are occurring in your life or in the lives of those close to you, you can plan a ritual to specifically generate healing.

Healing a Broken Relationship

The crisis of shattered trust and broken promises can lead to genuine atonement, forgiveness, reconciliation, and relationship renewal or, alternatively, to chronic resentment, bitterness, parting, and isolation. Since rituals are able to hold and express powerful contradictory feelings, such as love and hate, anger and connectedness, they enhance the possibility of relationship healing.

For Sondra and Alex Cutter, ritual provided a way to bury that past. The Cutters had spent seven of their twelve years of marriage in bitter arguments about a brief affair Alex had had just before their fifth anniversary. Sondra didn't want to leave her marriage, but she felt unable to let go of the past. Alex, in turn, had become extremely defensive about his behavior and was unable to genuinely show Sondra that he was sorry. In couple's therapy, Sondra and Alex were asked to bring two sets of symbols of the affair. The first set of symbols was to represent what the affair meant to each of them at the time it occurred. The second set was to symbolize what the affair had come to mean in their current life together. As a symbol of her feelings at the time of the affair, Sondra brought a torn wedding photograph to show that the affair meant a break in their vows. Sondra

was surprised by Alex's symbol: an old picture of his father, who had had many affairs. "I thought this was just what husbands did," said Alex. "I thought this was what made you a man, but I found out quickly that this didn't work for me and for what I wanted my marriage to be. Then we couldn't get past it." Sondra had never heard Alex speak about the affair in this way. Her belief that the affair meant he didn't love her and that he loved another woman began to shift for the first time in seven years.

As a symbol of what the affair meant currently, Alex brought the wheel of a hamster cage, remarking, "We just go round and round and round and get nowhere." Sondra brought a bottle of bitters, and said, "This is what I've turned into!" After a long conversation engendered by their symbols, Sondra said quietly, "This is the first time in seven years

(UN photo/John Isaac)

Rituals shape our relationships and give us a basis for a healthy society. Simply having a family meal together helps establish a stronger sense of self.

that we've talked about this without yelling and screaming." When the therapist asked if they were ready to let go of the past, both agreed that they were. They decided to revisit a favorite spot from early in their relationship and to bury these symbols there. During the ceremony, Alex cried and for the first time asked Sondra to forgive him, which she readily did. They followed this with a celebration of their anniversary, which they had stopped celebrating seven years earlier.

This healing ritual was created as part of couple's therapy, but you don't need the help of a therapist to create rituals to effect healing. Common to all healing rituals is a dimension of time—time for holding on and time for letting go. Selecting symbols to express painful issues generally allows for a new kind of conversation to emerge. Taking some joint action together, such as symbolically burying the past, can impart a new possibility of collaboration. Creating a ritual together can help you to rediscover the playful parts of your relationship, such as the couple who "put an affair on ice," placing symbols in their deep freezer and agreeing that they could only fight about the affair after they had thawed these symbols out!

A Ceremony for Grieving

There is no life that is lived without loss. We all experience the death of people we love and care for deeply. When healing rituals have not occurred, or have been insufficient to complete the grief process, a person can remain stuck in the past or unable to move forward in meaningful ways. Even the unhealed losses of previous generations may emerge as debilitating symptoms in the present. When this happens, new rituals can be created to address the need for healing.

Joanie and Jeralynn Thompson were identical twins who had a close and loving relationship. They went away to the same college and planned to graduate together. During their junior year, however, Jeralynn developed

Rituals connect us with our past, define our present life, and show us a path to our future.

leukemia. She died within the year. Before her death, Jeralynn talked with Joanie about how important it was that Joanie continue college and graduate. Joanie did go back to school after her sister's funeral, but she found it impossible to study. At the urging of friends, she took a year off in order to be with her family and begin to deal with the terrible loss of her sister. But a year turned into two years, two years into three. Finally, her family insisted that she go back to college. Joanie returned to school and finished all of her courses, but remained unable to do her senior thesis. She didn't graduate that June. "I don't know how I can graduate without Jeralynn," she told her mother. "It'll mean that she's really gone." Once her mother began to understand what was stopping Joanie from finishing, she talked with her daughter about how they might honor Jeralynn's life while still celebrating Joanie's entering adulthood with her college graduation. After developing a plan with her mother, Joanie finished her thesis in time to graduate the following December.

Joanie and her mother planned a special ceremony to be held two nights before graduation. They invited extended family and close friends, asking them to bring symbols of Jeralynn and to speak about her openly. During a very moving ceremony, many people spoke about what they thought Jeralynn would have wished for Joanie. One aunt made a video

that showed places the two sisters had both loved, and after showing it told Joanie, "These places still belong to you." Joanie's father brought photographs of several pets the twins had raised, carefully pointing out the individual contributions each twin had made to these animals. Then, in a five-minute talk, he highlighted the strengths and gifts of each young woman and gave Joanie permission to be her own person. People grieved the loss of Jeralynn openly and then embraced Joanie for finishing school and going on in life.

Several months later, settled in a new job as a teacher, Joanie talked about this ceremony and her graduation: "They all helped me to graduate. If we hadn't had our memorial first, I know all I would have been wondering about on graduation day was what my family was feeling about Jeralynn's death. Instead, all of it was out in the open. We could be sad together and then we could be happy together on my graduation day. They call graduation a commencement, an ending that's really a beginning, and that's what mine was. I miss my sister terribly—I'll always miss her—but my family and friends helped me take the next step in my life, and Jeralynn's spirit was right there with me."

Celebrating Recovery from Illness

Sometimes very important changes take place but remain unacknowledged. This may be because the changes are difficult to talk about, because they bring up the pain of how things used to be, or because no one had thought about how to mark the change. In our experience, recovery from medical or psychiatric illness is an aspect of change that is seldom marked by a ritual. Families, relationships, and the individual's own identity remain stuck with the illness label, and behavior among family members and friends remains as it was when the person was ill.

Adolescents who have recovered from cancer or adults who are now healthy after heart surgery often maintain an "illness identity," and others treat them accordingly. A ritual can declare in action that a person has moved from illness to health. Such a ritual might include a ceremony of throwing away no-longer-needed medicines or medical equipment, burning or burying symbols of a long hospital stay, or writing a document declaring new life and health.

After recovering from breast cancer, Gerry Sims had a T-shirt made that read HEALTHY WOMAN! She wore this T-shirt to a family dinner and announced to everyone that they were to stop treating her as a patient, and that, in particular, she wanted people to argue with her as they had before she became ill. Then she handed out T-shirts to her husband and children that read HUSBAND OF A HEALTHY WOMAN, CHILD OF A HEALTHY WOMAN. Everyone put on his or her T-shirt and for the first time spontaneously began to talk about what they had been through together during Gerry's year-long illness. They cried out loud to each other. Following this, Gerry's teen-age daughter picked a fight with her, just as Gerry had hoped!

A Rite of Passage

Like many life-cycle passages, a child leaving home is an event that carries deeply mixed feelings, including a sense of joy and accomplishment, fear regarding what lies ahead, sadness over the loss of relationships in their present form, and curious anticipation about what life will look like next. This life-cycle passage of leaving home may be even more difficult when the leaving is unanticipated or when the child has grown up with a handicap. Creating a leaving-home ritual whose symbols and symbolic actions speak to the many contradictory issues can ease this passage for everyone in the family.

Jennifer Cooper-Smith was born with some severe disabilities that affected her capacity to read, write, and speak. During her childhood she took the handicap in stride despite the cruel teasing of other children and despite coming from a family where high academic achievement was the norm. Through it all she taught her family a lot about perseverance in the face of enormous struggles and about building on strengths rather than focusing on weaknesses.

When Jennifer reached nineteen, since her disabilities would preclude her going to college, it was clear that high school graduation was to be her rite of passage. The family wanted to create a ritual that would both honor all that she had accomplished and send her forth into the adult world with confidence.

Jennifer wanted a party at a Chinese restaurant with her favorite festive food. Her mother and stepfather invited people who were important to Jennifer—extended family who lived far away, friends who had supported her, special teachers and co-workers from her part-time job. The invitation included a secret request for special items—poems, letters, photos, stories, drawings, and so on—to help make a "becoming an adult woman" album for Jenni. During the weeks before the party, her mom worked secretly to construct the album, which began at the time Jennifer joined the family as an adopted infant and included sections that marked significant stages of her development. Although the handicaps had sometimes made it difficult for both Jennifer and those around her to notice her growth and changes, this album recorded them for all to see.

When Jennifer arrived at the party, the album was waiting for her as a special symbol of her development. What she still didn't know, though, was that the album was open-ended, and a new section, "Becoming an Adult Woman," was about to be added during the party. After dinner, when people were invited to give their presentations to Jennifer, a moving and unexpected ceremony unfolded. Person after person spoke about how they experienced Jenni and what she meant to them, and they gave her their own special brand of advice about living.

Her grandma Dena gave Jenni a photograph of Dena's late husband—Jenni's grandfather—down on his knees proposing marriage. She spoke about enduring love and her wish that Jenni would have this in her life. Her aunt Meryle Sue read an original poem, "Portrait of Jenni," and then spoke through tears about what this day would have meant to Jenni's grandfather and how proud he would have been of her. Her cousin Stacey wrote a poem that captured who Jenni was to her and offered words about Jenni's future. Advice about men and what to beware of was given by Jenni's step-grandfather and received with much laughter. Photographs of strong women in history were presented.

Person after person spoke with grace and love and special stories about Jennifer's strengths. Her mother watched as Jennifer took in all that she was to people and the sometimes unknown impact that her own courage had had on family and friends. And then all who gathered witnessed the emergence of Jennifer, the adult woman, as she rose from her seat and spoke unhaltingly and with no trace of her usual shyness, thanking each person in turn for what they had given her in life, and talking about the loss of her grandfather and her wish that he could be with her today. She ended with all that she anticipated next in her life.

The weeks and months following this ritual were perhaps even more remarkable than the ceremony itself. Her family experienced a changed Jennifer, a Jennifer who moved from adolescence to young womanhood— starting a full-time job, auditing a community college course, traveling by herself, making new friends, and relating on a previously unseen level.

AS ALL OF THESE EXAMPLES ILLUSTrate, rituals ease our passage through life. They shape our relationships, help to heal our losses, express our deepest beliefs, and celebrate our existence. They announce change and create change. The power of rituals belongs to all of us.

Test Your Knowledge Form

We encourage you to photocopy and use this page as a tool to assess how the articles in **Annual Editi**[cut off] expand on the information in your textbook. By reflecting on the articles you will gain enhanced text informati[cut off] You can also access this useful form on a product's book support Web site at **http://www.dushkin.com** *online/.*

NAME: DATE:

_____

TITLE AND NUMBER OF ARTICLE:

_____

BRIEFLY STATE THE MAIN IDEA OF THIS ARTICLE:

_____

LIST THREE IMPORTANT FACTS THAT THE AUTHOR USES TO SUPPORT THE MAIN IDEA:

_____

WHAT INFORMATION OR IDEAS DISCUSSED IN THIS ARTICLE ARE ALSO DISCUSSED IN YOUR TEXTBOOK OR OTHER READINGS THAT YOU HAVE DONE? LIST THE TEXTBOOK CHAPTERS AND PAGE NUMBERS:

_____

LIST ANY EXAMPLES OF BIAS OR FAULTY REASONING THAT YOU FOUND IN THE ARTICLE:

_____

LIST ANY NEW TERMS/CONCEPTS THAT WERE DISCUSSED IN THE ARTICLE, AND WRITE A SHORT DEFINITION:

_____

ANNUAL EDITIONS revisions depend on two major opinion sources: one is our Advisory Board, listed in the front of this volume, which works with us in scanning the thousands of articles published in the public press each year; the other is you—the person actually using the book. Please help us and the users of the next edition by completing the prepaid article rating form on this page and returning it to us. Thank you for your help!

ANNUAL EDITIONS: Marriage and Family 01/02

Here is an opportunity for you to have direct input into the next revision of this volume. We would like you to rate each of the 41 articles listed below, using the following scale:

1. Excellent: should definitely be retained
2. Above average: should probably be retained
3. Below average: should probably be deleted
4. Poor: should definitely be deleted

Your ratings will play a vital part in the next revision. So please mail this prepaid form to us just as soon as you complete it. Thanks for your help!

We Want Your Advice

RATING — ARTICLE

1. The Intentional Family
2. The American Family
3. The Family: What Do We Really Want?
4. Boys Will Be Boys
5. Sex Differences in the Brain
6. Flirting Fascination
7. What's Your Love Story?
8. Protecting Against Unintended Pregnancy: A Guide to Contraceptive Choices
9. The Brave New World of Parenting
10. How Old Is Too Old to Have a Baby?
11. Shaped by Life in the Womb
12. The Cost of Children
13. Our Babies, Ourselves
14. Flying Solo
15. The Science of a Good Marriage
16. Will Your Marriage Last?
17. Men, Women & Money
18. Father Love and Child Development: History and Current Evidence
19. Do Parents Really Matter? Kid Stuff
20. Family Matters
21. Anatomy of a Violent Relationship
22. Resilience in Development
23. Sex & Marriage

RATING — ARTICLE

24. Shattered Vows
25. The Politics of Fatigue: The Gender War Has Been Replaced by the Exhaustion of Trying to Do It All
26. Do Working Parents Make the Grade?
27. Balancing Work and Family
28. Should You Leave?
29. Is Divorce Too Easy?
30. Smart Plan to Save Marriages
31. The Children of Divorce
32. Divorced? Don't Even Think of Remarrying Until You Read This
33. When Strangers Become Family
34. Elder Care: Making the Right Choice
35. Bereavement Events Among Elderly Men: The Effects of Stress and Health
36. Failing to Discuss Dying Adds to Pain of Patient and Family
37. To See Your Future Look Into Your Past
38. Getting the Word
39. What's Ahead for Families: Five Major Forces of Change
40. The Power of Secrets
41. Rituals for Our Times

(Continued on next page)

ABOUT YOU

Name   Date

Are you a teacher? ☐ A student? ☐
Your school's name

Department

Address   City   State   Zip

School telephone #

YOUR COMMENTS ARE IMPORTANT TO US !

Please fill in the following information:
For which course did you use this book?

Did you use a text with this *ANNUAL EDITION*? ☐ yes ☐ no
What was the title of the text?

What are your general reactions to the *Annual Editions* concept?

Have you read any particular articles recently that you think should be included in the next edition?

Are there any articles you feel should be replaced in the next edition? Why?

Are there any World Wide Web sites you feel should be included in the next edition? Please annotate.

May we contact you for editorial input? ☐ yes ☐ no
May we quote your comments? ☐ yes ☐ no